WAR

AGAINST

THE TALIBAN

WHY IT ALL WENT WRONG
IN AFGHANISTAN

SANDY GALL

B L O O M S B U R Y
LONDON · NEW DELHI · NEW YORK · SYDNEY

First published in Great Britain 2012
This paperback edition published 2013

Copyright © by Sandy Gall 2012
Map by ML Design

The moral right of the author has been asserted

No part of this book may be used or reproduced in any manner
whatsoever without written permission from the Publisher except in the
case of brief quotations embodied in critical articles or reviews

Every reasonable effort has been made to trace copyright holders
of material reproduced in this book, but if any have been inadvertently
overlooked the publishers would be glad to hear from them. For legal purposes the
Acknowledgements on pp. 371–373 constitute an extension of this copyright page

Bloomsbury Publishing Plc
50 Bedford Square
London WC1B 3DP

www.bloomsbury.com

Bloomsbury Publishing, London, New Delhi, New York and Sydney
A CIP catalogue record for this book is available from the British Library

ISBN 978 1 4088 2234 0
10 9 8 7 6 5 4 3 2 1

Typeset by Hewer Text UK Ltd, Edinburgh
Printed and bound by CPI Group (UK) Ltd, Croydon, CR0 4YY

MIX
Paper from
responsible sources
FSC® C020471

For Carlotta and Fiona, without whose incomparably greater knowledge, generosity in sharing it, and time and hospitality in Kabul and Islamabad, the task would have been beyond me; and for Michaela, my indispensable amanuensis and computer expert.

How can a small Power like Afghanistan, which is like a goat between these lions, or a grain of wheat between two strong millstones of the grinding mill, stand in the midway of the stones without being ground to dust?

Amir Abdur Rahman, on Afghanistan's relationship with Britain and Tsarist Russia, 1900

CONTENTS

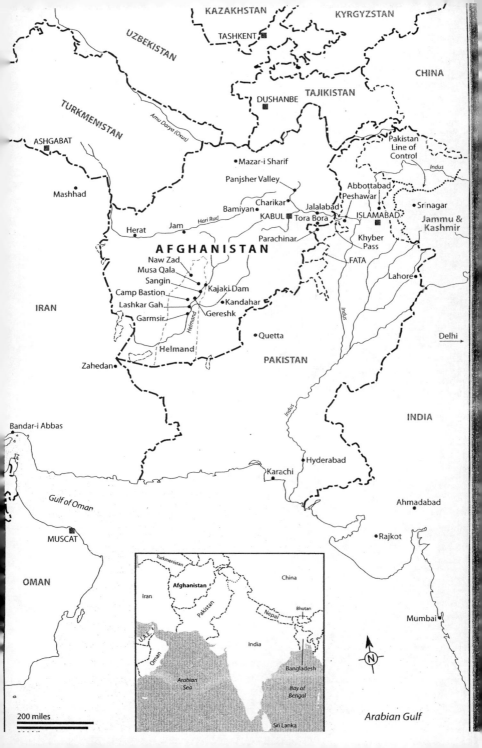

Foreword

Kashmir, Pakistan
December 1971

Since Partition in 1947, when British India, the Jewel in the Crown of Empire, attained independence and was divided into Hindu India and Muslim Pakistan, the two countries have been at one another's throats. The bloodletting at Partition was horrific. About 10½ million people were displaced amid scenes of bloodshed and violence which led to the deaths of another half a million, and the two new nations fought the first of their wars over Kashmir immediately afterwards.

Renowned for the beauty of its lakes and mountains, a romantic spot where in the days of the Raj young British newlyweds would spend their honeymoon on a houseboat, Kashmir was politically a time bomb. It was, in many ways, a microcosm of the old India. The ruler, a maharajah, was a Hindu. After Partition, he opted to join India, under pressure from Prime Minister Jawaharlal Nehru, himself of Kashmiri origin. But most Kashmiris were Muslims and when they rebelled, Nehru sent in the army. The first Indo-Pakistani War led to another partition, the capital Srinagar and the famous lakes falling to India, and Azad (Free) Kashmir going to Pakistan.

That was in 1948. Twenty-three years later, I found myself flying to Kabul en route for Pakistan on the outbreak of the Third Indo-Pakistan War, on 3 December 1971. Pakistan had closed its airspace and the only way in was by air to Kabul and then by road over the Khyber Pass to Peshawar.

One of the results of Partition had been to make Pakistan virtually ungovernable. Twelve hundred miles of hostile India divided East from West Pakistan and, apart from religion, they had little in common. Economically and politically West Pakistan was the dominant partner. The capital, then, was Karachi. Inevitably, East Pakistan developed an inferiority complex. To make matters worse, a disastrous cyclone struck the East in 1970. Elections that December returned the Pakistan Peoples Party to power in the West and the Awami League to power in the East. A dispute broke out as to who should rule, strikes followed and then a revolt in the East, which declared independence as Bangladesh. India backed Bangladesh and declared war on Pakistan. The outcome was predictable. Outnumbered three to one, and fighting a long way from home, Pakistan not only lost half its country but suffered a crushing defeat at the hands of the Indians. A whole army of nearly 90,000 men was taken prisoner and morale plummeted.

In Islamabad, I happened to meet an old friend, General, later President, Zia ul-Haq. He was like a man bereft. This latest debacle, Pakistan's third defeat in three wars, would leave deep wounds and lasting bitterness. Having completed the spectacular journey through the mountains of Afghanistan and over the Khyber we spent the night in Peshawar – where there was a blackout – and drove south the next day. When my ITN crew and I reported to the press office at army headquarters, Rawalpindi, we were told we could go on an army trip to Kashmir the next day.

We were taken to the front line. There was very little action. The Pakistanis and the Indians had a standard drill, the friendly artillery major in charge informed us. Every morning the Indians would shell the Pakistan lines, and every afternoon the Pakistanis would return fire. Feeling we ought to film some aspect of this war, having taken such trouble to get here, I asked the major what time he would be firing back.

'Oh, about four o'clock,' he said.

I looked at my watch. 'Unfortunately, they're taking us back at 3.30.'

'Oh, no problem,' he said helpfully. 'We can easily bring it forward half an hour and wake them up a bit early.' He smiled to show it was a ritual, nothing more.

The BBC, I remember, were also keen to film a bit of the action. We all chorused our approval. Five minutes later the obliging major sent ten or twenty shells hurtling across the sky to explode in Indian territory ten miles away. 'Will they respond?' I asked.

'No, no,' he said with a laugh. 'Tomorrow morning.'

Otherwise, there was no action on the Kashmir front. But in the months and years ahead, the Pakistan Army would recruit, arm and train many hundreds of guerrillas to fight in Kashmir. For them it would not be a ritual, but a bitter war. As the guerrillas became more experienced and more lethal, they would eventually carry out attacks like that, many years later, on Mumbai. The bitterness would grow and the chances of a settlement in Kashmir would become increasingly unlikely. But without such a settlement, it is difficult to see how peace between India and Pakistan can ever be established.

This book is about Afghanistan. But, as I will try to show, the key to that war lies at least partly in Pakistan, and in the Kashmir problem. We, in the West, have been slow to grasp that simple truth. Even the United States, with its vast resources, both material and intellectual, has not found an answer to the riddle: how do we persuade Pakistan to abandon its support for the Taliban and make peace with India? I do not pretend to know the answer, but I know it is important we apply ourselves to finding it.[1]

PART ONE

EARLY BATTLES

Zia and the ISI, 1970–1984

I'm sending four Special Forces people with you to make sure you're safe.

General Zia, Rawalpindi, 1984

I first met Zia, then a brigadier, in Amman, where he was deputy head of the Pakistan Military Mission to Jordan. It was just after Black September, 1970, when, after months of provocation and mounting fears of a PLO (Palestine Liberation Organisation) coup, the pro-Western King Hussein finally took action against them and their leader, Yasser Arafat. A close confidant of the King, Zaid Rifai, later Ambassador to London and Prime Minister, described to me how fraught the situation then was: 'The *fedayeen* had almost taken total control of Amman; the [Jordanian] Army was deployed in the Jordan Valley against Israel. On 15 September a parliamentary delegation went to see Arafat in an attempt to have him and his forces abide by Jordanian laws and leave the capital . . . if his real aim was to mount operations against Israel.' Arafat told the parliamentarians that the situation had gone out of his hands, that he could not control all the *fedayeen* and that all he could do was 'to offer King Hussein twenty-four hours to leave the country'.

When the parliamentary delegation reported this to the King, he immediately formed a military government and declared martial law. The commanding general telephoned Arafat and gave him an ultimatum: leave the capital with his forces or the army would drive them out. Arafat refused, so on 17 September the army was ordered to move against the *fedayeen*, of whom there were 70,000, according to Zaid Rifai, dug in all over the city. In the ensuing battle, the commander of the 2nd Armoured Division and his deputy were badly wounded and King

Hussein asked Zia, who had once been a tank commander himself, to take over. 'We flew Zia in a helicopter to the north [where the Syrian armour, camouflaged as PLO tanks, had invaded] and he took command,' Rifai recalled. Many observers believe Zia played a key role in the defeat of the PLO and Zia told me that the first person to congratulate him when he deposed Bhutto, the authoritarian Prime Minister of Pakistan, seven years later, was King Hussein.[1]

As the ITN correspondent in Jordan in the summer of 1970, I watched the storm clouds gather. The influx of Palestinian refugees following the Six-Day War of 1967, accompanied by fifty-two Palestinian and other international terrorist groups including the Baader-Meinhof gang, the Red Brigades and Carlos the Jackal, according to Zaid Rifai, had created a state within a state. Nearly half the population of Jordan and of Amman, the capital, were Palestinian and some quarters of the capital became no-go areas. Soldiers whose families lived in these areas stopped going home on leave in uniform: those who did were disarmed and insulted. The British military attaché at the Embassy told me he felt uncomfortable sitting in his car, in uniform, waiting for his wife to come out of the hairdresser's in the middle of Amman. *Fedayeen* with AK-47s slung over their shoulders strutted through the streets as if the capital belonged to them and pushed their way into the bar at the Intercontinental Hotel, jingling their collecting boxes arrogantly under the noses of Western guests. The message was clear: 'We're in charge here . . .'

One story, which I did not believe, and which Zaid Rifai said was untrue, but which captured the mood, had the King lying down in the road outside a barracks to stop his loyal Beduin troops, determined to foil any PLO coup, driving their tanks into the Palestinian townships. What is certainly true, however, is that King Hussein was twice ambushed and narrowly avoided assassination at the beginning of Black September. Driving from his hilltop palace at Hummar, ten miles outside Amman, into the city, 'to see what was happening', he came under attack at the Suweileh crossroads. The firing was so heavy that the bullets were 'dancing off the road like rain', in the words of Zaid Rifai. 'I begged the King to get into a ditch at the side of the road . . . One of the Royal Guards officers and I had the same thought . . . We both decided at the same time to physically protect the King.' They both jumped to cover him, collided in mid-air and fell on top of him. Their combined weight did not do the King's back any good. Zaid Rifai told me that when he went to see the King the next day, Hussein said: '"Never do that again. You're more bloody dangerous than the *fedayeen*." He was grinning but I knew he meant it.'[2] Although the King and Rifai escaped without serious injury, a sergeant of the guard was killed and four guards were wounded.

On another occasion Hussein was driving to the airport to meet his daughter, Alia, when his convoy was again ambushed. Luckily, he told me, one of the ambushers opened fire too early while they were still out of range. Despite that, Hussein and his guards were pinned down for about twenty minutes until they managed to extricate themselves.[3]

I arrived in Amman from London, via Syria, in the immediate aftermath of the fighting and checked into the Jordan Intercontinental. Also there was an old friend, Ed Hughes, who worked for *Time* magazine and was based in Beirut. Ed was a live wire, always full of ideas. 'Hey, there's a Pakistani brigadier here you ought to meet,' he told me. 'He's very well informed; you'll like him. He's also very hospitable and he'll ask us to his house for a curry. He's called Zia, Brigadier Zia ul-Haq.'

We met soon after in the lobby of the Intercontinental, which Zia seemed to patrol regularly. Spotting Ed, he bore down on us, impeccable in his well-pressed army uniform, with jet-black hair, very white teeth and a film-star smile. The smile was Zia's trademark. We shook hands and within five minutes he had issued his invitation to curry at his house the following night. Zia was a good host and although he did not drink, Ed and I were offered beer with our curry. Having been commissioned into the Indian Army during the war, Zia was very British in manner but very Muslim, I discovered, in his private life. Over dinner, he asked me if I was getting all the help I needed.

'Frankly, no,' I said. 'Being in television, we need pictures.' What I would really like, I added, was to spend some time with the King. We'd done several stories on the Palestinians and it was time we did the other side; but although I kept asking the Ministry of Information for an interview, nothing happened; and I did not think the King knew about my requests to see him.

Zia, who had listened attentively, said: 'Let me see what I can do to help. I'll talk to someone tomorrow.'

I did not set much store by his offer, but was pleasantly surprised when a mysterious figure in dark glasses arrived at the hotel next evening and without introducing himself said he understood I felt I was not getting the help I would like. I agreed that was so. Were we free tomorrow? he asked, adding he had something to show us that he thought would interest us.

'Yes, of course.'

'I will send a car for you,' he promised, as he left. As soon as I saw the car next morning with merely a crown and an Arabic number on the number plate, I knew things were looking up.

'Look, boys,' I said, 'this must be a car from the palace. We're in business.' We certainly were. The mysterious man in dark glasses turned out to be Moraiwid Tel, King Hussein's secretary, and brother of the tough Prime Minister, Wasfi Tel, later assassinated by the PLO in Cairo for his role in Black September. Half an hour later after the car dropped us at the air force base next to Amman airport, we were in one of Hussein's helicopters flying north behind him on his first visit to his troops on the Syrian border since Black September.

These were the soldiers who had repulsed a Syrian invasion force which, as fighting raged in Amman, had crossed the border early one morning in support of the PLO. Led by a large number of tanks, they had orders to drive down the road to Amman and overthrow Hussein. But owing to a feud between the Syrian President and his Defence Minister, Hafez al Assad, later to be President himself, Assad refused to commit the air force.* This left the Syrian tanks without air cover and Hussein's handful of ageing Hawker Hunter fighters rocketed and machine-gunned the invaders until they ran out of ammunition. Hussein's small air force proved decisive, but it was a near thing. Of his dozen or so Hawker Hunters, eight or nine were being converted and only two or three were operational. Luckily for the Jordanians, the Syrian air force having been grounded, the skies were empty.[4]

So this really was a victory celebration and it was an amazing scene, as

---

* Hafez al Assad was the father of Bashar al Assad, who in time became President of Syria.

the delirious Beduin troops hoisted Hussein shoulder high and carried him round and round the camp, shouting and singing in a spontaneous show of devotion, the dust thrown up by their feet obscuring the sun and investing the scene with an aura of tribal pageantry that might have come from the film *Lawrence of Arabia*. Old Harrovian though he might be, Hussein was first and foremost a member of the Hashemite dynasty, which stretched back 2,000 years, and which, as his secretary, Moraiwid Tel once explained, considered the Prophet as one of their own, although officially Hussein claimed to be a direct descendant. I don't think I, or either of my colleagues – hard-bitten newsmen – had ever seen anything like it. The story itself led *News at Ten* the following night and the cameraman, Alan Downes, won Cameraman of the Year partly on the strength of his superb photography that day.

I did not forget, however, that it was all thanks to Zia. Although I spent several days with him in 1977, just after he deposed Prime Minister Bhutto, it was not until 1984 that our paths really crossed again. I had already made one documentary film about the Soviet invasion of Afghanistan in 1982 and now, two years later, Zia intervened again, totally unexpectedly.

It all began in a suitably cloak-and-dagger fashion. Early in 1984 I received a call from a man in the Secret Intelligence Service (MI6), and was invited to lunch at a Soho restaurant. I knew him slightly from previous meetings with MI6, when I was collecting information for my first trip to Afghanistan in 1982. He now unfolded a fascinating story, which began with Mrs Thatcher's first visit to Pakistan to meet President Zia the year before. Pakistan had walked out of the Commonwealth in 1972, led by the Prime Minister, Zulfikar Ali Bhutto, who was angered by its recognition of newly independent Bangladesh, formerly East Pakistan. Five years later, in 1977, Bhutto was overthrown by General Zia ul-Haq and his fellow generals who accused him of leading the country to the brink of civil war.

'When the Prime Minister is ordering the army to open fire on fellow Punjabis who are demonstrating in the streets of Lahore, something has to be done,' Zia said.[5] Bhutto's arrest, subsequent trial and hanging after a controversial murder case – Zia was alleged to have influenced the Supreme

Court judgment which rejected Bhutto's appeal against the death sentence by one vote, after the resignation of one judge – made him a pariah in many eyes. But Western support for the *mujahideen* fighting the Russians, in the shape of arms and money, depended on Zia's cooperation and, almost overnight, the pariah became a sought-after ally. Hence Mrs Thatcher's visit.

Zia had considerable charm and the visit seems to have gone well. He arranged to take the Prime Minister and her party to the Afghan border. Torkham, the crossing-point, lies at the foot of the Khyber Pass, the historic route by which Alexander the Great and his successors invaded India and British generals in the heyday of Empire marched their men in the opposite direction on their way to invade Afghanistan. Mrs Thatcher was photographed standing beside a bemused-looking Afghan border guard with a rifle in his hand. It was good stuff for the newspapers and confirmed her reputation as a strong prime minister who was not afraid to step into the lion's den.

During her visit, my lunch host said, Zia had appealed for more press coverage of the war and apparently mentioned my name and the documentary I had made two years before as an example. The journey across the Pakistan border, which resulted in a film and book entitled *Behind Russian Lines*, was made without Zia's knowledge. I deliberately did not ask his permission to cross into Afghanistan since I did not want to risk a refusal. Zia's conversation with Mrs Thatcher was minuted in the normal way – later, under Tony Blair, when 'sofa government' took over, there was less minuting – and in due course a copy of the minutes reached MI6.[6] I had no idea, of course, that Zia had made these remarks and probably never would have known if MI6 had not picked them up. Zia went further, as far as I remember from the conversation in the restaurant, offering to support me if I decided to make another trip. There was no doubt, I was told, that Zia would not only welcome the initiative, but make sure there were no obstacles, certainly on the Pakistan side. 'Was I prepared to go?' was the next question. Yes, was the answer, but I would have to get ITN's approval and would let them know.

The answer was positive and a few days later I was able to say that ITN and I were ready to take up Zia's offer. What had come about largely through chance and a discerning eye at MI6, fitted in well with my own thoughts about a second visit to Afghanistan that summer. It would soon be two years since my first visit and the state of the war – who was winning or losing – was not much clearer than it had been in 1982. With only a trickle of news coming out of Afghanistan, it was in my view a good time to go. A few days later I flew to Islamabad with an ITN crew, a cameraman and sound recordist, who had both volunteered for the assignment. Paul Carleton was a very experienced and tough cameraman and Jon Hunt was a first-class sound man.

I went to see Zia at Army House in nearby Rawalpindi, the handsome colonial mansion built in the days of the Raj for the British Commander-in-Chief in the North-West Frontier Province and inherited by the Pakistan Army. He was in jovial mood, the famous smile much in evidence, although when he took me out into the garden to talk I wondered if he was worried about being bugged. It was possible. The Russians were furious at Zia's support for the *mujahideen* and the KGB would undoubtedly have been actively plotting against him. As we strolled across the neatly mown lawn among the rose bushes, I asked: 'Who have you arranged for us to go with, Zia?'

'Is there anyone you wouldn't want to go with?' he asked with a smile.

'Yes,' I replied. 'I wouldn't want to go with [Gulbuddin] Hekmatyar. In fact, I wouldn't go with him.'

Hekmatyar had a well-founded reputation for political assassination. Later, he was responsible for the deaths of two journalists, both friends, one Afghan and one British, as well as many other innocent Afghans to my certain knowledge. I once described him in the *Sunday Times* as the 'Afghan Pol Pot', which led him to protest to Sir Nicholas Barrington, British High Commissioner in Pakistan; some cheek, since Sir Nicholas had several times raised the murder with him of the ex-SAS British cameraman Andy Skrzypkowiak, with whom I made my third Afghan documentary in 1986 and who was killed by one of Hekmatyar's gangs in Nuristan in 1987.

Zia laughed easily. 'No, no, it's not Hekmatyar,' he chuckled.

'Who then?'

'Yunus Khalis,' Zia replied. 'They are very good people. You will like them.'

As long as it wasn't Hekmatyar, I didn't mind. I knew it would be a Pushtun group and I had decided in my own mind that, having travelled with Masud's Tajiks in 1982, I should try to assess the Pushtun side of the Resistance. But Zia had not finished. 'I'm sending four Special Forces people with you to make sure you're safe—'

'We don't need anyone to look after us, Zia, the Afghans will look after us,' I interrupted. What I really meant was that if we were making a film about the Afghan Resistance, I wanted it to be about Afghans and with Afghans and not through the prism of Pakistan Army intelligence.

He stopped in the middle of the lawn and looked me in the eye.

'I know you can look after yourself, Sandy, but I don't want to take any chances. I'm sending some of my best people with you and one of my best officers, Colonel Faisan. He and his three NCOs will look after you.' He grinned. 'I don't want anything to happen to you.' I could see Zia had made up his mind and since we were really in his hands, I did not argue any further. 'Is there anything else I can do for you?' he asked.

'Yes,' I said, on the spur of the moment. 'Could we take some SAM7s with us?'

He looked slightly surprised. 'It would make a brilliant picture if we filmed a Russian helicopter being shot down by a Russian missile,' I explained.

Zia got the point. 'Yes, of course,' he laughed. 'I'll ask them to send some with you.'

The SAM7 is a hand-held Russian ground-to-air missile, basically a long tube which one man can carry and operate from the shoulder. It would not fire until the target was within range and the operator had got 'lock-on'. This made it cumbersome, slow and with a low success ratio of only about one in ten. SAMs were bought on the open market by the CIA and then transported into Afghanistan on the backs of horses, which made one wonder how effective they were by the time they arrived on the battlefield. It was to be another two years before the US Congress finally agreed to the CIA's request to supply the *mujahideen* with the greatly superior STINGER. Its arrival, in the late summer of 1986, transformed the war and finally convinced President Gorbachev, many observers thought, that withdrawal was the only option. It was to take more than two years for this to happen, and by that time the once-feared Mi-24 'Hind' helicopter gunship had become much less effective.

We met Colonel Faisan (a codename) and his three NCOs when we left Islamabad for the border two days later. Faisan told me he had been trained at the American Special Forces headquarters at Fort Bragg, although the idea of the four-man team – one officer and three NCOs – is based on the SAS model. I thought the role of the NCOs was comparable in another way to what it was in the SAS. Officers might come and go, but the NCOs went on for ever. The senior one was a moustachioed warrant officer, thickset and reliable-looking, called Muslim; of the two sergeants, one, Pir, was a Pushtun with a ready smile and the other, Akram, tall and laconic, was, I guessed, a Punjabi.

This was the first time I had really got to know someone from the ISI; Zia had spelt out the acronym for me: 'Inter-Services Intelligence Directorate'. It is in fact only one of Pakistan's four intelligence agencies, but is by far the most powerful, and really represents the army's primal position in Pakistan society. Not only has the ISI all the powers and reach of the CIA or MI6 and MI5 rolled into one, with a strong dash of the KGB added, but where it differs from Western intelligence agencies is in its deep involvement in the domestic political scene, not just in security matters but in all aspects of life and politics in Pakistan, above all the threat from India. Imprisonment, torture and 'disappearance' or worse are part of its armoury and no questions are asked, either in the Pakistan parliament or anywhere else. The ISI is above the law, or, you might say, is the law.

To be its head is an almost certain stepping-stone to greater things. General Ashfaq Kayani, for example, the present Chief of Army Staff, was formerly head of the ISI. During the Russian War it was especially close to the CIA who always took its advice seriously – some would say too seriously – championing Gulbuddin Hekmatyar, for example, from his days as a student revolutionary in Kabul in the mid-1970s, even before the Russian invasion, and only dropping him in the mid-1990s in favour of the Taliban, when he failed to deliver and the ISI decided they were the better bet. To the astonishment of the British, the CIA were just as hooked on Hekmatyar as the ISI, accepting the spurious claim that Hekmatyar's Hisb-i-Islami fighters killed more Russians than any of the other *mujahideen* parties – a claim rightly pooh-poohed by the British. In fact, the ISI diverted the great bulk of the CIA's dollars to Hekmatyar because he was their man who, one day they hoped, would run Afghanistan on their behalf. The Americans saw the light in the end, although it took a long time. It was not until the 1990s that a high-ranking British politician and friend confided to me that 'the Americans have admitted to us for the first time that they were wrong about Hekmatyar and we were right' – that, of course, was after Hekmatyar had turned against his former paymasters.

Zia said he had sent Faisan and his NCOs specifically to look after us, but their familiarity with *mujahideen* ways suggested the ISI already had a good working relationship with the Yunus Khalis Party. This was no real surprise. From the very start, Zia had placed the conduct of the Afghan war firmly in the hands of the ISI and its then head, General Akhtar Rahman, a Pushtun. Zia and most of his senior colleagues were devout Muslims, fundamentalists who were determined to oppose the Marxist Russian occupation of Afghanistan, another Muslim country, in every possible way.[7] As the war expanded, there was little doubt in my mind that ISI advice to and influence over the *mujahideen* grew with it. In 1986, for example, I was told by the British that even American CIA agents in Islamabad were not allowed to speak directly to *mujahideen* commanders in the field. They were under strict orders to go through ISI channels only. This was typical of the possessive attitude the ISI always demonstrated, limiting American access to the *mujahideen*.

Zia, through the ISI, in reality ran the Afghan war. Once he had gained America's support he conducted the war to suit not only American policy but, increasingly, his own. In essence he was a straightforward, honest and honourable soldier, whose ambition, he once told me, was to celebrate the *mujahideen* victory by praying in the central mosque in Kabul. Some of his colleagues were not so straightforward, however, and Zia never got his wish. He was assassinated in August 1988, when his official C-130 crashed soon after take-off in southern Pakistan in an accident engineered, it was widely believed, by some of his most senior but disloyal fellow generals. The crash also killed the American Ambassador, Arnold Raphel, his defence attaché, and a number of senior Pakistani generals, including General Akhtar Rahman. No inquiry has ever got to the bottom of the crash, although an authoritative, joint American–Pakistan air force investigation reported that the cause was neither pilot error nor mechanical failure, but sabotage by persons unknown, and recommended another inquiry be held to establish the identity of those responsible. Typically of Pakistan, where the army remains the strongest power in the state, such an inquiry has never been held, despite continued pressure from Zia's two sons, Ijaz and Anwar.

The twin operation that had been planned for the Khalis group – and that we would film – also seemed to confirm a mixture of ISI influence and planning, not surprising since General Zia was its author. The first part was the attack on the government fort at Hissarak, which sat astride a well-trodden *mujahideen* infiltration route from Pakistan. Hissarak was strategically placed; with Kabul to the west and Jalalabad, the provincial capital of Ningrahar, to the north-east, both firmly in Communist hands. The *mujahideen* plan of attack, it seems, was perhaps not even to capture the fort, but simply to subdue it by sheer weight of fire, which Zia's planners would have seen as 'good television'. Hissarak was relentlessly rocketed, mortared and hammered by recoilless rifle fire to such an extent that the gunner ran out of ammunition, and Din Mohammed, who was deputy head of the Khalis Party and leader of our group, had virtually to call off the operation. The bombardment produced only minimal casualties to the well-dug-in defenders, as far as we could judge, but invited some dangerously accurate retaliatory rocket and mortar fire, of which we were on the receiving end on at least one occasion.

After three or four days it became clear the *mujahideen* had virtually no chance of capturing the fort. The heavy firing was done for the cameras, I concluded. This view was obviously shared by Abdul Haq, a well-known commander and brother of Din Mohammed. Abdul Haq, on his way to one of his own operations near Kabul, made some sarcastic comments about his brother's, or ISI's, battle plan, and dismissed Hissarak as a waste of time and ammunition.

Abdul Haq's main claim to fame in Britain was being photographed on the steps of Number 10 Downing Street with Mrs Thatcher. Her Foreign Office adviser, Charles (now Lord) Powell, recalls how, when Abdul Haq arrived at Number 10 and he was about to escort him up the stairs to Mrs Thatcher's office, he noticed his limp (Abdul Haq lost part of a foot on a Russian mine). But when he suggested they take the lift, Abdul Haq brushed the idea aside and fairly leapt up the stairs. Much later, just after 9/11, he was caught and killed by the Taliban for trying to raise a revolt against them.

About the only casualty we saw and filmed at Hissarak was a young farmer who was hit by a stray round while working in his fields. Sadly, he was about to celebrate his wedding, but as we passed through his village we found ourselves taking pictures of his funeral instead. In the Afghan tradition, his corpse lay in the open coffin, his face pale and peaceful as his friends filed past to pay their last respects and the family mourned in sorrow, the women keening a lament as at a Highland wake.

The second part of the Zia expedition was the ambush of a Red Army convoy in a steep-sided gorge on the Kabul–Jalalabad road. We walked and rode ten or fifteen miles to the top of the mountain ridge overlooking the ambush site, where the Kabul River, a green torrent tumbling down between huge boulders, ran parallel to the road and in some places only a few yards from it. Russian Army posts were sited at roughly half-mile intervals. The plan, explained by Colonel Faisan, sounded impressive in theory. About 120 *mujahideen* would assemble on the plateau above the ambush site where each one would be issued with a Chinese anti-tank mine and a length of yellow detonating cord. Each man was also given some sort of trenching tool. The plan was: they would descend to the road in the dark, dig holes in the verge beside the road and lay the mines, which would be detonated by remote control, in two batches. The first was intended to be set off just after the lead tanks had passed over them, in effect decapitating the convoy. Simultaneously, the second batch, placed just ahead of where the end of the convoy would halt, would also be detonated; finally, in the ensuing free-for-all, the *mujahideen* would rise from their cover on either side of the road and attack the main body of the convoy with RPGs (Rocket Propelled Grenades) and Kalashnikovs. If all went according to plan, the convoy, unable to escape forwards or backwards, would be annihilated.

So much for the theory. In practice, the *mujahideen* made so much noise going down the hill and planting the mines that the Russian sentries were well aware an ambush was being prepared – not for the first time at this spot, apparently. I had seen 'muj' walking about on the skyline before 'zero hour', and had remarked on it to Faisan. 'Why doesn't somebody tell them they'll be seen by the Russians if they walk around on the skyline?'

Faisan's reply would have done credit to a diplomat. 'They say the Russians are scared of them,' he explained deadpan, 'and so they turn their backs and pretend they haven't seen them.' Bravado over common sense, as it turned out.

While we were looking for a good camera position, I turned my binoculars on a Russian post just below us. As I focused I was surprised to see two Russian heads looking straight back at me and ducked back instinctively. But they made no movement so I concluded they had not seen me. We climbed back up the mountainside again and sat under a rock watching some helicopters droning overhead. Later, at about two in the afternoon a couple of Mi-24 gunships came overhead, circling, and someone said: 'That must be the convoy.' They remained overhead a long time, which suggested it was a big convoy; they can consist of as many as 250 vehicles, someone told us. In the afternoon, the *mujahideen* tested out the remote control exploder and primed eighty mines: large, yellow, plastic objects which looked for all the world like the jelly moulds Mrs Beaton might have used. Finally the *mujahideen* set off carrying their mines, the precious SAMs – with strict orders not to open fire until the helicopters had fired first – RPGs, recoilless rifles, Chinese 82-mm mortars, and the AK-47, which every *muj* who did not have a fancier weapon automatically carried.

With hindsight, that invaluable weapon of the know-all commentator, the ambush might have worked if the *mujahideen* had been left to their own devices. They are natural guerrillas, as they showed in many skirmishes against the British from 1838 – the First Anglo-Afghan War – onwards; against the Russians in the 1980s; and now again against the Americans and the British. What they are not so good at are conventional set-piece battles, which the Pakistanis, certainly in those early days, were always trying to push them into. The ambush in the gorge was too complicated an operation in my view – planting the mines in batches and detonating them by remote control – and did not give enough free play to the *mujahideen*'s natural guerrilla flair.

Having lost touch with Din Mohammed, who was no doubt having his own problems somewhere near the ambush site – he had disappeared without explanation the previous evening – we spent an uncomfortable night stretched out on a flattish piece of earth on which the *muj*, always hospitable, had spread some thin *pattus* (blankets). At around 4 a.m., Faisan got up and said we ought to move down closer to the scene of the action. We trudged down the slope with our porters but by the time we reached the rock which was our camera position, and clearly in view of the right-hand Russian outpost, it was light. Having set up the camera, and covered it with a blanket, we waited until eight, by which time the sun was so hot we retired to the shade. Shortly afterwards, the Russians started blasting the hillside with their tank cannon (we had seen three or four T-55s at the outpost the previous day).

Faisan, always the professional, explained that a Russian tank shell had a solid steel core and a very low, flat trajectory which meant a ricochet off hard ground would fly about twelve miles. A little later mortar shells started to come over, and, as the heavy 122-mm projectiles slammed down on the rocky hillside, I began to worry about having no camera. I went to have a look between rounds and saw it sitting disconsolately behind its rock, the blanket stirring in the slight breeze. Whether the Russians had spotted it or us, they certainly had the camera position bracketed. Finally Faisan volunteered to rescue it and, taking Paul Carleton and two porters with him, climbed down the little gully where we were sheltering. Paul took a couple of long lens shots of the road and solid lines of traffic held up in both directions. It was now clear even to a non-military eye that the ambush was well and truly blown. No convoy would be going through the gorge today. With the mortars coming in close every few minutes, Faisan suggested moving higher up the gully, where there was more cover. We had just completed the exhausting manoeuvre of hauling ourselves and the camera gear up the steep slope when word came that two Russian tanks were on fire below us, hit by rockets.

Faisan volunteered to go down to recce the situation, which I thought was sporting of him and almost beyond the call of duty, since he could have taken the view that it was our film and our job to run any risks involved. However I gladly accepted his offer and ten minutes later he came back to report that because of an overhang he could see the smoke but not the actual tanks burning; and three other tanks and at least one APC (Armoured Personnel Carrier) were still blasting away. I decided there was no point taking risks to film smoke if we could not actually see the tanks, so we stayed crouched in the gully as the mortars kept landing. Then, about midday, came the sound we had all been expecting: the unmistakable throb of the Mi-24 gunship; two in fact. Their beat came closer and they started to circle above us. No one had any doubt that they were going to launch a strike. After circling several times they did. It was a very unpleasant sensation, as I confided to my diary. 'You see the helicopter lining up, then you see the flash of the machine gun, then the smoke of the rockets firing and you wait for the "*Whoosh*" of the rockets. They went over our heads with a noise like a diving aircraft and exploded on the hillside above us with a terrifying roar. This was repeated half a dozen times, the target varying each time. Each time, one of the *mujahideen* Dashakas – Russian DShK heavy machine guns – fired back, in short bursts, but the Mi-24s were so high we did not fire our four SAMs. After about an hour, the Mi-24s departed and we went back to the more mundane business of being mortared.'

At this point Din Mohammed decided to pull out. Obviously no convoy was going to appear now and by staying put we were simply inviting more air strikes and other forms of attack. I fully expected the jets to come in but perhaps they had other business. Higher up we came across Din Mohammed observing operations from the shelter of a large rock. Faisan had said he was not well but he looked fine to me. He now gave a recoilless rifle gunner orders to attack the Russian post that had been mortaring us all day. High time, I thought. The excuse was they had been conserving ammunition. It went into action with a terrific *Whoosh!* and after several rounds the Russians retaliated with airburst shells from artillery about seven or eight miles away, according to Faisan who saw the muzzle flashes. Then the *mujahideen* let go with their mortar and more recoilless rifle fire. At the end of the day, as we climbed to the top of the mountain, Faisan reported that fifty mines had been set off just before the last *muj* withdrew, blowing up a third tank and an APC, although we were unable to verify any of these claims. The recoilless rifle was also said to have badly damaged the main Russian post and totally demolished the smaller one. Russian casualties were not known and no mention was made of Afghan losses. 'We came down the mountain to have our first tea of the day,' I added in my diary:

It tasted wonderful. I drank about a dozen cups. We then walked on to
the river where we had camped before, washed while the *mujahideen*
prayed and walked on to another sandy spot where we spread blankets
and ate mutton and bread: very good it was too.

I asked if Din Mohammed thought the Russians might move a force
ahead to ambush us and if so, shouldn't we press on? Faisan said Din
Mohammed agreed and that we would leave shortly. In fact, two hours
later, at about eleven, we started off, the moon having set. Luckily the
horses appeared and we mounted. It was a godsend, because they can see
in the dark much better than I can, at any rate, and we trekked on for
about three hours, climbing at one point up a narrow twisting mountain
pass. The track – mostly a dry river bed – wound round and round like
a corkscrew and after a fierce scramble to the top, during which Paul's
saddle slipped and he crashed to the ground, we came to our destina-
tion, a large village. There, gratefully, we collapsed onto our sleeping
bags. It had been a very long day.

Faisan remarked that the Russians reacted in a very unprofessional way,
making no attempt to come out of their positions and carry the fight to the
mujahideen. He laughed. 'They walk even less than the American GIs and,
apart from their Special Forces [*Spetsnaz*], hardly ever alight from their
vehicles.' The *mujahideen* have their faults, being noisy and undisciplined,
but, as I said to Faisan, luckily for them, their incompetence is matched by
the poor performance of the ordinary Russian troops, most of whom were
conscripts and had no stomach for the fight.[8]

A few years later, in 1995, when he retired from the army, Faisan offered to
introduce me to Taliban leaders he knew, which I felt would be of advantage to our charity, Sandy Gall's Afghanistan Appeal. As a result of my first
trip in 1982, my wife and I had started it in 1983 to provide artificial limbs
for wounded Afghans and orthoses for child polio victims. In 1995, when
the Taliban had only just taken control of Kandahar, Faisan suggested we
drive from Quetta, the capital of Baluchistan Province, to Kandahar where
he would arrange for me to meet the Taliban Governor, Mullah Hassan, a

close associate of the Taliban leader Mullah Omar. There was no chance of seeing the latter, I was told, but after about a week kicking our heels in an extremely primitive Taliban guesthouse – the only redeeming feature of which was that I had time to talk at length to Faisan – we finally did see Mullah Hassan for a brief and unilluminating meeting. After some small talk, and just as I was about to ask some serious questions, he scrambled out of his chair – he had lost a foot in the war – announcing it was time for prayers and stumped out of the room. End of interview.

Faisan was a persuasive apologist for the Taliban, whom he portrayed as having the best of intentions if sometimes rather an unfortunate manner of presenting them. Thus, although he did not deny that the Taliban had banned female education and closed girls' schools, he claimed this was only a temporary measure, which would be rectified in time, when conditions and funds permitted. Six years later, when the Taliban were driven from power, there was still no sign of any change. In fact, if anything the policy was even more firmly entrenched. Sitting on the threadbare carpet on the floor of our gloomy guesthouse, in between the uninspiring meals of rice and *nan*, I would listen patiently to his apologia and then tell him, as moderately as I could, that such a policy was simply unacceptable to the West and made any sort of dialogue virtually impossible. Faisan was a reasonable man but his spectacles, as far as the Taliban went, were in my view definitely rose-tinted. The ideological gulf between the Taliban and the West seemed unbridgeable.

Visually, and in every other way, I found Kandahar a disappointment. The modern city dates back only to 1761. Built on the grand scale by Ahmad Shah Durrani – the dashing young cavalryman who founded the great Durrani Empire – with huge walls surrounded by a moat and pierced by six massive gates, Kandahar was designed to impress the approaching traveller, friend or foe. The walls were pulled down in the 1940s and when I first visited it in the mid-1990s it had become, thanks to years of war and neglect, not much more than a heap of sandy ruins. Somebody had built a garish new house, which we passed whenever we drove to or from our guesthouse. Otherwise nothing seemed to have changed since the days of the founder. You hardly ever saw women in the streets, and if you did they were shapeless bundles, wreathed in black. The traffic lights at one intersection in the centre of the city were festooned with yards and yards of shiny black and rust-brown cassette tape, torn from the players of offending cars by the zealous religious police, and left fluttering in the wind as a warning to other miscreants that music, like all other forms of enjoyment, was forbidden. Although bin Laden, who had been a guest of Mullah Omar there, was no longer in residence, Wahhabism, an extremist Muslim sect with views endorsed by the Saudi Royal Family, was still rampant. It reminded me of something Dame Flora MacLeod once told me when I interviewed her at her home, Dunvegan Castle, on the Isle of Skye. The 'Wee Free' Church had just 'banned' piping on Skye (the home of the bagpipe) as 'the work of the Devil'. Unlike the Taliban, however, few people on Skye, least of all Dame Flora, paid much attention to the Wee Free, and its ban was ignored.

But Faisan had other friends in Kandahar, apart from the mullahs he had helped to put in power. They were educated, middle-class Afghans who, I suspected, had little sympathy for the Taliban; engineers who were working on the regeneration of the silted-up canal system in neighbouring Helmand, built by the Americans in the sixties as part of the Helmand Valley Project, which itself was based on the Tennessee River Valley Authority. Like so much else in the country, it had fallen into disrepair during and after the Russian occupation. One day they offered to take us to Sangin, north-west of Kandahar, on the Helmand River. But first we went to visit an old friend of Faisan's, Mullah Naqibullah, a once-powerful *mujahideen* commander and leader of the Alikozai tribe. The Alikozai had controlled the Arghandab Valley, which in turn controlled the approaches to Kandahar. When Mullah Omar took over Kandahar in 1994, Naqibullah had made a deal with the Taliban and then been tricked and sidelined.

A big, powerful Pushtun, he was now virtually under house arrest on his brother's farm outside Kandahar where he complained the Taliban had allowed him to keep only a dozen rifles for his personal protection. Unfortunately, since I had no Pushtun, the conversation that ensued passed me by, except for the odd crumb of information that Faisan let fall. It was only as we left and everyone shook hands that Mullah Naqibullah addressed me in English for the first time. 'When you next see Commander Masud,' he said, 'please give him my best wishes.' As we drove away I told Faisan in some surprise what Naqibullah had said. 'Oh, yes,' he replied, 'he's a good friend of Masud's. He's also a member of Jamiat [Jamiat-i-Islami, the largest and mainly Tajik *mujahideen* party].' That would have been one reason the Taliban did not trust him. Later, in what was seen as a deliberate assassination attempt, the Taliban planted a roadside bomb which blew up his car and left Naqibullah with serious injuries from which he eventually died.

We drove on to Sangin, arriving in late afternoon, and drew up at the police station. It had a large garden and we arranged to camp out there for the night. The Taliban police chief at first seemed doubtful about the British guest, but Faisan's friends must have been very persuasive – they sat up most of the night, talking to the police chief – for he not only invited me to stay but next morning offered to show me round the town. 'Can I take my camera?' I asked tentatively.

'Yes, of course,' was the surprisingly positive answer.

After a frugal breakfast of *nan* and *chai* (unleavened bread and tea), the police chief, armed with an old British Lee–Enfield .303 – which made me wonder if he was secretly pro-British, since most self-respecting police chiefs owned a Russian Kalashnikov or, better still, a Kalakov – loaded us all into his Toyota pick-up and drove us into Sangin. The first thing I noticed was that almost every male citizen we saw was also making for the centre of the town carrying household utensils of every shape and size, from pots and pans and buckets and bowls to a tin bath which one gentleman was transporting balanced on his head, all of them filled with a strong-smelling, dark brown paste known as 'brown sugar', or raw opium. When converted into heroin, it is not only the world's most lethal and most expensive drug, which thousands of young men and women in the West, and in neighbouring countries like Pakistan and Iran, are addicted to and dying from, but its international sale is funding and fuelling the Taliban insurgency which is also killing and maiming thousands of young American, British, and other NATO soldiers and countless Afghans. Heroin is a scourge of biblical proportions and no one seems to be able to control it.

All these opium growers were making for the bazaar where dozens of shops were doing a roaring trade, their fronts open to the street, the owners lolling in chairs with their merchandise stacked in open white sacks behind them.

'Is it all right to take a picture?' I asked the police chief.

'Yes, yes, go ahead.' He gave an obliging wave of his hand.

The merchants were not so obliging. One or two turned away; others remonstrated angrily in Pushtu with the police chief. I did not need a translator to tell me my photography was highly unpopular. But the police chief simply ignored the objectors, continuing the tour, rifle in hand and a smile on his face, as if determined to show me everything. Buying and selling opium was presumably perfectly legal and so, I imagined, was taking photographs in a public place like the bazaar.

Had I been on my own, I knew, it would have been a very different story. This became clear when we reached the car to find Faisan in a state of considerable agitation. The Special Forces officer, who had been so cool under fire from the Russian Mi-24 gunships and heavy mortars during the ambush in the gorge, met me with something close to panic.

'Where have you been?' he asked abruptly.

'Oh, we just went round the bazaar and I took a few photographs . . .' – I must have sounded infuriatingly offhand.

'We have to get out of here immediately. These people are extremely hostile. They've been complaining, saying to us, "Why did you bring these people [meaning me] here to destroy our living." They even started to rock the car. We must leave at once.' I realised that Colonel Faisan did not want to have to report to the British Embassy that I had fallen victim to an angry mob of opium merchants in Sangin.

After I had said a hasty goodbye to the police chief, who seemed oblivious of Faisan's nervousness and the reasons for it, I hurriedly got into the car and the tight-lipped driver edged his way through the crowd which seemed to be increasing in size and indignation by the minute. As we finally got clear, he put his foot down. Faisan kept looking back to see if were being pursued. 'I don't trust these people,' he said. But no one tried to follow us and half an hour later he had regained his usual unflappable demeanour. It was about then that he twisted in his seat again, and pointed out of the window. 'This is Maiwand,' he said, 'where as you know the British suffered one of their greatest defeats in Afghanistan.' His voice betrayed a certain relish, I thought. As the flat green battlefield unrolled peacefully before our eyes, invoking fragmentary recollections of the British rout and of Malalai, the Afghan Joan of Arc, encouraging her countrymen by waving her veil as a standard and shrieking her *landay:*

> *Young love, if you do not fall in the battle of Maiwand,*
> *By God, someone is saving you as a token of shame.*

Faisan gave a little smile, as if to say he was glad not to have to report another defeat, at Sangin this time.

Eleven years later, from 2006 to 2010, Sangin acquired the reputation in the British Army of being the most dangerous town in Helmand, and therefore Afghanistan. British troops, from 3 PARA onwards, found themselves fighting for their lives to hold the district centre against successive waves of Taliban fighters determined to drive them out. In those four years the British lost more than a hundred men in Sangin, with many more wounded. But the Taliban never took the district centre.

* A *landay* is a non-rhyming couplet popular in the Pushtu-speaking areas.

The Coming of the Taliban, 1995–2001

As so often in Afghanistan, you had to take a chance and hope for the best . . .

. Author, on visiting the Minaret of Jam, 1995

After saying goodbye to Faisan I flew to Kabul from Kandahar airport, built by the Russians and now, six years after their departure, looking distinctly the worse for wear. In Kabul I met two of my daughters, Carlotta and Michaela. We had planned a trip to the famous Minaret of Jam, which meant flying to Herat and then travelling a considerable distance overland. Few people had been to Jam – the travel writer Freya Stark of course was one, but that was a long time ago and she, no doubt, had a good dragoman, or the Afghan equivalent.

Jam was hidden in the mountains east of Herat, and it was difficult to discover the best route. Would we have to cross the river, the Hari Rud? Was it fordable at this time of year? Could we drive all the way? Would we need horses? And so on. As so often in Afghanistan, you had to take a chance and hope for the best. Then, in the mid-1990s, people were still very friendly and the threat of kidnap, which has become a much greater risk, was virtually non-existent. All three of us were excited but not daunted by the prospect of the adventure.

We wangled a free flight to Herat on a Russian-built cargo plane, which had seen better days. There were no seats and I remember standing for most of the two- or three-hour flight beside a bulkhead at the top of which were some cables and other components tied with wire. They say Russian planes need a minimum of maintenance, being less sophisticated than their Western equivalents, and it was anyone's guess when our Antonov had last been serviced. However, it got us there.

Herat is the most attractive of all Afghan cities, close to the Iranian border, imbued with Persian art and history and boasting a superb mosque and spectacular citadel, recently restored by the Aga Khan, a generous benefactor who has done much to revive Afghanistan's cultural heritage. Nancy Dupree describes the city in her guidebook in her inimitable fashion: 'Thirty-two thousand stately jack pines, planted by the Governor Abdullah Malikyar during the 1940s, escort the traveller out of Herat,' she writes. 'On the way, about 13 km/8 mi. after leaving the Governor's office, one notes a roofless mausoleum by the roadside to the right. Inside, among a jumble of tombstones, two headstones mark the final resting places of the ill-fated Shah Mahmud Sadozai and his son Kamran. Shah Mahmud ruled at Kabul from 1801–03 and again from 1809–1818 when he lost his throne to the Barakzai brothers. Fleeing to Herat he ruled that city until his son Kamran set him aside in 1821. He died in his bath in 1829 and rumour suspected that he had been murdered by his son. Power however rested in the hands of the wily Chief Minister, Yar Mohammad, who, tiring of maintaining the facade, suffocated the debauched Kamran in 1842.'[1] This is a supremely Afghan story, by no means exceptional in that country's turbulent history, which nobody recounts better than Nancy Dupree. Knowing something of it helps one to understand what is happening there today: the fighting, killing, politicking, corruption and general chicanery is nothing new and really quite moderate compared to what has happened there before.

Hamid Karzai, Afghanistan's President since 2004, is no Mahmud of Ghazni (988–1030), son of a Turkish slave and great general, whose reign ushered in 'one of the great renaissances of the Early Islamic period',[2] and at whose court were said to reside 400 poets and 900 scholars; nor is he another Amir Abdur Rahman (ruled 1880–1901), the founder of modern Afghanistan who welded together, by force when necessary, Afghanistan's patchwork of peoples and tribes into its first semblance of a nation state. He, one feels, would have dealt more successfully with the Taliban.

Afghanistan has a habit of producing long periods of savage conflict alternating with bursts of great artistic creativity. Herat has seen both. Genghis Khan and Tamerlane fought beneath the walls of its Citadel, but it was Tamerlane's son, Shah Rukh, who, using 7,000 workmen, restored and embellished them. And it was Shah Rukh's wife, Gowhar Shad, who built the minarets which Robert Byron described as 'the most beautiful example in colour in architecture ever devised by man to the glory of his God and himself'. Alas, most have been destroyed, some by earthquakes, others deliberately knocked down in 1885 by the British at the insistence of the Amir Abdur Rahman who feared a Russian attack and wanted to ensure a clear field of fire. The Russian attack never materialised but sadly, as Nancy Dupree points out, 'these great works of art were irretrievably lost'.

The Ghorids (1148–1202), originally mountain chieftains, ruled briefly but produced the masterpiece of the Minar-i-Jam, or Minaret of Jam. At 213 feet, it was the tallest minaret in the world when it was built about 1190 by their last and greatest king, Ghiyasuddin (1157–1202). His name is emblazoned on the minaret with the epithets: 'Sultan Magnificent! King of Kings!' Forgotten for centuries, the minaret was rediscovered in 1886 by Sir Thomas Holdich, a British official working for the Afghan Boundary Commission, but lapsed into oblivion again until it was sighted by a pilot flying between Herat and Kabul. Nancy Dupree says the same Governor of Herat who planted the 32,000 jack pines, Abdullah Malikyar, announced that it still existed in 1943 but it was not until 1957 when a French archaeologist, André Maricq, and the president of the Afghan Historical Society, Ahmad Ali Kohzad, visited the site, that the 'full significance of this astounding discovery was appreciated'.[3] More importantly, it is the only well-preserved architectural monument from the Ghorid period and as such is, Dupree writes, of 'immense importance' for students of medieval Islamic architecture.

We made a very small archaeological contribution ourselves by agreeing with the local UNESCO office to take with us an Afghan architectural engineer, Dr Najimi, who would carry out a survey of the Minaret of Jam. None of UNESCO's high-powered foreign archaeologists would undertake the mission for security reasons and, in any case, UNESCO Afghanistan said it could not afford their equally high-powered fees.

We discovered the minaret had a considerable tilt, not quite as pronounced as that of the Leaning Tower of Pisa, but still enough to worry the conservationists. It stands on the south bank of the Hari Rud, just above the entry of a tributary which was slowly eroding the minaret's foundations. Dr Najimi's mission was to investigate how serious the erosion was and to recommend a solution. While he did his research, we explored the interior of the minaret which consists of three cylindrical tiers of fired brick, each more slender than the one below and separated by corbelled balconies. Inside, twin spiral staircases rise to the first balcony from where a single staircase climbs to the top, enabling the most daring and agile climbers to reach the small circular arcade which surmounts the minaret and from which they can lean out dizzily, and wave to people below. We climbed the first two tiers; the third we thought looked rather shaky and, to our shame, we did not attempt it. But the views of the valley, from narrow windows cunningly set so as not to spoil the exterior design, are still, as Nancy Dupree says, breathtaking.

The exterior is superbly decorated with intricately carved brickwork in Persian blue, as vivid, it seemed, as when it was first fired, depicting the 19th Sura of the Koran called Maryam, which recounts the story of Mary and the Virgin Birth, of Prophets Abraham, Isaac, Jacob, Moses, Aaron, Ishmael and Enoch, and of Adam and Noah. It relates also 'how they were guided by the revelations of the Merciful', warns unbelievers of the punishments of Hell, and promises those who embrace the Faith the glories of the Garden of Eden.

Why the minaret is there, standing in solitary magnificence in a narrow valley, surrounded by barren mountains, remains a mystery. A minaret is, after all, the part of a mosque from which the muezzin calls the faithful to prayer; but there is no mosque at Jam, only the vivid green Hari Rud which flows from central Afghanistan westwards to the Iranian border, near Herat, before looping north and losing itself in the deserts of Turkmenistan. Was this once the site of Firozkoh, the Ghorid capital, which has disappeared? And what is the significance of a Jewish cemetery which existed near the minaret in the Ghorid period? We crossed the river to inspect the ruins of a small fortress and some watchtowers but, the experts say, they can hardly be all that remains of the great city of Firozkoh. Watching Dr Najimi taking his measurements and doing his calculations, and admiring the minaret from different angles, we had to conclude that, even after the passage of eight centuries, it remains an enigma.

On the third day we started off back to Herat, climbing up the almost dry bed of the tributary to the village where we had spent the first night, and then walked over the hills to where we had left our vehicles. It was a long drive back to Herat and halfway there we broke down, forcing us to leave Dr Najimi and his son, to their chagrin, behind. It was a case of *sauve qui peut*, although I still have feelings of guilt. But we had an appointment with Ismail Khan, the Governor of Herat and a famous former *mujahideen* commander during the Russian War. He was a close ally of Masud and a pillar of the Northern Alliance.

I asked him about the threat from the Taliban who had by now gained control of the south. Dour and rather uncommunicative – perhaps he was worried – he dismissed the question in a few words. 'The Taliban? We're not worried about them,' he said. Two months later they had inflicted a crushing defeat on his army and reinforcements flown in by Masud. Ismail Khan was forced to flee. It was a shattering defeat for the Northern Alliance.

The fall of Herat took everyone by surprise. Taking over the Pushtun south was one thing, but this put another complexion on Taliban ambitions. Herat's sophisticated, Persian-speaking inhabitants looked down on their new rulers as barbarians. More surprises were to follow and a year later, in September 1996, the Taliban juggernaut, trained and directed by the Pakistan Army and financed by the Saudis, was at the gates of Kabul. Outnumbered and outflanked, Masud made a strategic withdrawal to his old stronghold in the Panjsher, inflicting heavy losses on his pursuers who, despite repeated attempts, never succeeded in forcing their way into the valley. Instead, in 1997 and 1998, the Taliban turned their attention to the north, launching new blitzkriegs, slaughtering thousands of Hazaras and Uzbeks in Mazar-i-Sharif and the Hazarajat, and laying waste to much of the countryside. In 1999 and 2000, with Pakistani and Arab al Qaeda reinforcements, they captured Kunduz and Taloqan, finally squeezing Masud into the north-east corner of the country, although he kept the Panjsher and through it a lifeline across the Amu Darya River border to Tajikistan, now technically independent but still heavily influenced by Moscow: it was his sole link to the outside world.

Although under constant pressure from the Taliban, who had the very considerable resources of Pakistan's ISI intelligence machine and Saudi petro-dollars behind them, Masud was undefeated five years after his withdrawal from Kabul. His was still the only effective resistance to the Taliban when, two days before 9/11, he was assassinated by two Arab al Qaeda suicide bombers posing as television journalists. By then, in the view of Western defence sources in Islamabad, he had his back to the wall and was unlikely to have survived very much longer, unless he received substantial help from the West. Masud, however, was a great survivor and had often proved the pessimists wrong. For those five long years, he had fought the Taliban virtually single-handed. Of the other top Northern Alliance commanders, the most powerful, the Uzbek General Dostum, was forced by the Taliban to flee to Turkey; the second most important, Ismail Khan, after being driven out of Herat took refuge in Iran but was later captured by the Taliban and imprisoned for two years before escaping again. From the Taliban's point of view, it must have seemed only a matter of time before they gained control of the whole country.

As the millennium approached, with Osama bin Laden under Taliban protection, the Americans were at a loss to know how to deal with an enemy who had already carried out three major attacks on American targets: the bombing of the World Trade Center in New York on 26 February 1993, which killed six adults, one unborn baby and injured more than a thousand (an attack planned by Ramzi Yousef, the nephew of Khalid Sheikh Mohammed, the al Qaeda mastermind of 9/11); the simultaneous blowing up of the US embassies in Nairobi and Dar-es-Salaam on 7 August 1998, with a loss of hundreds of lives, mostly Africans; and the suicide strike on the US Navy destroyer USS *Cole* at Aden on 12 October 2000, which killed seventeen American sailors and wounded thirty-nine. It was only after 9/11 that the United States intensified their demands for the handover of bin Laden. Mullah Omar was to be given a choice: 'Hand over bin Laden and his al Qaeda network or be attacked,' as Kathy Gannon, the well-informed Associated Press correspondent in Pakistan writes in *I is for Infidel*, her account of the American intervention. President Musharraf, who until then had 'supported the Taliban wholeheartedly', was urged by Washington to put pressure on Mullah Omar to deliver the al Qaeda leader.

Musharraf sent General Mahmud Ahmed, the head of Pakistan military intelligence, the ISI, and a small party of clerics to Kandahar for talks with the head of the Taliban. Kathy Gannon describes General Ahmed as 'a religious zealot very much like Mullah Omar. He had been central to the military takeover of Pakistan in 1999 by General Pervez Musharraf. A hawk with pan-Islamic visions, he had been a staunch supporter of *jihadis* both from Pakistan and elsewhere. This was the man Musharraf sent to negotiate with Mullah Omar.'⁴ But Ahmed had a message for Mullah Omar 'quite different' from the one that Washington had asked Pakistan to convey, according to eyewitnesses and ISI officials, Gannon claims. 'He took the slow-talking Taliban leader aside and urged him to resist the United States. He told Mullah Omar not.to give up bin Laden.'⁵

General Ahmed made several more trips to Kandahar, Kathy Gannon states, and warned Mullah Omar that the Americans would rely heavily on bombing and the ground forces of the Northern Alliance. But there was no progress in handing over bin Laden. This should not have surprised the Americans. Mullah Omar was bound by the tribal code of *Pushtunwali*, 'the Way of the Pushtun', which lays down strict rules governing *melmastia* (hospitality), *badal* (revenge), and *nang* (honour). In the case of hospitality, any stranger who has asked for and been given shelter (as bin Laden had) is entitled to his host's protection whatever he has done, even if he has committed a crime against his host's family. In fact a story is told of how a stranger who asked for shelter turned out to be the murderer of his host's elder son. The host did not realise this when he took the man in. But when his younger son saw the man, he immediately recognised him and told his father, who said: 'There is nothing I can do about it, I have offered him my hospitality.' During the night, the younger son got up and killed his brother's murderer. Next day, he confessed to his father, who was horrified that the iron laws of hospitality had been broken in his house by his own son. He then felt honour bound to kill his second son.

In the case of Mullah Omar, *Pushtunwali* and political interest coincided. Interestingly, the Saudis, who deprived bin Laden of his citizenship and passport in 1994 after differences with the King, and who obviously had much more clout with Mullah Omar than the Americans, also asked Mullah Omar to extradite him, after the bombing of the American embassies in East Africa in 1998. But even their request was rejected. 'Even if all the countries in the world unite, we would defend Osama by our blood,' was Mullah Omar's answer.

In 2001 the Taliban's steady march towards increasingly extremist policies caused international outrage with the blowing up of the Buddhas of Bamiyan. Since the sixth century the two giant Buddhas had gazed out from their red sandstone cliff over the fertile fields of Bamiyan, watching over the valley which, for more than 1,400 years, had drawn thousands of Buddhist pilgrims from China, Japan and the rest of the Far East to the great Buddhist centre and monastery. 'To us, Bamiyan is Afghanistan and Afghanistan is Bamiyan,' a former Japanese Ambassador is reported as saying. It seemed at one stage that Mullah Omar did not disagree. In 2000 he issued an edict forbidding any damage to the Buddhas and proclaiming they were part of Afghanistan's heritage. Why the change? Extremist mullahs and possibly al Qaeda under the urging of the puritanical bin Laden agitated for their destruction, harping on Islam's ban on the representation of the human form, and insisting they were 'idols'. Even the Mongol conqueror Genghis Khan, whom the American anthropologist and historian Louis Dupree describes as 'the atom bomb of his day', spared the Buddhas when he razed Bamiyan and slaughtered every living thing in it in 1221.[6] But Mullah Omar finally succumbed to extremist pressure and the Buddhas were dynamited in March 2001.

And then, six months later, out of the blue – almost literally – came Osama bin Laden's thunderbolt: 9/11; September 11th, 2001. Overnight the world changed. Less than a month later, on 7 October 2001, America began bombing Afghanistan in retaliation, bringing down the Taliban government and driving it out of power.

3

Tora Bora 1, 1982–2001

Wanted: dead or alive.
> President George W. Bush on the hunt for Osama bin Laden,
> October 2001

One of the great ironies of the American intervention in Afghanistan after 9/11 was that its success depended to a great extent on the army of the Northern Alliance, created by the guerrilla leader, Ahmed Shah Masud, who despite being the only effective opponent of the Taliban and thus of al Qaeda in Afghanistan from 1996 to 2001, was never really supported by the United States.

The core of the Northern Alliance army consisted of Masud's Panjsheri guerrillas, or *mujahideen*, hardened in the fire of the Red Army's helicopter gunships and Su-25 fighter-bombers during repeated punitive raids into the valley throughout the 1980s. The Panjsher was strategically close to the Salang Highway and Tunnel – the highest in the world when it was built by the Russians in 1964, and the pipeline through which most of the Red Army's supplies came, including fuel for their tanks and jets. It was also the most important road in the country since it connected the Soviet Union via Uzbekistan with Kabul, the capital, and the big air base at Bagram. Masud's *mujahideen*, often under the particularly daring Commander Panah, regularly attacked Russian convoys on the Salang, making Masud a dangerous opponent. The Russians tried long and hard to eliminate him, without success.

Peasant farmers, artisans and shopkeepers from a tightly knit community, with an exceptionally strong esprit de corps, the Panjsheris responded as one to Masud's call to arms. In 1982, when I first visited the valley with a television crew to film how the resistance was faring – there was very little news available then in the outside world – we were impressed by the strength of Panjsheri morale. Proud of their Tajik blood, they were even

boasting that once they had got rid of the Russians, they would start liber-
ating their cousins across the Amu Darya River border, in what was then
the Soviet Republic of Tajikistan.[1]

Arriving by chance in mid-August at the start of Panjsher Six – the sixth
offensive the Russians had launched against the valley since they invaded
Afghanistan at the end of 1979 – we witnessed the indiscriminate bombing
of villages and a scorched-earth campaign which would have brought less
determined opponents to their knees. One day we were bombed at very
close range in a tiny hamlet – some of our more panicky escorts thought it
was because we had been betrayed by Russian spies on the ground or in the
sky; the ubiquitous reconnaissance Antonov always seemed to be circling
– so we could appreciate at first hand the terror inflicted on the women
and children of this poor valley. I still have a vivid memory of meeting a
man by a stream one day and our guide, Yahya, I think, one of Masud's
brothers, telling us the man's house had been bombed and his whole family
of eight killed.

Once the Russians had withdrawn, after a two- or three-week 'search
and destroy' operation, which heavily disrupted the daily life of the valley,
killing and maiming many civilians and livestock but few *mujahideen*,
Masud outlined his future strategy. First, he said, it was pointless and
dangerous for him to remain in the Panjsher where he had become a sitting
duck, with the odds against him surviving steadily worsening. He intended
therefore to leave the valley and establish a headquarters in the north.
Secondly, and as a logical extension of the first decision, he would set up a
political and military coalition drawn from the northern Tajik and Uzbek-
speaking provinces of Badakhshan, Takhar, Kunduz, Samangan, Balkh,
(capital, Mazar-i-Sharif, the most important city in the north), Jowzjan,
(capital, Shiburghan) and Herat in the west.

The new body would be called the Shura-i-Nazar, or Council of the
North, later renamed the Northern Alliance. Among its early leaders with
Masud were men like Ismail Khan from Herat, a former professional
soldier. Only much later would the Uzbek warlord, Abdul Rashid
Dostum, whose headquarters were in the Qala-i-Jangi (War House), a
massive, mud-walled Beau Geste fort at Shiburghan, and who was then a
general in the Afghan Communist army, become one of its leaders. So

successful did the Northern Alliance become that after playing a key role in the defeat and withdrawal of the Russians in 1989, three years later, in 1992, Masud led it to victory over President Najibullah's Russian-trained army, ousting his rump Communist government and capturing Kabul. That was perhaps the zenith of the Northern Alliance's military success. The West, however, to their lasting discredit, ignominiously failed to support the Rabbani–Masud government in the ensuing civil war, which did more damage to the capital and killed more of Kabul's inhabitants than the entire Russian occupation. This was the first time the West let Afghanistan down in its hour of need. The second was after 9/11.

Commander Masud, or *Amir sahib* (pronounced *Omer sa'ab* in the Panjsheri dialect) as he became to his men, saw the Northern Alliance as the nucleus of a national army, which did not materialise until after his death and the overthrow of the Taliban. He had gained the support of a number of prominent Pushtuns in other parts of the country, notably the influential Kandahari commander, Mullah Naqibullah and Haji Qadir, the Governor of Ningrahar, both opponents of the Taliban. Haji Qadir, later one of President Karzai's Vice-Presidents and Minister for Urban Development, was shot dead leaving his office in Kabul in July 2002, the victim of a blood feud with the family of Haji Zaman, one of the Pushtun militia commanders at Tora Bora, Osama bin Laden's mountain stronghold.[2]

Throughout the Russian War and its aftermath, the Americans blew hot and cold about supporting Masud. The CIA was divided between pro- and anti-Masud factions, as was the State Department; the antis reflecting the ISI's long-term bias against Masud which coloured US policy throughout the entire period of the Russian occupation and Taliban rule, right up to his assassination, aided and abetted by the ISI, many of Masud's closest associates believe. Masood Khalili, who was sitting next to Commander Masud, acting as his interpreter when the bomb that killed Masud went off, seriously injuring him, is convinced the ISI were part of the conspiracy. The consulate in Pakistan's London Embassy, under ultimate ISI control, issued the two al Qaeda-trained Tunisian suicide bombers, posing as television journalists, with multiple entry visas valid for a year – unheard of for journalists normally – and facilitated their journey through Pakistan and across the border to Afghanistan, carrying their bomb with them.

Despite the anti-Masud lobby seeming always to have been in the ascend-
ant, the CIA was quick to recognise after 9/11 that only Masud's Northern
Alliance could help them make the Rumsfeld–General Franks 'light footprint' plan work. As the CIA got ready to launch its sortie into the war zone,
blacked-out helicopters would land at night on the shingle in the middle of
the Panjsher River, near Masud's guesthouse at Astana, with, on one occasion at least, communications equipment on board.[3] This was the vital link
with Dushanbe, the capital of Tajikistan, which Masud himself had set up
and which enabled him in those last few years to beat the Taliban blockade;
and from which the CIA and the American invasion now profited.

The arrival in late 2001 of two senior CIA officials, Gary Schroen and
Gary Berntsen, and a handful of assistants, their suitcases bulging with crisp
new $100 bills, and orders to link up with Generals Dostum and Atta
Mohammed in the north and Masud's own people on the Kabul front, was
too late, alas, to save Masud, but not his legacy. In the skies above them,
carrying enough high explosive to obliterate half Afghanistan, came the full
weight of the US Air Force, which soon started hammering the Taliban into
submission. On the ground, a ready-made army, raring to go, were the *mujahideen* of the Northern Alliance who, having been on the back foot for years,
were now itching to get their revenge. Without this army-in-waiting it is
hard to see how the United States could have mounted their retaliatory
Operation Enduring Freedom as quickly, effectively and cheaply. In fact,
without it they would have had to launch a full-scale expedition, deploying
thousands of American troops, which would have seriously interfered with
another, altogether more ambitious campaign with which President Bush
himself, his Vice-President, Dick Cheney and Secretary for Defense, Donald
Rumsfeld, were much more concerned: the invasion of Iraq. As we shall see,
the obsession with Iraq was to bedevil the whole Afghan campaign.

But to begin with, the CIA plan to defeat the Taliban worked on the
whole much better than anyone could reasonably have hoped. This was
certainly true in the north and centre. In the north, where the CIA relied
on the two commanders, Dostum and Atta Mohammed, the combination
of Northern Alliance *mujahideen* and the fearsome firepower of the B-52s
and ground-attack aircraft wreaked havoc on the black-turbaned guerrillas
who had no experience of this kind of warfare. They began to give

themselves up; at first in tens and twenties, then in their hundreds, and eventually in their thousands, as they were surrounded and finally surrendered at Kunduz, in the north. General Dostum made the headlines when he led a charge on a Taliban outpost on horseback, at the head of his cavalry – a quixotic touch the media loved – but the real damage was done by the air cavalry, the US Air Force.

In the Kabul area, Masud's successor, General Fahim, kept urging the Americans to start bombing the Taliban front line, about thirty-five miles north of the capital and just south of the Northern Alliance-held town of Charikar. Pressure built up from Pakistan and the United Nations to stop the Northern Alliance occupying Kabul – there was hysterical talk of a bloodbath – but it was a totally unrealistic demand since the Northern Alliance were the only troops on the ground and Taliban morale was disintegrating. I visited the front line just before the fall of Kabul on 13–14 November and was briefed by some of Masud's commanders, including Bismillah Khan and Gul Haider, before they marched on the capital. They were impatient that it had taken the Americans so long to bomb the Taliban front line, which they did not have the firepower to overwhelm on their own. The American overall commander, General Tommy Franks, a tough, no-nonsense Texan, refused to be rushed, but eventually, when the Taliban rout in the north was complete, gave the order to bomb. The US Air Force blasted a hole in the Taliban front line, putting to flight an al Qaeda Arab unit holding the central sector and the Panjsheri *mujahideen* strolled into the capital virtually without firing a shot.

It was a different story, however, in the Pushtun south, where Mullah Omar, the Taliban leader, was preparing to flee Kandahar for the safe haven of Pakistan, and Osama bin Laden had already moved from Jalalabad to his mountain redoubt at Tora Bora, a natural stronghold used by the *mujahideen* in their struggle against the Russians and which he had later extensively fortified. As the instigator of the 9/11 attacks on the United States, the first time in history an enemy had attacked the continental United States since the British Army and Royal Navy bombarded the city of Baltimore in 1814,[4] the Saudi terrorist mastermind was America's Public Enemy Number One. 'Wanted, Dead or Alive', as President Bush put it, metaphorically donning his Stetson and strapping on his Colt .45,

Wild West-style. His death – or capture – was President Bush's main stated priority. Which makes it all the more surprising that he did not order Rumsfeld, who had remained inflexible to all requests, pleas, arguments and demands from the CIA, to send in American Rangers and Marines, as well as Special Forces, to catch bin Laden.

Tora Bora, forty miles south-west of Jalalabad, is Pushtun country and the Northern Alliance had little or no pull there. Most local Pushtun leaders were pro-Taliban and pro-bin Laden, who had assiduously cultivated them over the years, giving them generous amounts of money, arms and other perks. But not all. One exception was the small non-Pushtun Pashai tribe which, although also from the Jalalabad area, had fought with the Northern Alliance against the Taliban. Its senior commander, General Hazrat Ali, was given command of the Tora Bora operation. Despite his Northern Alliance background, however, Hazrat Ali seems to have played an equivocal and indeed obstructive role, largely, no doubt, because he was reportedly given a hefty bribe of $300,000 by bin Laden to help him escape, according to a senior Afghan intelligence source.[5] I found him evasive and uninformative when I tried to interview him in Kabul in 2005.

The second senior commander, Haji Zaman Ghamsharik, a former military commander of Jalalabad, drug smuggler and adventurer, who had been in exile in France during the Taliban period and was specially flown back to Afghanistan to take part in the Tora Bora operation, was reported by the same intelligence source to have received an even bigger bribe: $800,000. Rivals and enemies Hazrat Ali and Haji Zaman may have been, their mutual animosity later becoming very apparent at Tora Bora, but ultimately the lure of Saudi gold must have encouraged a deal. Haji Zaman took over the ceasefire 'negotiations' at Tora Bora, while Hazrat Ali, supposedly in command, simply disappeared. I never succeeded in meeting Haji Zaman who was killed in an allegedly Taliban suicide bomb attack in Jalalabad, in February 2010, although tribal sources claimed it was a blood feud killing.

The third and much more junior commander was Haji Zahir, then aged twenty-seven, and son of Haji Qadir, the pro-Western, anti-Taliban Governor of Ningrahar Province. Zahir was a nephew of Abdul Haq, the famous *mujahideen* leader who had just been murdered by the Taliban for trying to raise a local rebellion against them. Of the three, Zahir had much the strongest motive for trying to kill or capture bin Laden, although his poorly trained border police would have been no match for the fanatical, fight-to-the-death warriors of al Qaeda. He told me Haji Zaman received a bribe of 'maybe a million, maybe two million dollars' from bin Laden for arranging the fake ceasefire, which allowed him and allegedly 800 of his followers to escape from Tora Bora.[6]

Speaking of the actual operation, Haji Zahir said he and his two fellow commanders were each given the area they were supposed to cordon off. He did not know who made 'the plan', meaning the operational plan, 'but I know Marshal Fahim introduced General Ali to the Americans'. One day, according to Zahir, when the three militias were all deployed on the mountain, and the Americans were bombing, Haji Zaman announced he had arranged a ceasefire. Al Qaeda had agreed to surrender at 8 a.m. the next morning. Haji Zahir said he did not see the point of the delay. 'If they wanted to surrender why didn't they do so right away? So I refused to take part in the ceasefire and kept my men in their positions on the mountain,' he said.[7]

At about the same time he saw a local tribesman, named Elias Khel, who knew every path through the mountains that led from Tora Bora to Pakistan, being given 'a satellite telephone and $20,000 or $30,000 dollars' by Hazrat Ali. A former *mujahid*, Khel came from a local family of butter carriers, and since boyhood had regularly crossed the mountains carrying fresh butter in a wooden frame on his back to sell in the Pakistani town of Parachinar, a journey of fifteen to twenty miles each way. He knew 'every stone of Tora Bora', according to Haji Zahir, who described him as bin Laden's 'right-hand man' who led him and his party over the mountains to Pakistan during the fake ceasefire.[8] Next morning a B-52 bomber turned on its afterburners to produce contrails and wrote the figure 8 followed by the letters NO to demonstrate that the Americans did not recognise the ceasefire. But by that time, Haji Zahir said, 'Al Qaeda had all gone. No one was there.' The main body of al Qaeda fighters escaped, and only a few stragglers were taken prisoner. Haji Zahir said his men captured twenty-one al Qaeda, one of whom confirmed bin Laden had been at Tora Bora. 'He [bin Laden] visited them one day,' Haji Zahir quoted the prisoner as saying, 'told them to fight hard against the enemy, had a cup of tea and then left.' Other reports told of how bin Laden was on the radio frequently at one stage, apologising to his followers for getting them trapped at Tora Bora.

Hazrat Ali's brother-in-law, Commander Mohammed Musa, who commanded 600 troops at Tora Bora, said: 'Al Qaeda fought very hard with us. When we captured them, they committed suicide with grenades. I saw three of them do that myself.'[9] One day, he says, Haji Zaman told him al Qaeda wanted to escape from the village of Ghalanjali in the mountains. 'Al Qaeda said: "We want to surrender to the United Nations. We want a ceasefire," to which Zaman replied: "We'll accept a ceasefire at 4 p.m. in the afternoon."'[10] This contradicts the timing – 8 a.m. the following morning – given by the US Delta Force commander at Tora Bora, a major who uses the pen name Dalton Fury in his racy, first-hand narrative of the battle, *Kill Bin Laden*.[11] He writes that Zaman had changed the time when he would contact al Qaeda by radio to 8 a.m.

The discrepancy may of course simply reflect the general lack of coordination, to put it mildly, on the *mujahideen* side, although a more sinister and mercenary motive is more likely. That night, Commander Musa added, al Qaeda and the Taliban all escaped to Pakistan. 'We only captured thirteen people . . . We did not want the ceasefire to happen. It was Haji Zaman who agreed to it.'[12] US forces were not involved in the fighting, according to Commander Musa. 'There were six American soldiers with us, US Special Forces, they coordinated the air strikes . . . My personal view is: if the Americans had blocked the way out to Pakistan, al Qaeda would not have had a way to escape.'[13]

There were in fact only 'about ninety or so',[14] mainly American, Special Forces at Tora Bora, according to Dalton Fury. Of the total 'three dozen' were British – twelve SBS (Special Boat Service) and 'two dozen' Royal Marine Commandos, who were mainly at Bagram airport and only made a brief appearance at Tora Bora. Of the fifty or so Delta commandos at Tora Bora only forty were 'in the mountains';[15] the remainder were in a support role at the Schoolhouse, their temporary base.

Dalton Fury blames Haji Zaman as the organiser of the fake ceasefire and describes how, in one incident, when Fury wanted to push on up the

mountain to monitor the 'ceasefire' process of which he was highly suspicious, Zaman's *mujahideen* levelled their guns at the Delta men and for an
ugly few minutes it looked as if there would be a shoot-out. Delta, outnumbered and under orders to cooperate with their Afghan 'allies', backed
down. But the inference seems clear: Zaman did not want Delta to interfere with his lucrative ceasefire deal with bin Laden, and was prepared to
open fire on the Americans if they got in his way. This incident demon-
strates better than anything else the unreliability of the Pushtun militias at
Tora Bora, something that the CIA's old hands were well aware of and had
warned against.

Which raises the question: Who approved the Hazrat Ali–Haji Zaman
partnership? Was it a deal struck between Marshal Fahim, representing the
Northern Alliance, the two militia commanders (Hazrat Ali and Haji
Zaman) and US Special Forces? It is hard to believe the CIA were involved,
since Gary Berntsen was highly sceptical of the militias and was pressing
for a battalion of Rangers. The most exhaustive study of Tora Bora
published so far does not answer the question.[16] One can only conclude
that Rumsfeld and Franks, who were not prepared to use their own ground
troops, although they were there, ready and waiting, gambled on the militias being up to the task – and got it wrong. It seems a strange decision,
given the uniqueness of the opportunity to eliminate Osama bin Laden, an
opportunity that would not recur for ten years. The answer may well lie in
Rumsfeld's unorthodox, even quirky, views on 'light footprint, risk averse'
warfare, criticised by the then British Chief of the Defence Staff, Admiral
Sir Michael [now Lord] Boyce as 'incompetent strategic appreciation'.[17]

Stationed a short helicopter flight away, at a base near Kandahar, were
one thousand US Marines whose commander, Brigadier General James
Mattis, said his men could have sealed off Tora Bora but his offer to do so
had been rejected; and another thousand troops from the US Army's 10th
Mountain Division were split between Bagram air base, north-east of
Kabul, and another base across the border in neighbouring Uzbekistan,
also within helicopter range. Their commander, Lieutenant Colonel Paul
Lacamera, said later that his men had been ready to deploy anywhere in
Afghanistan since mid-November, but they too were not called on. The
question remains: Why?

Conditions at Tora Bora, 6,000–10,000 feet or more above sea level, could hardly have been worse. Temperatures were below freezing, with deep snow on the ground, and it was still Ramazan (Ramadan), the month of fasting when devout Muslims do not eat or drink, not even water, during the hours of daylight and then stay up half the night making up for it. Ramazan is notorious for being a time when very little gets done because people are half asleep in the day and awake much of the night, eating. As they set foot on the mountain, Dalton Fury says, one of the first things he and his men noticed was that in the late afternoon, as the light began to fade, and the prospect of *iftar*, the evening meal which breaks the daily fast, filled their thoughts, the *mujahideen* turned their backs on al Qaeda and headed down the mountain as fast their legs would carry them.[18] Far from being committed to trying to kill or capture bin Laden, they were simply putting on a show – for money. It did not take Delta long to realise that neither General Ali nor his men had any appetite for the fight.[19]

This is what Dalton Fury says about the military prowess of the Afghan militias he saw at Tora Bora. 'Afghans are afternoon fighters by nature,' he writes, and their methods are straight out of 'Barbarian Tactics 101: Sometime after midday prayers they would muster with AK-47 rifles, PKM machine guns and RPGs as far forward in the foothills as they safely could. After clustering around, seemingly as if nobody knew who was in charge on that particular day, they would plough straight uphill, firing wildly. It was a good show that apparently was played out to convince the watching reporters that General Ali's forces were on the offensive. But it was also grossly ineffective.'

Fury dismisses their tactics as 'centuries-old tribal warfare, more symbolic than savage, more duty than deadly, more for spoils than scalps. No one was supposed to really get hurt. The skirmishes would last a few hours, then the fighters would do some looting, call it a day and retreat down the ridgelines, giving back to al Qaeda any of the day's hard-earned terrain . . .'[20] Hazrat Ali's intention was to maximise the bombing to save as many of his troops' lives as possible, Fury says, and Colonel Ashley, the Delta Force commander in Afghanistan, was similarly wary, although for different reasons. Ashley's caution was meant to 'stave off our natural impetuousness and was hard to dispute, for he still carried with him his experiences in the deadly streets of Mogadishu'. (This is a reference to the notorious 'Black Hawk Down' disaster when the Americans had two Black Hawk helicopters shot down, nineteen men killed in action and more than seventy wounded in the Battle of Mogadishu in October 1993. The US subsequently withdrew from Somalia in 1995.)

Ashley's point was well taken, Fury writes, but it made them wonder how America would react to hearing a commander state, '"Let them [the Afghans] finish the job. This is about using surrogate forces; it's their war." As much as I respected both of their positions, I also disagreed with them and so did my men. We did not like hearing such statements while the rubble was being cleaned up from the attack on the World Trade Center.'[21]

The Senate Report tells the same story: 'The Delta Force commandos had doubts about the willingness and ability of the Afghan militias to wage a genuine assault on Tora Bora. Their concerns were underlined each time the Afghans insisted on retreating from the mountains as darkness fell, and their suspicions were confirmed by events that started on the afternoon of 11 December, the fake ceasefire.'[22]

Haji Zaman approached Fury and told him that al Qaeda fighters wanted to surrender. All they needed to end the siege was a twelve-hour ceasefire to confirm that they had lost their resolve under the relentless bombing and wanted to give up. But Fury remained suspicious:

'This is the greatest day in the history of Afghanistan,' Zaman told Fury.

'Why is that?' asked the dubious American officer.

'Because al Qaeda is no more,' the Afghan said. 'Bin Laden is finished.'[23]

CENTCOM (Central Command) headquarters in Florida refused to back the ceasefire, suspecting a ruse, but the official history records that it agreed reluctantly to an overnight pause in the bombing to avoid killing any surrendering al Qaeda fighters.[24] Haji Zaman, who negotiated by radio with representatives of al Qaeda, initially told Fury that a large number of Algerians wanted to surrender. Then he said that he could turn over the entire al Qaeda leadership. Such a 'bold promise' only increased Fury's suspicions.[25] By the morning of 12 December, no al Qaeda fighters had appeared and the Delta Force commander concluded that the whole episode was a hoax. Intelligence estimates suggested that as many as 800 al Qaeda fighters escaped that night, although 'bin Laden stuck it out'.[26]

Dalton Fury says there were two plans to attack bin Laden, both from the direction he would never anticipate, the southern side of the mountains.[27] 'The idea to come in from the south using oxygen to get the drop on UBL [Usama/Osama bin Laden] from behind was concocted in late November/first day or so of December 2001. It was disapproved before we ever reached Bagram ... The Gator mines idea surfaced around 9 December, after we had been at Tora Bora for several days and acquired an understanding of the lay of the land and the situation. This was disapproved as well. So, both these ideas happened *prior* to the 12 December ceasefire fiasco.'[28]

Fury gives a detailed description of the effect these air-dropped, anti-personnel Gator cluster mines would have had on a body of men escaping along one of the trails which link Tora Bora and Parachinar, on the Pakistan side of the border: 'First guy blows his leg off, everybody else stops,' he says. 'That allows aircraft overhead to find them. They see all these heat sources out there. Okay, there is a big group of al Qaeda moving south. They can engage that.' That proposal was rejected too, Fury says, although the manufacturers claim that after a preset period of at most fifteen days, the mines would self-destruct, and after forty days the batteries would run out, rendering them harmless. In other words, in six weeks the trails would be safe again.[29] And few if any local travellers would be using these trails in the depth of winter when snow would block most of the passes.

The last word should belong to Dalton Fury. After six years of pondering the significance of the battle at Tora Bora, he writes: 'We were naïve back in December 2001 to think that Westerners could invade a Muslim country and rely on indigenous fighters to kill their Islamic brothers with tenacity and impunity.'[30]

In addition, at Tora Bora, he adds, the local militias were fighting al Qaeda and Osama bin Laden. 'We might as well have been asking for them to fight the Almighty Prophet Mohammed himself. What motivation did the Afghan Muslims possess for hunting down, raising their rifles, sighting in and actually shooting an al Qaeda fighter, much less the revered leader?' He was convinced, he says, that not a single one of our *muj* fighters wanted to be recognised in their mosque as the man who killed Sheikh bin Laden.

Dalton Fury thus confirms the criticism made by the most senior CIA men at Tora Bora. Gary Berntsen, for example, said he was sceptical from the beginning of the reliability of the Pushtun militias assigned to Tora Bora, who were mainly from Ningrahar Province. Haji Zaman's men at Tora Bora, for example, would have been in the main pro-Taliban and pro-bin Laden and anti-American. Tajik, Uzbek and Hazara fighters from the Northern Alliance, on the other hand, were not only intensely anti-Taliban, for very good reasons, but they were just as bitterly anti-al Qaeda. The Tajiks above all would never forgive or forget the assassination, two days before 9/11, of the Tajik Northern Alliance leader, Ahmed Shah Masud, at the hands of two Arab suicide bombers, who they believed had been trained and dispatched by bin Laden. But there were no Tajiks or Uzbeks, loyal to Masud and General Dostum, at Tora Bora. There were some Pashai militias under the command of Hazrat Ali, but although technically in charge, since he seems to have been sponsored by General Fahim, Masud's successor as head of the Northern Alliance, his commitment was doubtful, to say the least. When the chips were down at the time of the fake ceasefire, he was noticeable by his absence.

Fury is right too when he writes that 'the Afghan military and tribal leaders had goals that were much different from our own. They were out to accumulate personal fortunes and political power, to clear the opium fields for business again and protect the drug distribution routes ... not to avenge the Americans killed on 9/11.'[31]

While all this was happening, of course, General Tommy Franks was well into planning for the next war – the invasion of Iraq. In his memoirs, *American Soldier,* Franks described getting a telephone call on 21 November from Rumsfeld relaying the President's orders while he was sitting in his office at MacDill Air Force Base in Florida. Ironically, Franks and one of his aides were working on air support for the Afghan units being assembled to push into the mountains surrounding Tora Bora. Rumsfeld said that the President wanted options for war with Iraq. Franks replied that the existing plan was out of date and that a new one should include lessons about precision weapons and the use of special operations forces learned in Afghanistan.

'Okay, Tom,' Rumsfeld said, according to Franks. 'Please dust it off and get back to me next week.'[32]

Franks said his reaction was: 'Son of a bitch. No rest for the weary.'[33]

Tora Bora 2, 2001–2011

Gary, I want you killing the enemy immediately.
Cofer Black, CIA Counter-Terrorism Chief, October 2001[1]

Although the initial stages of Operation Enduring Freedom, the American campaign to overthrow the Taliban regime in retaliation for 9/11, were outstandingly successful, the attempt to kill or capture Osama bin Laden and destroy his al Qaeda organisation at Tora Bora, which would have been the final *coup de grâce,* proved a failure. It was in fact the first serious blunder of the Bush 'War on Terror'.

This emerges clearly from the 2009 Senate Report on Tora Bora. It frankly admits that removing bin Laden from the battlefield then would not have eliminated the worldwide extremist threat.[2] But the decisions that opened the door for his escape to Pakistan, the report claims, allowed bin Laden to emerge as 'a potent symbolic figure who continues to attract a steady flow of money and inspire fanatics worldwide'. The failure to finish the job represented a lost opportunity that 'forever altered the course of the conflict in Afghanistan and the future of international terrorism, leaving the American people more vulnerable to terrorism, laying the foundation for today's protracted Afghan insurgency and inflaming the internal strife now endangering Pakistan'.[3]

This failure and its 'enormous consequences' were not inevitable, according to the report. 'Cornered in some of the most forbidding terrain on earth, he [bin Laden] and several hundred of his men, the largest concentration of al Qaeda fighters of the war, endured relentless pounding by American aircraft, as many as 100 air strikes a day,' the report continued. One 15,000-lb bomb, nicknamed a Daisy Cutter, so huge it had to be rolled out of the back of a C-130 cargo plane, 'shook the mountains for miles'. It seemed only a matter of time before American troops and their Afghan allies overran the remnants of al Qaeda 'hunkered down in the thin, cold air at 14,000 feet'.[4]

Bin Laden expected to die, the Senate Report says, and drafted his last will and testament at Tora Bora on 14 December 2001. Details did not emerge, however, until the following October when *Al Majalla*, a Saudi-owned magazine published in London, claimed to have obtained a four-page copy of it through one of the magazine's reporters in Kandahar. *Al Majalla*'s editor-in-chief, Hani Nakshabandi, said: 'He [bin Laden] did write the will as someone saying goodbye,' and claimed it showed him as 'dying' or 'going to die soon'.[5]

As we know, however, he not only survived but escaped.

According to Mr Nakshabandi, the will was signed: '"Your brother, Abu Abdullah Osama Muhammad Bin Laden', and dated '14 December 2001, Afghanistan'. It expresses 'disappointment with the Taliban, who had harboured him in Afghanistan, speaks of betrayal, and urges his children to shun al Qaeda'.[6] It continues in critical vein: 'Even amongst the students of religion, only few stood their ground and fought, and the rest either surrendered or fled.' But 'despite the setbacks,' the purported will says,

we will be victorious against the US and the infidel West even if it takes tens of years. My last advice is to the *mujahideen* everywhere . . . Put aside for the time being fighting the Jews and the Crusaders, and instead devote your efforts to purifying your groups from the agents and the cowards and those impostors who claim to be scholars amongst you.

As for you, my sons, forgive me if I failed to devote more of my time to you since I answered the call to *Jihad* . . . I have carried the burden of Muslims and their causes, and have chosen a dangerous path and endured hardship, disappointment and betrayal. If it wasn't for betrayal, things would be different today.

This is the most precious advice I can give you. I also want you to stay away from al Qaeda.

He asks his sons not to follow in his path and seek leadership. To his wives, he writes:

> May God reward you generously. You have been very supportive to me. You recognised right at the start that the path will be paved with land mines and other obstacles. Don't consider marrying again, and devote yourselves to your children and guide them to the right path.

Peter Bergen, an American journalist said to have done the first Western television interview with Osama bin Laden in 1997, in his translation of the same document writes: 'Allah bears witness that the love of *Jihad* and death in the cause of Allah has dominated my life, and the verses of the sword permeated every cell in my heart . . .' His advice to his wives is both stricter and more flowery. 'O women kinfolk! Do not ever use cosmetics or imitate the whores and mannish women of the West . . .'[7]

Against all the odds, however, bin Laden would live to fight another day. The bombing took a heavy toll but somehow he managed to survive. In his memoir, *Inside CentCom*, General Michael DeLong, second-in-command to General Tommy Franks, gave a lively account of the campaign: 'We were hot on Osama bin Laden's trail. He was definitely there when we hit the caves,' he wrote, apparently contradicting his superior's remark about there being 'no evidence' bin Laden was at Tora Bora. DeLong later retracted his statement.[8]

He makes clear, however, that Rumsfeld himself thought bin Laden was at Tora Bora. 'Every day during the bombing, Rumsfeld asked me, "Did we get him? Did we get him?" I would have to answer that we didn't know.' DeLong even said that intelligence suggested bin Laden had been wounded during the bombing before he escaped to Pakistan, a conclusion reached by many journalists. But he also shared Rumsfeld's view that large numbers of US troops could not be deployed at Tora Bora 'because the area surrounding Tora Bora was controlled by tribes hostile to the United States and other outsiders'.[9]

This point is debatable, to say the least. The Governor of Ningrahar Province, which includes Tora Bora, Haji Qadir, was pro-West and anti-Taliban. His son Haji Zahir, the youngest of the three militia commanders at Tora Bora, was also opposed to the Taliban and al Qaeda. The Taliban had already fled south to Pakistan, and no one else could have offered any real resistance. In addition, Parachinar, the main Pakistani town in the area, just south of Tora Bora, through or past which bin Laden almost certainly escaped, is mainly Shia and would therefore not have been sympathetic to the extreme Sunni bin Laden and his al Qaeda followers, a point which may have escaped Rumsfeld and his generals.

Bin Laden is thought to have escaped from Tora Bora on or about 16 December and about ten days later, on 27 December, Al Jazeera television broadcast a tape, in which 'a visibly aged bin Laden' declared, 'I am just a poor slave of God. If I live or die, the war will continue.' As Peter Bergen observed: 'His choice of words seemed to confirm his recent brush with death. Bin Laden, who is left-handed, did not move his entire left side in the thirty-four-minute transmission strongly suggesting he had sustained a serious injury during the battle.'[10]

The man in charge of CIA operations in Afghanistan, Gary Berntsen, was an old hand in the secret world of the CIA. He was working at the organisation's counter-terrorist centre in Washington in October 2001, not long after 9/11, when his boss, Cofer Black, summoned him and gave him his orders: 'Before Gary Schroen deployed, I told him I wanted bin Laden's head in a box,' he said. 'I want that, and more from you . . . It's now your time to make war. Gary, I want you killing the enemy immediately.' He left the next day for Afghanistan.[11]

Berntsen says he was confident that the al Qaeda leader would make his last stand at Tora Bora and he was proved right when bin Laden's voice was intercepted and identified there by Jalal, the CIA's most experienced bin Laden listener.

It was at this point or just before it that Operation Enduring Freedom took the wrong turning, according to the most senior CIA officials and other commanders on the spot.[12] From the outset, Berntsen says, he was 'sceptical' about relying on Afghan militias 'cobbled together at the last minute' to kill or capture the man who ordered the 9/11 attacks.[13] 'I'd made it clear in my reports that our Afghan allies were hardly anxious to get at al Qaeda in Tora Bora.' He also knew that the relatively small number of Special Forces and CIA men available were not enough to stop bin Laden from escaping across the mountains. As Berntsen puts it in the Senate Report:* 'We needed US soldiers on the ground! . . . I'd sent my request for 800 US Army Rangers and was still waiting for a response. I repeated to anyone at headquarters who would listen: "We need Rangers now!" The opportunity to get bin Laden and his men is slipping away . . . Day and night I kept thinking: we need US soldiers on the ground! We need them to do the fighting. We need them to block a possible al Qaeda escape into Pakistan.'[14]

But General Franks was adamant. 'No American boots on the ground' were his orders, or more probably Rumsfeld's, which he unhesitatingly passed on. However infuriated he must have been, Berntsen chose to be diplomatic. 'Franks,' he said, 'was either badly misinformed by his own people or blinded by the fog of war.'[15]

At one point, he recalled an argument at a CIA guesthouse in Kabul with Major General Dell Dailey, then commander of US Special Forces in Afghanistan. Berntsen said he renewed his demand that American troops be sent to Tora Bora immediately and Dailey replied by repeating Franks's instructions, explaining that he feared alienating Afghan allies – the Rumsfeld line. 'I don't give a damn about offending our allies!' Berntsen shouted. 'I only care about eliminating al Qaeda and delivering bin Laden's head in a box!'[16]

Another long-serving CIA officer, Michael Scheuer, who was chief of the CIA's Osama bin Laden unit from 1996 to 1999, and then special adviser to his successor from 2001 to 2004, was sharply critical of the war plan for Tora Bora because of its reliance on Afghan allies of dubious loyalty. 'Everyone who was cognizant of how Afghan operations worked would have told Mr Tenet [George Tenet, CIA director] that he was nuts,' Scheuer said later. 'And as it turned out, he was . . . The people we bought, the people Mr Tenet said we would own, let Osama bin Laden escape from Tora Bora.'[17]

A third highly experienced CIA officer, Gary Schroen, added his voice to the chorus. The Senate Report says that Schroen, who had spent years cultivating members of the opposition to the Taliban, 'bemoaned the reliance on local tribal leaders to go after bin Laden and guard escape routes. Unfortunately, many of those people proved to be loyal to bin Laden and sympathisers with

---

* Berntsen uses exclamation marks to emphasise his concern that the most wanted man in the world was about to slip out of the Americans' grasp.

the Taliban and they allowed the key guys to escape.' Schroen, who was by then retired, said as much when interviewed on television in May 2005.[18]

The scepticism of the CIA's old hands was reproduced in countless media reports which delighted in the old chestnut, 'You can rent an Afghan, but you can't buy one' – leading cynics to wonder if the only people who did not know it were Donald Rumsfeld and Tommy Franks. American forces never had a clear idea how many al Qaeda fighters were arrayed against them, the Senate Report says. Estimates ranged as high as 3,000 and as low as 500, but the consensus put the figure around a thousand – at least until so many escaped during the fake surrender.

Although the British SBS had only twelve men at Tora Bora, according to Fury, their main task was to provide support, mainly secure communications, to all the main Northern Alliance commanders, including Generals Dostum and Atta Mohammed in the north, Ismail Khan in Herat in the west, and Commander Masud's successors, Generals Fahim and Bismillah Khan, on the Kabul front.

I remember arriving at Masud's guesthouse at Astana in the Panjsher Valley in November 2001 and being met at the top of the steps by a young Englishman in civilian clothes.

'Is Jan Mohammed here?' I asked.

'Who?' he asked.

'Jan Mohammed. He runs the place.'

'Oh,' the young man said in a public school accent. 'We're actually setting up communications for Tony Blair's special envoy to the Northern Alliance, Paul Bergne.'

'Do you mean there's no room for us?' I asked.

'No, I'm afraid not,' the young man replied. 'Sorry.'

Bergne, once described as a character from a John Buchan novel, was one of the most distinguished Foreign Office linguists and Intelligence officers of his day. He spoke fluent Arabic, Persian (Farsi in Afghanistan) and several other Oriental languages. Unfortunately we were in a hurry to find a place to stay and I never met him.

However, the SBS now proposed reinforcing its contingent at Tora Bora with fifty or sixty more of its elite troops already in the country, in order to carry out a second attack on al Qaeda in support of Delta from the Pakistan side of the border. Despite not having all the clothing and equipment they would have liked, the SBS – being highly trained in mountain warfare – were confident they could make a success of the operation. This is what they had been trained for. But, like all the other proposals, even from someone as senior as Gary Berntsen, the SBS offer was 'turned down flat', presumably by Rumsfeld.[19]

About the same time, Delta Force and SBS troops pushing up the mountain one day received reports that 'a very tall figure' had been seen, which could be bin Laden. 'A frantic *muj* commander keyed his radio and began trading transmissions with another *muj*. Some of the fighters excitedly reported seeing a figure that they believed to be Usama bin Laden moving among a group of several dozen enemy fighters,' Dalton Fury wrote. 'They lost sight when he disappeared into a cave.'[20]

The Delta snipers who acted as air controllers immediately called base. 'The Admiral [a Delta controller for the US Air Force] broke into the net and summoned all available aircraft to check in with him and stack up while Murph [another Delta controller] plotted the exact target location.' Dalton Fury voices what everybody else must have been thinking: 'Could this be it for bin Laden?'

The first bombs exploded with tremendous effect, igniting something flammable, 'and multiple flashes and secondary explosions lit up the valley like an outdoor rock concert . . .' Fury's dramatic description gives some idea of just how terrifying the American onslaught must have been for those on the ground. 'More GBU-31 bombs saturated the cave complex with enormous power . . . impact after impact shook the ground and detonated even more secondary explosions. Fireballs rose into the air and shrapnel and debris raced over their heads and rattled off the rocks.' The bombs rained down on the cave for the next two hours, but somehow bin Laden escaped, if indeed it was him.[21]

At sundown, the *mujahideen* retreated as usual, Fury says, but the Delta snipers were unwilling to give up their chance 'to nail bin Laden' and stayed on the steep ridgeline for the next two days and nights in sub-zero temperatures, although without proper cold weather gear. 'They were certain,' Fury adds, 'that they were as close to bin Laden as any Americans had been in years, certainly since 9/11', and they were 'hell-bent on ensuring that some American pilot would wake up soon and hear that it was his bomb that killed the al Qaeda leader'.[22]

Radio traffic revealed al Qaeda morale crumbling and bin Laden author-ising 'his battered subordinate units to surrender'. The last signal intercepts of bin Laden's voice from the day before, 14 December, 'indicated obvious distress'. Meanwhile the attacks continued. 'The British [SBS] who went into the mountains to keep Haji Zaman motivated,' Fury writes, 'radioed back that scores of al Qaeda fighters had decided to quit, opting to remain in the present world for the time being. Martyrdom would have to wait. Having lost their will to fight, they dropped their weapons and walked off the battlefield.'[23]

'Al Qaeda had lost its nerve,' Fury writes, 'and it appeared that their leader also was cracking. But was he really in a panic? Or was he just putting some fighters out there to surrender as a ruse to buy time and stall our attack, hoping to get breathing room to slip out the back door? Even when things are looking good, you have to consider other possibilities.'[24] Fury admits the fog of war seemed to be closing in.

His frustration at the limitations imposed on Delta's operations by Rumsfeld and Franks emerges strongly at this point: 'Throughout the Tora Bora operations, no Delta operator killed anyone in any other way than by dropping bombs on their heads [as ground controllers for the US Air Force]. Some of the best snipers, explosives experts and knife fighters in the world were forced to curb their enthusiasm because the Afghan *muj* had to be in the forefront, and their hearts were not in it.'[25]

Fury says in *Kill Bin Laden* he was against using the thousand-odd US Marines flown into Kandahar at the start of the American invasion, explaining it would have been difficult if not impossible to deploy conven-tional units north of the mountains, because Delta had no helicopter capacity, having to use local porters and donkeys for everything they needed, or else carry it themselves. They were sharing their water with the *mujahideen* and even ran out of food at the end. 'Moreover,' he says, the *muj* commanders, Hazrat Ali and Haji Zaman, 'threatened to walk away if conventional forces showed up.'[26] The same lack of transport had been the problem with the Royal Marine Commandos and like them, 'they would have had to hump it for miles just to get to the foothills'.[27] As a result, Fury states, the Royal Marines spent most of their time at Bagram airport, only moving to Tora Bora for four hours when it looked as if Delta had a 'good bead' on bin Laden and were then flown back to Bagram when that proved to be a false alarm.[28]

However, Fury wrote, the US Marines might have made the difference if used in another way. 'Had they been committed to assist the Pakistan Army in blocking the key passageways that threaded out of the Tora Bora mountains, or at least to keep those new allies honest about sealing the border, we almost certainly would have captured and killed more fleeing al Qaeda. And we might even have bagged bin Laden. Leaving the back door open gave the rat a chance to run.'[29]

The Senate Report places the blame firmly on Rumsfeld and Franks. 'The decision not to deploy American forces to go after bin Laden or block his escape was made by Secretary of Defense Donald Rumsfeld and his top commander, Gen. Tommy Franks, the architects of the unconventional Afghan battle plan known as Operation Enduring Freedom.'[30] Rumsfeld was concerned that too many US troops in Afghanistan would create an 'anti-American backlash and fuel a widespread insurgency'. Reversing the recent American military orthodoxy known as the Powell doctrine, the Rumsfeld–Franks, or Afghan model, as the Senate Report called it, 'emphasised minimising the US presence by relying on small, highly mobile teams of Special Operations troops and CIA paramilitary operatives working with the Afghan opposition'.[31]

Even when his own commanders and senior intelligence officials in Afghanistan and Washington argued for more US troops, Franks 'refused to deviate from the plan'. He had enough men to execute 'the classic sweep-and-block manoeuvre' to attack bin Laden and prevent his escape, although it would have been a dangerous fight across treacherous terrain, and the deployment of more US troops and the resulting casualties would have contradicted the risk-averse, 'light footprint' model formulated by Rumsfeld and Franks. 'Commanders on the scene and elsewhere in Afghanistan, however, argued that the risks were worth the reward,' the Senate Report says.[32]

Berntsen and his colleagues in Afghanistan were not the only CIA men to doubt the commitment of the Afghan militias at Tora Bora. Even George Tenet, CIA director at the time – despite being described by the CIAs Michael Scheuer as 'nuts' for putting his trust in the main Pushtun militia force at Tora Bora, commanded by Haji Zaman (Ghamsharik) who arranged the fake ceasefire – states in his memoir, *At the Center of the Storm*, that it was evident from the start that aerial bombing would not be enough to 'get' bin Laden at Tora Bora. Troops needed to be in the caves, he wrote, admitting that the Afghan militiamen were 'distinctly reluctant' to put themselves in harm's way and there were not enough Americans on the scene. He claims, however, that senior CIA officials lobbied hard for inserting US troops.[33]

Henry Crumpton, the head of special operations for the CIA's counterterrorism operation, and chief of its Afghan strategy, made direct requests to Franks. Crumpton had told him that the back door to Pakistan was open and urged Franks to move more than a thousand Marines, who had set up a base near Kandahar, to Tora Bora to block escape routes. But the CENTCOM commander rejected the idea, saying it would take weeks to get a large-enough US contingent on the scene and bin Laden might disappear in the meantime.

At the end of November, Crumpton went to the White House to brief President Bush and Vice-President Cheney and repeated the message that he had delivered to Franks. He warned the President that the Afghan campaign's primary goal of capturing bin Laden was in jeopardy because of the military's reliance on Afghan militias at Tora Bora. He also showed the President where Tora Bora was located in the White Mountains and described the caves and tunnels that riddled the region. The CIA man questioned whether the promised Pakistani forces would be able to seal off the escape routes and pointed out that they had not yet arrived.[34] In addition, Crumpton told the President that the Afghan forces at Tora Bora were 'tired and cold' and 'just not invested in getting bin Laden'.[35]

According to the author Ron Suskind in *The One Percent Doctrine*, Crumpton sensed that his earlier warnings to Franks and others at the Pentagon had not been relayed to the President. So Crumpton emphasised to Bush that 'we're going to lose our prey if we're not careful'. He recommended that the Marines or other US troops be rushed to Tora Bora.

'How bad off are these Afghani forces, really?' asked Bush. 'Are they up to the job?'

'Definitely not, Mr President,' Crumpton replied. 'Definitely not.'[36]

Yet President Bush seems to have done nothing about it; at least the

Rumsfeld–Franks policy did not change. Possibly a lack of follow-through, which was only too common in Bush's first term, according to a senior Western diplomat.[37] He would give orders to Condoleezza Rice, his National Security Adviser, saying what he wanted done in general terms – 'he was not famous for being a detail man . . . But veterans like Dick Cheney and Donald Rumsfeld wouldn't always pay too much attention to her . . . and it wouldn't get done.'[38]

Regardless of the exact number of enemy fighters, assaulting Tora Bora would have been difficult and probably would have cost many American and Afghan lives, according to the Special Operations Command's history. Its 'tightly worded' assessment was: 'With large numbers of well-supplied, fanatical AQ [al Qaeda] troops dug into extensive fortified positions, Tora Bora appeared to be an extremely tough target.'[39] Dalton Fury, however, who knew the ground better than anyone, thought it was 'worth the risk to the force to assault Tora Bora for Osama bin Laden', as he told the Senate Foreign Relations Committee staff. 'What other target out there, then or now, could be more important to our nation's struggle in the global War on Terror?'[40]

It is perhaps no coincidence that the Chairman of the Senate Foreign Relations Committee which produced the critical 2009 Tora Bora report was Senator John Kerry, who, in his campaign for the presidency in 2004, accused George Bush of making a major error at Tora Bora by letting bin Laden escape when 'we had him surrounded'. This in turn drew angry denials from President Bush and Vice-President Cheney who said that Kerry's criticism was 'absolute garbage', and a riposte from General Franks that there was 'no evidence' that bin Laden was at Tora Bora at the crucial time – a remark which most commentators dismissed out of hand, including the Pakistani journalist and author Ahmed Rashid who considered it rare for an American general to be so 'partisan'.[41] In short, Tommy Franks seems to have been 'leant on' to protect his superiors – President Bush, Vice-President Cheney and Secretary Rumsfeld.

Bin Laden himself had already given the answer a year before by boasting how he, his Egyptian deputy Dr Ayman al Zawahiri, and 300 fighters had survived the heavy bombing before escaping from Tora Bora. 'The bombardment was round-the-clock and the warplanes continued to fly over us day and night,' he said in a clip released on 11 February 2003 by Al Jazeera television. 'Planes poured their lava on us, particularly after accomplishing their main missions in Afghanistan.'[42]

The Senate Report sums up the failure of the Rumsfeld–Franks strategy like this: 'The vast array of American military power, from sniper teams to the most mobile divisions of the Marine Corps and the Army, was kept on the sidelines. Instead, the US command chose to rely on air strikes and untrained Afghan militias to attack bin Laden and on Pakistan's loosely organised Frontier Corps to seal his escape routes.' On or around 16 December, two days after writing his will, 'bin Laden and an entourage of bodyguards walked unmolested out of Tora Bora and disappeared into Pakistan's unregulated tribal area. Most analysts say he is still there today.'[43]

This appeared to have been confirmed less than a year later, in 2010, by a very senior Afghan intelligence source who told me that Osama bin Laden was in the Miranshah area of North Waziristan, considered the most lawless and militant of all Pakistan's tribal areas, under ISI (Pakistan's Inter-Services Intelligence Directorate) 'protection', which meant, the source said, that 'no one can get to him'. In addition, and according to a NATO source, both bin Laden and al Zawahiri were said to be living 'comfortably in houses, not caves', not far apart. That, at least, was partly true.

The information that bin Laden was in North Waziristan – ironically his compound in Abbottabad was known to the locals as Waziristan House – seemed eminently likely. Wild, mountainous, semi-independent and right on the Afghan border, North Waziristan is today a hotbed of terrorist activity. It had always been rebellious. For many years in the 1930s and 1940s, when it was still part of British India, British-officered tribal levies pursued an elusive rebel leader, the Faqir (priest) of Ipi, up and down its valleys and over its steep and jagged mountains without success. The Faqir had his own *lashkar* (army), made his own primitive mortars and other weaponry, carried out countless attacks on the British and defied every attempt to kill or capture him. He died peacefully in 1960, still at large, the bin Laden of his day.[44]

It was not until the early hours of Monday, 2 May 2011, when twenty-four US Navy SEALs (Special Operations Forces), twelve in each modified Stealth Black Hawk, helicoptered across the border from Afghanistan – hurtling above the Khyber Pass, over the Kabul River and the lights of Peshawar, and then swooping down to attack a secretive, shuttered, concrete compound in the staid Pakistan military town of Abbottabad – that all these guesses and suppositions were proved to have been spectacularly wrong. To virtually universal shock and surprise, the world's most wanted terrorist was found to have been living not in the wilds but right at the heart of Pakistan's military establishment, not just for five or six months but for five or six years, since 2005 in fact, and in a nearby village for two years before that.

Did Pakistan's all-seeing and all-knowing military intelligence agency, the ISI, or the most secret part of it, the so-called 'S Wing', know all along he was there? Most journalists, analysts and Western politicians think they must have known. The British Prime Minister David Cameron said bin Laden must have had a 'suppport system' in Pakistan. But Pakistan, of course, denied the suggestion vociferously.

Named after a British colonial administrator called Sir James Abbott, and only seventy-five miles from the capital, Islamabad, Abbottabad is full of retired Pakistan Army officers; only a mile or so away is the Kakul Military Academy, founded at independence in 1947, and the local equivalent of Britain's Sandhurst. Just a week before, General Ashfaq Kayani, the Chief of Army Staff and Pakistan's top soldier, had addressed the assembled cadets and told them proudly that the army had broken the back of terrorism in their country.

When the news broke of the SEAL raid, and the death of bin Laden, after the first reaction of disbelief, the ingeniousness of the deception became apparent. The last place one would look for America's Public Enemy Number One was among the well-manicured lawns, golf course, polo grounds and retirement villas of Abbottabad. Also, Waziristan had become too dangerous. American drones – unmanned aircraft – equipped with Hellfire missiles, ceaselessly patrolled the skies 30,000 feet above the rugged landscape, ready to strike without warning at any militant foolish or unwary enough to betray their whereabouts. Thousands of militants have been killed by drones in the past two or three years in Waziristan.

In the first eye-witness account of the raid written by one of the SEALs involved, 'Mark Owen' – real name, Matt Bissonnette – claims bin Laden was mortally wounded by a snap shot when he peered out of his third-floor bedroom door to see what was happening. On the stairs below, the 'point' SEAL saw him and opened fire. Seconds later, entering the room they found bin Laden in 'death throes' on the floor, and pumped several more bullets into his prone body. The team leader radioed headquaters 'Geronimo [code name for bin Laden] EKIA [Enemy killed In Action]'. The SEALs also shot and killed bin Laden's son Khalid, his senior courier al Kuwaiti, his brother Abrar and his wife. They left minutes later, taking with them bin Laden's body which was flown to an American aircraft carrier, the USS *Carl Vinson*, in the North Arabian Sea, where it was washed and wrapped in a white sheet, sealed in a weighted canvas bag and committed to the deep. The raiding party also took time to scoop up a huge haul of secret al Qaeda files on computer disks and hard drives and departed, before the Pakistanis knew what had hit them: mission accomplished, leaving behind an angry and bewildered Pakistan Army and establishment.

The SEALs were sent in on the express orders of President Obama who, along with his Vice-President, Joe Biden, his Secretary of State, Hillary Clinton, Secretary for Defense, Robert Gates and the rest of his White House team, sat tensely on the edge of their chairs on Sunday night, 1 May, Washington time, watching the live feed of the raid from the other side of the world, as it was recorded, second by second and minute by minute and relayed by an American surveillance aircraft circling above Abbottabad. One can almost feel the tension captured by the official photograph: the anxiety, the hope, the fear that it might go wrong. But it went amazingly smoothly except for the mechanical failure and crash of one of the helicopters. Then, with bin Laden's body and his private al Qaeda archive on board, the SEALs flew out, unscathed, victorious. As President Obama announced: 'Justice has been done.'

One can only guess at the impact bin Laden's death must have had and must still be having on al Qaeda and the Taliban network. If the Americans can track down and eliminate Osama bin Laden, is any enemy safe? Mullah Omar must be wondering if he is the next in line. In Waziristan and elsewhere it may well have caused a ripple of fear. The Haqqani clan, who are closely affiliated with both al Qaeda and the Taliban, also have a base there. They are considered by the ISI as important 'strategic assets'. Led by Maulavi Jalaluddin Haqqani, a famous *mujahideen* commander during the

Russian War, whose son, Sirajuddin, now runs the organisation, the Haqqanis are said to be responsible for some of the worst terrorist atrocities, such as the attack on the Indian Embassy in Kabul in 2008. Although the Indians are said to have had a warning, the Embassy was open for business; more than twenty civilians, including Indian diplomats and Afghans queuing for visas, were killed and fifty-seven injured. The CIA claimed afterwards they intercepted mobile telephone messages between the Haqqani terrorists and their ISI minders in Pakistan at the time of the attack. The Americans considered this as conclusive evidence of their long-standing suspicion that the ISI was masterminding terrorist attacks against India and the West, using a variety of organisations it supported, or had set up, trained and financed itself.

The Mumbai attacks, also in 2008, in which 164 people were killed and 308 wounded, were on a much greater scale and brought India and Pakistan to the brink of war. Lashkar-e-Taiba (LeT), the Army of the Pure, which champions independence for Kashmir, claimed responsibility. One of Mumbai's largest railway stations and two of its biggest hotels, including the historic Taj Mahal, were bombed, set on fire, heavily damaged and guests shot indiscriminately. The operation was conceived as a seaborne invasion launched from Karachi by ship, from which the terrorists sped to the Mumbai seafront in inflatable rubber boats, landed and then fanned out to their respective targets. The planning, funding and execution suggested a major backer.

Although LeT has its headquarters near Lahore, the centre of terrorism in Pakistan is in North Waziristan. The Americans want the Pakistan Army, which receives billions of dollars a year from the United States, to go in and clean it up. This the Pakistanis have so far refused to do, although they have in the past at least turned a blind eye to the increasing number of Predator drone strikes the Americans have made against al Qaeda and Haqqani militants there. From fifty-three in 2009, the number of strikes more than doubled in 2010, to 118, an average of nearly ten strikes a month, and more than 2,000 militants – and civilians – were killed, according to American statistics.

Is Pakistan the ally or the enemy? Both is probably the most accurate answer. Some say the war cannot be won as long as the ISI continues to back the Taliban. And so far the ISI shows no sign of changing its policy. One experienced ISI watcher told me: 'It never has and it never will.'[45]

5

The British in Kabul, 2001–2002

The US don't do nation-building.

Major General John McColl, British Commander ISAF, Kabul, 2002

In the early, optimistic days of the post-9/11 Anglo-American intervention in Afghanistan, at the end of 2001 and the beginning of 2002, the way ahead must have seemed fairly straightforward. While the Americans concentrated on hunting down al Qaeda, the British volunteered to get life back to something like normal in Kabul itself. In a small way their presence must have generated, in Afghan terms, some of the euphoria which bubbled up in Britain at the end of the Second World War. The first step was taken on 20 December 2001 when the United Nations Security Council in New York voted to dispatch a peacekeeping force to stabilise Afghanistan, still reeling from seven years of war and chaos under the Taliban. At the moment of the vote, the Taliban, who had been blasted out of power by a combination of American bombing and 'boots on the ground' provided by the anti-Taliban Northern Alliance, were in the process of surrendering en masse. Tony Blair, the British Prime Minister, who believed passionately in intervention in a humanitarian cause (East Timor, Sierra Leone and the Balkans were recent examples), as well as hankering after the role – in conjunction with America – of the 'world's policeman', offered to send 3,000 British troops to Kabul. To differentiate it from the American al Qaeda task force deployed for Operation Enduring Freedom, the peace-keeping contingent was named the International Security Assistance Force, or ISAF, under the command of Major General John McColl (later General Sir John McColl), NATO's deputy SACEUR (Supreme Allied Commander Europe). Apart from the British, fifteen other NATO countries contributed troops to ISAF, later increased to more than twenty.

The Security Council resolution also established, in accordance with the Bonn Agreement (December 2001) that ISAF would provide a protective umbrella for an Afghan transitional administration to be set up, with Hamid Karzai, the future President, as chairman. The foundations were being laid for a new and, it was hoped, a more peaceful and democratic Afghanistan.

The agreement reached at the Petersberg, sometimes known as the German Camp David – a spectacular mountain-top hotel turned government conference centre overlooking the Rhine near Bonn – called for 'a broad-based, gender-sensitive, multi-ethnic and fully representative government' and the creation of a central bank, a supreme court, an independent human rights commission and an independent commission for the convening of an emergency Loya Jirga (grand council) by June 2002, which would decide on a new transitional government. Elections, both presidential and parliamentary, would follow, and a new constitution. The old king, Zahir Shah, was to be given the title 'Father of the Nation'. Bonn was a victory, the author Ahmed Rashid says, for the Northern Alliance, which gained the lion's share of cabinet seats, including the key portfolios of defence, interior, intelligence and foreign affairs, plus three of the five vice-presidential posts.[1] The Pushtuns, who made up about 40 per cent of the population, were not amused; but they, for the most part, had acquiesced in the Taliban tyranny. Only the Northern Alliance, thanks to Masud, had actually fought the Taliban.

Britain felt it knew something about Afghanistan, having played the Great Game there for two centuries from 1809, and been involved in three Anglo-Afghan wars. That era, although it ended peacefully at the conclusion of the Third Anglo-Afghan War in 1921, when put alongside all the other invasions which the Afghans had endured over the centuries, from Alexander the Great in the fourth century BC, to the Russians in the twentieth, left them with a deep-seated distrust of all foreigners. It is a feeling which is still very evident today. Yet, despite Britain's record in Afghanistan, I rarely detected any personal animosity towards me as an ordinary British traveller, although that was during the Russian War. At Gandamak in 1984, for example, near the spot where the British made their last stand in the winter snow 142 years before, the headman greeted me warmly: 'Welcome to Gandamak, we still remember Macnãghten here' – a reference to Sir

William Macnaghten, British envoy to Kabul, whom the Afghans assassinated in 1841.

Historically, Afghanistan has suffered the twin misfortune of being on the traditional invasion route from Asia to India, as well as being a small and weak neighbour of a Great Power, Russia. The Communist coup of 1978, the bloodbath that followed and the Russian invasion and occupation (1979–89) not only killed more than a million Afghans and destroyed most of the country's infrastructure, but displaced more than 5 million refugees and radicalised Afghan society. Extremism was un-Afghan. One friend, a highly intelligent woman from one of the most distinguished monarchist families, would say to me: 'We Afghans have always been moderate in our religious beliefs. Never extremists. This is something new.'

Many of the Afghan boys educated in Kabul or one of the other main cities, under a more or less moderate system – the better-off ones in Westernised high schools like the French-founded Istiqlal Lycée and the German High School in Kabul – found themselves, as refugees, going to much more extreme *madrassas* in neighbouring Pakistan. Children from poor families especially, in places like Peshawar and other towns in what was then the North-West Frontier Province, received an education that was free but often limited to the culture of the Koran and the Kalashnikov. *Jihad*, or Holy War, was the main subject on the syllabus. Increasingly, in those *madrassas*, young boys were raised on a diet of religious extremism and hate for the West, above all America.

The Russians finally withdrew in 1989, leaving behind a puppet government under President Najibullah, which survived until 1992 when the *mujahideen* drove them out of Kabul. While the West looked the other way, civil war laid waste to much of Kabul and finally led to the emergence of the Taliban. Their early promise to establish law and order soon degenerated into ruthless conquest. In 1996, Kabul fell to their blitzkrieg, planned and directed by the Pakistan Army's ISI and financed by the Saudis, although Masud made a masterly withdrawal from the capital to his old stronghold of the Panjsher Valley. Two years later another Taliban offensive to try to capture the north was again planned by the ISI and financed by the Saudis. Prince Turki al-Faisal, head of Saudi intelligence, visited Kandahar in June 1998 and agreed to provide 400 new Japanese pick-up trucks, the preferred Taliban battle-wagon, while the ISI prepared a war plan with a budget of 2 billion rupees (£3,125,000).[2] By 2000, only the extreme north-east remained outside the Taliban grasp.

The darkest days of Taliban misrule came in 2001 when, in March, the two great sixth-century Bamiyan Buddhas were blown up on the orders of Mullah Omar; and on 11 September (9/11), when al Qaeda suicide bombers flew two crowded passenger jets into the Twin Towers in New York, a third into the Pentagon in Washington while a fourth crashed in a field in Pennsylvania, killing nearly 3,000 civilians, on the orders of the Saudi terrorist, Osama bin Laden. Retaliation followed in October, when the US Air Force launched an intensive bombing campaign, which, in partnership with Northern Alliance ground troops and American and British Special Forces, drove the Taliban from power.

For a brief period, Afghanistan stood on the threshold of a new beginning. Hopes were high, and expectations even higher. Despite the chaos and destruction the Taliban had left behind, the mood was buoyant. Most Afghans hoped for a phoenix-like rebirth from the ashes of a disastrous past. King Zahir Shah eventually returned to his homeland after an exile of thirty years. Endless delegations, dignified tribal leaders clad in long cloaks and splendid turbans, came from far and wide, and especially the Pushtun south, to greet him as Father of the Nation, even if he was no longer King. His return after so many years, a symbol of what now seemed a golden age of peace and plenty, brought with it hopes for a better future. It was into this war-weary but expectant, and indeed hopeful, country that the first British troops to be on active duty in Afghanistan since 1921 cautiously stepped.

Major General John McColl, a distinguished-looking former tank commander, who arrived in Kabul in January 2002, paints a dark picture of the capital the Taliban had just fled: of a city completely deserted at night, when there was a curfew. A city with virtually no private cars, just yellow taxis. Government ministries had 'absolutely no capacity, there was no middle class; they had all either been marginalised, or fled, or in some cases killed. So there was no capacity in the government, no capacity in the commercial life of the capital or the country.' Post-Taliban Afghanistan was a failed state to an extraordinary degree, the antithesis to Iraq, McColl said. 'Iraq had money, it had a middle class; it had all sorts of infrastructure and investment over years.'[3]

McColl's second-in-command, Brigadier (now Lieutenant General Sir) Barney White-Spunner, arrived before his boss, soon after Christmas, at the head of 16 Air Assault Brigade, which included 2 PARA, in what was described as very cool weather – in fact it was freezing. They were out on patrol for the first time on 11 January. In February, in a piece of pure hearts-and-minds diplomacy which would have gladdened the heart of General David Petraeus, one imagines, the brigade helped to organise a football match between ISAF and an Afghan team. Lawrie McMenemy, the former Southampton and Northern Ireland coach who was once a Coldstream Guardsman, and Gary Mabbutt, the former England and Spurs player, flew to Kabul to coach the teams. The match was played before a crowd of 30,000 excited locals in the stadium where the Taliban had carried out public executions, shooting the men and stoning to death women convicted of adultery. The contrast could not have been more striking, a point not lost on the Kabulis.

Brigadier White-Spunner was struck particularly forcibly by the bleakness of the city, possibly because many years earlier, as a young backpacker, he had seen Kabul through the smiling prism of a British Embassy garden in summer. Now, in the cold and gloom of a shattered city in winter, it was very different. 'It really was a sorry sight,' he recalled. 'The whole southern part of the city was effectively ruined. And although people were quick to blame the Russians, it was pretty clear that most was destroyed in the civil war.'[4] Between 1992 and 1996, civil war had raged with Masud's Tajiks fighting a bitter struggle against the combined forces of Hekmatyar's Hisb-i-Islami, Dostum's Uzbeks and the Shia Hisb-i-Wahdat. Masud's Tajiks won in the end, but the damage was horrendous and hundreds if not thousands of civilians were killed.

'There was a complete breakdown in services,' Brigadier White-Spunner recalled. There were no municipal services, and so the British set up an embryo municipal administration and police force under Yunus Qanooni, the Interior Minister. The British ran the ambulance service because there wasn't an ambulance service at all. 'It was absolutely apparent then that the damage was much deeper, physically and actually mentally, to people's confidence than anyone had quite anticipated and what actually struck me particularly,' White-Spunner explained, 'was that people, particularly the intelligentsia, looked back to the Russian days as being a bit of a halcyon era.' There were a lot of people who had been gainfully employed, particularly their wives. 'My interpreter's wife, for example, had been teaching at Kabul University under the Russians, and was very distinguished in her field, and lost her job under the Taliban.'

The second thing that struck Brigadier White-Spunner was the degree of expectation that people associated with the arrival of the British. 'They really did think that the West owed them a considerable debt of gratitude, and many Afghans said to me: "We got rid of the Soviet Union by defeating the Russians and we've got rid of the Taliban." Maybe that was a little hasty, as we know now. But there was an expectation that a lot of very good things were going to happen. There was an expectation that the aid money was going to flow.'[5]

Barney White-Spunner's previous visit had been in the 1970s when Afghanistan was very much part of the hippy trail to India. After hitchhiking and travelling by local bus round the country, he arrived at the British Embassy, one of Britain's grandest, built by the Viceroy, Lord Curzon, in 1919. (Peter Levi, the poet and writer, described it as 'looking as if it had been supplied complete by Harrods'.[6]) He had an introduction to the First Secretary, a friend of one of his sisters, who lived in a cottage in the garden compound. Banging on his door, rucksack on his back, filthy after weeks of sleeping rough, young Barney was nevertheless welcomed like a VIP and served tea in Embassy bone china by a uniformed retainer.

He never forgot it, in fact he remembered it very vividly when, in 2001, having had a 'fairly hazardous' drive in from Bagram airport, with the advance party of 16 Air Assault Brigade, he found his way to the Embassy, or what was left of it. The Embassy staff was 'just Stephen Evans, the first Ambassador', who had 'a cottage in a corner of the same compound . . . Absolutely everything was destroyed round the main Embassy building [which was] in embers and no water, no power'. In 1995 a Kabul mob, in protest at alleged Pakistani interference, and encouraged, it was said, by the Rabbani government, marched on the Embassy, which the British had handed over to Pakistan, as agreed at Partition in 1947, ransacked it, set it on fire and in effect destroyed it.

In the middle of this chaos and destruction, I was standing there with
Brigadier Peter Wall [then Chief of Joint Force Operations and now a
General and Chief of the General Staff] looking at the general hopeless-
ness of the situation, when who should appear . . . but the same orderly
with, it seemed, the same tray and the same tea cups which he'd kept all
the time since the 1970s and obviously been guarding ever since . . . I'm
happy to say the Foreign Office gave him an MBE for guarding the
Embassy.[7]

Brigadier White-Spunner's first challenge was to restore law and order,
which, he says, was 'relatively easy' because he had Gurkhas with him who,
through 'universal Bollywood Hindi, made themselves very well understood in Kabul . . . The problem rather was getting the Northern Alliance
to realise that we didn't mean them harm; that we were only there to
help . . . Obviously [Ahmed Shah] Masud was no longer with us . . . but
his heirs and successors – Mohammed Fahim, the Defence Minister, and
particularly Bismillah Khan [a Masud commander who became Afghan
Army Chief of Staff and later Interior Minister] the man who in my book
deserves the credit for taking Kabul – were enormously helpful in accepting our presence . . .' A lot of people thought they were Russians, because
they were hiring Russian aircraft, Antonovs and Ilyushins.[8] Brigadier
White-Spunner may have laughed at the idea of British troops being
mistaken for Russians, but I often experienced the same reaction travelling
through the countryside in the 1980s. Nowadays, almost any foreigner is
taken for an American. There was no doubt, however, about the warmth of
the welcome. 'The majority of people in Kabul were happy to see the
British,' he said. 'About half were very happy and a further 30 per cent were
a bit bemused; they didn't quite know what the British were doing, and
there was some hostility, but very little to be honest in Kabul. In the north,
in Mazar-i-Sharif – they were looking at expanding over the Salang Pass –
the British were very warmly welcomed.' It was 'a great pity' that they did
not exploit that welcome and 'take the mission forward then', White-
Spunner reflects.

It was frustrating that ISAF was restricted to Kabul, although General
McColl visited Ismail Khan in Herat and he went up to the north to talk

to Generals Dostum and Atta Mohammed who, although both Northern Alliance, were still at each other's throats.[9] Given the subsequent attitude of President Karzai to the British, and above all the Americans, it is strange to hear General McColl say he found Hamid Karzai – then the head of the recently formed transitional administration, whom he saw frequently – a great admirer of ISAF. Karzai welcomed its stabilising influence in the capital, and kept urging its expansion to other major cities – Kandahar, Herat, Mazar-i-Sharif and so on. He told McColl he was receiving delegations from all over the country, all asking for an ISAF presence. 'There was a feeling that the international community had at last come to the help and aid of Afghanistan,' McColl recalled. 'They saw the security that was in Kabul both in terms of inter-ethnic tensions but also in terms of general security [including] crime . . . they wanted that and they felt the international community would provide it.'[10] They were also astute enough to realise that once there was a military presence other elements of the international community's presence would follow – aid and government support – so there was a groundswell of pro-ISAF support. Karzai would often say to the British general: 'We need to deploy ISAF more broadly.'[11]

McColl did an analysis and talked to various senior American and British officials to see if it was possible. But 'there were a number of problems', he noted, the first being the American preoccupation with the pursuit of al Qaeda. 'There was a feeling that any distraction from that would be unhelpful.'[12]

The obsession with the hunt for al Qaeda seems, in retrospect, to have been a red herring. As Lakhdar Brahimi, the UN Secretary General's Special Representative for Afghanistan, 2001–04, told me, by that time, and apart from a few minor members, al Qaeda were long gone, most of them with, or at the same time as bin Laden, when he escaped from Tora Bora into Pakistan in December 2001.[13]

The second objection, General McColl says, and that was a 'doctrinal thing, which I think was certainly prevalent in the US but flowed I suspect from higher, probably from [Secretary of Defense Donald] Rumsfeld and that was "the US don't do nation-building". You have heard that cry and that was certainly the doctrinal cry at the time . . .'

Admiral Sir Michael [now Lord] Boyce, who as Chief of the Defence Staff had the task, he says, of 'cobbling together' the ISAF coalition, clearly upset Rumsfeld – who was against ISAF – when he said in an interview in 2001 that 'we were going to be in Afghanistan for a very long time'. Rumsfeld exploded: 'Who the hell is this guy Boyce, what does he know about anything? We will be out of there within no time at all. What an idiot he is' . . . Boyce's only comment was: 'We know who was wrong, anyway.'[14]

More to the point, Lord Boyce, who insisted before the invasion of Iraq on receiving an 'unequivocal assurance' from the Prime Minister, Tony Blair, that the war was legal and that British military leaders and their troops would not be prosecuted for war crimes,* is highly critical of Donald Rumsfeld's strategic judgement. Acknowledging the 'fantastic speed at which they [the Americans] went through Iraq, supported by ourselves : . . We provided a third of the armour capability, we the Brits, which people forget about' . . . Lord Boyce said, 'Rumsfeld's . . . passion was network-centric warfare, in other words you could do everything by clever technology'. The 'anorexic forces' sent into Iraq and the 'failure to sort out Iraq properly by not having enough boots on the ground' meant 'they won the war by a hair's breadth'.

'Rumsfeld', he says, 'believed everything could be done by remote control, by unmanned air vehicles . . . and didn't appreciate the need for boots on the ground . . . Everything had to be done either by cash or by clever bombing, overhead surveillance, satellite surveillance and then knocking out this bit here and that bit there and therefore you didn't have to put people on the ground because that was a waste of resources. History one day should write it down in blood as being the perpetrator of many deaths, as a result of his, in my view, incompetent strategic appreciation'.

General McColl, in Kabul meanwhile, was stymied on both counts – the expansion of ISAF and Rumsfeld's refusal to be involved in nation-building 'something that other people could do, other people being probably the Europeans, I should imagine'.[15]

McColl also noted 'tremendous sensitivity' about the mission among the Europeans, 'because it wasn't a NATO operation, as you will recall, it was a coalition of the willing'. There was a feeling that 'it was a step into the unknown . . . into a part of the world that they didn't fully

---

* in his evidence to the Chilcot Inquiry, 3 December 2009

understand . . . that they were overextending themselves. There was also, from a parochial UK point of view, the feeling that if the mission became more expansive and more ambitious, with a whole load of challenges which weren't fully understood . . . then people would be less inclined to step up to the plate to get involved and take the leadership.'[16] The British, in other words, did not want to discourage a potential successor who might take over from them. The Turks were finally persuaded to do so in 2002.

'After the first couple of months, the biggest problem became this complete lack of coherence of the international, political aid effort,' according to Brigadier White-Spunner.[17] At the Tokyo Conference, an international conference on reconstruction assistance to Afghanistan in January 2002, countries promised 'staggering sums of money. This was faithfully reported in Kabul and people did genuinely think all this was going to translate into concrete projects. Of course, like so many aid programmes it translated into so many offices in Kabul . . . and actually into complete inability to turn that commitment of cash into proper aid projects.'

Brigadier White-Spunner did not blame the Department for International Development (DFID), as some people did; there had been far too much 'DFID-bashing', he said. He did think, however, that the British were 'institutionally' not well set up to do reconstruction, even fifteen years after the Balkan conflict started: 'Governments were quick to use armed forces because they were organised, ready to go and because they had a degree of coherence and reliance.' But there was no equivalent mechanism to do the 'absolutely critical bit of these expeditionary operations, which is to get the aid and the civil governance going, and it's a big gap'. In his view, as in so many things, 'the Americans had learned very quickly. They were not good at it originally but they had got much better at it . . . much quicker than we had.'[18] A British journalist embedded with American troops remarked on how, whereas American middle-ranking commanders could dish out thousands of dollars to deserving villagers, the most the British commander could do in a comparable case was to offer the local farmers a supply of seeds.

Brigadier White-Spunner thought the success of the British operation to disarm Albanian insurgents in Macedonia in 2001, which he commanded – a peacekeeping mission which was accomplished rapidly and successfully – had generated over-optimism in London and other

Western capitals. Nobody had appreciated that Afghanistan in 2001 'was a very different operation, because no one realised quite how damaged it was. There was an obvious urgency to get in there; there was a quick military task to be done, but once we had stabilised the situation there was something of a political standstill.'

The other thing that no one realised was how much damage the drought – the worst in memory – had caused. To make matters worse, the Taliban had smashed all the irrigation systems in the villages that were 'anti them'. The situation was so critical that in May 2000, Eric de Mul, the UN coordinator for humanitarian aid in Afghanistan, urgently appealed for $1.8 million to feed the starving victims. The scale of the challenge in Afghanistan, Brigadier White-Spunner, added, was underestimated as was the degree of reconstruction needed. So too was the 'sheer geography of the country in terms of getting troops round it'. Above all, however, what went wrong was that there was 'no proper plan as to what should happen once Kabul fell . . . I cited the Macedonian example, the idea that you would go in, you would get rid of the bad guys, the Taliban, you would get Karzai and the Northern Alliance together, you give them some aid money, and they would look after themselves. It was very similar to Iraq. There was no proper plan for what the military called Phase Four – or reconstruction.' In addition, 'the international community proved incapable of keeping its aid and reconstruction promises and of providing one, focused advice to President Karzai'.

Brigadier White-Spunner admits to being 'rather a fan' of President Karzai. 'I know things have gone wrong now, but then we saw him as a very brave and honourable man. He was physically, personally, brave.'[19]

On 8 October 2001, the day after the Americans started to bomb, the future President, the only one of the Karzai brothers not to have decamped to America, got on the back of a friend's motorbike and set off for the Afghan border, which they crossed clandestinely and headed for the outskirts of Kandahar, where they spent the night with friends. Two days later Hamid Karzai arrived in a small village near Tarin Kot, the dusty, dirty, impoverished little capital of Uruzgan, where Mullah Omar, the Taliban leader, grew up. He met local leaders who promised their support, provided he was backed by the Americans, and became convinced the country was ripe for revolt.

Karzai had two narrow escapes: the first when, a few days after the end of the Bonn Conference in December 2001, a misdirected American 2,000-lb bomb exploded almost on top of his party, killing three American soldiers, seven Afghans and wounding many others. Ahmed Rashid says Karzai's face took the blast but, almost miraculously, he suffered no major injuries. Karzai's Green Beret escort, Captain Jason Amerine, who was badly wounded himself, recalled ten years later in an interview with Christina Lamb: 'By sheer luck Karzai was further along the ridge and only slightly wounded in the shoulder . . . I didn't have it in me to tell him the headquarters had done it.'[20] The second close shave came when the Taliban, having discovered Karzai was inside Afghanistan, pursued him, and were closing in, when his CIA escort managed to send an SOS asking urgently for rescue. It came just in time. Karzai and his team were helicoptered out, narrowly escaping capture and almost certain death.

'I did feel very sorry for him,' Brigadier White-Spunner says, 'because he was getting advice and promises from all sorts of international bodies and there was no one plan. [Zalmay] Khalilzad [a Neo-Con Afghan-American who worked for the State Department] tried for a bit when he was the American Ambassador . . . but then he was taken away.' Karzai, White-Spunner says, 'did not have the one thing he really needed – one body to deal with . . . So there was no proper plan, a complete inability to live on the aid and reconstruction . . . Because he had no idea of how to spend it . . . enough was promised, but the problem was spending it and also, some of the plans for spending it, reconstruction projects, were quite ludicrous. They were based on how money would have been spent in a Western democracy.'

One aid agency, which he declined to name, objected strongly to the army running the ambulance service in Kabul because the ambulances they were using were not up to Western standards. 'We had quite a bit of a battle about it. And when we proved that we were saving lives nightly they backed down.' Somebody else said that they could not do a well-digging project round Kabul because they had not done a 'full gender survey'.* 'That was the sort of thing that one was up against . . .'

---

* One British aid worker commented that the idea was not as daft as it might sound because of the difficulty women often had leaving the house, to fetch water for example, so it made sense that they should be consulted.

Another mistake, he suggested, was not expanding outside Kabul. 'I don't know what would have happened if we'd gone down into Kandahar and Helmand, but I expect in those heady days with the Taliban on the back foot we would have been able to achieve quite a lot. Because you'd have been able to work with [Governor] Ismail Khan in Herat and [Governor] Gul Agha Sherzai in Kandahar . . . One would have been able to work with local administrations based on what was practical and effective . . .' Another difficulty was the lack of any effective means of communicating what ISAF was trying to do. When the British arrived there was very little media, only a few hours of television a day, very little radio, no print media and the only successful way of getting their message out was through the mullahs. Brigadier White-Spunner found the Islamic leadership in Kabul 'absolutely fantastic . . . probably the most supportive'. They described how they had been 'besmirched' by the Taliban – probably because they had been appointed by the previous Rabbani–Masud government. He used to have regular meetings with the then chief mullah on Thursdays and he would assemble all the main mullahs in the Kabul area 'fairly regularly' before Friday prayers and 'expound some of the messages'. As a result the Friday prayers message was usually 'very supportive' of the British. Another ingenious way of promoting their message was by selling kites with 'ISAF' printed on them.[21]

Just before he left Kabul in June 2002, General McColl told me he thought it had been a mistake not to have deployed 20,000 troops in Afghanistan instead of 3,000, which would have made it possible to extend ISAF's presence all over the country, as Karzai kept pressing for and indeed the State Department under Colin Powell supported.[22] At the same time, McColl felt the media placed too much emphasis on what had gone wrong in Afghanistan, and that the question should be: 'What's gone right?' His answer to this was: 'We have had double digit economic growth every year since we arrived; we have had this extraordinary growth in education; in health; we have had a democratic process which has now gone through several cycles.' It was absolutely right, he agreed, to point out the problem of drugs, corruption, the lack of security, all areas which needed attention. 'But let's not forget what has gone right.'[23]

Brigadier White-Spunner agreed with McColl's suggestion that ISAF should have been expanded to possibly 20,000. He thought the British were slow to realise that they should have been more widely based because of the need to 'consolidate on the opportunity that had been created'. That had been a mistake. 'And I think it's absolutely right [to say] that the administration in Washington got distracted by Iraq and saw Afghanistan almost as a campaign won. I think you've also got to look at the motives in going in there. I think the American motive was very much to have a go at al Qaeda and . . . try to get Osama, very soon after 9/11. I don't think much thought had been given to what happened after that, quite similar to Iraq, really. There was a sort of diktat to do this – destroy bin Laden and al Qaeda.'

Also, there were those who thought it might have been better not to have gone straight in 'but to have shown 9/11 for the horror that it was to civilisation and say to the government of Pakistan "You can't condone this, you should give Osama bin Laden up, or put him on trial yourselves."' But it had been 'very rushed, very like Iraq, and no thought of what was going to come afterwards: not enough thought.'[24]

————

Kabul changed dramatically in that first six months, McColl recalls, going from no cars, only taxis, to traffic jams. 'People flooded back from Pakistan . . . They had a problem with returning refugees. It became a booming and vibrant city.' Yet, despite the vibrancy, Afghanistan in 2002 was a 'failed state'. Although 'there were degrees of failed state . . . this one was right at the bottom. You would go to a ministry, have a conversation with someone, and realise it was one-man deep. You were speaking to somebody who spoke reasonable English and gave you the impression of being reasonably competent but the minute you walked out of the door and tried to get hold of his chief of staff, or PA, or a branch to deliver something, the whole thing fell apart.'[25]

Even if Donald Rumsfeld was not interested, someone had to make a start on nation-building.

The International Security Assistance Force 'kicked off the training of the Afghan Army', McColl says and the 1st Battalion, Afghan National Guard marched off the square in about May that year (2002). 'That was the first 500. Now of course, (late 2009), we are talking about an army which is about 80,000- to 90,000-strong; a police force that is 90,000-strong, so it's gone from 500 then, and it really was 500, up to an institution now which is really becoming increasingly capable.' The old Afghan Army basically had dispersed. The majority had gone back into civilian life, including 'the fighting elements' of the Taliban and the Northern Alliance. 'We had no desire to use the army of the Northern Alliance,' General McColl told me. The new army would reflect the country itself. 'For example the first battalion of the Afghan National Guard had a proportional ethnic make-up, about 35 per cent Pushtuns – and Tajiks and Uzbeks in a quota system, the boss being Pushtun, the number two being a Tajik. The next time it was going to be the other way around, so it was very much designing and developing an Afghan National Army [ANA] which the whole country would respect.'[26]

Unfortunately, the original intention that the army should reflect the national make-up does not seem to have taken root. Instead, Pushtuns have fought shy of making a career in the military, saying they do not want to join a 'Tajik army'. In fact, according to the official figures, the army is almost equally made up of Tajiks, Uzbeks and Hazaras with very few Pushtuns. General McColl was surprised when I said as far as I knew the ANA was still almost entirely made up of northerners and still had a very small percentage of Pushtuns in it. As one experienced Western observer put it: 'It is a vicious circle. Pushtuns won't join because they don't want to fight other Pushtuns in the shape of the Taliban, or because they don't want to be in a "Tajik army". So, of course, the army remains basically non-Pushtun.'

Overall, General McColl feels ISAF's initial performance, even if Kabul-centric, was successful. 'I felt that the progress that we made in six months was as much as we could reasonably have expected. We had had the Emergency Loya Jirga, which was the last thing we did, where the country came together, the leadership came together.' He admits there was a lot of criticism of the grand council, 'in that it included "the usual suspects" [meaning warlords]. All of that is true, but on the other hand we could not have started with a clean sheet of paper. The country was what it was . . . and we had to make use of those leaders . . . There was some very robust debate, people jumping up and saying neither of you should be here, you should all be . . . They were able to do that because we were there. Had we not been there it would have been a rather different discussion.'

'In the event,' General McColl said, 'ISAF had enabled the Afghans to begin the process of moving towards some kind of democratic electoral process and in that respect I thought we had made progress.' They had made progress in terms of the 1st Battalion, the Afghan National Guard,* and they had also seen significant development in terms of the capacities of the ministries; but it was still very Kabul-centric.

General McColl said he 'was conscious that there was a need to develop the writ of the Afghan national government across the country and in order for that to happen there would need to be some kind of international support . . . some kind of expanded international role.' He then spoke about what was perhaps the most significant political failure which blighted what might otherwise have been considered a successful start to the reha-bilitation of Afghanistan. 'I think, looking back on it, what we did not have was a feel for what was happening to the Taliban and exactly what condition they were in . . . They had of course fled across the border and effectively disappeared into the south, into Pakistan . . .' What they were not able to do, General McColl said, was to get a clear picture of how the Taliban would regenerate themselves. 'I don't think at that stage we would have predicted that they would have risen and got back the capacity that they have, in the time they had.'[27]

General McColl left Afghanistan in June 2002, when the rebirth of the Taliban had barely started, so he can hardly be blamed for the failure to foresee how they were, eventually, to make such an astonishingly successful comeback. His successors, however, are less easily exonerated. Where was the military and diplomatic intelligence that should have picked up the warning signals? Once again it is impossible not to point the finger at the obsessive demands generated by the war in Iraq, mainly on the Americans, but also, to a lesser degree, on the British, dragged along in their wake. One man realised very clearly what was happening: Francesc Vendrell, former UN and EU Special Representative for Afghanistan in Kabul from 2001 to 2008. He tried to warn both the British and Americans about the

---

* Now the Afghan National Army, ANA.

Taliban revival – masterminded by the ISI – which was already visible in 2002, 2003, and 2004, he says, but no one paid any attention.[28]

Even in 2006, Dr Vendrell says, when the British were deploying more than 3,000 troops to Helmand, 'everyone knew' British soldiers were being killed by Taliban 'who were either linked to Pakistan or based in Pakistan'. It was not until 2007, Vendrell says, that the British and Americans realised what was really happening. One wonders why Karzai, himself a Popalzai Pushtun from Kandahar with a multiplicity of tribal and political connections in the south, did not react. Vendrell talks about his 'blindness' towards Pakistan. Karzai, better than anyone, knew who the Taliban were and also understood the ISI connection. Mullah Omar had offered him the job of representing the Taliban at the UN, which he was on the point of accepting, according to Ahmed Rashid, when he discovered that Pakistan was already running their foreign policy.

The secret regeneration of the Taliban, under the noses of the British and the Americans, must qualify as one of the great conjuring tricks of history: although it was not so much a rabbit which the ISI magicians pulled out of the hat; more a spitting cobra.

With the proviso that '20/20 hindsight is a great asset', General McColl argued, 'I think you can be forgiven for being surprised by the way in which the Taliban were able to come back . . .' There was absolutely no doubt in his view that 'the majority of Afghans were delighted to see the back of them . . . They might have welcomed them when they turned up in Kandahar [in 1994] to bring order to chaos, but certainly by the time that we were there, in 2002, the overwhelming view . . . was they were pleased to see the Taliban go.' This would undoubtedly have been the view in Persian-speaking Kabul, which was always hostile to the Taliban. 'So I think it would be fair to say the idea of the Taliban philosophy was dead; it was seen to be flawed and dead, which is not to say the movement was dead; it was the philosophy that was dead,' McColl added. The majority of people in Afghanistan had experienced it and it did not meet their expectations. They were glad to see the back of it. If you were analysing the ability for it to resurrect itself, you would probably have taken the view: No, actually now that we've got rid of them and they no longer have their hands round the throat of the country they will not be able to get back there, because the people don't want them. That was the 'overwhelming feeling among the populace, I think it was understandable . . . that it should be thought that we had the advantage.'

General McColl admits the resources and intelligence that they had in Pakistan and southern Afghanistan were 'pretty limited' largely because of Iraq. Which leads him to a frank summing up: 'I think the analysis would be that had we not been distracted by Iraq, had we had the full weight of those resources, had we had the desire to provide security across Afghanistan and therefore the broader international community's presence, securing governance and economic development, had we done that from the outset then it would have been very, very difficult for the Taliban to come in. But we gave them a window of opportunity. I think that is what history will say.'

General McColl does not mention Pakistan's ISI, which, we now know, took advantage of America's almost total absorption in Iraq to start to rebuild the Taliban from 2002. As a Haqqani district commander told the British researcher Matt Waldman, the ISI not only actively encouraged the Taliban who had taken refuge in Pakistan, but also members of the Haqqani group to go back to Afghanistan.[29] The commander described how he and many former Talibs and *jihadi* fighters had been living in Pakistan, doing ordinary jobs, when, in 2003/2004 the Pakistani military and ISI actively tried to 'reconnect' them, encouraging them to return to fight in Afghanistan. If they went back, the ISI said, they would give them money, weapons and support.[30]

Even if a lot of Afghans, as General McColl suggests, did not want to see the return of the Taliban, they really had no means of stopping them. Once the repatriation movement started, they went back in droves. They flooded back to their farms and villages, funded, retrained and rearmed by the ISI, and found no one standing in their way. In fact, in many cases they would have been treated like returning heroes, reoccupying a political vacuum, without opposition from the government in Kabul. They were there, waiting, armed to the teeth, when the British arrived in 2006.

At this juncture, neither the United States nor Britain had any time to spare for Afghanistan. Iraq was the only game in town, as the Americans say. As deputy commander in Iraq in 2004, General McColl recalls that 'the resources flowing in from the US to try and resolve the crisis – and it was a crisis in Iraq at that time – were immense'. Afghanistan did not just take second place; 'it wasn't just a second order, it was of a different order totally . . . The allocation of resources in the widest sense – hardware, men, money and brainpower – between Iraq and Afghanistan, were worlds apart.'[31]

Not only was there a crippling lack of intelligence, again because of the emphasis on Iraq, but more seriously even, an almost deliberate ignorance and lack of curiosity as to what the Pakistanis were up to. The British old India hands and above all the Americans believed Musharraf when he told them he was 100 per cent on their side when it came to fighting terrorism, which included the Taliban. And when challenged about the sinister activities of the ISI, Pakistan would deny any official role, and blame a few 'rogue elements'. It took a long time for the penny to drop.

Speaking in November 2009, General McColl defended the decision to send British troops to Helmand – Afghanistan's largest province and its biggest producer of opium – in 2006, despite a lack of clarity in the intelligence picture. 'If we had not gone into Helmand,' he argued, the Taliban, having strengthened their grip there, would undoubtedly have made a move 'on Kabul and the north and west of the country' and it would have been very difficult to dislodge them. By 'putting a foot on the ground' in conjunction with our allies to improve security, we had encouraged Pakistan's 'counter-terrorist and counter-Taliban activities' on their side of the border – in other words to confront the Pakistani Taliban in Swat, Malakand, Bajaur but not, most crucially, in North Waziristan, which they would not, he suggests, have otherwise done.

'We needed,' General McColl explained, to give the south 'a degree of security to allow governance and economics to develop. The other option, frankly, was the option we are faced with now; to withdraw and cede that part of the country to the Taliban and just say "that's it, it's over to you". And if we did that, what would happen shortly after? We would find life very difficult in the centre, in the north, and then we would cede that to them as well. I accept the point that in the deployment of operations some things don't always turn out as you might have expected. Occasionally, operational circumstances surprise you and this is one of them. However,

I don't accept that it was the wrong thing to do. I think it was the right thing to do.'[32]

McColl also disputes that the British went in with too few troops and resources originally: 'No, we did an analysis which indicated that that was the right level of resource in conjunction with allies' (mainly the Canadians and Americans). As things turned out, however, it required more troops.

> We deployed initially I think the figure was 3,500 or 4,000 . . . and we are now up to 9,500. So clearly we have put more resources in, in response to a situation which has developed in a dynamic way, but that is the nature of operations. Look at Northern Ireland.

> 'Now, had we had complete clarity and visibility and our intelligence was perfect, we probably would not have gone in with the resources we did, we would have gone in with more but it wasn't so . . . You can't hide the fact that we went in with too little, okay, but on the other hand this is a dynamic operational situation and perhaps it is unreasonable to expect us to get the level of resource exactly right.

He also rejects suggestions that Afghanistan is another Vietnam in the making; he does not see it as a total disaster, but rather as a manageable problem capable of solution.

> There has been . . . significant progress in Afghanistan in the GDP, the economic wealth of the country, health, education, infrastructure; all of these things they're making significant progress on. The areas that are a problem are security, narcotics and corruption.

> So, on the question of, is it winnable, I come back to this central idea of what does the population want? Well, any poll you read tells you that the Taliban have about 5 per cent support across much of the country and 95 per cent don't want them. Now, they don't necessarily support the government because they have misgivings about the government, but they absolutely don't want the Taliban . . . What we have got to do is . . . give them first of all some sort of security and back it up in parallel with . . . more troops, more focus on governance, in other words a civilian surge and more focus on economics.

This, in effect, was what the McChrystal surge, approved by President Obama in late 2010, did.

Did he think that we could do it? 'I absolutely think we can, I absolutely think that we must and I think that the only thing that will defeat us is the internal commentary in our respective countries. I don't think the Taliban will defeat us.'

So what does success look like? General McColl says the answer is to build up the Afghan security forces to the state where the West can hand over to them. For him it means 'some kind of security environment and that means sufficient troops; it means sufficient Afghan national security forces'.[33]

This leaves, however, one vital ingredient out of the equation: Pakistan and the ISI, to which we will come later.

The Great Game in the South, 2005

It would be a bit like moving another gang into the East End of London.
They [the Taliban] weren't going to like it.

Lieutenant Colonel Henry Worsley, London, 2009

In 2005 a youthful-looking Royal Green Jacket officer, Lieutenant Colonel Henry Worsley, was sent on what Kipling might have described as a mission inspired by the Great Game. But rather than spying on Russia's penetration of Afghanistan in the nineteenth century, Worsley was instructed to act as ambassador-cum-spy for Tony Blair's twenty-first-century adventure to pacify the drug-growing Afghan south. The British would send more than 3,000 troops to Helmand to implement a tripartite plan comprising security, governance and development. The objective was the peaceful reconstruction of a country racked by more than thirty years of revolution, war and occupation. It was a brave new venture, unlike any others the British had undertaken in Afghanistan over a period of nearly 200 years; ventures which, although always in the end militarily victorious, embroiled them in a series of disastrous and costly wars. As I write, in 2011, the outcome of the latest venture hangs in the balance.

Worsley's mission was to sell the Blair plan to the Afghans, what the Army calls 'info ops' – information operations – and also to report back to London what sort of reception the exponents of the latest Great Game mission would encounter. In other words, to carry out a recce, spying out the conditions in which the tripartite plan would be implemented.

Worsley travelled light, went all over the south 'with freedom and ease', he says, 'with only five vehicles protected by fifteen soldiers'. Some journeys lasted three days, driving across the desert and gravel plains and camping out in the wadis. 'It was like being on safari. We walked up the main bazaar roads with berets and body armour and then sat out in the sun drinking tea and eating dried peas with the District Chief and his Head of Police, whilst some of the soldiers played football with the local children.' It was 'an interesting juxtaposition with what was soon to happen', Worsley reflects. 'Looking back I am amazed I wasn't killed! I suppose we posed no threat at that time.'[1]

Despite the relaxed atmosphere, he reached a very definite conclusion: 'One thing was very clear to me . . . when the Paras [3rd Battalion, The Parachute Regiment] were going to arrive [in Helmand] in April or May 2006, there would be a reception party for them. There was no doubt about that.' The implication was that it would be a hostile reception.

Worsley visited all of Helmand's thirteen administrative districts to spread the word the British were coming. He found the locals already knew, although their information was faulty. 'Certainly the elders knew we were coming . . . [but] all they thought we were going to do when we arrived was to eradicate poppies.' He tried to disabuse them by explaining the three-pronged policy: the establishment of security, accompanied by the improvement of governance, which together would allow economic development to flourish. The army, which he represented, would be responsible for security but he could only talk about governance and development because the Foreign Office and DFID were not with him on the ground.

'Of course they didn't have anyone from the Foreign Office or DFID with them because they weren't allowed to come so far forward and rarely got out of Kandahar in those days. So it was quite tricky to speak up on their behalf.'[2]

With little or no hard intelligence he and his limited staff were unable to 'paint the picture actually of what the Taliban were doing', but at the same time, 'we were seeing it every day. I knew they were around.' He was well aware the arrival of more than 3,000 British soldiers could spell trouble. 'It would be a bit like moving another gang into the East End of London. They [the Taliban] weren't going to like it.'

He made his concerns clear and got into trouble in London when he was quoted in the *Sunday Telegraph* as saying that the advent of the British would be like 'stirring up a hornets' nest'.[3] He said the journalist had put words in his mouth, 'but I didn't disagree because it was clear to me that

that was going to happen'. Added to which 'there just wasn't that level of expectancy from the British military'.

Nor, one might add, from the politicians.

Wherever the fault lay – lack of intelligence or lack of foresight, or both – Brigadier Ed Butler, the commander of British troops who arrived in mid-2006, had not been expecting such 'a brutal entry into the province' as Henry Worsley, with whom Brigadier Butler later spent some of his R&R, put it. 'They were expecting a fight but nothing more.'[4]

Worsley says he will 'never forget, and it [has] come back to haunt me since, the words from three separate elders in, I think, Naw Zad, Musa Qala and Gereshk' – three of the principal towns in Helmand. He recalls the first elder 'standing up at the end of one of my talks just explaining what we were coming to do, wagging his finger at me. I can see him now, his long grey beard, an elegant man, wagging his brown finger at me saying: "Don't you ever forget that the only difference between you and the Russians is that you are supposed to be bringing development to this country; make sure you deliver it." Then he sat down. Of course I didn't have anyone from the DFID with me and I tried to reassure him that DFID were hot on our tail and once we had made the place safe, they would be doing all their good work. He listened to that, but he just wagged his finger . . .

'Another man I remember,' continued Worsley, 'a very similar-looking guy . . . asking: "Have you got the patience? We saw all this activity for the first five years after the Russians left, a lot of investment from the international community across the world particularly America and Europe but it [only] lasted five years. Have you got the patience to see this through?" This was a rhetorical question, whereupon he just sat down. That right now is a telling comment because I think we are running out of patience. We want things done quickly.'

The third man Henry Worsley remembers specifically talked about personal security:

'Listen, we don't want development. I don't want a new well in my village. I want to be safe, I want to be able to go to my local policeman and tell him I have a problem, because my house has just been robbed.

And I want to have a police force I can trust and I want a safe country.'
So he enjoyed hearing that the Afghan Army were coming. The Afghan
Army were pretty popular; actually the police were not. And if we could
do something about the police and make the place safe [for] him, that
was all that mattered. The development, the well or the new road can
come much later. He wanted to sleep well in his bed at night. So those
three elements were very important and I think it still rings true today,
particularly the one on patience.[5]

Colonel Worsley's account raises a number of questions. The arrival of
the British had been well publicised in the British media, and everyone had
heard the Defence Secretary Dr John Reid's famous remark, which seemed
perfectly sensible at the time, but also came back to haunt him. British
troops were in Afghanistan to help the Afghan reconstruction effort and
'would be perfectly happy', he told a press conference in Kabul, 'to leave
without firing a shot'.[6] The mission, after all, was development. Admittedly
the elders, according to Worsley, thought the British were coming to 'eradicate the poppy'. Had the story about destroying the poppy crop been
spread by the Taliban, who had been moving back into Helmand and the
rest of the south and rebuilding their organisation since 2002? Secondly,
despite his warning that there would be a 'reception party' when the Paras
arrived, why had this message not rung alarm bells at the Ministry of
Defence in London and at Number 10 Downing Street?

Whitehall, however, seems to have been completely caught on the
wrong foot by the seriousness of the situation in Helmand. The headline
of a lengthy analysis carried out by *The Times* in June 2010 was provided
by Major General (then Brigadier) Andrew Mackay, who commanded in
Helmand in 2007: 'They went into Helmand with their eyes shut and
fingers crossed' was his pithy critique. The paper went on: 'He is not
alone. A succession of military and civilian officials, interviewed by *The
Times*, indicated that warnings about under-resourcing and over-ambi-
tion were made lower down the chain of command during the planning
process, but were not considered sufficient for a significant rethink by the
top brass.'[7] It added: 'The charge sheet includes institutional arrogance
and an overkeenness to deploy to Helmand to compensate for a troubled

campaign in Iraq. In addition, there is evidence of another British intelligence failure, this time an underestimation of the threat rather than the
overestimation that was made on weapons of mass destruction before the
downfall of Saddam Hussein.'[8]

Lieutenant Colonel Stuart Tootal, commander of 3 PARA, which was
the spearhead of 16 Air Assault Brigade and took the brunt of the early
fighting in Helmand, attributes the failure to 'wishful thinking'.[9] The decision-makers, in his view, had the wrong 'mindset' for Afghanistan. 'There
was a definite feeling,' he says, 'that it was going to be a peaceable operation, they would not need that many resources, and that it was a pretty
straightforward mission. Whenever anyone raised issues or concerns, the
reaction was: "Oh, you're rather over-egging it, it's all going to be rather
benign."' Colonel Tootal recalled one occasion when he was talking about
his contingency planning and what he would do if his troops got into
trouble: he was actually taken aside by a very senior Marine colonel and
told: 'Well, I shouldn't worry too much. You won't have any problem from
the Taliban . . .'

'Well, quite clearly we did,' is Tootal's response. 'It showed there was no
proper intelligence.'[10]

However, what little intelligence they had, he says, was sufficient to give
an indication that there was likely to be trouble. For example, eighteen
policemen sent down to the south by the new British-backed Governor,
Mohammed Daud, were 'massacred and murdered . . .' That told them for
a start that security forces might have some trouble in the area in which
they were about to arrive. And in the north, Governor Daud had to send
200 militia up into the Sangin Valley after four district chiefs had been
murdered. 'There was a sense that the Taliban were coming in and there
was an unholy alliance with the drug lords and a combination of the two
coming together . . . that was happening.'

Because of the wrong mindset, Tootal contends, when the fighting
started people at PJHQ (Permanent Joint Headquarters, Northwood,
Middlesex) and at the MOD were quite slow to make the appropriate
response. 'Although, for example, we were having vicious firefights which
could last for six hours, people were still questioning why we needed our
own artillery although on numerous occasions the artillery I'd been using

was keeping my people alive.' So again he did not see enough in the senior echelons of the MOD and in some parts of the Army of 'this focus on combat. This is what the British Army now does. There was a need for an intellectual shift to change the mindset. And that definitely wasn't happening in 2006, which is partly why we ran into trouble in Afghanistan the way we did.'[11]

There were four other reasons why the British venture into Helmand was doomed to failure from the start, according to Colonel Tootal: first there was the much-debated issue of resources. There were clearly not enough troops, he says. 'If you did your normal calculations, the number of the population and areas to be covered, 1,200 combat troops out of a force of 3,000, most of whom would never go on patrol, quite frankly it was barking mad to think that one battle group could dominate an area the size, effectively, of Northern Ireland, where it had taken 16,000 British troops at its [the Emergency's] height and the support of a first-world police force [the Royal Ulster Constabulary] in the 1970s, '80s and early '90s. So the metrics were wrong.'

His most trenchant criticism, however, he reserves for the helicopter issue. Three PARA did not have enough helicopters in Afghanistan, Tootal declares, despite repeated claims by the Prime Minister, Gordon Brown, that they did. 'We had six Chinooks of which at best five would be available. Quite frankly a brigade needs twelve Chinooks, that's what the Americans have, and that's one battle group, at any one time. So we were significantly below the number of aircraft needed. We made a number of calculations before we went to Afghanistan and we didn't have enough troops just to do the peacekeeping mission . . . and with what we were forced to leave to the outstations, Sangin, the Kajaki Dam, Musa Qala, Naw Zad, not only were we stretched for general resources but we had real risks in stretching helicopter hours to cover all those outstations.'

It also meant, he said, that casualty evacuation was never guaranteed. He had to make decisions about leaving badly wounded men on the ground, needing to be airlifted out, for hours on end. 'I needed that time to reduce the threat against the aircraft . . . and that was partly forced on us . . . by the first problem I mentioned, wishful thinking and the fact that there were not enough helicopters, not enough troops, and we didn't have the right kinds of equipment.' Not every member of his battalion who went out on patrol had night-vision gear, and the gunners of 7 Royal Horse Artillery used in the OMLTs' (Operational Mentoring and Liaison Teams), nickname 'Omelettes', were 'woefully ill-equipped'.[12]

The third problem, Tootal says, was the poor command and control structure. He is especially critical of the UK decision to sideline Brigadier Ed Butler and make him COMBRITFOR (Commander British Forces) but without tactical control and to 'bring in an outsider who didn't know the Brigade'. This was 'full Colonel Charlie Knaggs, ex-CO Irish Guards, who I think tried to do the right thing but had a struggle to do it,' he says. 'Butler was the man to do the tactical commander's job and they brought in someone less able and less qualified.'[13] Moreover he, Knaggs, was subordinate to a Canadian Brigade Commander who reported to an American two-star (major general), 'so I had these triple reporting lines'. Sometimes Tootal reported direct to Charlie Knaggs and sometimes direct to Brigadier General David Fraser, the Canadian Brigade Commander, and he also had to report to the commander, Ed Butler, who was his old Brigade Commander. 'We had mutual trust and respected each other. We should have been allowed to work together right from the start . . . It was flawed and wasn't something that would have been recognised in any decent Staff College.'[14]

Colonel Tootal says they suffered as a result. To take Butler away as Brigade Commander was a fundamental mistake, although it was rebalanced and readdressed by General Sir David Richards (later Chief of the Defence Staff) when he took command in Helmand in July 2006. 'He changed the command arrangements pretty quickly because he's a pragmatic guy and he realised it was wrong.' But a procession of chiefs and senior officers had signed up to the original structure, which made you 'wonder how much experience they'd really had to make that decision', Tootal says. 'The one thing you really don't need is an unwieldy, complex, fraught-with-risk, inefficient way of doing business.' Operations had to be as clear and simple as possible, 'making a form of order out of chaos and that's what operational success is all about. It definitely caused us problems, slowed things down and caused risk.'[15]

Tootal himself was a typical Para. Brigadier Ed Butler recalls an all-action occasion when they were putting down in hostile territory, with

Colonel Tootal 'grabbing the machine gun from the young, apprehensive RAF door gunner, as the Chinook . . . approached a "hot LZ" [Landing Zone] in Helmand. Stuart, as CO, proceeded to provide suppressive fire for his paratroopers on the ground until it was appropriate for his TAC [Tactical Headquarters] to land on. All in the finest spirit of the Airborne fraternity!' Butler adds with a grin. 'Often said and more importantly I genuinely knew that his paratroopers would have, and did, on numerous occasions follow him to the end of the Earth. I also think that Stuart and I shared that rare bond of total trust between commanders that is only really seen on the battlefield.'[16] Although small and slight, Lieutenant Colonel Tootal once described to me how he had to go through the tough Para training routine known as 'milling', when two trainees wearing head guards and 16oz boxing gloves stand toe to toe and, for sixty seconds, hit their opponent as hard and as often as they can. Most recruits, Tootal says, finish covered in blood. He was no exception.[17]

In another strong indictment of the tripartite scheme proposed by Tony Blair and his Defence Secretary Dr John Reid, Tootal identifies the fourth problem as there having been 'no joined-up plan' with DFID and the Foreign and Commonwealth Office. There was 'lots of talk about a comprehensive plan but actually rubbish in delivery. It's easy to chat, harder to do. DFID and the FCO wouldn't leave Lashkar Gah,' he says, 'they always hid behind FCO rules.' Most damning of all is his account of the way DFID blocked his and his medical officer's plan to help out the local hospital in Gereshk, in southern Helmand, where 3 PARA had just arrived. When the MO visited the hospital, to be greeted warmly by the surgeon and anaesthetist, he noticed a pile of unwashed, bloodstained sheets. They had a washing machine, they explained, still in the packing case in which it had arrived from the United States Agency for International Development (USAID), but no running water. 'Don't worry,' the MO said, 'our engineers can sink a borehole and you'll have running water in no time.' But they had reckoned without DFID. Tootal was told in so many words to 'mind his own business'; 3 PARA were not to get involved, it should be left to local NGOs (non-governmental organisations). Unfortunately the NGOs never got around to it.[18]

Although this was exactly the sort of quick-impact project that could win over hearts and minds in the local community, Tootal says: 'I wasn't allowed to fix one washing machine . . . even though the hospital wanted it. DFID said this was not something soldiers should do. But they never went and fixed it themselves. I said: "We don't care if we don't do it, it's not a turf war but the point is someone has got to do this because there's a fundamental requirement"; and they came up with lots of excuses.'[19] The Afghan NGO commissioned by the Department of International Development to deal with the problem 'never went to the hospital, they might have done since, but not during our time . . . It was lacklustre. They [DFID] didn't have their best people there: they rotated out every two weeks, they did only six weeks in theatre, they'd go back on holiday, they lived in air-conditioned containers, they didn't "do" living in tents. They just weren't up to the hunt and so consequently the military tended to lead which wasn't always ideal.'[20]

Colonel Tootal quotes General Sir Frank Kitson, considered one of the British Army's foremost authorities on guerrilla warfare, who said the military often has to be secondary and subordinate. But there was no way it could be in Helmand, says Tootal, 'because DFID and the FCO basically didn't have the spunk to do it properly'. It all came back to the mindset, he says, and adds that there was another lesson of counter-insurgency: 'be pretty clear about the kind of operation you're getting into, the conflicts you're going into and what the implications are'. You need 'joined-up people who can deliver . . . DFID and the FCO were not joined-up and delivering people'.

'Sadly,' he continues, 'the British military is delivering; they did so in 2006 and they continue to do so today; but then they're not supported by the right resources and the right strategy.'[21]

───────────

Another critical view of the Helmand operation – equally harsh – came from Captain Leo Docherty, former aide-de-camp to the Brigade Commander, Colonel Charlie Knaggs. In September 2006 he described it to Christina Lamb of the *Sunday Times* as being 'a textbook case of how to screw up a counter-insurgency'.[22]

'Having a big old fight is pointless and just making things worse,' said

Docherty, who became so disillusioned that he resigned from the Army that August. 'All those people whose homes have been destroyed and sons killed are going to turn against the British,' he said. 'It's a pretty clear equation – if people are losing homes and poppy fields, they will go and fight. I certainly would. We've been grotesquely clumsy – we've said we'll be different to the Americans who were bombing and strafing villages, then behaved exactly like them.'

Captain Docherty's criticisms, the first from an officer who had served in Helmand, came during the worst week so far for British troops in Afghanistan, with the loss of eighteen men. They reflected growing concern, Christina Lamb wrote, that forces had been left exposed in small northern outposts (known as 'platoon houses') of Helmand such as Sangin, Musa Qala and Naw Zad. Pinned down by daily Taliban attacks, many had run short of food and water and had been forced to rely on air support and artillery.

'We've deviated spectacularly from the original plan,' Docherty told the *Sunday Times*. 'The plan was to secure the provincial capital, Lashkar Gah, initiate development projects and enable governance . . . During this time, the insecure northern part of Helmand would be contained: troops would not be sucked in to a problem unsolvable by military means alone.' According to Captain Docherty, the planning 'fell by the wayside' because of pressure from the Governor of Helmand, who feared the Taliban were toppling his district chiefs in northern towns.

Docherty traces the start of the problems to the British capture of Sangin on 25 May 2006, in which he took part. He says troops were sent to seize this notorious centre of Taliban and narcotics activity without night-vision goggles and with so few vehicles they had to borrow a pickup truck. But even when they had established a base in the town, the mission 'failed to capitalise on their presence'. Sangin had no paved roads, running water or electricity, but because of a lack of support his men were unable to carry out any development, throwing away the opportunity to win over the townspeople.

'The military is just one side of the triangle,' he says. 'Where were the Department for International Development and the Foreign Office? The window was briefly open for our message to be spread, for the civilian population to be informed of our intent and realise that we weren't there simply to destroy the poppy fields and their livelihoods. I felt at this stage that the Taliban were sitting back and observing us, deciding in their own time how to most effectively hit us.'[23]

Eventually the Taliban attacked on 11 June, when Captain Jim Philippson became the first British soldier to be killed in Helmand. British troops had been holed up in their compound with attacks coming at least once a day and seven British soldiers had been killed in the Sangin area. 'Now the ground has been lost and all we're doing in places like Sangin is surviving,' says Docherty. 'It's completely barking mad. We're now scattered in a shallow meaningless way across northern towns where the only way for the troops to survive is to increase the level of violence so more people get killed. It's pretty shocking and not something I want to be part of.'

Colonel Tootal, who also resigned from the Army after he returned from Afghanistan, in November 2007, partly because of what he considered the shameful treatment of his wounded soldiers, spoke positively to me in February 2010, however, about the high morale of British troops in Helmand.

I don't think there is a problem with army morale, but I think there is a leadership problem and I think there's a lack of leadership in defence as a whole. David Richards could change that . . . I think he certainly has the intellectual faculties and the moral courage to change that. He's a different thinker and of course people have high expectations of him . . .

The key thing is that people have got to follow his lead . . . soldiers have to stop being what he would call second-rate politicians, start being bloody soldiers. When a minister asks: 'Can you do so and so?' And you say: 'Yes, [but] we can only do it with thirty-two helicopters or twenty-two helicopters, not with six.' If told to get on with it of course you'll get on with it; but too many people I saw during the planning in the run-up to Iraq, too many people were offering politically acceptable options. Instead of that, you have to say: 'Here's clear military advice; minister take your choice. We'll do whatever you want us to do but be aware if it's an option that's not properly resourced, there'll be a penalty and a risk you need to sign up to publicly.' That's how business does it and we could learn a lesson from that and I think that's a lack of leadership.

Did it come from the top of the Army? I asked him.

No, I think from the top of defence actually. I spent almost two years in the MOD working for David Richards but also under [General] Mike Jackson in 2004, 2005 . . . It's not just generals. It's generals, civil servants, the other services and the politicians. [It needs] someone at the top to say I want Afghanistan sorted out, alongside the Americans, with the right resources. If this country wants another twenty, thirty, forty Chinooks, it can have them. It just has to accept that there are other things that have got to give in the Defence budget, like our Typhoon fighters, which deliver not a jot of capability to Afghanistan. That's the logic, and it comes right back to my original point: lack of intellectual thinking, the ability of people to say I'm going to take my service cloth (army, navy or air force) off; even though I've been a jet fighter pilot all my life doesn't necessarily mean we need jet fighters. We don't think like that. This is public money and so these people who're paid lots of money have a duty to us as taxpayers to be a little less parochial, be a little less self-centred in terms of their careers . . .[24]

He added that he found it very disheartening to hear people stand up and say 'the commanders have everything they've asked for'. It was not true, of course. 'They're going to be tight-lipped about what they say, naturally, and sidestep the issue in the rather hackneyed phrase we used to use in 2006: no commander would ever say they have enough resources, whether it was Caesar or Napoleon.' The key question was, did they have enough resources to do the task to the optimum of their ability? The answer was no. Did the middle-ranking officer corps, the middle-ranking and junior NCOs, and the foot soldiers, feel they were properly resourced? No, they did not. 'So we need to grip that, we need to address it.'[25]

Much criticism was levelled at Gordon Brown for his penny-pinching attitude to defence spending during his ten-year reign as Chancellor of the Exchequer (1997–2007). One of his most vocal and persistent critics was, and remains, General Lord Guthrie, a former Welsh Guards officer who served in the SAS and was Chief of the General Staff before becoming Chief of the Defence Staff (CDS, 1997–2001). He makes no secret of his disapproval of Gordon Brown's attitude to the funding of the armed forces. 'I feel very strongly . . . that he has been very unsympathetic to defence when he was the Chancellor, when I had to deal with him and I went to see him. He was very unsympathetic, whereas Blair was sympathetic. I suspect why he [Brown] was unsympathetic was because Blair was sympathetic; and I am serious about that . . . the animosity [between the two] was much, much worse than anyone realises.'[26]

He went on: 'When times were good and we were rich and other departments were being given money, the Army was given as little as they could get away with . . . and they will say, well in real terms you had an increase every year, but . . . of course it didn't keep pace with what we were doing in the Balkans and in Sierra Leone [where] we were heavily engaged.'

Throughout the Helmand campaign, but especially in the last couple of years, the helicopter issue dominated the argument about the equipping of British troops in Afghanistan. Gordon Brown and his ministers insisted that there were enough helicopters and that the alleged shortage was not the reason for the steady rise in the number of British casualties. Interviewed in *The Times* on 25 July 2009, Lord Guthrie said: 'Peter Mandelson said this week he was convinced that no one had been killed through lack of helicopters – well, I don't believe that's so. And when Alistair Darling [Chancellor of the Exchequer, 2007–2010] says we will give the Army everything it asks for, that is patently not true.' To anyone who had been on the ground in a war, 'helicopters are obviously better than winding columns of troops who can be seen miles away in a cloud of dust. They are easy to ambush and having more helicopters would avoid much of that. Helicopters give you huge flexibility . . . The helicopters are the thing that would save lives and actually make the Army more effective.'[27]

In another passage, Guthrie explained: 'In the end it's about money. When we could have made a decent investment, we didn't,' a reference to the 1998 Strategic Defence Review's recommendation, among other things, to more than double the number of Chinook and Merlin heavy-lift helicopters, which was 'dumped unceremoniously' by Defence Secretary Geoff Hoon in 2004 on instructions from Brown. 'Gordon Brown focused on health and education rather than on defence. That means we're not prepared. When you suddenly realise the body armour doesn't work, or the vehicles haven't got the right protection, you have to throw money at it very quickly which means you are paying way over what you would have paid if you had been sensible about planning. It's no good the Prime Minister one moment saying success is all-important and then for the sake of a few extra helicopters and 2,000 men allows the mission in Afghanistan to fail. You can't go to war in a penny-pinching way.'[28]

Lord Guthrie told me that Gordon Brown's lack of interest in defence was 'certainly not a Labour thing – old Labour were extremely patriotic and some of our best Defence Secretaries were from the Labour Party. But Gordon Brown doesn't understand the military.' When Chancellor, he said, Brown was the only Cabinet minister who refused to attend briefings with the heads of the armed forces. 'I was very upset that he wouldn't come and hear our side.' The only time he did was to talk about the future of Rosyth docks, in Fife, where Brown also has his constituency.

There is a story, possibly apocryphal, that one day General Guthrie, as CDS, went to see Tony Blair, with whom he got on well – despite declining the invitation to call him 'Tony' as Blair urged him to do, an invitation he is said to have also extended to the Queen. On this occasion, Guthrie was lobbying Blair for more funding for the armed forces. Blair told him to go and see Gordon Brown, then Chancellor of the Exchequer, who under their power-sharing agreement was in charge of the economy. Guthrie said he knew what that meant and demurred, persisting that he wanted the Prime Minister's approval. To no avail: Blair refused to get involved. So, reluctantly, Guthrie went to see Gordon Brown who, as he expected, stonewalled and finally said: 'You think I'm unsympathetic to defence, don't you, General?' Guthrie is said to have answered: 'No, Chancellor, I don't think you're unsympathetic to defence.' Pause. 'I think you're f****** unsympathetic to defence!' Even if it is apocryphal, it probably reflects Lord Guthrie's real feelings for Gordon Brown.[29]

7

Ed Butler and Musa Qala, 2006

There was no unified NATO plan, no unity of command . . . there was no real 'one campaign' plan.

`Brigadier Ed Butler, London, 2010

Ed Butler was one of the British Army's youngest and most decorated brigadiers, winning the Distinguished Service Order when commanding the SAS in Afghanistan in 2001 and 2002. Four years later, he went back again to command 16 Air Assault Brigade. The grandson of Rab Butler, who had been Home Secretary under Harold Macmillan, and son of Adam Butler, also a Tory MP and a junior minister under Mrs Thatcher, Ed Butler (Eton and Exeter University) was no stranger to the political scene.

Before going to Afghanistan as commander of 16 Air Assault Brigade in 2006, Butler had done his homework and realised that they could expect a hostile reception from the Afghans if not, in Worsley's words, such a 'brutal entry into the province'. He was expecting a fight, as Worsley said, 'but nothing more'.[1] He must have known, too, that the NATO command and control structure would be less than well organised.

In his book, *16 Air Assault Brigade*, the military writer Tim Ripley says: 'Because of NATO politics, the UK decided not to put Brigadier Butler's headquarters in Helmand. From April until July he had to stay up in Kabul in his capacity as Commander British Forces or COMBRITFOR in Afghanistan and could only make brief visits to forward units . . . At this crucial part of the campaign, the command of British forces was spread across five headquarters.'[2] Although in a crisis Butler could speak directly to the commanding officer of 3 PARA, Lieutenant Colonel Stuart Tootal, the command set-up created much 'multi-national command tension'.[3] Coalition and NATO operations across southern Afghanistan were bedevilled by 'national caveats and differing objectives', Ripley writes. Senior British officers complained that the arrangements were 'confusing and sub-optimal'. A lot of these criticisms are still valid, although the British themselves were not entirely blameless, being 'very reluctant' to cede responsibility to commanders in the field, according to one senior British Army source.[4]

Ed Butler at least had the advantage of having been in Afghanistan before. 'I knew the nature of the terrain,' he recalls, 'how physically demanding it was going to be for men, machines and equipment. I knew that just surviving and operating and doing routine operations was going to be a huge challenge.' Even if you took the enemy out of the equation, it was going to be difficult to survive there, as difficult as surviving in any desert, he told me.[5]

'I knew from my experience the Taliban, like the *mujahideen*, were extremely effective fighters, very brave, very tenacious. We were in their backyard. As we said from the middle of 2005 onwards, when we started the planning, we expected a reaction. That when we put our size twelve boot in the middle of this, something was going to happen. There was going to be a reaction in Helmand Province.' But the briefings they were given in late 2005 and in early 2006, before the brigade deployed to Helmand, underestimated the ground and the enemy, Brigadier Butler says. 'This was one of my takeaway bullets to the senior officers who had come down to listen to our updates and plans.' Rather than a lack of intelligence per se, Butler saw it as 'a lack of analysis of the intelligence that we had or should have had. We were not directing the very few strategic assets or operational assets into finding out . . . whether it was the ground or the Taliban or the people of Helmand, how they were going to react to us coming.'

Running through his analysis like a leitmotif, or rather two leitmotifs, are on the one hand the lack of 'intelligence, understanding [and] appreciation of the specific threats and challenges' which they faced in Helmand; and on the other, the fact that the issue of Afghanistan was repeatedly dwarfed by Iraq and its demands. They weren't directing 'the strategic assets of GCHQ [the Foreign Office intelligence listening post] and the rest into Helmand', because they were 'very much focused on Iraq . . .

which was going badly wrong in terms of Nimrods* and everything else.'
MI6, Butler says, 'were engaged, but again not in terms of really finding
out . . . One of the issues we faced – and it is slowly improving – was the
lack of human intelligence, very few human sources. [It was] the same for
the Canadians in Kandahar or the Dutch up in Uruzgan later on . . . I
know we didn't have very good intelligence. We didn't understand the
tribal tapestry of Helmand, we had very little clue about the nature of the
tribalism, the warlordism, the narco-criminality, the Taliban.'[6]

   'On reflection, he says, 'if the British hadn't been in Iraq and had said
in 2002, when we were up in Kabul, "Right, in two years' time or four
years' time . . . we are going to expand the NATO mission," and had
gone about it in the conventional Staff College way ("Okay, let's start
directing our assets, let's get our experts onto it, let's look into it while we
sit rather conventionally behind the start line, let's gather all the knowledge, let's have some advanced force operations, let's build up a real
picture as we did in Iraq"), that would have been a great improvement.'

   But the British didn't do that, and to make matters worse the Americans
diverted all their satellite surveillance of southern Afghanistan, and the
intelligence back-up that went with it, to Iraq. As Butler says, ascribing a
reason for failure which would become all too familiar in the months and
years to come: 'I think a lot of it was the physical issue of Iraq, it was draw-
ing [down] vast resources, from the Americans too, and my judgement
was . . . the physical resources had to be there because we were in danger
of losing [the Iraq war] before the Petraeus surge [in 2007] and the balance
started to turn.'[7]

   Brigadier Butler desribes how he became 'quite frustrated' by the way in
which Iraq continued to dominate resources. The assumption was that as
the requirement in Iraq diminished, more men and equipment would be
diverted to Afghanistan. 'We would be increasing our forces in Afghanistan
then, not just boots and vehicles, but planes and intelligence-gathering
systems and everything else; but that never happened because Iraq was still
going 100 per cent and we were picking up the crumbs.'

---

* A reference to the fourteen British servicemen killed when an RAF Nimrod Maritime
Reconnaissance aircraft blew up during air-to-air refuelling and crashed near Kandahar on
2 September 2006.

Another major issue in 2005–06 was the lack of strategic direction as to what Britain and NATO were trying to achieve in Afghanistan. 'What were our strategic and political objectives; not only from a UK perspective, but also from an international perspective? Because in 2001 [it was] very clear. We had one mission: counter-terrorism. Kick out al Qaeda, destroy the training camps, bring the perpetrators of 9/11 to justice; make sure they cannot make another attack. That was counter-terrorism. Bang.' That was very successful, Butler says. 'It all happened . . . the Northern Alliance and everything else, and it all snowballed. Few people went, but we achieved it . . . The Taliban were politically, militarily and morally defeated. So we had the opportunity and I could sense it then, in 2002.' But, he goes on to say, it was 'a huge frustration' to see the emphasis shift to Iraq.

He recalled that as the Americans set off for Iraq, they would say: '"Right, we are off to do unfinished business. We are off to Iraq to kick out Saddam, where Bush Senior failed, Bush Junior is going to do it." That was the NAAFI talk, the cookhouse talk. And it was them saying they were just going to "kick arse" here, hitting al Qaeda and senior Taliban.' In other words, Afghanistan was just a sideshow; the real target was Saddam.

Butler is also critical of the 'ill-thought-through nation-building' policy of installing a new, democratic government under Karzai and holding elections in 2004. 'That thinking was only coming from . . . those who were based in Kabul. But over the intervening years,' Butler says, 'we went on to do counter-insurgency, nation-building, state-building, economic reconstruction and counter-narcotics.' So NATO, under the British, had five different missions, with no priorities set and no resources allocated to those. And what emerged was confusion.

Did he blame the Blair government?

'I have reflected on this,' he says. 'We can kick the government. If we had set our foreign policy objectives, our national strategic objectives, what our security policy was, and then out of that the military would say: "Right, what can we do to support it?" But that was never really set.' Butler explains that he was asking these questions from his headquarters in Colchester in 2005 and they were falling not so much on deaf ears as on 'busy ears that were all in Iraq'.

The answer was – and they were still saying this as late as the second half of 2005 – 'Well, we aren't sure if it's just going to be an expanded Provincial Reconstruction Team in Lashkar Gah, or whether it's going to be 2,000, but it certainly isn't going to be more than 3,150 troops.' We were saying: 'Fine, but what do you want us to do with them?' So that lack of political and military objectives was a failing.

The fault lay, he believes, with the senior military for not demanding clearer answers to their questions: 'What do you want the military to do [about the Blair–Reid tripartite plan for reconstruction in Helmand]?' The joint campaign plan for Helmand, Ed Butler recalls, was very much recon-struction-focused and with very little emphasis on the military contribution, which he describes as a 'naive approach' and – to borrow Stuart Tootal's phrase – 'wishful thinking':

I mean you had the military line of operation, the governance FCO-led thing and the development led by DFID and this was going to happen simultaneously and they thought it would all advance at the same time . . . it was almost one day the military would do something, the next day it would be the FCO, the next day DFID, but it would all proceed uncontested, no contingency, no plans for contact with the enemy. What they were very surprised about [was] the huge disagree-ment and bad relationships which started to emerge.

The bad blood between the soldiers and the FCO and DFID representa-tives, ordered to stay put in Lashkar Gah, was perhaps not so much surprising as inevitable given the lack of planning. There was also a lack of realism in London about the likely reaction of the local inhabitants who would see the arrival of the British as another invasion.

The military line of operation started to accelerate way away, because there was Stuart Tootal and the 3 PARA Battle Group fighting for their lives. DFID said: 'Well what about us?' We said: 'Well, there are oppor-tunities.' And there were plenty of opportunities to do development work projects, the same on the government side. But they didn't seize them because they didn't have the capacity, because they hadn't resourced them. There were only four or five people from the other government departments in Lashkar Gah over that period in 2006. Now they have eighty . . . which is great, but we had four or five. They couldn't get out; they didn't have the clearances. It wasn't the fault of the tactical people there, they wanted to do more, but Whitehall had put these constraints on them.[8]

Adding to the sense of muddle and confusion which prevailed was the mind-boggling complexity of the NATO plan, or multiplicity of plans. If there is such a thing as a recipe for disaster, this must be it or very close to it. Here is how Brigadier Butler described it:

We as a brigade came up with a plan, but there were about four or five other plans all running . . . The vast majority of our time and effort in 2006 was just to deploy the force into Afghanistan, which was not an inconsiderable feat over some several thousand miles, all by air . . . Then there was the Canadian plan in Kandahar: they were our superior head-quarters. But we had no plan or directive from the Canadians of what we were going to use our force for. It was just get the force in, that is a big logistic effort, and then see what goes. But we had no plan from the Canadian commander or his headquarters, which was again growing out of nothing, to be fair . . . Then we had the ISAF plan, which was under an American, General Eikenberry [later Ambassador in Kabul], he was a three-star [Lieutenant General]. So we had one American plan under him . . . we had the counter-terrorist plan under Operation Enduring Freedom, and then we had the NATO plan coming out of Brunssum, in the Netherlands; and we had David Richards who took over as the ISAF Commander in July starting to work up his plan. So actually there were five or six different plans all running . . .

As well as all those, Brigadier Butler explains,

You could times it by the power of two for each plan because every nation had their own development department and their foreign office and their own security services all having their own plans and ideas, and if you times that by thirty-six with all the other troop-contributing nations, then . . . you had thirty-six or thirty-seven different definitions of success and failure, different end states, different risk appetites, resources they were prepared to put in, different rules of engagement, different red cards [national caveats] etc., etc. But there was no unified, NATO plan, no unity of command. And overarching all of that – we were saying this in 2006 – we required an Afghan plan. It was an Afghan problem; they needed to come up with a plan which we, the international community, would support. But Karzai and his government did not have the capacity, or the competence or the appetite or the strength to come up with a plan saying: *Right, this is what we are doing . . .*, because that is Afghanistan: you were never going to bring it together as a unified nation.

But underneath all that planning, you had to ask: 'What was the plan? Well there wasn't really a plan,' Butler adds; 'there was no real, one campaign plan.'[9]

Brigadier Butler set very limited objectives for the brigade, which was going to take three to four months to deploy, he says, because first of all 'the physical size of the deployment pipeline was only so much', and because all the resources, the strategic air, logistics and everything else, was going into Iraq. His priorities were to establish the headquarters and base in Lashkar Gah,* the provincial capital of Helmand, establish relationships with Governor Daud and the other government departments, establish a base in Gereshk, and 'most importantly, continue to build up Camp Bastion [British Army HQ], because work didn't really start on that until late 2005. In 2006 they were still putting the perimeter fence around and Stuart Tootal and his men were all in tents.'

The brigade plan was very simple: to build up the force and the triangle between Lashkar Gah and Camp Bastion and establish the David Richards 'ink spots', small government-controlled enclaves from which security would radiate outwards, enabling reconstruction and better governance to

---

* Lashkar Gah, the capital of Helmand, means 'Place of the Soldiers'.

develop. Eventually the ink spots would join up. 'And then over time they would expand out of that triangle (it was then called a lozenge because it stretched up the Sangin Valley). They judged they just about had sufficient resources to man three bases . . . Stuart [Tootal] said they needed to have influence up the Sangin Valley, because that was clearly where the main enemy "arterial" [thrust] would come; down the Sangin Valley, cross over the highway and then into the relatively secure area of the triangle.'

Butler and his staff were saying that 'the enemy were going to respond and the war-fighting season was going to start after the poppy season'. They were receiving reports, Butler recalls, of 'a plan by the Taliban saying "our fathers and their fathers are scratching in their graves ready to rip out the sons and grandsons of those infidels whom we kicked out three times previously". This was all very effective – we laughed it off in the UK, but it was quite serious; but more importantly it was galvanising a lot of the people against us and they wouldn't want us there, a vast majority of the Afghans . . .'[10]

Security first, then development, but make sure you deliver it, is what Henry Worsley's Helmand elders told him. Unfortunately, looking back over the past ten years in Afghanistan, one has to admit that the West has struggled to provide sufficient security or development, at least in the Pushtun east and south. Brigadier Butler points out that the plan agreed at the Tokyo Conference in January 2002 promised Afghanistan $5 billion (more than £3.8 billion), according to the official communiqué. 'Well, none of that had made it down to Helmand and Kandahar,' Butler asserts. Like all big donations, as was always the case, 'these things don't deliver. So big expectations, big liberation after thirty years of oppression, we, the West, were going to come in and make a difference. Well, in those intervening years, from 2002–06, we had done nothing, so already they were quite dubious. They wanted us to come in, they wanted us to kick out the Taliban; they hated the Taliban and what they were doing, was our view, but we had let them down. So when we did arrive and made no impact in terms of making their lives better, they became increasingly disillusioned.'[11]

Early on in their tour, Ed Butler says, he came to the conclusion that the British in Helmand were facing three opposition groups: the Taliban, backed up by foreign fighters (mainly Pakistanis, Arabs and Uzbeks, plus a few Chechens, often al Qaeda-trained); the narco-criminals; and the former regime warlords – 'the Dostums [Uzbek General Abdul Rashid Dostum] and everyone else'. 'Each of those groups wanted to have and keep failed-state status and the British were coming in to try to say well, actually, they wanted it to be a successful state. So it isn't just an issue of fighting the Taliban and creating security. All these people don't want you to be there and they still don't want us to be there . . . A lot of time and money had to be spent . . . trying to marginalise them, reconcile them, and pay them off.'

The long-established Governor of Helmand was a local·tribal leader called Sher Mohammed Akhundzada, whom the British were determined to oust as corrupt and incompetent, despite President Karzai's support for him. I asked Brigadier Butler if Akhundzada was part of the three-part opposition?

'I would put him as part of it,' he replied. 'There was a symbiotic relationship between all three of those groups. I think he [Akhundzada] would class himself as a mini quasi-warlord. But he was as much in the narco-criminality and making a considerable amount of money out of it.' Butler thought he had considerable influence and hold over Karzai. But whether it was because he might spill the beans about Ahmed Wali Karzai, the President's younger half-brother who was to be assassinated in July 2011, and was said by American and British diplomats to be deeply involved in the drug trade, one could only speculate. Akhundzada was very influential, Butler continued, and even after he was replaced by the British nominee, Governor Daud, the British continued to blame him for 'hindering progress on the governance side, and continually undermining Governor Daud's position and credibility and credentials and everything else . . . He [Sher Mohammed] went around saying: "Daud's hopeless, he doesn't listen to anything . . ."'*[12]

---

* Sher Mohammed Akhundzada was Governor of Helmand from 2001–2005 when President Karzai finally acceded to British insistence on his removal and replacement by Mohammed Daud, a former communist who joined the anti-Russian resistance in the early 1980s. Akhundzada, from a prominent family of the Alizai, the largest tribe in Helmand, was sacked after nine tons of opium were found in his office. He said he had forgotten to hand it in to the authorities. Karzai later made him a senator. The real reason the Presi-

Lieutenant Colonel Worsley had predicted, with classic British under-statement, that the Taliban would arrange a 'reception party' for the British. In fact, all hell was let loose about three weeks after the British arrived. In *Danger Close*, his account of 3 PARA's battle for survival in Helmand, Lieutenant Colonel Stuart Tootal writes: 'Some who made the decision to send us hoped it would be completed without a shot being fired, but the Taliban thought differently.' During its six-month tour of duty, he writes, 3 PARA fired nearly half a million rounds of ammunition in a level of sustained combat that had not been seen by the British Army since the end of the Korean War. The battles took place across wild desert plains and in the foothills of the Hindu Kush. To add to their troubles it was oppressively hot, as 3 PARA and the rest of the Battle Group fought desperately to defend 'a disparate number of isolated district centres', acting as garrisons in what became known as 'platoon houses'. General Sir David Richards says it was only after they began establishing these that the Taliban 'really started to fight'.[13] The British were sucked into these battles willy-nilly, the ferocity of the Taliban offensive leading to a barrage of SOS calls for help from the embattled Governor Daud and his micro-managing President in Kabul.

The intensity of the conflict, Tootal adds, stretched resources to break-ing point as 3 PARA, undermanned and suffering from critical equipment shortages, became involved in a deadly battle of attrition against a resur-gent Taliban determined to drive British troops from Helmand. But it was the raw courage and fighting spirit of British soldiers that forced the Taliban to blink first. After months of vicious close-quarter fighting they won what Colonel Tootal describes as 'the break-in phase of the battle for Helmand' in an unforgiving campaign that larger British forces continued

---

dent was reluctant to dismiss him, however, was the closeness of their family relationship. Sher Mohammed was a brother-in-law of the President's late half-brother, Ahmed Wali Karzai. They were married to sisters – so there was a strong family bond, very important in Afghanistan, as well as a narco-mafia connection, and on top of everything else, Karzai's belief that Akhundzada was the right man to keep the Taliban out of Helmand. To the British, getting rid of Governor Akhundzada may have seemed sensible at the time. Now, with hindsight, removing someone who may have been venal, but knew how to hold the complicated tribal jigsaw together, was probably a mistake. Certainly Daud, who was not a local figure, and therefore did not have his predecessor's tribal expertise, was not judged a success.

to fight until relieved by the US Marines. Three PARA won many medals
for gallantry, including a posthumous VC and George Cross, but there was
a price to pay, Stuart Tootal says. 'Fifteen members of the Battle Group
were killed in action and another forty-six were wounded.'[14]

Brigadier Butler was widely criticised for implementing the policy of
'platoon houses', garrisoned by 'penny packets' of paratroopers in the
various district centres of Helmand. In his own defence, Butler argues
that neither he nor Tootal had any alternative because Governor Daud,
with President Karzai's telephonic support, repeatedly asked for British
troops to be flown to a whole series of district centres under threat of
being overrun by the Taliban: 'The enemy engaged us in a fight straight
away,' Butler recalls. 'We had this challenge and tension between deploying the force, which was not inconsiderable, but also employing the force
at the same time. There was Stuart, as soon as he got another platoon
in . . . being pitched into battle because the enemy, funny old thing,
were going to take us on.'[15]

Both the Army and Whitehall had misread the situation, Butler
claims, and describes as 'crazy' the fact that the British 'had an Interim
Operating Capability [IOC] and a Full Operating Capability [FOC]'
called the Text Book. 'This was again,' he asserts, 'where the senior military let us down: people would say to me . . . and I couldn't believe it . . .
"Ed, you are not meant to be fighting. Why are you and Stuart Tootal
fighting before you have FOC?" And I'd reply: "The enemy are having a
go at us!" And they would say: "Why are you fighting, because you're not
yet at an IOC? You don't need your big guns and everything else because
you are not at Interim Operating Capability?" And I'd say: "Wait a
minute, the enemy are taking us on. Here we are having this fight . . . so
what do you expect us to do? We are defending ourselves, we are defending the force which is coming in."'[16]

What followed, says Butler, was a 'great debate' in which he was 'quite
heavily criticised', both in the UK and at the UN: 'The Taliban were
surrounding and about to overthrow the district commissioner and the
head of police in Musa Qala. And Governor Daud said: "What are you
going to do about it? My people are being killed, my policemen are being
kicked out and people are starting to leave Musa Qala, and my credibility

nor – whom you have come to support – is being undermined? mustn't allow the black flag of Mullah Omar – this was the first y had used the expression – to fly over any of the district centres. se why have you come here? We have invited you in, you have got onal support and the first time we need you to help us, you are us."'17

with what amounted to an ultimatum, Brigadier Butler sent up finder Platoon team with about 300 militia who 'saw off' the and 'chased them all the way up to Baghran' in northern Helmand. eration was a 'huge success' and changed people's perceptions. 'But posed a dilemma, because when the Taliban launched another Governor Daud asked: "Well are you going to do it again?"' er's answer was that they did not have enough forces. 'We can just manage Lashkar Gah and Gereshk . . . because we were still trying the forces in and Musa Qala started . . . and then Sangin started to essure on . . . They had a lot of very late-night discussions and Daud ring up President Karzai – it would go straight up on the mobile , or the ping-pong phone as they called it – and say "They are letting wn, Brigadier Butler and Co. are refusing to give their help; the e of Musa Qala are being killed, threatened and injured and being ff and they are going to be flying the Taliban flags and ripping down fghan flag by tomorrow morning."'18

tler described the atmosphere as 'very emotional'. When he tried to ss or debate tactics, Governor Daud would say: "'No, this is very rtant we cannot be overrun." So this argument went on, and we didn't hat much support from the UK because they didn't understand it.' as Brigadier Butler has said in another context, his words were falling so much on deaf ears as on 'busy ears that were all in Iraq'. Butler's mma was that the brigade's role was to provide security for the FCO DFID's good works, but as the Taliban offensive increased in tempo, British were unable to cope. 'The first time that Daud asked for help the British had to say "No, we cannot do this." His rejoinder was: "If are not going to help, you may as well go home now."'

utler clearly felt isolated and let down. Not only was there no strategic ction from the UK, too busy with Iraq and viewing Afghanistan as a sideshow, but he was even being asked: 'Why are you fighting?', which he must have found infuriating. It was also quite obvious from 3 PARA's first contact with the Taliban that 'these people clearly don't want us here'.[19]

Brigadier Butler says Karzai and Daud were putting pressure on Colonel Tootal and himself, but it was the local tribal elders who were putting pressure on Governor Daud: 'They would ask him, why aren't you helping us? And he would turn to us.' The old solution, according to Butler, was to say it was just a local tribal problem, and let the tribal elders and militia handle it. Butler complained there was a lack of clarity about their role. Were they a peacekeeping force, peace force, reconstruction force or nation-building? Again the confusion.

On the ground, Butler makes plain, the British were under constant pressure to intervene militarily. 'And then suddenly we were into a war-fighting mode which this government didn't want to declare to the public. We had gone in saying one thing and it was all in the backdrop of Iraq. We had already had cash for honours, David Kelly's suicide, no weapons of mass destruction. Prime Minister Blair's legacy years were all starting to unravel and we were about to get into another major fight which we hadn't defined to Blair, or the public or Parliament, what we were really doing there.'

Butler says success in one town simply meant more demands from Governor Daud for reinforcements in other places under Taliban attack. After Musa Qala and Sangin, recalls Butler, 'the call went out for help from Naw Zad and the Kajaki Dam . . . Each town said: "Come and help us, the Taliban are coming in and killing us and terrorising us." Whether they were or not, one wasn't there to know.'[20]

Musa Qala was undoubtedly the defining episode in Brigadier Butler's third tour in Afghanistan and his command of 16 Air Assault Brigade. Musa Qala, which in Pushtu means 'the House of Moses', is a typical central Helmand town, surrounded by fields of opium poppies, intersected by deep irrigation ditches, furnace-hot in summer and with a population, 99 per cent Pushtun, of about 10,000. Throughout the 2006 war-fighting season it had been hotly contested by succeeding 'human waves' of Taliban fighters, mainly young locals, who hurled themselves against the Paras' defences day and night with a grim determination and a high rate of casualties reminiscent of the Chinese in Korea and later the Vietcong in Vietnam. Their propaganda tells them the British and Americans and the other NATO troops are 'invaders', and as mainly non-Muslims, 'infidels' who have come to destroy the poppy crop and thus deprive them of their living. The Koran forbids all intoxicating substances, including alcohol and drugs, but this does not stop the Taliban exploiting huge quantities of opium and heroin, which brings in billions of dollars and, to a great extent, finances their insurgency.

Musa Qala was half-destroyed by the fighting, the bazaar closed and many of the inhabitants had fled. In September 2006, the elders, angry at the destruction of their town and the disruption of their lives, let it be known that they wanted both warring parties, the British and the Taliban, to stop fighting and leave the town. The Shura (Council of Elders) would take over the administration. Because of the intensity of the fighting 3 PARA had been involved in since their arrival, and the casualties they had suffered, Brigadier Butler, as Commander of British Forces (COMBRITFOR), wanted a breathing space for tactical reasons and flew to Musa Qala from Camp Bastion to discuss the situation with the Shura. After negotiation, he agreed to a ceasefire, to pull out the Paras, provided the Taliban also withdrew, and leave the administration of the town to the Shura.

In his account of the Musa Qala ceasefire, which was to put him at loggerheads with General Sir David Richards who was just taking over as the NATO commander, and therefore Butler's superior, and also at odds with the Americans, Butler makes the point that in the tradition of tribal fighting, 'the Pushtun love attacking forts'. One result of the Taliban concentration on Musa Qala was that nothing was happening in Gereshk or Lashkar Gah. It allowed Butler to get the rest of the brigade in, but DFID missed its opportunity, he says.[21]

They had a plan, but they hadn't planned to exploit 'this great big vacuum where they could have done lots of development and reconstruction and that could have made a difference because there were no attacks. I think we had one shooting in Gereshk in about six months and towards the end there was a little bit of a skirmish. We had two suicide bombings in Lashkar Gah in April but nothing else. Garmsir then flared up . . . so we did have this other opportunity [but] because it wasn't resourced or planned for by the other government departments, we missed it.'

In those three months, Butler explains, the Taliban threw themselves hour-in, hour-out against the platoon houses: 'and it got to such a stage, and we were saying openly, that we were doing more destruction than construction. We were killing a lot of ordinary Afghans, we were levelling a lot of Naw Zad and Musa Qala and elsewhere.'

The pressure of the fighting had disrupted the normal annual farming cycle, Butler continues, including the poppy crop. Business was bad and children weren't going to school. Tribal elders in Sangin and Musa Qala were putting pressure on Governor Daud to come up with a plan. The British produced a fourteen-point plan for those two districts 'which was all actually about Afghan autonomy . . . a tribal solution . . . I could see the gains . . . they would do their own self-protection, they would elect their own police chief, look after their own security, they would do their own reconstruction, so basically we were negotiating.'

This was happening against the backdrop of more casualties, increasing threats to aircraft and helicopters being shot down, Butler explains. After the Nimrod crash near Kandahar on 2 September 2006, in which fourteen personnel were killed,* the Chief of the Defence Staff (CDS), Air Chief Marshal Sir Jock Stirrup, and the government said: 'We cannot afford another strategic asset to be lost.'[22]

Meanwhile in the field, Brigadier Butler and Colonel Tootal were worrying about the risk of not only losing one helicopter when picking up a casualty, but of losing 'two if we have to send the second one in'.[23] Even with a seriously injured casualty they could not risk flying them out in the day, and at night the Taliban had 'a very complex matrix of air-defence systems'.[24] The worst scenario, which deeply worried Butler and Tootal, was that a helicopter, trying to evacuate a badly wounded paratrooper, would be shot down and then a second helicopter, going to the rescue, would also be shot down 'so rather than just having one guy bleeding to death we may have twenty . . .' All the time, as Butler puts it, the clock was ticking, 'but the prize as I saw it was the tribal solution. Luckily . . . the

---

* The crash was later found to have been caused by a fuel leak.

tribal elders turned round and said . . . "We can guarantee the security, you go and tell your British troops to stop firing and the Taliban will stop firing and then we want to have a dialogue." So we sat down with Governor Daud that evening and I said: "Yes, if you can guarantee that the Taliban will stop the attacks then I will tell my soldiers to stop firing."' Butler lists the advantages: if there was a ceasefire, there would be no casualties; there would be no threat to helicopters, nor to the strategic imperative not to lose a helicopter. 'I was told very clearly by the CDS and by the Chief of Joint Operations: "Don't lose a helicopter . . . it will lose the war, potentially. If we lose a Chinook with people on the back we will certainly lose it, politically . . . If we have two . . . We had already sent quite a lot of people back in body bags, we had a total press exclusion, no embeds; the media were turning against us because we weren't providing information to them, so it was a real mess.'[25]

David Richards on the other hand – who had just started Operation Medusa, west of Kandahar, the first NATO offensive operation in history – said, according to Butler: '"No, I need you up there as a sort of flank secured," which Sangin, Kajaki and Musa Qala were doing. "Frankly, Ed, if you pull out not only will you destroy the reputation of the British Army but also you will destroy NATO's credibility that we are an effective fighting force. So you stay put." And I replied: "General, the probability of losing a helicopter is incredibly high. It is in the high 90s; it's a certainty. I have talked to the helicopter pilots . . ."' Butler said he was not prepared to have his troops in any of those platoon houses – 'without disregarding the reputation of the Army, without disregarding the political backdrop', and he was not prepared to have his paratroopers in a forward location without any form of casualty evacuation. He was just not ethically and morally and personally going to live with it so he would pull out. They had what Butler describes as 'quite a discussion' about this. 'General Richards told me: '"No, you will stay put," and I said: "I am not wearing my hat as a tactical commander who reports to you. I am wearing my National Contingent Commander's hat as commander of British forces, COMBRITFOR, and have received very clear political direction from the Chief of the Defence Staff on behalf of the government that we are not to lose a strategic asset, therefore you will pull out."' Butler said he did not know if Air Chief Marshal Sir Jock Stirrup (CDS) was concerned about having casualties that they could not pick up. As far as he was concerned, 'I am not going to be sitting here in ten years' time saying: I put paratroopers there with no casualty evacuation. Luckily all that was saved by the bell of coming up with this tribal solution [of the ceasefire].'[26]

Butler says it happened about forty-eight hours before he was going to pull British forces back. Next day the British and the Shura sat down in the desert and talked it through. Butler says he could see then that this was the prize; this was Afghan autonomy. It was not a national plan; the British were not going to change their lives. They could make their lives better but they were not going to make them different. 'Afghanistan to me,' Butler says, 'is a tribal solution . . . It gives them their own authority, because the people of Musa Qala want to run themselves, they don't want to be run by a Sanginite or a Helmandi, they want to look after themselves, their family, their tribe, and we are trying to impose a centralised government on them, which will have all the conventional ways of doing government business. So that is what I said.'

Brigadier Butler, who was clearly and impressively ahead of his time in wanting an Afghan solution, says he found the Shura's approach 'tremendously exciting. They discussed their aims and objectives. They knew this was all part of the fourteen-point plan we put together.' The basis of the agreement that day was a five-kilometre exclusion zone around each district centre, where there wouldn't be any fighting. The power of the mullah, the tribal elder, in Musa Qala was greater than that of the Taliban, Butler says, adding: 'and actually a lot of the Taliban were local fighters so that was easy. Even the more senior [Taliban] were under the control of the tribal elders. They wanted us out totally, the elders, and we said: "Well actually, you know, we have got to have some [government] representation."' On reflection, Butler felt they should have trusted them. Most of his military colleagues, however, were critical. 'Certainly the Americans were very vocal and vociferous about what the British were doing: we were dealing with the Taliban, we were walking into a trap, [Lieutenant General] Eikenberry and [Major General] Freakley particularly.'

At the time, Butler says, people couldn't understand the need to negotiate, although opinion was changing. 'I think people do understand that you are going to have to do reconciliation; it is a tribal thing, you are going to have to talk to a Taliban, you are going to have to have novel solutions. What we were doing then, in 2006, was two or three years too early.'

It was not only Butler; General Sir David Richards, as we will see later, was also well ahead of his time.

Brigadier Butler said he did not use the 'red card', the national caveat which gives every NATO member country the right to follow its own rules. The Germans, for example, are notorious for insisting on numerous caveats, partly because Germany considers Afghanistan a humanitarian, peacekeeping mission and not a war-fighting one. 'In effect I didn't pull it out of my pocket with David Richards, but I said: "No, I am going to do what I think is right. I am going to play by National Contingent COMBRITFOR rules here rather than obeying who is my senior commander." And he was like: "I am a British officer and the senior officer here. You are going to do as you are told." I said: "Thank you General. I have three different bosses. I have you; I have Air Chief Marshal [Sir Jock] Stirrup and General [Sir Nicholas] Houghton, Vice Chief of the Defence Staff." They were all in my reporting chain; which one did I obey? He said: "You obey me." And I said: "I am being pulled in a number of different directions here, it is quite uncomfortable."'

After they had had a heated discussion Brigadier Butler said: '"General, thank you for that. We are both right but we are both wrong, but I bet you don't speak to any of the other three dozen National Contingent Commanders in just the way you have spoken to me?" He gave me a broad grin.'

Butler said he also played the 'yellow card' (a joke, based on a football referee showing a player the yellow card as a warning) on a number of occasions with Major General Freakley, the American commander in charge of the Canadian contingent. He was a very good, experienced tactical soldier, Butler says, but what he recognised from previous occasions working with Americans before 9/11, was that two-star generals were not politically aware and it was only when you were above that that you began to become more politically attuned. He says that General Freakley couldn't understand at all why Butler was saying: '"Well your military plans are great; Operation Mountain Thrust was wonderful, but London is a bit concerned about this; we need to see evidence of what reconstruction you are going to do and what is behind it. We need to see what you are going to do with the aid projects," and Freakley said: "What the bloody hell has London got to do with this?"'[27]

Butler describes General Freakley as 'classic American, heavy metal. Very good at putting physical assets together' and, mimicking his style, adds: '*I understand all this region, so we will just pour in.*' Butler describes having 'a couple of fairly major disagreements with him and with General Eikenberry (he was the three-star) on the same issue of trying to articulate what London's concerns were about casualties, about lack of reconstruction, about this confusion over the mission, what John Reid had said, that Iraq wasn't going well . . .'[28] When Butler said Blair was worried about his legacy, and the cash for honours controversy, Freakley responded by saying: '"What the hell then, this is a war zone, it has got nothing to do with it," and I would say: "It has got everything to do with it, the way the British military and the psyche and the government works [is] what I am here for" . . .'[29]

It took Brigadier Butler a little time to grasp that their misunderstandings were partly due to linguistic confusion. The expression 'National Contingent Commander' was the term the Americans used for the chief logistician. They thought it was a bit odd because they knew Butler had a Special Forces background and would ask: 'Why is Brigadier Butler as a chief logistician telling me I can't do this for political concerns in London?' Butler says it took him 'a few days to twig this'.[30]

Apart from the ludicrous confusion between being in charge of logistics on the one hand and a national contingent of soldiers on the other, Butler spoke of American unfamiliarity with the concept of a coalition. In Iraq, for example, 'where the Americans had always been dominant . . . the lead nation . . . they had never had this and this is why it was easier for [General David] Petraeus and [General Stanley] McChrystal then, because they had to worry less about the coalition interests and everything else. They understood it now; but coalition-building and maintaining the relationship . . . was a very time-consuming business. You had to listen to everyone . . . to understand their politics, what their hosts, their capital cities, were saying.'

Brigadier Butler gives an example of the political sensitivities a British commander had to be aware of: 'We have an election coming up, we may not be able to have a major operation this month . . . "Well, that's ridiculous," someone might say. Well maybe,' Butler agreed. 'Tactically you are absolutely right, it is ridiculous, but if we were to lose twenty British soldiers this month it would influence the outcome of the general election . . . When the summer fighting season kicks off this year there will be handbrakes put on the military commanders to go easy, don't take too many risks . . . But the Americans never understood that and they couldn't get it, so my yellow card would come out. They never understand the red card issue; they didn't understand what we were doing – so that reflected on a number of rows which General Freakley and I had. The story has grown as to how close we came to having a major punch-up. I don't think it went that far.'

More significant, perhaps, was 'the lack of "campaign continuity". What the British were doing in Iraq and also did in Afghanistan for the first two years was that each Brigade Commander would come up with fresh ideas and fresh plans and say, "I am doing it this way . . ." I think it was [the Defence Secretary] Des [now Lord] Browne who said to me: "Ed, I cannot understand this because there was you, demanding you needed helicopters. The [Royal] Marines turned up straight after and they demanded . . . their [BV Arctic] vehicles. And [Brigadier] John Lorimer [who commanded 12 Mechanised Brigade in Helmand] turned up and said: 'Well, we want tanks.'"'

Des Browne said he responded in good faith and tried to get them what they wanted but they kept on changing their minds. 'He was absolutely right because we didn't have one central military plan run by Headquarters. They had their Permanent Joint Headquarters [PJHQ] in Northwood but they did not have a deployed headquarters forward. 'The Kandahar plan, rotating between a Dutchman and an American and a British General, was almost running in isolation, and little Helmandshire was going on with its own foreign policy, its own reconstruction.'

According to Butler, Des Browne was right: 'the PJHQ should have said: "Right, this is the plan, Brigadier X, you are turning up here and you are getting off there. This is what you are going to achieve, these are your resources get on and do it." They hadn't taken a campaign kind of approach, which they are only now in the last year [2010] starting to do, with General Nick Carter in Kandahar . . .' Brigadier Butler says that what was needed, in his view, was unity of command, one plan which everyone works to, a NATO plan which McChrystal was now 'gripping'. 'As the Americans are by far the biggest troop-contributing nation, we do exactly what they say and what they want.'

Butler forecast – correctly – that the British would hand over all of Helmand to the Americans, which in effect is what has happened. 'We are going to subsume the north to them and the south and we will have a bit in the middle, but if you want my private view . . . they [will] control all of the south. What we should turn around and say is: "What do you actually want [from the British]?" And they will say: "We want some Special Forces, we want some specialist air, we want as much ISTAR [Intelligence and Surveillance system] as you can give us and . . . the biggest supporting group of people which you can provide, whether that is an all-arms battle group or an all-arms brigade, which we can pick up and do x, y, z [with], because what we really like about you Brits is you are dynamic, you get a task, you go and do it . . ."'

Summing up, Brigadier Butler says: 'Rather than trying to spread ourselves so thinly, with 10,000 people [the British contingent in Helmand] he would argue: Let's have 5,000 people who we can resource, train, equip and actually start to regenerate the rest of the Army with . . . It may be 3,000 people, the Americans will not mind because they can always fill the numbers behind us, even though it is quite tight for them. But we have got to do it properly . . . We lost a lot of people in Sangin, which is a motive. Some think we came out of Basra with our tails between our legs. We don't want to do the same in Helmand.'[31]

Brigadier Ed Butler resigned from the Army in June 2008, citing as his main reason his son telling him he 'didn't want a part-time dad'. He also said he was 'frustrated' by 'inadequate resourcing and insufficient strategic direction for the Afghan deployment'.

PART TWO

CORRUPTION AND BAD GOVERNANCE

Patronage or Corruption

Crudely put, within Helmand Province, my sin was not so much one of talking to the enemy, but one of doing so in such a way that the Provincial Governor had no financial stake in the enterprise.

Michael Semple, 'Afghanistan Then and Now', 2008

•

Patronage, or corruption, has always been part of the Afghan scene, as the Irish scholar-diplomat Michael Semple pointed out in a lecture he gave in 2008.[1] In the early decades of the Durrani Empire (1747–1978), provinces were quite explicitly 'farmed'. A provincial governor, he said, received his appointment on payment, and was expected to recoup the investment from revenue of the province. The institutional legacy was still there, Semple says, and informed the attitude of some of the old-fashioned governors, who viewed a governorship as a 'licence to tax any economic activity that requires some form of government blessing'.[2]

In 2007, Semple was working as a political officer for the European Union, based in Kabul, engaged in persuading middle-ranking Taliban commanders and their fighters to come over to the government, a policy now known as 'reintegration'. Semple's account of the dramatic end of his mission, ordered apparently by President Karzai himself, starts with the wonderfully sardonic words: 'My moment of international infamy came on Christmas Day 2007 when the spokesman of Hamid Karzai designated Michael Semple and Mervyn Patterson [a friend and colleague] as a threat to the national security of Afghanistan.'[3] Patterson, who worked for the United Nations, was blameless, according to Semple, and was not involved in his mission. Yet both were declared *persona non grata* and given forty-eight hours to leave the country.

Through a combination of briefings to diplomats and leaks to the press, Afghan government figures let it be known that their 'sin was unauthorised negotiation with the enemy, the Taliban', and even suggested they were plotting the handover to them of south-west Afghanistan. The episode certainly required some explanation, Semple says. 'Firstly my contacts with the Taliban were coordinated with the government of Afghanistan. So how come they threw me out? Secondly, negotiations with the Taliban have subsequently been held up by [President] Hamid Karzai and many others as·the great hope for progress towards peace in Afghanistan. So how come they threw me out for working with their people to pursue a cause that they now champion?'[4] That was in 2007. Since then, President Karzai's enhanced enthusiasm for a negotiated settlement with the Taliban – until recently at any rate – makes his original reasoning seem all the more eccentric.

In his lecture, published as a booklet, Semple set out the causes, effects and implications of the episode, which includes a section headed: 'An historical perspective on storms in teacups. Point one: The history of court conspiracies targeting foreigners in Afghanistan predates even the colonial intervention,' and begins with Mountstuart Elphinstone's diplomatic mission of 1809. Elphinstone's arrival in Kabul coincided with the rumour that the King, Shah Shuja, later deposed and replaced by Dost Mohammed who, in 1839, in turn was deposed by the British and replaced by the same Shah Shuja, was 'on the point of giving up our property to plunder'.[5] The whole town, Elphinstone wrote, was 'in a ferment; people were running up and down in all directions, getting their arms in order, and lighting their matches, and a great mob soon assembled at our gates'.[6] Indoors, meanwhile, the British, who were entertaining local VIPs, kept their nerve. Captain Pitman quietly doubled the guards; Afghan friends helped to defuse the situation and the King 'decided not to encourage the rumour'.[7]

The incident ended up as a mere footnote in Elphinstone's mission report. 'But anyone,' Semple says, 'operating in the Afghanistan of the twenty-first century should be aware of the degree of continuity in political praxis. The potency of disinformation in the fragmented court politics of contemporary Afghanistan should not be underestimated.'

His expulsion started, he describes, in the 'extremely overt location' of the Helmand Governor's sitting room. 'He had responded to a British Embassy request to provide some suggestions on how to deal with the Taliban who did not fight during the NATO and Afghan Army operation to recapture Musa Qala [in 2007].'[8] He quotes Elphinstone as saying that Afghan battles are 'generally not so much determined in the cavalry charge as in the decisions of key *khans* and their followers to change sides'.[9] Accordingly, a couple of Afghan government colleagues, in the run-up to the Musa Qala operation, spent their time working the telephones 'to contact any Helmand Taliban commander that any of us had a number for. Speaking as one Afghan to another, the government colleagues told the Taliban that something really big was about to happen in Musa Qala and advised them to get out of the way.'[10]

Because it was Afghanistan, Semple says, 'many of the men receiving these calls expressed their great amazement that the Afghan government could ever have considered them hostile in the first place. They promised to keep their men out of the battle and some of them did indeed extricate themselves just in time.' The challenge was 'how could we build on the momentum gained by this one tactical decision not to fight and provide an opportunity for these young men to stay off the battlefield more permanently.'

He continues: 'If it be a sin to advocate peaceful reintegration of young Afghan men as an alternative to bombing them, then I be a sinner, and unrepentant.'[11] His thinking was very much in step with that of General David Petraeus, the guru of modern American counter-insurgency (COIN) doctrine, and of General Stanley McChrystal, later overall American commander in Afghanistan. But despite that, it was as a sinner that he was seen by President Karzai, who only a few months later was to stake his presidential reputation, precarious as it was, on talking to the Taliban.

After the recapture of Musa Qala, Semple says he spent most of the Eid holidays in the Afghan Ministry of the Interior, working with the Deputy Head of National Security, developing his project ideas. No government agency had any plan for follow-up with these non-fighting Taliban and so three deputy ministers participated enthusiastically in developing the idea for what had 'poetically been described as a scout camp'. The Deputy Interior Minister, according to Semple, said that when things were final-ised his ministry would authorise a private sector company to run the camp. 'The deal we came up with was that batches of young men would be put through a six-week course, under retired Afghan Army education branch instructors, doing literacy, physical exercise, religious education, the Afghan constitution and health education.'[12]

A committee of provincial government chiefs and members of the British Provincial Reconstruction Team (PRT) would screen the young men, based on how well they did on the course, and recommend them for employment. They had already received a request from one of the big contractors involved in the repair of the Kajaki Dam (the huge hydro-electric scheme to provide power for half the south, built by the Americans in the 1960s) that was looking for labour about the time the young ex-Taliban would be graduating. 'The idea,' Semple summed up, 'was simple, good, timely, appropriately coordinated and was still in the consultation stage.'

He travelled to Lashkar Gah with Afghan colleagues who had worked on the plan, including a Ministry of Interior delegation, to brief Afghan and British officials there. They had a good briefing, Semple says, with PRT staff and the Afghan provincial police chief. Semple then went to the Governor's residence and was 'barely fifteen minutes' into talking through the idea with him when, in what he describes as a prepared move, the Governor called on the local NDS (National Directorate of Security) chief, a tribal ally, to arrest the Afghans who were with Semple. The Governor then rang the President's office in Kabul and announced that he had 'done as planned'.

'And in a sense that was that. I was not arrested and because Afghan hospitality still trumps all, I continued as guest of the Governor.'[13]

Semple rang numerous friends, all of whom promised to help but proved unable to do anything, including Amrullah Saleh, director of the Afghan NDS, who assured him his department had no quarrel with him (a veiled message meaning 'it is the President, not me, brother'). 'It was he [Saleh] who laughed and said that the Governor was having me expelled from Helmand – I would have to return to Kabul.'[14] Semple's first concern was to secure the release of the three Afghans with him, but confesses it soon became evident there were 'no strings in Helmand strong enough' to get them out.

'Classically,' Semple says, 'the Helmand NDS chief, who was only too delighted to have recovered some cash belonging to another project from the pocket of an Afghan colleague, said to him so confidently: "In future we really must work together and then nothing like this will ever happen."'[15]

Christmas Eve, 2007, Semple flew back to Kabul only to be told on that the government had 'PNG-ed' him (that is, declared him *non grata,* in effect expelling him) and he only had Christmas Day xing Day to wind up his affairs. He did the rounds of various minis- deputy ministers, 'some of whom had shared much worse times e, when we were together in the mountains in the days when they he resistance against the Taliban government. I am honoured that ous Afghan friends expressed their distress at what was happening. am not at all surprised that all reported back that when they tried to the President [Karzai], he was very angry.'

on Burke, the *Guardian* and *Observer* South Asia correspondent, had ed to this most aptly, Semple says, as 'manufactured ire'.16 It was also ical theatre, he suggests. 'They were manufacturing the case, and were y not angry.' One 'very dear minister', with whom he had worked ly, 'reported back that he told the President that he did not feel like ng on in Afghanistan if friends of Afghanistan like Michael [Semple] Mervyn [Patterson] were not allowed here. But I knew this was not a ning matter. And that was it.'17

ne of the more extraordinary twists in this convoluted tale – the ghost Elphinstone may have emitted a chuckle at this point – was the role, or her the non-role, of Mervyn Patterson.

Mervyn is from Northern Ireland and is one of the world's leading perts on the tribes of northern Afghanistan,' Semple explains. The head the UN's Analysis Cell, he had been on a fact-finding mission to elmand and he and Semple had doubled up to share the UN helicopter at flew them there. 'In other words he was neither involved in nor briefed en the "scout camp".' Nor was he involved in Semple's Taliban contact ork. 'Mervyn had not talked to a Talib since their government threw him ut of the country for taking photographs of a wrestling match. Including Mervyn in the expulsion order was a masterful contribution to the politi- cal theatre. His crime was drinking a cup of tea with the Achakzai Governor, nothing more.' Semple's conclusion was: 'If you see the whole thing as an Afghan round of the Great Game, the capricious move against Mervyn is not collateral, it is poetic.'18

As deputy to Francesc Vendrell, then the European Union's Special

Representative in Kabul, Michael Semple had responsibility for the reconciliation programme, which was part of the EU mandate, and worked on
it for three years. Where appropriate he was to make practical arrangements to facilitate commanders' peaceful reintegration. Semple says he
worked quietly behind the scenes. It gave him and his office 'tremendous
insights' into the factors driving the insurgency, and how the failures of
governance were contributing to the revival of the Taliban.

'The first message the government of Afghanistan gave out during the
expulsion episode was essentially: "Thou shalt not negotiate." However it
raised the profile of the idea of political engagement with insurgents as a
complement to military action, which, over the past year [2008] had
shifted from being a 'fringe idea' to being "a main plank" of strategies to
turn round the situation in Afghanistan. Even to the extent that I, the
original enthusiast, caution people not to represent this as the golden
bullet.' In conclusion, Michael Semple adds, the incident highlighted that
there was 'no coherent Afghan government approach to political engagement with the Taliban and yet one was direly needed'.

Perhaps most significantly of all, Semple says that his and Patterson's
PNG-ing raised doubts about the nature and quality of the relationship
underpinning the whole international intervention in Afghanistan, that
between the President of Afghanistan and his international partners. At
the start of the Bonn process in 2001, the United Nations had undertaken
to support the stabilisation of a renewed political system in Afghanistan.
But when put into practice, that meant supporting the government of
Afghanistan and hoping that it would build a stable political system. And
with a centralised constitution, and little sign of checks and balances,
supporting the government of Afghanistan effectively meant propping up
the President.[19]

Even if one laughs off the PNG-ing of Patterson and himself as an act of
political theatre, Semple argues, and given that 'everyone is disposable', the
act of expulsion was indeed 'gratuitous, unreasonable and a breach of
faith', and indicated that the 'strategically key relationship was decidedly
shaky'. Despite the fact that Semple was an Irish citizen working for the
European Union, the government spin was carefully crafted to focus on
Britain, he says. 'They made me the bizarre choice to symbolise Perfidious

Albion.' Constructive, coordinated, legitimate activities were deliberately misrepresented to give the impression that 'Michael and the British were scheming with the Taliban to weaken the Afghan government.' Such fanciful suggestions created doubt and suspicion and undermined the cooperation between Afghans and international bodies that was essential to the success of the mission in Afghanistan. The strategically vital relationship was simply not reliable.[20]

Of more strategically relevant practical consequences, perhaps, Semple says, was President Karzai's decision to sabotage the appointment of Lord (Paddy) Ashdown as Special Representative of the Secretary General of the United Nations. After initially indicating his support for the appointment, in the aftermath of the expulsions the President gave such 'negative briefings' about the appointment that Lord Ashdown 'quite rightly' turned it down. 'Just about every commentator concluded that the Ashdown appointment was sabotaged because someone had tipped off the President that Ashdown would be a very effective coordinator who would have ensured that the international community in Afghanistan basically spoke with one voice.'[21] Given the acuteness of the crisis in the country, the idea that the West's sole partner in Afghanistan should consider this a 'bad thing' further called the central relationship into question.

Finally, Semple said he warned his boss, Francesc Vendrell, that despite the good progress he was making in the reconciliation of mid-level Taliban commanders in Helmand, 'the Provincial Governor scented money and might create trouble. The issue was, when viewed from a tax-farming perspective, that reconciliation of Taliban was a potential revenue-raising activity, because foreigners were interested in supporting it. Crudely put, within Helmand Province, my sin was not so much one of talking to the enemy, but one of doing so in such a way that the Provincial Governor had no financial stake in the enterprise.' The Governor had ordered the arrest and search of the Afghan members of their delegation and seized the money from their pockets, 'with the eyes almost popping out of his head'. A member of the Pushtun Achakzai tribe, he had recently succeeded, Semple says, in getting another Achakzai appointed as head of provincial security. 'The tribal link to the intelligence chief was important, as it meant that the Governor had a cooperative security agency to move against us.

While the NDS had our Afghan colleagues in detention, the only issue that NDS showed any interest in was financial – where was the money.'[22]

Semple ends with another quotation from Elphinstone, describing the Achakzais he had met 200 years before: 'Their manners are rough and barbarous, but they are not quarrelsome among themselves . . . They are not hospitable; they have no mosques; and seldom pray, or trouble themselves about religion . . . All tribes are loud in their complaints against them and the Douranees [Durranis] will hardly acknowledge them for clansmen.'[23]

In many ways life in Afghanistan, especially in the rural areas and, above all, among the Pushtuns, who still set great store by their tribal code, *Pushtunwali*, has changed little in the past two centuries. In the mountains and deserts existence for the ordinary Afghan is as hard as it ever was. The imperative for self-preservation is absolute and tribal loyalties are paramount. Hospitality is the hallmark of *Pushtunwali*; honour – family honour especially – the touchstone. In her book *Afghan Frontier*, Victoria Schofield writes that, most important of all, quarrels have to be settled honourably. 'In the time of the British, they arose frequently over issues such as *zar*, *zan* and *zamin* (gold, women and land)'[24] – three things of supreme importance to Pushtuns. Rudyard Kipling adds a fourth dimension in *The Ballad of the King's Jest*, that tragic tale which, like *The Ballad of East and West*, distils the magic but also reflects the harshness of the Frontier:

> Four things greater than all things are
> Women and Horses and Power and War.

9

The Narco State

If you are looking for Mother Teresa, she doesn't live in Afghanistan.
Former CIA officer, Kabul, quoted in the *New York Times*,
27 October 2009

The debate about corruption lies at the heart of present-day Afghan politics. In fact it could not be more central, since the ramifications led and lead to President Karzai himself and his family, and more specifically to his late younger half-brother, Ahmed Wali Karzai, who, until his assassination on 12 July 2011, was the President's eyes and ears and political enforcer in Kandahar. Although officially Chairman of the Kandahar Provincial Council, his real influence stemmed from being his brother's personal representative in the drug-rich south. He was often referred to, only half in jest, as the 'King of Kandahar'. Immensely powerful and widely feared for his connections and forceful personality, he was a controversial figure and strongly disapproved of by a number of senior American military and diplomatic officials. The previous head of American military intelligence in Afghanistan, Major General Michael Flynn, once drew a caustic parallel with the notorious Prohibition gangster, Al Capone: 'The only way to clean up Chicago,' he commented, was to get rid of Capone. 'If we are going to conduct a population-centric strategy [the cornerstone of General Petraeus's counter-insurgency theory] in Afghanistan, and we are perceived as backing thugs, then we are just undermining ourselves,' was another Flynn jibe.[1]

Ahmed Wali Karzai's assassination, which followed a string of suicide bombings of high-level targets by the Taliban, came as an enormous shock even to a country inured to bloodshed and Taliban atrocities. It soon emerged, however, that it almost certainly had nothing to do with the Taliban, but was the result of a personal quarrel – there is said to be 'bad blood' in the family – and the killer, Sardar Mohammed, also a Popalzai, was virtually one of the family. Ahmed Wali knew him intimately and trusted him as an old family retainer who had served him in the past as a bodyguard. Even more disturbingly, the killing took place not during his usual morning conference at which, as tribal leader and prominent local politician, he held court regularly to a host of fellow tribesmen and petitioners. Sardar Mohammed arrived early and asked for a private meeting with Mr Karzai, saying he wanted to show him some papers. He was carrying a pistol but given his status in the household this was normal practice and raised no suspicions. According to the *New York Times*, when Mr Karzai emerged from an adjoining room, sat down and started to read the papers, Sardar Mohammed, without warning, drew the pistol and shot him twice in the head and once in the hand, killing him almost immediately. A relative said he was using drugs, not uncommon in that part of the world, but would not elaborate.

Hearing the shots, Mr Karzai's bodyguards burst into the room, too late to save him, and fatally shot Sardar Mohammed. At Ahmed Wali's funeral in Kandahar next day, his brother, the President, surrounded by tribal dignitaries, leaned down to give his brother a farewell kiss, declaring he had been martyred. 'This is the life of all Afghans,' he added, meaning that every Afghan family had suffered the same sort of loss.

It was widely believed by foreign diplomats and officials in Kabul that Ahmed Wali was deeply involved in the hugely lucrative business of opium and heroin smuggling. There had been numerous media reports to that effect over the years, quoting Western diplomats. Possibly the first of these was Carlotta Gall's article in the *New York Times* on 19 November 2004, headlined 'Afghan Poppy Growing Reaches Record Level, UN says',[2] while a senior American officer in Kabul was also quoted by the paper more recently as saying: 'If it looks like a duck, and it quacks like a duck, it probably is a duck' – meaning Ahmed Wali Karzai. 'Our assumption is that he's benefiting from the drug trade,' the officer added.[3]

In October 2009 the same newspaper reported that Ahmed Wali Karzai was a CIA agent or informant and had been on their payroll for several years. He subsequently denied taking any money from them. The CIA must have known all the drug allegations against Ahmed Wali Karzai and evaluated them, but presumably still adhered to the old maxim, attributed originally to Franklin D. Roosevelt, who is said to have remarked of the Nicaraguan dictator, Anastasio Somoza, whom he had invited officially to Washington: 'He may be a SOB [Son of a Bitch], but he's our SOB.'[4]

In *Seeds of Terror*, a detailed account of how heroin is 'bankrolling' not only the Taliban and al Qaeda, but the Afghan government as well, the American journalist Gretchen Peters writes that one report on drug-related corruption within the Karzai administration, compiled by the UN and described to the author, mapped out a complex system of kickbacks – very similar to the one existing inside the Taliban. UN researchers had identified thirty-six districts across Afghanistan – either in poppy-producing areas or along smuggling routes – where governorships, customs and police postings were the most sought after. The report estimated that officials who won 'plum assignments' stood to earn hundreds of thousands of dollars a month in 'dirty money' (bribes). 'One indicator was the huge sums they would have to "kick upstairs" just to hold on to their jobs,' Peters writes. According to one researcher who contributed to the report, top police officials in lucrative districts had to pay as much as $40,000 (£25,000) a month in bribes to keep their posts, she adds.[5]

One UN researcher who worked on the study concluded that the man who had been at the top of the organisational chain was Ahmed Wali Karzai. 'He's been implicated in multiple US intelligence reports seen by the author as having ties to the drug trade and Western diplomats say NATO has intercepted him reportedly making deals on the telephone.' As with other senior officials and insurgent commanders who profit from drugs, 'you won't see Ahmed Wali actually touching the trade', Peters quotes a UN official who worked on the report as saying. 'He has influence over who gets what position – and that gives him extraordinary power.'[6]

The President's sibling stoutly denied his ties to the drug trade repeatedly in the media. But in private he was 'less coy', says Peters, adding that a 'European envoy [unnamed] who dined with Ahmed Wali at the splendid Kandahar mansion he calls home, once asked him: "Where did the money come [from] for this incredible house?" Ahmed Wali smiled and said: "Everything you see here was paid for with drugs."[7] The story, of course, may be apocryphal.

The British General, Nick Carter, who commanded in southern Helmand in 2010, told me that in his capacity as the senior NATO official in Kandahar he saw Ahmed Wali Karzai regularly. There was no evidence that he was rich, he said, and he lived in a 'humble abode in downtown Kandahar'. General Carter said, 'he is a political player – I see all the political players – you couldn't have a security solution if you didn't talk to all the political players. I have to see him. There is no way that I could produce stability in southern Afghanistan if I didn't talk to everybody . . . [if you don't] they will end up doing something that is completely out of control.'[8]

'What would you say about the allegations that he is deeply involved in the drug trade?' I asked.

'Show me the evidence,' General Carter replied.

'Why is it always said he is a senior player in the drug trade?' I asked.

'There is no evidence to say that he is involved in the drug trade and there is no evidence to suggest he is rich – none at all,' he answered.

This is the party line, of course, and General Carter was speaking on the record as a senior, and respected, NATO commander.

I asked if Ahmed Wali Karzai had a country house?

'No – his brother does. Qayum [the eldest brother] has a veritable palace in Kandahar with manicured lawns: a distinguished residence. He is an American citizen, as is the other brother, Mahmood. Mahmood has significant business interests in Afghanistan. They are not popular particularly.'[9]

The truth about Ahmed Wali Karzai's house seems to lie somewhere in between, according to a Western journalist who knows Kandahar well. It was neither 'incredible' in the words of Gretchen Peters's anonymous European envoy, nor a 'humble abode' as General Carter describes it. It belongs or belonged to an exiled Afghan drug baron who either lent or rented it to the late Mr Karzai; three storeys high, clad with slabs of marble and spacious enough to accommodate sixty or seventy tribal visitors and petitioners at a time.

Another story I was told in Kabul in 2010, may also, or may not, be apocryphal; namely that Ahmed Wali Karzai left Kabul airport for Dubai one day with $40 million in cash. Even if true, however, it would not be a record. The transportation of huge sums of cash from Kabul to Dubai and beyond has become almost routine in the past few years. In November 2010, WikiLeaks published a diplomatic cable from the American Embassy in Kabul to Washington saying a former Afghan Vice-President, Ahmed Zia Masud, a brother of the late guerrilla leader, Ahmed Shah Masud, was found to be carrying $52 million in cash on arrival at Dubai airport and was allowed to continue without being questioned. (He was, presumably, travelling on a diplomatic passport.)

Since 2008 there has been a stream of reports in mainly American newspapers of approximately $10 million in cash per day being flown to Dubai from Kabul. Afghanistan has few exchange control rules: you can export as much money as you like provided you declare it, have paid your taxes and can satisfy the authorities the money did not come from 'corrupt sources'. Judging by the huge flow of money from Kabul to Dubai on a daily basis, it would seem that, for whatever reason, Afghans do not find these conditions hard to meet.

As to the President himself, Gretchen Peters claims that Karzai, an ethnic Pushtun who derives much of his political support from the Pushtun-dominated south, has long resisted efforts to curtail poppy cultivation. He has consistently refused to dismiss, much less prosecute, high-level officials in his administration widely believed to be tied to drugs, Peters claims, prompting some former officials to conclude that he is protecting relatives and cronies suspected of earning enormous profits. She quotes one American official, Thomas Schweich, who was the State Department's senior counter-narcotics official in Afghanistan and who wrote in an 'unusually frank' article in the *New York Times*, quoted by Peters, that 'Karzai is playing us like a fiddle'.[10]

Schweich relates how he first met President Karzai on a clear, crisp day in Kabul in March 2006 when President and Laura Bush, Secretary of State Condoleezza Rice, and the American Ambassador Ronald Neumann attended the dedication of the new US Embassy building in the Afghan capital. He says he took to heart Karzai's strong words about the Afghan drug trade. Over the next two years, however, Schweich writes, he 'would discover how deeply the Afghan government was involved in protecting the opium trade – by shielding it from American-designed policies.' While it was true that Karzai's Taliban enemies financed themselves from the drug trade, so did many of his supporters. At the same time, 'some of our NATO allies [above all the British] have resisted the anti-opium offensive (including aerial spraying) as has our own Defense Department, which tends to see counter-narcotics as other people's business to be settled once the war-fighting is over.' The trouble, Schweich adds, 'is that the fighting is unlikely to end as long as the Taliban can finance themselves through drugs – and as long as the Kabul government is dependent on opium to sustain its own hold on power'.[11] He then goes on to forecast in the article that 'the US would spend billions of dollars on infrastructure improvement; that it and its allies would fight the Taliban; Karzai's friends would get rich off the drug trade; he could blame the West for his problems; and in 2009 he would be elected to a new term'. As a piece of political prophecy, it is hard to fault.

The *New York Times* report claiming that Ahmed Wali Karzai was on the CIA payroll said he had been paid 'for a variety of services', including 'helping to recruit an Afghan paramilitary force that operated at the CIA's direction in and around . . . Kandahar'. The paramilitaries, known as the Kandahar Strike Force, had been used in raids against suspected insurgents and terrorists but have been accused of mounting an unauthorised operation against an official of the Afghan government.

Ahmed Wali Karzai's close relations with the American military were claimed to have led to the lease to the CIA and American Special Forces of a large compound outside the city, which used to belong to Mullah Omar, the Taliban leader, now believed to be under ISI protection in Quetta or Karachi. The compound was also used by the Kandahar Strike Force. One senior American official described Wali Karzai as having been their 'landlord'. The *New York Times* said the arrangement with Wali Karzai had created 'deep divisions' within the Obama administration, and complicated the relationship with the President.

Both military and political officials, the *New York Times* report added, said the evidence, though largely circumstantial, suggested that Wali Karzai had made himself probably the richest and most powerful figure in the south, partly through his control of half a dozen road bridges over the Helmand River. Through his private militia he controlled all traffic across those bridges and levied heavy taxes on trucks carrying opium or heroin to Kandahar and elsewhere. That, the anonymous official said, was the basis of his fortune: bridge tolls.[12]

It is not to say, of course, that he was not involved in many other money-making projects, the article continues. Hundreds of millions of dollars in drug money are flowing through the southern region, and nothing happens in southern Afghanistan without the regional leadership knowing about it. American officials say the opium trade, the largest in the world, directly threatens the stability of the Afghan state by providing a large percentage of the money the Taliban needs for its operations, and also by corrupting Afghan public officials to help the trade flourish. The Obama administration has repeatedly promised to crack down on the drug lords who are believed to permeate the highest levels of President Karzai's government. Administration officials had pressed him to move his half-brother out of southern Afghanistan, but he refused to do so. The CIA's close connection with Wali Karzai sent the wrong signals, many American officials feel, and undermined the 'push to develop an effective central government that can maintain law and order and eventually allow the United States to withdraw'.[13]

His behaviour is said to have caused 'anger and frustration' among many members of the Obama administration, and the 'Mafia-like way that he lords [it] over southern Afghanistan makes him a malevolent force'.[14] Other Western officials claim that Wali Karzai supervised the production of hundreds of thousands of fake ballots for his half-brother's re-election campaign in August 2009. He is also believed to have been responsible for setting up dozens of so-called ghost polling stations – existing only on paper – that were used to manufacture tens of thousands of fake votes.[15]

On the other hand, there is a more cynical – or realistic – approach, depending on your point of view, that corruption is endemic in Afghanistan: the United Nations rates it as the second most corrupt country in the world, after Somalia. The *New York Times* quoted a former CIA officer with first-hand knowledge of Afghanistan as saying the agency relied heavily on Ahmed Wali Karzai, and often based undercover agents at compounds he owned. Any connections he might or did have to the drug trade 'mattered little' to CIA officers 'focused on counter-terrorism missions . . . Virtually every significant Afghan figure has had brushes with the drug trade,' he added. 'If you are looking for Mother Teresa, she doesn't live in Afghanistan.'[16]

The debate over Ahmed Wali Karzai, which began when President Obama took office in January 2008, intensified in June when the CIA's paramilitaries, the Kandahar Strike Force, shot and killed Kandahar's Provincial Police Chief, Matiullah Qati, at the office of a local prose-cutor. The circumstances surrounding Matiullah Qati's death remain mysterious and unexplained, according to the *New York Times*. And it is unclear, for instance, the paper says, if any CIA agents were present.[17] Officials say the gun battle broke out when Mr Qati tried to block the strike force from freeing the brother of a fellow member who was being held in custody.

'Matiullah was in the wrong place at the wrong time,' Wali Karzai is reported to have said when interviewed. Counter-narcotics officials repeat-edly expressed frustration over the unwillingness of senior policy-makers in Washington to take action against Wali Karzai – or even begin a serious investigation of the allegations against him. In fact, they say that while other Afghans accused of drug involvement are investigated and singled out for raids or even rendition to the United States, Wali Karzai seemed immune from similar scrutiny.[18] He also helped the CIA 'communicate with and sometimes meet Afghans loyal to the Taliban'. To the average Afghan, the answer is easy. As the brother of the President he was above the law: untouchable.

***

For a precise, insider, if less colourful, account of the rampant corruption that prevails in Afghanistan, one has to turn to Dr Ashraf Ghani, a puck-ish, quicksilver academic with an apparently total recall of figures who was his country's first post-9/11 Finance Minister. As a young man he studied at the American University in Beirut, then at Columbia, Harvard and Stanford Universities in the US, joining the World Bank, where he worked for ten years, in 1991. After 9/11 and a twenty-four-year absence, Dr Ghani returned to Kabul in 2001 and joined the Afghan government. In January 2002 he became chief adviser to President Karzai and in November was appointed by the UN to advise Lakhdar Brahimi, the UN Secretary General's Special Representative to Afghanistan, working with him on the Bonn Agreement which set up a democratic system of government for post-Taliban Afghanistan. He turned down the offer of a post in Karzai's 2005 government, choosing instead to return to academic life as Chancellor of Kabul University. He stood as a candidate in the 2009 presidential election, coming third after Karzai and Dr Abdullah, the main challenger.

When I asked him what he thought had gone wrong in Afghanistan, he replied that the international community had no serious interest in Afghanistan between 2002 and 2004. They were unconvinced that Afghanistan could really function. It was of complete marginal interest. The United States and Britain were preparing to go to war in Iraq. Basically, he said, they were not ready for what the post-9/11 world meant. 'It was a paradigm shift of enormous significance . . . and at the Tokyo conference of January 2002, the [financial] pledge by the USA was less than that of India.'[19]

This attitude placed a heavy burden on a very small group of Afghans who 'had to persuade the world that you are actually worth paying attention to', Dr Ghani said. 'And when I became Finance Minister in July of 2002 there was not one cent in the Treasury, literally, because they gave $1.6 billion to the UN Agencies and $40 million to the Afghan government.' Dr Ghani explained that the funds had been pledged but not yet committed or transferred, so there was no cash in the Treasury. They had a functioning bureaucracy with a lot of dedicated people but 'we were being stuffed'.[20]

So first, he explained, it was a serious lack of attention to what Afghanistan needed. The World Bank estimated that Afghanistan had lost $20 billion in infrastructure damages and lost growth opportunities. 'I had to break my back with a team of Afghans to prepare a document that put [together] a $26.5 billion, eight-year public works finance programme . . . we got $8.2 billion for the first three years but the

Germans who were hosting the conference wanted $1 billion to be the mark of success. So we were approached in those initial years with a very miserly attitude – that is one example.'

The second was Iraq. 'The day the invasion took place was the worst day for me and the Afghan government,' Dr Ghani recalls. 'I knew what it entailed and I explained it and nobody, of course, wanted to hear.' Everyone's attention was diverted: 'all the oxygen was taken out'. Without Iraq they would have been judged under the microscope. 'It would have been a two-way dialogue regarding reforms, growth etc . . . But by comparison with Iraq we looked so good that everybody ignored [us],' although, as he points out, the 'fundamental deterioration' was setting in. There had been a complete change in Washington in the way the Bush administration reacted to bad news from Afghanistan. 'Only [in] the last six months did they start . . . acknowledging that there was a problem.'[21]

Then there was the question of warlords, which did not exist on 9/11. 'We had the Taliban on one side and Ahmed Shah Masud [on the other].' Northern Alliance leaders like General Dostum and Ismail Khan were abroad, in exile. But after the American intervention, 'all these strong men that came back were like orphans. They had forgotten nothing and learnt nothing. So the government was hampered from all sides.' Then, Dr Ghani says, 'unfortunately, we got the world of contractors', most of whom, with one or two honourable exceptions, had a 'negative' influence. 'The international contractors descended on us which, when I was in finance, I controlled. But subsequently it really became so we ended up with parallel governments much stronger in the way of resources than the Afghan government, without any accountability and with extremely limited transparency. You take the UN agencies: they have not issued a single report to the Afghan public as to what they have achieved, with what amount of money.'[22]

Some reports were coming back from UNOPS (the United Nations Office for Project Services), documenting 'massive fraud and mismanagement and outright corruption'. As a result, Dr Ghani said, 'a new political class emerged that used its political position to acquire economic assets and financial gain. It was linked to very weak accountability to the Afghan public. Institutions were used for private, factional or ideological sectional gains rather than for the purpose of the national interest.' Dr Ghani sees the largest problem as being the lack of 'a coherent, national strategy for Afghanistan. So in the process of dividing the country among different partners, for Britain, Helmand has become Afghanistan; for Germany, it is Kunduz; for Italy it's Herat, for Spain it's Baghdis . . .'[23]

There were compensations, however, at least initially, Dr Ghani pointed out. The interim transitional government set up at the Bonn Conference contained strong personalities who sometimes disagreed, but when they did agree, Ghani says, 'the implementation was very easy because power was concentrated in the Cabinet'. That meant that 'everybody was inside the tent' and 'there was a mechanism to hammer out major issues'. After 2004, when Karzai was elected President, however, the Cabinet was no longer all-powerful: 'government officials, particularly Governors with an independent power base, started behaving very arbitrarily vis-à-vis the population', he says. Dr Ghani rejects the idea that arbitrary behaviour was in any way normal practice in Afghanistan: 'No, Afghan governments have been extremely accountable,' he says.

As more and more power was concentrated in the hands of the President, he could remove any governor, however powerful, whenever he wished. This meant the 'system of governance did not evolve and accountability was really weakened very considerably'.

Summing up what has gone wrong, Dr Ghani explains that the new Afghan elite forgot who their master was and what kind of people they were dealing with. 'The Afghan people cannot be abused and take it lying down. We are not a colonised people,' he says. Afghans have never been forced to submit, either by an army of occupation or by their local institutions. You have to gain their consent and that is what makes them distinctive. Unless consent is gained, through persuasion and delivery, the system starts ripping apart. 'The predatoriness of officials and their desire to make up in a very short time what in some other countries would take twenty to thirty years of bribery . . . this was a very strong driver. The failure to deliver justice and to really focus delivery of justice had been very important,' Dr Ghani observes. 'Our international partners misread the welcome and the Afghan population felt that the guests were not behaving like guests but like hosts . . . We have a very distinctive cultural tradition.

We are incredibly respectful of our guests as long as they understand the rules that they are guests and not the master of the house.'[24]

I suggested some people thought the President had begun to arrogate too much power to himself?

He agreed. There was 'a steady change' to ignore the rule of law, Dr Ghani said. The constitution provided the road map: 'I come back to the contrast between the interim transitional government, which had a very well-delineated series of benchmarks.' He had helped to design those and moved into the government to help implement them, with his colleagues' help. Once Karzai became President, 'he had no script, he had no idea as to what was required of him in a definitive way'. The international community failed, Dr Ghani claims: 'They did not draw up a script because they were not capable.' The international community, he continues, became partners to oust the Afghan reformers. 'We were extracting too high a price from them and they lobbied for our removal.'

'People like yourself?' I asked.

'Yes, absolutely,' he replied. 'Among their international partners were some who did not like strong Afghan leadership . . . They left a President who was extremely talented politically but had no experience in managing and had not acquired the experience of managing. They left him . . . without a script and simultaneously made him the centre of all the decision-making. They started running to him for everything which led to both the arrogance of the office of the presidency and its separation from other institutions. No systematic attention was given to the balance of power, to parliament or the judiciary. Because they didn't have a strategy, everybody's behaviour became tactical,' he asserts.

The case of Dr Spanta* was one episode of ignoring the law, he said. Then there was Kai Eide, the Special Representative of the UN Secretary General, who had the specific task of holding the Afghan presidential elections on time and democratically. 'And what did he do?' Dr Ghani asks rhetorically. 'He ignored the Afghan constitution and wasn't paying any attention to the fact that the elections were coming in May.'

---

* In 2007 Parliament passed a vote of 'No Confidence' in the Foreign Minister, Dr Rangin Spanta. President Karzai refused to recognise the vote and appealed to the Supreme Court who backed him, thereby restoring Spanta's status as minister. See Chapter 19.

'At this point there was a hiatus?' I suggested, referring to the gap of several months when Karzai's term had run out and he was no longer, constitutionally, President.

Dr Ghani's reply was caustic. 'A hiatus because: where is the UN? The UN spent $1 billion on the Afghan election and we still do not have an electoral roll. Then they read the constitution which said the elections were required in May. So when did they wake up? They woke up in January and then said it was impossible to hold elections in May.'

At this point Dr Ashraf Ghani appeared to point the finger at Kai Eide, saying he had been very much involved in breaking the rule of law.

But that was not his task, Dr Ghani says. He had a mandate from the Security Council 'specifically itemised to actually help support a democratic election and what did he do?' He functioned like the President's Chief Whip and Campaign Manager, Dr Ghani claims.[25] 'When we have a UN office blowing up into fragments in the middle of an election between the Special Representative [Kai Eide] and his deputy [Peter Galbraith] what does that say to you? Everything that Mr Eide was told by candidates and by the other Afghan stakeholders regarding a free and fair election fell on deaf ears.' He saw his duty as being to please the Karzai executive and he ignored the larger field, Dr Ghani says. 'So consequently when we wake up all of a sudden it is a flawed election. Hello. Didn't we tell you months in advance? Didn't Afghan society, civil society, tell you months in advance? Didn't Afghan women's groups tell you to invest in Afghan political parties ... tell you in advance? So either there was dysfunctional deafness, or there is incompetence.'[26]

I said there had been talk in the Western media of a transitional authority which would have bypassed the President and brought in a prime minister figure.

'But Kai Eide had zero interest in this,' Dr Ghani replied. 'He blocked it completely.'

'Had that been a possibility?' I asked.

'Absolutely. It was a possibility. The alternative would have been to keep the President but really turn him into a transitional figure with very strong limitations on the functions of the government. But he didn't do that. Mr Kai Eide did not lift a finger to make the Afghan elections democratic. It was one-sided. He was partisan. He was not neutral and he was not focused on democracy, or focused on the corruption of his own officials, and when massive evidence became available he ignored it. He had a mandate from the Security Council. What more did he need?'

Why didn't the Americans, I asked, put pressure on Kai Eide? After all, he was the servant of the Security Council?

'The Obama administration had just come to power – the post (you know the American system) required filling. The previous Ambassador [William 'Bill' Wood] had ignored the elections; the new one took a long time until confirmation came . . . Ambassador [Karl] Eikenberry really tried to level the playing field, but it was too late.'[27]

Dr Ghani, who believes corruption is destroying Afghan society, says there are 'seven drivers of corruption' in Afghanistan, based on the fact that there are 'seven illicit sources of production of wealth and each one eats through the moral fabric'.

The first of these, he says, is drugs. 'International drug traffickers made between $460 and $600 billion out of Afghanistan's heroin trade in the past eight years. Afghan drug traffickers made $18 billion and 1.8 million Afghan farmers made $6.3 billion.' This, Dr Ghani says, eats through the institutions which govern security and the rule of law – such as the judiciary and the police.

'Then there is illegal smuggling coming in as oil – millions of tons of oil – pharmaceuticals, etc. That is another driver because it subverts both the moral fabric and affects contracts.' Thirdly, Dr Ghani says there is 'a chain of corruption in international contracting that is hair-raising; roughly only between 10 and 30 cents out of every dollar ends up in Afghanistan'. He then tells the story of a new road that was contracted out to a big American firm in the Washington 'beltway' for $125 million. Shortly after getting the contract, the company 'subcontracted it to a firm from a regional country [probably Pakistan, India or China] for $80 million. And what was the contribution of the first firm to the second firm? One engineer, for the life of the project, to supervise the second firm. So, I mean, $45 million for one engineer is not bad money.'

'Why did no one stop it?' I asked.

'It is an entrenched system. The [Afghan] Minister of Finance has nothing to do with that. It is the USAID [United States Agency for International Development] chain of contract. It doesn't go through the Afghan budget. These [deals] are contracted in Washington and then they go and they tell you consequently the price of roads is one of the highest prices of anything.'

Dr Ghani gave another example, concerning two schools which were next to one another and had exactly the same specifications. One was built by a programme that he had designed, called the National Solidarity Programme, a programme for development. That school cost, he believed, $25,000 (£15,600). Next to it is a school built through USAID contracting. That building cost $265,000 (£165,600), more than ten times as much. The Afghan contractor built both schools, 'but one was done through a community project and the other built through this international chain of contracting. So that is a fact.'

The fourth driver of corruption, Dr Ghani says, is bureaucracy. The imports are legal 'but then the merchants are making the bureaucracy partners in corruption . . . If you are an Afghan producer you face the nightmare that the imported foreign goods pay much less in customs duty, or nothing, while the raw material is taxed to the core and you yourself are taxed for everything.'

Then there is land.

'The price of land has gone through the roof in Shahr-i-Nau [a fashionable residential and business area near the centre of Kabul]. A quarter of an acre of land was now going for as much as $5 million. So therefore the dispute over property, the forging of books, subversion . . . taking bribes is a risk.'

All of this, Dr Ghani explains, leads to the seventh 'driver of corruption': the 'sale of offices'. 'If you are in a position such as a clerk of court or the police official of a district . . . you measure your income not by your salary but by real income, [meaning] what is produced via corruption . . . There is a domestic component and a national component and we need to tackle both in order to be able to fix the system.' The source of the money, says Dr Ghani, is mainly drug money: 'The drug money is a tough issue. We have also our illegal exports – gems: emeralds, lapis [lazuli], everything else, antiquities. Take our wood. The best wood comes from Kunar. It is smuggled to Pakistan . . . It is not allowed to be sold in the Afghan market but it is being sold to Pakistan, millions of cubic feet. Then its "crushed-up" version comes back and is sold in Kabul, so the price of wood that should normally be very low is high.'

I pointed out that the President's half-brother, Ahmed Wali Karzai, had, in his final years, come in for a lot of criticism. Did he think that Wali Karzai had been as bad as he was said to be, and if so why hadn't the President done something about it? Or was it part of Afghan culture, family ties being so strong, that he could not have acted against his brother?

'Let me tell you a story,' Dr Ghani replied, 'about the King who ruled from 1826 to 1839 and then from 1843 to 1863. His name was Dost Mohammed; his was the first famous encounter with the British.* His brother had been the Grand Wazir [Prime Minister]. He rebelled and then was blinded and killed by the King . . . Three of his older brothers were ruling Kandahar. They besieged Kabul without success and Zabul, his elder brother, came and said that, according to Afghan custom, he should yield. Dost Mohammed's reply was: "State interests and family don't mix."'

It was not a question of Afghan custom, Dr Ghani said. 'Kinship and kingship is always going to clash in this country. State interests overcome kinship. Kingship and kinship are not compatible.' He went on to say he had known Wali Karzai 'very briefly when I was chief adviser to the President'. As Minister of Finance he had no dealings with him and had not investigated him, so he could not really comment, he said.

Then I asked: 'Do you feel the President does enough to stop corruption, to set an example?'

'No, he has not done enough.'

'Do you feel he is to blame for that?'

'Constitutionally, he is obliged. That is his duty and in this regard he has judged state interest probably differently than what his constitution mandated him to do.' The constitution 'is crystal clear', he said. It

---

* He was deposed by the British, who thought he was pro-Russian, at the beginning of the First Anglo-Afghan War.

stipulates 'an honest, accountable, functioning government. He has not created that. There is no dispute over this. He himself is clearly acknowledging that corruption is a major problem and that it has worsened. All the signals are there as well as the perception. Afghanistan ranked 114th on transparency internationally in 2005. In 2010 it ranked 179 out of 180. Only Somalia is worse.'

Dr Ghani then joked about a local wit, a poet, who wrote: '"Oh, poor Afghanistan, even on corruption you cannot be Number One." I think that sums it up,' he says with a smile.[28]

By way of comparing Afghanistan's position in the world drug league, journalist Gretchen Peters gives figures from the UNODC (United Nations Office on Drugs and Crime) which show in 2007, for example, the global illegal drug trade was worth $400 (£250) billion a year – then more than the entire US defence budget.[29] Dr Ghani cites Afghanistan's figures as being between $460 and $600 billion over a period of eight years.[30] Illegal drugs made up 8 per cent of global trade, compared to 7.5 per cent for textiles and 5.3 per cent for motor vehicles.[31] In 2007 an estimated 12 per cent of the Afghan population 'was tied to the poppy industry' on average, with much heavier concentrations in the south and east. Opium made up between 30 and 50 per cent of Afghanistan's GDP, and it was not just the insurgents who benefited, Peters claims. 'Key allies in the CIA and US military-led effort to hunt down al Qaeda and the Taliban [warlords and their allies, for example] are themselves known to run massive drug rings,' she writes. Senior officials in the Karzai administration have been involved as well, Peters claims, and 'efforts to fight corruption have stalled badly'.[32]

In 2009, the global figure for the illegal drugs trade fell to $320 billion a year, according to the UNODC World Drug Report. In an accompanying commentary on 'Corruption in Afghanistan', published in January 2010, Antonio Mario Costa, former UNODC executive director, says of bribery, as reported by the victims: 'The problem is enormous by any standards. In the aggregate, Afghans paid out $2.5 billion in bribes over the past twelve months – that's equivalent to almost one quarter (23 per cent) of

Afghanistan's GDP. By coincidence, this is similar to the revenue [which] accrued [to] the opium trade in 2009, which we have estimated separately at $2.8 billion. In other words, and this is shocking, drugs and bribes are the two largest income generators in Afghanistan: together they amount to about half the country's (licit) GDP.'[33]

President Karzai 'raised eyebrows' when in 2007 he appointed Izzatullah Wasifi as his anti-corruption tsar. Wasifi had been convicted two decades earlier for trying to sell $2 million-worth of heroin to an undercover drug officer in Caesar's Palace, Las Vegas – an act Wasifi described as 'a youthful indiscretion'.[34] Once again, it would seem, anyone in the magic circle of family and tribal cronies is above the law.

Perhaps most troubling of all, in the light of President Karzai's notorious reluctance to take on the drug trade, Peters says, were persistent reports that his immediate family members, including his late half-brother Ahmed Wali Karzai, and other cronies were taking an active role in coordinating it, and have been posted to positions along trafficking routes around Afghanistan.[35] 'Karzai's record with counter-narcotics is even worse than his record of going after corruption,' a Western official complained to Peters.[36]

Doug Wankal, however, a former Drug Enforcement Administration agent who later ran the Counter-Narcotics Task Force at the US Embassy in Kabul, took a different view. 'Afghanistan's biggest problem isn't drugs,' he said. 'It's corruption.'[37]

They are, in fact, two sides of the same coin, Peters believes. It is not only in Afghanistan that the Taliban insurgency flourishes; it is anchored in, directed and financed by and through Pakistan. So is the drug trade.

Gretchen Peters says in her summing up in *Seeds of Terror*: 'We must stop thinking about Afghanistan's drug and insurgency problems as isolated issues and understand that this country – and the region as a whole – will remain a problem until a comprehensive, holistic strategy is adopted. The nexus of terrorists and traffickers is as much a threat to the West as it is to South and Central Asia. The campaign against it must be global in scope, reach and purpose. The ultimate goal should not be the end of the Taliban and al Qaeda, but the creation of prosperity and stability in Afghanistan and the greater region. We owe it to the citizens of Afghanistan and it would make ours safer, too.'[38]

Although Karzai, under Western pressure, has sacked the odd blatantly corrupt minister, like Mohammed Adel, the Minister of Mines and Industries – who was accused of taking a $20 million bribe to give the $3.2 billion contract to exploit the world's largest copper deposit at Ainak, in Logar Province, to a Chinese company – he has done nothing to curb, let alone stamp out, corruption involving family and cronies, including another brother, Mahmood, with interests that include banking and property development, and also said to be hugely rich.

Opinions about corruption, its extent and its importance, differ among responsible Afghans themselves.

The former head of Afghan intelligence, Amrullah Saleh, who resigned in May 2010, once told me the problem of corruption needed to be kept in perspective. 'The West cannot disassociate itself from Afghanistan by saying Afghans are corrupt, because corrupt Afghans are not the enemies of the West. The enemies of the West are the Taliban and al Qaeda, and they are not defeated yet. I don't say it [corruption] is not there, but I don't think it is the centrepiece of the crisis. I don't deny it is there.' He complained of the frustration he felt with Afghan judges: 'You may ask some of your British officers . . . Sometimes I burst out of the meetings against our own [people].' He cited the case of a suspect who was jailed without trial for three years because he was unable to pay a bribe of $60,000. 'We have those cases. I do not deny it. But I think if we entirely focus on a wrong problem – I don't say it is not a problem – forgetting or ignoring or creating a deficit of attention to the big problem, we will not be able to solve it. The big problem is the Taliban and al Qaeda and Pakistan.'[39]

In *Seeds of Terror*, however, Gretchen Peters's key message is that fighting corruption and official involvement in drug trafficking in Afghanistan is as crucial a challenge to rebuilding the country as defeating the Taliban. A central reason the Taliban insurgency is now flourishing, she says, is the failure of the Kabul regime and the international community to establish good governance in Afghanistan. Peters argues that it is not possible to treat the Taliban insurgency and the opium trade as separate issues. She also quotes executive director of the UNODC, Antonio Maria Costa, as appealing in 2006 for a radical change in NATO operations in Afghanistan 'to stop the vicious circle of drugs funding terrorists and terrorists protecting drug traffickers'. 'NATO forces should change their tactics and destroy heroin laboratories, disband opium bazaars, attack opium convoys, and bring to justice the major narco-traffickers,' Costa declared.[40]

Four years after Costa's appeal for a change of approach, in October 2010, a senior British drug official told me: 'the military are a lot more engaged in counter-narcotics operations than they were, at least down here [in Helmand]', although he admitted it was not the same everywhere else. Helmand however is the gold mine.[41]

Sherard and the French

It's a deal: you don't attack me, I don't attack you.

Afghan Defence Ministry official, Kabul, 2008

In September 2008, *Le Canard Enchaîné*, the French equivalent of *Private Eye* in Britain, leaked what purported to be a confidential briefing given by the British Ambassador, Sir Sherard Cowper-Coles, to his newly arrived French colleague, Jean-François Fitou, Deputy Ambassador to Kabul. Sir Sherard, vastly experienced in diplomatic hot-spots, having served as Ambassador to both Israel and Saudi Arabia before Kabul, was chosen as an ideal troubleshooter by Tony Blair in 2005, when he realised things were going wrong in Afghanistan. Sir Sherard brought to the daunting new job not only a shrewd political brain and an enviably fluent turn of phrase, but also an infectious *joie de vivre* which brightened up the drab social scene in Kabul. Invitations to his dinner parties were much sought after, despite the fact that he said he had difficulty finding the right chef.

As a professional diplomat he was known for his straight talking and therefore it came as no great surprise that Sir Sherard should be quoted as saying in the leaked story that 'the American strategy is destined to fail'. According to the *Canard Enchaîné* version, M. Fitou's confidential diplomatic telegram to the Quai d'Orsay and the Elysée Palace also quoted him as continuing: 'The current situation is bad, the security situation is getting worse, so is corruption, and the government has lost all trust . . . The presence of the coalition, in particular its military presence, is part of the problem, not part of its solution.' It added: 'Foreign forces are the lifeline of a regime that would rapidly collapse without them. As such, they slow down and complicate a possible emergence from the crisis.'[1]

Sir Sherard was also quoted as saying that despite public statements to the contrary, 'the insurgency, although still incapable of a military victory, has the capacity to make life more and more difficult, including in the capital'. There was 'no option, however, other than to support' the Americans in Afghanistan. 'But we must tell them that we want to be part of a winning strategy, not a losing one.'[2]

Then came a sentence which undoubtedly upset the bureaucrats in London and Washington, less perhaps in France, the French being more pragmatic, but which many seasoned observers probably agreed with. 'Within five to ten years,' Sir Sherard continued, according to the *Canard Enchaîné*, the only 'realistic' way to unite Afghanistan was for it to be 'governed by an acceptable dictator', adding that 'we should think of preparing our public opinion' about such an outcome.[3]

Le Canard had the Ambassador as being critical of both American presidential candidates, who both pledged to increase troop numbers in Afghanistan. In the short run, 'it is the American presidential candidates who must be dissuaded from getting further bogged down in Afghanistan', he is quoted as saying.[4]

British officials responded that the comments attributed to the Ambassador had been distorted and did not reflect official British policy, adding sententiously: 'It's not for us to comment on something that is presented as extracts from a French diplomatic telegram, but the views it quotes are not in any way an accurate representation of the government's approach,' said a Foreign Office spokeswoman. She confirmed, however, that the two men did have a meeting, but said that the British Ambassador's comments were taken out of context. As for M. Fitou, a senior French official said, he was a 'responsible and precise diplomat who would be unlikely to misreport a conversation'. He added 'it was a "diplomatic disaster" that could put French soldiers at more risk'.[5]

It later emerged that M. Fitou had indeed had a meeting with a British diplomat, but not Sir Sherard. He had had lunch with Sir Sherard's deputy the day before sending the telegram. Sir Sherard commented privately and in public – for example on the BBC Radio 4 *Today* programme on 16 November 2010 – that he had never said, let alone believed, that Afghanistan needed an acceptable dictator, on the grounds that there was nothing to dictate with.[6] Even if the *Canard*'s report was inaccurate, there is little doubt that Sir Sherard was deeply sceptical of America's policy in Afghanistan, especially the emphasis on military victory at the expense of diplomatic engagement. That may have been true in 2008, but the Americans would certainly contest its validity in 2011.

Only a month before, something much more disturbing had made the headlines in the French media. A recently arrived unit of French Marine paratroopers was ambushed while on patrol near their base at Sarobi, halfway between Kabul and Jalalabad, in an area they had just taken over from the Italians and which seemed perfectly peaceful. It was clearly a set-up. The Taliban knew they were coming and about a hundred fighters were waiting in a prepared ambush as the French climbed up the pass. Just before they reached the top, the insurgents opened fire. The battle lasted all day and most of the night and by next morning the French had lost ten killed and twenty-one wounded. Despite being accompanied by a detachment of the Afghan National Army, the Marines were outgunned and pinned down. It was the worst loss of life the French had suffered since the bombing of a French barracks in Beirut in 1983, in which fifty-eight French paras were killed. It brought the total number of French servicemen killed in Afghanistan by then to twenty-four (compared to 116 British and 574 Americans) since 9/11.

'In its struggle against terrorism, France has just been hit hard,' President Sarkozy said, before flying out to Afghanistan to pay his personal respects to the dead.

Grief turned to rage a few days later when it emerged that the Italians, from whom the French had taken over, had been bribing the Taliban not to attack them. Regular payments were apparently being made by Italian intelligence agents, said to be a common Italian practice in other parts of Afghanistan. But in Sarobi the Italians apparently neglected to tell the French of the arrangement when they handed over. However it was not only the Italians who paid off the Taliban, one anonymous Afghan official disclosed. Lots of NATO contingents did it, he claimed, giving the Canadians in Kandahar as one example. In fact, another source said, the only NATO troops who did not buy off the Taliban were the Americans and the British, and in this case obviously, the French.[7] The Italian government described British press reports about Italian bribery as 'totally baseless' and said it had 'never authorised any kind of money payment to members of the Taliban insurrection in Afghanistan'.[8] But a senior Afghan intelligence official suggested otherwise. 'I certainly can confirm that we were aware that the Italian forces were paying the opposition in Sarobi not to attack them,' he said. 'We have reports of similar deals in Herat Province by Italian troops based there under the NATO umbrella.'

'It's a deal: you don't attack me, I don't attack you,' the official said, adding that the practice was passed on from one foreign contingent to another and it was likely that senior commanders were 'either involved or turned a blind eye to it'.[9]

Three years later, on 12 August 2011, *The Times* reported that confidential telegrams from the American Embassy in Rome to Washington, published by the Italian magazine *l'Espresso*, revealed that President Bush had intervened with the Italian Prime Minister, Silvio Berlusconi, in May 2008, asking him to ensure the practice was stopped. Pressed, Mr Berlusconi 'agreed this should be stopped', but nothing seems to have been done and just before he paid an official visit to Washington later in 2008 the American Ambassador in Rome wrote that Italian support in Afghanistan had been 'undermined by Italy's growing reputation for avoiding combat and paying ransom money and protection money . . .'

The Ambassador warned that if true, 'Italian actions are endangering Allied troops'. *L'Espresso* also quoted its own intelligence sources for 'credible evidence' that 23 million Euros (£20 million) were made available to Mr Berlusconi's office for 'security and information activities for the Prime Minister' in 2004–2006, the first two years of the NATO campaign in Afghanistan.

Only a week after the leak of Sir Sherard's alleged criticisms of American military policy by *Le Canard Enchaîné*, the British commander in Afghanistan, Brigadier Mark Carleton-Smith, another decorated ex-SAS commander, told the *Daily Telegraph* in an interview published on 8 September 2008 that the war against the Taliban was unwinnable. It was the first time it had been said so dramatically in public. Under the headline 'War in Afghanistan cannot be won, British commander . . . warns', he went on to say the British public should not expect 'a decisive military victory', adding that he believed groups of insurgents would still be at large after British, American and other NATO troops pulled out. The previous

June he had claimed British forces had reached a 'tipping point' against a weakened Taliban whose leadership had been 'decapitated' by the killing of six important commanders. But he now believed it was 'time to lower expectations and focus on reducing the conflict' to a level which could be managed by the Afghan army. 'Talking to the Taliban could be an important part of that process,' he said.

On 6 October, just before he left Afghanistan, the Brigadier was quoted by *The Times* as saying his troops had 'taken the sting out of the Taliban' during 2008, but at a heavy cost. His brigade suffered 32 killed and 170 injured during its six-month tour of duty. Two PARA alone lost 11 soldiers, most of them killed by roadside bombs or other explosive devices.

He was also quoted by *The Times* as saying that in the areas where the government had no control, the Afghan population was 'vulnerable to a shifting coalition of mafia, mad mullahs and marauding militias'. In other areas, however, progress was being made and children were going back to school. 'We are trying to deliver sufficient security for a degree of normalisation,' he said.

But it was in an interview with Alastair Leithead of the BBC for *Panorama*, broadcast on 3 November 2008, that he summed up best, in his own opinion, why the Helmand war was not winnable. They were in Garmsir, south of Lashkar Gah, the capital of Helmand, which Brigadier Carleton-Smith described as having been 'a battlefield', but where they had established a 'degree of security round the district centre', leading to a 'very significant economic regeneration'. Despite the local population being still cautious, he thought they were 'beginning to sense a degree of optimism for the future'.

Garmsir is close to the Pakistan border, making it easy for Taliban fighters to infiltrate. 'It means that I am operating against an open flank,' the Brigadier said. 'From the Taliban perspective clearly they have a tactical and military advantage because it means that they are able to recruit, train, equip and importantly regenerate and regulate their losses with relative impunity . . . which is why there is no exclusively military solution to the nature of the insurgency in Afghanistan – armies have never governed Afghanistan.'

On the subject of talking to the Taliban, which the Americans were still resisting at that stage, he said there were 'elements of the Taliban with whom there will be no negotiation . . . [or as General Sir Graeme Lamb put it two years later, there were 'reconcilables' and 'irreconcilables'.] There will be elements of the Taliban who – for various reasons of disenchantment and disenfranchisement in Helmand, where for the last thirty years government has been a very unfamiliar thing and good government almost an oxymoron – that actually there is a political accommodation and settlement to be had.'

'I think when set against the wider context of what we are trying to achieve in Afghanistan of leaving Afghanistan for the Afghans, in a much more stable secure country and one that no longer represents a strategic threat to the United Kingdom; I think that probably has been a price that is worth paying.'

Looking back two years later, Brigadier Carleton-Smith recalled that what he was saying then was that there was 'no military solution in isolation without that overarching political settlement . . . The idea that . . . the Taliban represented a military force that could be defeated conventionally in the field was flawed – particularly when it was an organisation that enjoyed safe havens across the border in Pakistan in which they could recruit, retrain, re-equip and regenerate with near impunity . . .'[10]

British strategy, he continued, was to isolate the centres of population from Taliban interference, 'to marginalise the Taliban's influence' and to give the local tribal elders the tools with which to speak to their people, to establish the conditions for 'rudimentary public administration', to hold the ring while the capability of the Afghan security forces was growing – the Army in his day but now increasingly the police – to 'reduce the Taliban tactical military threat to a level that the Afghan security forces could deal with. I think that is what we are seeing happening today,' he concluded.

Like his predecessors, Ed Butler and General Sir David Richards, Brigadier Carleton-Smith understood that a political settlement was the only practical solution in Afghanistan.

Brigadier Carleton-Smith was not the first British Commander in Helmand to run up against the problem of Taliban safe havens and to point out that they were crucial to the outcome of the war – a point senior Americans like Admiral Mike Mullen and Ambassador Tomsen have only recently insisted in public Pakistan finally does something about.

The Girl Who Ran Away from Her Husband, 2010

How can we reconcile with them [the Taliban]?
>   'Aisha' quoted in *Time* magazine, July 2010

In the summer of 2010, *Time* magazine shocked its readers by printing a heartbreaking picture on its cover of eighteen-year-old Aisha, once a pretty young Pushtun woman, now horribly disfigured by having had her ears and nose cut off by her own husband for running away from him. The headline on *Time*'s cover, opposite the picture of Aisha's ravaged face, was: 'What Happens If We Leave Afghanistan'. It was a statement, not a question.

The story begins when Aisha, only twelve, and her younger sister were given away to another family under a tribal custom for settling disputes, known as *baad*. Aisha's uncle had killed a member of this family and 'to settle the blood debt her father gave the two girls to the victim's family'.[1] When she was fourteen, the official age of puberty, Aisha was married to a young member of the aggrieved family. As a young Talib,* the husband was away most of the time, so Aisha and her sister were housed with the in-laws' livestock (often stabled on the ground floor of a farmhouse) and frequently beaten, she is reported as saying, as punishment for their uncle's crime.

In desperation, Aisha decided to run away. But her husband tracked her down in Kandahar and took her back to Uruzgan, their home province where Mullah Omar, the Taliban leader, was brought up. Late one night, according to *Time*, the Taliban came for her and 'dragged her to a mountain clearing near her village . . . Shivering in the cold air and blinded by

---

* Meaning literally 'student', but by extension 'insurgent'.

the flashlights trained on her by her husband's family, she faced her spouse and accuser.' The frightened girl pleaded that her in-laws had treated her like a slave and beaten her and if she had not run away she would have died. 'Her judge, a local Taliban commander, was unmoved.' Later he would tell Aisha's uncle that she had to be made an example of to stop other girls in the village doing the same thing.

'The commander gave his verdict and men moved in to deliver the punishment. Aisha's brother-in-law held her down, while her husband pulled out a knife. First he sliced off her ears. Then he started on her nose. Aisha passed out from the pain but awoke soon after, choking on her own blood. The men had left her on the mountainside to die.'[2]

In Pushtun culture, a husband who has been shamed by his wife is said to have lost his nose. From the husband's point of view, he would have been punishing Aisha in kind. American aid workers took her, traumatised by her ordeal, to the 'Women for Afghan Women' shelter in Kabul, and arranged for her to be seen by a psychologist. Gradually she began to recover, learning to do handicrafts, but showing little interest in her studies. *Time* describes her telling her story 'in a monotone, her eyes flat and distant, only becoming animated at talk of some kind of political accommodation with the Taliban. "They are the people that did this to me," she says, touching the jagged bridge of scarred flesh and bone that frames the gaping hole in an otherwise beautiful face. "How can we reconcile with them?"'*

This is the much-debated question that faces Afghanistan as the committee set up by President Karzai after the Peace Jirga (consultative grand council) in Kabul in June 2010 reviews the cases of jailed Taliban with a view to charging or releasing them. Most Afghans, especially in Kabul and the north, having experienced the brutalities and privations of Taliban rule between 1996 and 2001, when they were driven out by American bombing and Northern Alliance ground troops, have no desire to see them back in power. The conditions for the 'reintegration' of rank-and-file Taliban and the 'reconciliation' of higher-ups are tightly enough drawn, as Hillary Clinton, the American Secretary of State, made clear in Kabul on 20 July 2010. 'Any

---

* Aisha later went to America for reconstructive surgery.

reconciliation process,' she said, 'must require that anyone who wishes to rejoin society and the political system must lay down their weapons and end violence, renounce al Qaeda and be committed to the constitution and laws of Afghanistan which guarantee the rights of women.'[3]

This would seem to be watertight, but *Time* points out that Article 3 of the constitution, for example, states that no law may contravene the principle of Sharia law, although 'what constitutes Sharia [law] has never been defined . . .'

This may be true of the Afghan constitution, but the basic precepts of Sharia law are well known to the majority of Muslims, above all to Muslim judges, lawyers and politicians. The most controversial are for a group of *haram* offences, which carry severe punishments. These include pre-marital sexual intercourse, sex by divorced persons, extra-marital sex, adultery, false accusation of unlawful intercourse, drinking alcohol, theft, and highway robbery. *Haram* sexual offences can carry a sentence of stoning to death or severe flogging, and theft is punishable by amputation. In the autumn of 2010, a young couple – the young man married, the girl, Sediqa, nineteen and single – were sentenced to be stoned to death for adultery in a village in Kunduz, northern Afghanistan. Sediqa was said to have run away with the young man after her father sold her in marriage to an older man, without telling her. She was finally shot to put her out of her agony. Local villagers, many of whom were involved, say they were forced to take part in the stoning by the Taliban.

The stoning and Sediqa's death were filmed by mobile phone and widely circulated on the internet. The Provincial Governor called for the culprits to be brought to trial, and the publicity put President Karzai under pressure to take action. But so far only one arrest has been made and Afghan human rights campaigners are sceptical that any trial will take place.

Liberal opinion in Afghanistan was taken aback when in March 2009, President Karzai signed a new Shia Family Law, which women's groups believed would essentially legalise rape. Specifically, the measure negated the need for sexual consent between married couples, tacitly approved child marriage and restricted a woman's right to leave the home unaccompanied by a male relative. Shinkai Karokhail, a woman MP who campaigned against the legislation, called it 'one of the worst bills passed by the parliament this century'.⁴ The most controversial parts of the law dealt explicitly with sexual relations. Article 132 requires women to obey their husband's sexual demands and stipulates that a man can expect to have sex with his wife at least 'once every four nights' when travelling, unless they are ill. The law also gives men preferential inheritance rights, easier access to divorce, and priority in court. A report by the United Nations Development Fund for Women, UNIFEM, warned: 'Article 132 legalises the rape of a wife by her husband.' Critics accused President Karzai of an election ploy, charging that he rushed the bill through parliament in a bid to appease Islamic fundamentalists ahead of elections in August 2009.

The man behind the Shia Family Law bill, Sheikh, or Ayatollah, Asef Mohseni, was described as 'an ambitious maverick who has his fingers in many pies, is venerated by his supporters and deeply reviled by his opponents'. In some ways he symbolises the complex ethnic mix of Afghanistan, being a Shia with strong links to Iran, a *qizilbash* (originally Persian-speaking Shia mercenaries of Turkish origin), born in Kandahar and a Pushtun speaker. Asef Mohseni is the owner of Tamadon (Civilisation) TV, a privately owned television station with a 'visual outlook and religious content remarkably similar to Iranian state-run television channels'.⁵ Mohseni, it is said, has the potential to act as a unifying figure, bringing together the Shias and the Sunnis, the Pushtuns and the Hazaras. This, in turn, may explain why President Hamid Karzai didn't appear to hesitate to sign the law, presumably to secure Mohseni's support in the (then) upcoming presidential elections. According to Zareen Taj, a Hazara human rights campaigner who lives in the United States, Mohseni 'has a dark past history of human rights violations' and 'pushed this law to please extremists and to move his political agenda forward'. She claims that 'One of the results of this law will be an increasing hostility towards the Hazara community in general and Hazara women in particular.'⁶

Despite a general outcry, Karzai insisted on proceeding with the law. Sixteen months later, in August 2010, he guaranteed that any agreement with the Taliban would not be made at the expense of women's rights. But one former senior official says Karzai will be unable to extract satisfactory terms from the Taliban because he is negotiating from a position of such weakness that he will not be taken seriously.[7] Unlike Northern Ireland where, after a long and bitter struggle, the IRA finally agreed to peace talks, believing they could achieve more through the political process than by terrorism, the reverse is true in Afghanistan. The Taliban read all the signs as meaning the Americans – and the rest of NATO – are preparing to withdraw from Afghanistan and that they have only to wait to achieve victory. They are convinced time is on their side and President Obama's much-publicised statement that he would announce the start of the withdrawal of American combat troops from Afghanistan in July 2011 simply confirmed their view. Karzai, however, who was reported to have lost all faith in his Western allies, meaning America and Britain, was said to be pinning his hopes on his talks with the Taliban.[*][8]

The loss of confidence was mutual. A leaked diplomatic telegram of 6 November 2009, from Karl Eikenberry, the American Ambassador in Kabul, to Secretary of State Hillary Clinton, opposing General Stanley McChrystal's request for 40,000 more troops, was highly critical of Hamid Karzai. 'President Karzai is not an adequate strategic partner,' the Ambassador stated. 'The proposed counter-insurgency strategy assumed an Afghan political leadership that was both able to take responsibility and to exert sovereignty in the furtherance of their goal – a secure, peaceful, minimally self-sufficient Afghanistan hardened against transnational terrorist groups. Yet Hamid Karzai continued to shun responsibility for any sovereign burden, whether defence, governance or development. He and much of his circle did not want the US to leave and were only too happy to see them invest further,' Eikenberry wrote. 'They assume we covet their territory for a never-ending "War on Terror" and for military bases to use against surrounding powers,' he added. 'Beyond Karzai himself, there is no political ruling class that provides an overarching national identity that transcends local affiliations and provides reliable partnership.'[9]

In a second telegram, dated 9 November, he expressed new concerns, stating that in a Public Broadcasting Service interview on 7 November,

---

* This was before the assassination of former President Rabbani, appointed head of the High Peace Council for negotiations with the Taliban. He was killed by a suicide bomber trained by Pakistani Intelligence, the ISI.

Karzai sounded bizarrely cautionary notes about his willingness to address governance and corruption. This tracked with his 'record of inaction or grudging compliance in this area'.[10]

The telegrams – one four pages, the other three – also represent, according to the *New York Times*, a detailed rebuttal of the counter-insurgency strategy advocated by McChrystal, then the top American and NATO commander in Afghanistan, who argued that a rapid infusion of fresh troops was essential to avoid failure against the Taliban. The telegrams showed, the *New York Times* said, that Eikenberry repeatedly cautioned that deploying sizeable American reinforcements would result in 'astronomical costs' – tens of billions of dollars – and would 'only deepen the dependence of the Afghan government on the United States. Sending additional forces would delay the day the Afghans will take over, and make it difficult, if not impossible, to bring their people home on a reasonable timetable,' he wrote on 6 November. An increased US and foreign role in security and governance would increase Afghan dependence, at least in the short-term, he argued.

Later the Ambassador, without explaining why he had changed his mind, said his concerns had been dealt with, and that he supported the McChrystal plan. But it was not clear what might have changed about his assessment of President Karzai as a reliable partner, the *New York Times* said, adding that 'the strong language of the cables might increase tensions between the Ambassador and the Karzai government, especially as world leaders were meeting in London on Thursday to discuss a much-debated Afghan plan to reintegrate the Taliban. It also coincided with a strong effort by the administration to mend ties with Mr Karzai.'[11]

Western observers in Kabul say President Karzai, as head of an independent, sovereign country, is tired of being pilloried, as he sees it, in the American media and when under pressure is liable to let his tongue run away with him. After several outbursts, on 7 April 2010 *The Times* of London put it like this: 'The Americans are furious, his own supporters are incredulous and opposition politicians think that he is mad. In three successive outbursts he blamed foreigners for the election fraud of 2009, accused Western troops of meddling in his country's internal affairs and even threatened to join the Taliban.'

According to *The Times* article, the next day Karzai suffered 'two key blows' as a Taliban spokesman ridiculed his offer and, worse, the White House seemed ready to give him the diplomatic cold shoulder. Speaking of the Afghan leader's 'planned visit to Washington on 12 May 2010, Robert Gibbs, President Obama's official spokesman, said that the visit was still on, but added: "We certainly would evaluate whatever . . . further remarks President Karzai makes, as to whether it is constructive to have that meeting." Scoffing at the idea that the Afghan leader might join the insurgents, Zabiullah Mujahid, the Taliban spokesman, told *The Times*: "It's just a game he is playing. He is trying to show people he is not under the control of the Americans but it's completely false . . . If he really wants to join the Taliban, first he should face justice. He should face justice for bringing foreign troops to Afghanistan. He should face justice for all the crime which has happened during his rule in Afghanistan, and for the corruption and for what is going on now. Then we'll decide whether we will join with him or not."[12]

The Times reported in the same article that it was at a closed meeting of Afghan parliamentarians in Kandahar on Saturday 3 April 2010 that the 'increasingly eccentric President – who is still smarting from a failed attempt to change the election law – threatened to join the Taliban'. Karzai was quoted as having said that the Taliban could be seen as a legitimate resistance movement, telling MPs: 'If I come under foreign pressure, I might join the Taliban.' The paper noted that Karzai's remarks were made 'after the Afghan parliament had voted down a presidential decree' which 'in effect would have neutered Afghanistan's independent election watchdog. "It was against the constitution",[13] the paper quoted an MP as saying.

At the same meeting 'one parliamentarian said that President Karzai claimed there was "a fine line between resistance and revolt. If I don't get this decree passed, this revolt will turn into a resistance and I will join it."[14] Even President Karzai's supporters, the paper continued, 'were worried that he might have gone too far. MPs who usually back him refused to speak publicly. One said anonymously: "We can't stand by and allow one person to ruin our relationship with the world." White House officials were quick to point to America's sacrifice in "blood and treasure" in the hostile terrain of Afghanistan. Haroun Mir, director of Afghanistan's Centre for Research and Policy Studies, said: "Without the foreign troops, he wouldn't last one minute here.'"[15]

Few Afghan women will be inclined to accept Karzai's approaches to the Taliban as reassuring. The stoning of women accused of adultery, the public executions in the Kabul stadium, the cutting off of hands and other brutalities are too fresh in people's minds. The closing of girls' schools and university faculties, and, equally unpopular, forbidding women to go out to work even if they were their family's sole breadwinners is too recent to be forgotten, or forgiven. The northern minorities – the Tajiks, Uzbeks, Hazaras and the rest – will not accept a settlement which puts the Taliban back in power, in any significant manner. Karzai, with the presidential gravy train travelling at full speed, seems to be impervious to criticism, apparently believing he can talk the Taliban into a deal acceptable at least to him and the Pushtun south. Again, this may have been true then, but Rabbani's assassination seems to have brought about a radical change in Karzai's thinking.

While diplomats, statesmen and even the generals accept that the long-running war will only be brought to an end by a political solution, the Americans have seemed reluctant to talk to the Taliban in the past, although as I write, in 2011, there are signs of dramatic changes. President Obama is reliably reported to be committed to negotiations for a peace settlement and American negotiators are said to be talking to senior Taliban officials.[16]

At the end of the Vietnam War, Henry Kissinger's top-secret talks with the North Vietnamese in Paris, despite being conducted from a position of relative weakness – given that the Americans had pulled out virtually all their troops by then, leaving the South Vietnamese to take on the might of the Communist North virtually single-handed, apart from airpower – finally brokered a peace settlement. It was the best he could do but it left the Communist North in charge of the whole country. Ultimately, some sort of settlement with the Taliban will have to be found, but people like Amrullah Saleh and Dr Abdullah, the former presidential candidate who forced Karzai into a run-off in 2009, will not accept another quasi-Taliban government in Kabul – nor will the Americans or the British.

In August 2010, Karzai suddenly fired another broadside, announcing the closure of all private security companies in Afghanistan by the end of the year. Although he had let off a warning shot in November 2009, saying all private security firms would be closed down within two years, he accelerated the process by cutting the timescale in half.

Most companies were taken by surprise. The US State Department spokesman, Philip Crowley, was polite but disbelieving: 'As we stand here, it's hard to envision where the Afghan government can assume all of the . . . security responsibility in Afghanistan four months from now.'[17] Nobody said it was a bad idea, but nobody thought it was realistic either. The facts speak for themselves: nearly 30,000 armed men, mostly Afghans, are currently employed by more than fifty registered private security firms. In Kandahar and other parts of the insurgency-ridden south, there are said to be also scores of unregistered firms. Some of the security companies, it is said, are little more than locally engaged mercenaries 'running shakedowns' at checkpoints, while others provide sophisticated protection crucial to diplomats and senior officials of the UN and other international agencies. One of the most costly – and therefore lucrative – aspects of fighting the insurgency is the protection of the supply convoys carrying fuel, water, ammunition and food from Karachi, Pakistan's largest city and port on the Indian Ocean, across Sind, Punjab and the North-West Frontier (now called Khyber Pakhtunkhwa), over the Khyber Pass and into Afghanistan. In the second half of 2010, following a border incident in which an American helicopter fired on and killed three Pakistani soldiers, the Pakistan authorities closed the border and appeared to turn their backs while militants killed the drivers and set fire to more than a hundred petrol tankers waiting to cross into Afghanistan. After several weeks of mayhem, and profuse apologies by the Americans, the border was reopened.

Ironically, it is only when they reach Afghanistan that the convoys can count on safe passage. Each stretch of the two main roads, from the border at Spin Boldak to Kandahar in the west, and from the Khyber to Jalalabad and Kabul in the east, is controlled by the Taliban, or Taliban-associated gangs. They control all traffic on their patch, levying high tolls on every vehicle which goes through their checkpoints. Refusal to pay is met by confiscation or destruction of the vehicle and cargo, or worse. At the top of the pile will be the American contractor, probably some mammoth organisation which has already made a fortune out of its activities in Iraq, with offices in Washington and which has been awarded the contract by USAID. They take their large cut and subcontract to a Pakistani company for the first part of the journey and then to an Afghan contractor, controlled no doubt by one of the Afghan mafias, for the final part of the journey, through Afghanistan. To guarantee delivery, large sums of protection money have to be paid to the Taliban – as Britain used to pay the Khyber tribes for safe conduct of their armies in the nineteenth century. Indirectly, therefore, the Americans are helping to fund the Taliban insurgency, which, through its suicide bombers, ambushes and IEDs, is killing NATO troops on a daily basis.

Now President Karzai was threatening to close down all private security companies, good and bad, by the end of the year. He referred to them as 'thieves by day and terrorists by night', yet another of his now frequent off-the-cuff, anti-Western remarks. That may well cause more gnashing of teeth in Washington, but, more importantly, the disbanding of the private security companies may simply increase the influence of the Taliban.

Outside the corrupt magic circle of Kabul – its suburbs choked with flamboyant millionaires' concrete palaces, each more vulgar than the last, built cheek-by-jowl in what might be called Kabul Kitsch Baroque – poverty abounds. Despite the delivery of $35 billion in aid during the past eight years, more than a third of Afghans (9 million) live in 'absolute poverty' and about the same number are only slightly above the poverty line, according to a report by the UN's Geneva-based Office of the High Commissioner for Human Rights (OHCHR). It blames corruption in Afghanistan, and the failure of the international community for ignoring the basic needs of the people.

Another UN agency, the United Nations Development Programme (UNDP), also underlined Afghanistan's desperate condition, designating it as the poorest country in the world, coming bottom (135th of 135 countries) in its 2009 Human Poverty Index and either bottom or near bottom in categories such as 'life expectancy' and 'literacy'. The UNDP report drew a parallel between 'abuse of power' and poverty. 'Abuse of power is a key driver of poverty,' the report stated. 'Vested interests frequently shape the public agenda.'

The twenty-six-page report, however, also criticised the international community for placing too much emphasis on security and too little on long-term development, a remark that NGOs may find gratuitous and uninformed. Many NGOs working in Afghanistan faced increased security risks in 2010. A party of eight foreign eye specialists and their assistants – six Americans, one Briton, one German and two Afghans – were murdered in Badakhshan in August, and a young Scots aid worker, Dr Linda Norgrove, kidnapped in Kunar, was killed in a failed rescue attempt by American Special Forces in the Korengal Valley in October. Other statistics cited in the report make disturbing reading. More than eight years after the Americans and their allies ousted the Taliban, Afghanistan had the world's second worst maternal mortality rate and the third worst child mortality rate. 'Only 23 per cent of the population have access to safe drinking water, and only 24 per cent of the population above the age of fifteen can read and write, with much lower literacy rates among women and nomadic populations,' it said.

A spokesman for the UN Human Rights Office said the world was failing to address these problems despite pledging a new beginning for the country at the Bonn Conference in 2001. Perhaps the most shocking conclusion was that for many Afghans, the only way to survive was to take up arms and perpetuate the 'vicious circle' of war and poverty that has plagued the country for decades.

'The government is often unable to deliver basic services, such as security, food, or shelter,' the report said. 'Widespread corruption further limits access to services for a large proportion of the population,' it found, accusing Afghan officials of advancing their own interests at the expense of the general population. It warned that 'a growing number of Afghans are increasingly disillusioned and dispirited' about prospects for a better future. While conflict with Taliban and al Qaeda insurgents is a factor in the nation's growing poverty, foreign aid was not being properly distributed even in areas of relative stability. As little as 15 per cent of food aid reaches the poorest people, the report said. 'Food distribution is mostly in the hands of those who are in a position of power.' They look for opportunities to increase their personal wealth and this often occurs at the expense of the poor who are rarely given priority. Without using the word, the report obliquely criticises the system of warlords. 'Local governance has shifted from leadership that is accountable to communities to individuals who control military or financial resources,' it says.

Provincial Governors, the report continues, who are appointed by President Karzai, 'rarely enjoy the support of their constituents, which deepens the gap between decision-makers and the population'. In what is clearly an attack on the Karzai government, it says national leaders are perceived to exercise political power 'on the basis of personal relationships through a patronage system. The lack of political will on the part of Afghan leaders and the country's international partners to address a long history of abuse, nurtures the prevailing culture of impunity.' Many Afghans see foreign intervention as aimed at 'short-term objectives rather than challenging entrenched and abusive power structures', the report says. All in all, an indictment no less damning coming from an organisation which is itself much criticised for corruption and inefficiency.

The State of the Insurgency, 2008

*Perhaps the grossest error of all was President George Bush deciding . . .
to charge off and invade Iraq, ignoring what was happening in
Afghanistan.*

Senior Western diplomat, Kabul, 2008

•

It was a lovely summer's evening in Kabul in 2008. The cool air from the
surrounding mountains, dispersing the heat of the day, flowed along the
empty streets and into the quiet gardens of the city like some magical river,
making a pool of silence as the dusk descended. Although by daylight
Kabul is a city under siege, battered and broken by thirty years of Russian
war and occupation, civil war, Taliban misrule and now a growing insurgency, at night it is a different place.

In 2008 it was still a pleasure to be abroad in this ancient royal city, with
its memories of British as well as Afghan rule, where Babur, the first and
most civilised of the Moghul emperors, was happiest. Despite his ancestry
– he was descended from Tamerlane on his father's side and from Genghis
Khan on his mother's – he was a man of taste and learning, steeped in
Persian art and literature and that other great passion of the Moghuls,
making gardens. He was remarkable in other ways too, enormously strong
and fit. He could run uphill carrying a man on each shoulder, it was said,
and always swam twice across every river he came to, including the Ganges.
His gardening masterpiece is Bagh-i-Babur – Babur's Gardens – which he
created in Kabul to embellish his marble tomb. On it is inscribed in
Persian: 'If there is a paradise on earth, it is this, it is this, it is this.'

The vicious fighting of the civil war in the 1990s all but destroyed
Babur's Gardens and tomb, the odd stray bullet chipping its marble. It
was more or less on the front line between the warring factions and I

remember driving past it during a lull in the fighting and worrying about getting across before the shooting started again. Like many people in Kabul, I wondered if the roses would ever bloom there once more. But thanks to the dedication of a small band of enthusiasts and craftsmen, and to the generosity of the Aga Khan, it has been lovingly restored and sometimes, when there's enough water, across the sloping lawns and between the rose beds, a crystal-clear stream cascades over marble slabs in the classic Moghul style.

· For all the splendours of Delhi, which Babur conquered in 1526, he always pined for Kabul, 6,000 feet up in the rarefied air of the Hindu Kush, especially in the heat of summer. 'The climate is extremely delight-ful,' he wrote, 'and there is no such place in the known world.' His verdict is still valid today, although the second half of the sentence might now be true in a way he did not originally intend. His gardens are an oasis in the desert of razor wire and concrete blast walls, pillboxes, checkpoints and armed guards which is present-day Kabul.

I wonder what Babur, in his wisdom, garnered over many years, from many wars, defeats and victories, would make of the present situation, especially if he had heard it described in detail by a host of clever twenty-first-century men and women: soldiers, diplomats, historians, businessmen and women and architects, American, British and Afghan, as I had in the past few weeks, sometimes with shocking frankness.

The bare bones of it were most starkly exposed by what was happening in Helmand in the south, where 8,000 British soldiers were engaged in some of the most vicious fighting the British Army had experienced since the battle of the Imjin River in Korea in 1951, certainly far fiercer than anything the British encountered in Aden, Malaya, Kenya or Cyprus, and certainly much worse than Northern Ireland. To find a closer parallel one is tempted to go back to the disaster at Maiwand in 1880 and even further back, to the last stand of the British at Gandamak in 1842, where they fell one by one in the bloodied snow. As one senior Western diplo-mat put it, 'It's a very serious fight we're engaged in.' So why and how had we arrived at this point? His answer was because the road to hell is paved with good intentions.[1]

• In 2001, the story went, Britain was part of what was essentially an

American 'imperial expedition' to avenge what happened on 9/11, when al Qaeda terrorists using hijacked airliners as missiles destroyed the World Trade Center – the Twin Towers in New York – part of the Pentagon Building in Washington and crashing a fourth airliner in Pennsylvania, killing around 3,000 innocent people, and seek out those responsible for the atrocity. And in the aftermath of that, with the collapse of the Taliban regime, we, the Allies, sought, with the support of many well-intentioned Afghans, to establish a near-perfect Western liberal democracy. But the good intentions of the Bonn Conference foundered on the realities of Afghanistan.

One of the biggest mistakes was to believe that a lasting political settlement could be made without accommodating what the same Western diplomat describes as 'the strand of conservative religious Pushtun nationalism of which the Taliban are the expression both on the Afghan side and even more obviously on the other, Pakistan side of the Durand Line'[2] (named after the British officer, Sir Mortimer Durand, who in 1893 negotiated the border between Afghanistan and what was then British India, now Pakistan, with the Amir, Abdur Rahman).

But other mistakes were made, mistakes of implementation, and mistakes of choice about individuals. Perhaps the grossest error of all, says the diplomat, was President George Bush deciding 'while the job here had not been done, to charge off and invade Iraq, ignoring what was happening in Afghanistan'.[3] We are now living with the consequences of those mistakes, and the situation is very serious. Throughout the Pushtun belt – extending from just north of the Kabul to Jalalabad road in a great arc through the south, up to Herat in the west and even in patches like Kunduz in the north – the 'virus of insurgency is spreading and the situation deteriorating'.[4]

In 2008, things were bad but not yet catastrophic. We were not quite going over the precipice. Kabul was not surrounded and the government was not about to collapse, although three years later, as I write, that may no longer be as true as it was. In 2008 we had 50,000 coalition troops in Afghanistan and an Afghan Army of 60,000; now the figure is more than 130,000 coalition troops, mainly American, and 150,000 Afghans. And while those troops remain, and they will remain, the situation here is not going to disintegrate. But the trend is downwards.

Similarly in politics, the high hopes kindled by the Bonn Conference and its timetable for a presidential election in 2004 and parliamentary elections in 2005 gradually died out, to the despair of many Afghans. 'Talk to people in Kabul,' says the Western diplomat, 'and they are worried, very worried, from the President down to people in the streets who can no longer leave the city for picnics at the weekend, let alone visit their families north of the Salang tunnel, or anywhere to the south and east of the city – at least they don't feel safe doing so.'

So we had, they all agreed, some serious problems: an insurgency which was spreading; an insurgency which had many strands; 'not just the old guard Taliban loyal to Mullah Omar. There were the younger Taliban; the "have-a-go" Taliban; the $10-a-day Taliban; and there were the local thugs and warlords. There were all sorts of networks and groups and individuals. And what was happening was that they were reinfecting areas where the Afghan government was not present in any meaningful way. And the saddest thing was seeing the way in which the human talent in this country was living in Harrow or Wealdstone, or Baltimore or California, or in north-west Germany. But no longer here.'[5] An entire generation of talent had left; because of the *jihad*; because of the fighting once Kabul fell to the *mujahideen* in 1992; and again once the Taliban took Kabul in 1996. 'Many of them returned in the early years after 2001, but too many of them have left again.'

It was true, the informant said, that there were still many patriots in Afghanistan. Many individuals of talent and commitment who had stuck it out. 'Men who graduated from the military academy in '78 or '79 and then went on to serve under the Communists, to serve in one capacity or another during the fighting against the *mujahideen* and then, extraordinarily, under the Taliban.'[6] He cited the example of a patriotic, Soviet-trained Afghan officer who rose to an important position in the Afghan air force under the Taliban. He said he was the only man in the Defence Ministry who had a desk, because the Taliban believed that desks were an infidel creation and that there was something vaguely blasphemous about having a desk. So he would sit in his office while these mullahs consulted him about the way an air force should be run. But he also described how he was at one of the great shuras in Kandahar in 2001 when the Taliban decided whether they would or would not accede to the demands of the Americans and the United Nations 'to cough up Osama bin Laden and al Qaeda'.[7] The Afghan officer claimed that there had been a very vigorous debate and he believed that in time the younger moderates would have prevailed, and it might have been possible to reach a settlement before the West invaded Afghanistan.

Every Afghan I spoke to agreed that the American decision in 2002 to switch almost its entire war effort from Afghanistan to Iraq had had disastrous consequences for Afghanistan. The British also realised that it had serious consequences for them, although in a different way. To fight two wars, Iraq and Afghanistan, simultaneously, led to the serious overstretch of Britain's relatively small and weak army and economy. And when, in 2006, Prime Minister Tony Blair agreed to help out the Americans who wanted to transfer more troops to Iraq, by sending 16 Air Assault Brigade to Helmand Province, they found themselves as we have seen short of reliable intelligence on Taliban activity because American satellite surveillance of the south had been diverted to Iraq.[8] But even more serious were the defence cuts ordered by the then Chancellor of the Exchequer, Gordon Brown, who imposed a complete guillotine of £1 billion on defence spending in September 2003, only six months after the invasion of Iraq. This was revealed in a letter from Brown to Blair, leaked to *The Times*. As a result, 16 Air Assault Brigade found themselves seriously under-resourced, particularly with regard to helicopters. Shortage of helicopters meant, among other things, more deaths and casualties from roadside bombs.

Despite the overstretch, and thanks to the huge budget the Labour government allocated to foreign aid, dispensed via the much-criticised Department for International Development (DFID), Britain was still the second largest bilateral donor to Afghanistan, handing out in 2008 about £120 million pounds a year from a total spend of about £1.6 billion of taxpayers' money, most of which went to support the military effort in the south. 'Despite the many mistakes we made,' one senior official said, 'the policy that we are pursuing now is in my view the only sane policy, which is a policy of Afghanisation, of putting the Afghans – Afghan security forces, Afghan civil servants, Afghan ministers, front and centre, as far and as fast as possible. It's a policy of civilianising the effort, of putting it under civilian direction. And it's a policy of trying to get what is a dysfunctional international effort here into a more coherent shape.'⁹

While a lot of people agreed that this was the only policy that would work in the long term, they also knew there were a number of obstacles. As one observer explained: 'The first difficulty is the lack of capacity in the Afghan government. Sixty per cent of the police officers in Helmand are said to be addicted to heroin or opium. Half the representatives of the nine ministries in Helmand can neither read nor write. There are 140,000 teachers on the books of the Education Ministry · in Afghanistan, but the Education Minister [until 2008], Hanif Atmar, reckoned that between 20,000 and 30,000 of those teachers could neither read nor write.'¹⁰

The Spanish diplomat Francesc Vendrell, Special Representative for Afghanistan for the UN and EU in Kabul for many years, said in 2005 that President Karzai had one year 'in which he could do almost anything'. He was legitimately elected in his view, and there was no parliament. The constitution provided that in that year the Cabinet would be the legislature. But Karzai missed the opportunity. He undertook virtually no reforms and that is when Vendrell and his colleagues began to question Karzai's commitment.¹¹ As a leader, he says, 'he's indecisive. He listens to the last person who comes to see him. So he can't quite make up his mind. He's also a bad manager, but he's not the only head of state who's a bad manager. The trouble with him is that he has not entrusted management to someone else . . . So he runs a chaotic presidential office and in particular he micro-manages . . . any small issue goes right up to him. He has literally no time to think strategically, to think in terms of long-term objectives, he is just constantly dealing with the latest crisis or small problems that arise.'¹²

Then there was what Vendrell described as the President's 'blindness' towards Pakistan, matched only by the West's myopia in regard to the rebirth of the Taliban. It was quite obvious that the Taliban, in late November 2001, went back home to their villages, left their weapons there and the 'big guys', Mullah Omar and his senior commanders, known later as the Quetta Shura, went across the border to the tribal areas of Pakistan. President Musharraf had vowed he was now undertaking a 180-degree change of policy. Francesc Vendrell said he thought that rather than taking Musharraf at his word, they should have tried to verify if it were true: 'A lot of us kept saying in 2002, 2003 or 2004 that the Taliban were regrouping; there was a Quetta Shura, there was [Gulbuddin] Hekmatyar [the Hisb-i-Islami warlord and former darling of the ISI], in the north . . . But Western countries weren't interested in listening. Karzai then went public, he was constantly attacking Pakistan, probably not the best idea, but probably the only way he had of letting off steam . . . So I would say it was only in 2007 that the UK and the US began to look at Pakistan and to express their concern. Until then, even when British troops had already arrived in 2006 in Helmand, everyone knew that some of the British soldiers being killed were being killed by Taliban who were either linked to Pakistan or based in Pakistan.'[13]

Another diplomat put it like this: 'One went to meetings with President Karzai and you saw him pulling the levers of power and they were not connected to anything – they came away in his hand. There was a thin crust of educated and dedicated people, but all too often below the surface there was nobody to implement the best-laid plans of the international community.'[14]

So that was one problem, the lack of capacity on the part of the Afghans. The second, the same source observed, was that leading this enterprise was a quasi-imperial power, the United States, that was not fit for purpose. 'It didn't understand what it had got itself into, it couldn't admit to itself what it was doing, it did not have the systems, the constitution, literally, the knowledge, the understanding or the resources to drive this great enterprise through in the way that it needed to be driven through. There was no one in charge of this, for example, in Washington [in 2008]. The person nominally in charge, Hillary Clinton, the Secretary of State, was also running the State Department and a great deal of the rest of American foreign policy.' There was a lieutenant general in the National Security Council, the diplomat explained, 'who had been designated by President Bush as the War Czar, but he was also dealing with Iraq, and he was only a three-star general. There were four American military command chains in Afghanistan. The CIA station in Kabul was far larger than the American Embassy, and it was not under the control of the American Ambassador.'[15]

On the other hand, he says: 'America was being incredibly generous, incredibly brave, incredibly dedicated. But it did not yet have the systems, and the application, and the coordination necessary for an enterprise as serious as this. And if you multiplied the deficiencies of the leader of this enterprise, and applied them several times to the pathetic performance of the European Union, of the United Nations, of all the other contributors, of NATO . . .'[16]

One cynical observer of the scene I spoke to said: 'If you've been to the ISAF headquarters, it looks like some sort of Club Med without the French. People striding around, happier wearing the uniform of combat than actually engaging in combat.'[17] He described a 'wonderful cameo' of General Sir David Richards, then ISAF Commander, walking past his headquarters and coming across a scene of a whole lot of Spaniards having a barbecue. 'There are many NATO contributors who do not realise that we have a war on. The UN has not stepped up to the plate; the EU has boasted about its police mission here, but the European Union police will not go out after dark, and will not go to a party unless they wear a flak jacket all evening. They are just not serious.'[18]

Then there is the question of Afghanistan's neighbours, which to give him his due, President Obama recognised from the very beginning needed to be brought into the equation. 'Afghanistan has a series of neighbours, and near neighbours,' a senior Western diplomat told me, and they 'need to be part of the solution: Pakistan, Iran above all, India, Russia, China, Saudi Arabia.' All of them could contribute one way or another to solving this problem. All of them had an interest in a stable, successful, prosperous Afghanistan. But for reasons having to do with ideology in Washington, they had not been seriously engaged. And they needed to be engaged.

'Take Iran for example. Iran had three separate policies towards Afghanistan. Its main policy was one of support, including lots of money for President Karzai. It had a separate policy, run by its Intelligence Ministry, of support to the Northern Alliance. It had a third policy, run by the Jerusalem Corps, the al-Qods Corps of the Revolutionary Guard, of supplying just enough weaponry to the Taliban across the southern desert to poke the British and the Americans in the eye, and to turn up the heat if we started doing anything really silly in or against Iran. Iran could contribute in a serious way. It was a major investor in western Afghanistan;

it was suffering far more than any other country apart from Pakistan from the export of Afghan drugs, and yet America and its allies failed seriously to engage it.'[19] A small example of how close relations between the two neighbours can be was reported widely, and somewhat embarrassingly, when President Karzai's plane was delayed at Tehran airport in August 2010, waiting for the arrival of the Iranian Ambassador to Kabul, Feda Hussein Maliki. He eventually hurried on board clutching a plastic bag stuffed full of Euro notes in packets which he handed to Karzai's chief of staff, Umar Daudzai, a former Afghan Ambassador to Iran. Karzai himself is reported to have said the Iranians often gave him money, as did the Americans, which he and his staff used for 'expenses'. The Western media described it as a palace 'slush fund' and said a lot of it went personally to Umar Daudzai, whose daily briefings to Karzai were said to be consistently anti-American and anti-British.

'So we have some problems,' the Western diplomat continued. 'But what we also have is an understanding of those problems.' Much had been achieved since 2001, he said. Millions of Afghans had access to health care; 5.5 million Afghans now had mobile phones; the economy was growing by about 12 per cent a year. All of that would be in danger if the West simply walked away. 'That would not be realistic politics; it would not be responsible politics. And no British Prime Minister was ever going to go to Washington and tell an American President that Britain was simply going to march out of Helmand.'[20]

That was the scene in 2008. Much changed from January 2009, when Barack Obama, elected forty-fourth President of the United States in November 2008, actually entered the White House and took over the reins of power. One of his first and most important policy decisions, reflecting his more decisive and much better-informed grasp of the Afghan war, was his appointment of General Stanley McChrystal as his overall commander in Afghanistan, undoubtedly on the recommendation of General David Petraeus, the head of US Central Command which includes the two war zones of Afghanistan and Iraq. General McChrystal, who was head of US Special Forces in Iraq under Petraeus, and credited with hunting down and capturing the Iraqi dictator, Saddam Hussein, called for a new strategy in Afghanistan, one that put the security of the Afghan people first, and was based on a surge of 30,000 more American troops. Ironically, when General McChrystal was dismissed by President Obama in June 2010, he was replaced in Kabul by General Petraeus, considered to be the person best qualified to bring the war to a satisfactory conclusion.

It was Petraeus, the author of modern American counter-insurgency doctrine, who masterminded the successful surge in Iraq. He struck me, when I met him in London, as looking more like a fresh-faced scout master than a hard-bitten veteran. A youthful fifty-eight, Petraeus is one of the new breed of American soldier-scholars. A fitness fanatic, he jogs daily and does umpteen press-ups (push-ups in American English) before breakfast and is at his desk almost before anyone else. He graduated top at Staff College, has a BSc from the United States Military Academy and a PhD in International Relations from Princeton. His remarkable success in Iraq led, perhaps inevitably, to suggestions that he might be a future presidential candidate, following in the footsteps of Dwight D. Eisenhower. He denies, however, any political ambitions.

In his comprehensive review of the war and request for more troops after he took command in Afghanistan in June 2009, General McChrystal wrote that if substantially more troops and resources were not committed to the Afghan theatre, the war against the Taliban might be irrevocably lost. It was a dire forecast. But first, he argued, the strategy must be radically changed. 'Our strategy,' he wrote, 'cannot be focused on seizing terrain or destroying insurgent forces; our objective must be the population. In the struggle to gain the support of the people, every action we take must enable this effort . . . Preoccupied with protection of our own forces, we have operated in a manner that distances us – physically and psychologically – from the people we seek to protect. In addition we run the risk of strategic defeat by pursuing tactical wins that cause civilian casualties or unnecessary collateral damage. The insurgents cannot defeat us militarily; but we can defeat ourselves.'[21]

This emphasis on reducing civilian casualties became one of the hallmarks of the McChrystal strategy. He was determined to tighten the rules on the use of air strikes to a point that the seemingly inevitable 'own goals' would be virtually eliminated. Civilian casualties, month after month, year after year, nearly always involving women and children, have done more to turn the ordinary Afghan against Western forces than almost anything else. Each year, since 2001, the toll has grown, beginning in December 2001 with the American air strike on a convoy travelling to Kabul to celebrate Hamid Karzai's installation as the new head of state. A convoy of friends and supporters from Paktia, close to the Pakistan border in Eastern Afghanistan, were mistaken for a force of Taliban and attacked. Fifteen of the convoy passengers were killed and fifty inhabitants of local villages wounded. Paktia's tribal council declared it was a 'mistake' and that a local enemy had deliberately misled the Americans. 'A spy told them they were Taliban,' a council spokesman said.

But when you looked closer it turned out to be more complicated. Paktia had always been pro-Taliban, the home of the powerful Haqqani clan, which had close ties to al Qaeda. The head of the clan, Jalaluddin Haqqani, was a prominent *mujahideen* leader against the Russians, when he got to know Osama bin Laden. He was later appointed military commander by the Taliban, but has now handed over to his son Sirajuddin. To escape military pressure from the Americans, the Haqqanis moved to North Waziristan, in Pakistan's FATA (Federally Administered Tribal Areas), courtesy of the Pakistan Army, where they are said to have about 6,000 trained fighters and are considered an important strategic 'asset' by the army's military intelligence wing, the ISI. Many of the Afghans in the convoy had been in the Taliban, which was an almost entirely Pushtun movement – one was a deputy minister – but as good Pushtuns were now behind Hamid Karzai. They had been 'fingered' by opponents as Taliban, a frequent occurrence which the Americans, in their hunt for the remnants of al Qaeda, had neither the inclination nor the reliable intelligence to investigate, and they presumed the supporters guilty. It was very much the old 'shoot first and ask questions later' approach which McChrystal, and his mentor and successor General David Petraeus, were anxious to reverse.

If the attack on the convoy was a political fiasco as well as a humanitarian disaster, six months later, on 1 July 2002, there followed an even more heart-rending catastrophe: the wedding party massacre, when US jets bombarded the village of Kakarak in Uruzgan, north of Kandahar. Guests

were celebrating the union of two prominent local families with a traditional *feu de joie*, firing volleys of gunfire into the sky. Suspicious American
pilots thought they were under Taliban attack and opened fire, killing and
wounding a huge number of innocent people. The *New York Times* quoted
figures of fifty-four dead including one entire family of twenty-five – many
of them women and children – and more than 120 wounded.[22]

There have been literally hundreds of similar incidents in the following
years, with casualties running into the thousands – no one knows exactly
how many – mainly in the Pushtun south and east. Recently released
figures estimated that more than 2,700 civilians were killed as a result of
military action in 2010, up 15 per cent on the year before. The United
Nations says 75 per cent of deaths are down to the Taliban – although the
Taliban say the figures are one-sided. According to the BBC news website,
2010 was the 'bloodiest year for a decade'.[23] The north remained largely
unscathed until in Kunduz, in August 2009, despite McChrystal's best
efforts, up to 142 people, including more than a hundred civilians, were
killed in an air strike called in by the local German NATO commander,
reacting to the Taliban hijack of two diesel fuel lorries. Advised by a single
local Afghan informant that no civilians were involved, he passed this on
to strike command only to find that the Taliban had abandoned the two
hijacked tankers and invited the inhabitants of a local Pushtun village to
help themselves to the stolen diesel. Most of the victims turned out to be
not Taliban, as alleged, but local villagers.

In his campaign to stop these 'friendly fire' blunders, which have
angered and alienated countless Afghans, turning popular opinion
against all foreign troops – whether American or NATO – and infuriating President Karzai, General McChrystal made a good start, judging by
what the head of Afghan intelligence, Amrullah Saleh, told me in
November 2009. 'General McChrystal,' he explained, 'has done more
than fifty operations in the past two months with either no or very little
civilian casualties.'[24] Kunduz was the exception, but he probably did not
class it as a McChrystal operation.

The emphasis on protecting the people stems directly from General
Petraeus's COIN doctrine, which turned on its head what until then had
been the deeply ingrained US military approach, typical of the early stages

of the counter-insurgencies in both Iraq and Afghanistan. It can best be summed up by the Wild West stereotype, the old, hard-nosed, sheriff-style approach. Soldiers ordered to search a house after an incident would routinely kick, or break, the door down. That was the first insult. Then, if they forced their way into the women's quarters, that was a second, even more unforgiveable insult to the family honour, which under *Pushtunwali*, the tribal code of honour, could only be expunged by blood. These cultural gaffes, especially the invasion of the women's quarters – out of bounds in Afghan society to all males apart from members of the family – caused enormous offence, and deeply alienated the local population. To force your way into a Pushtun *qala* – and if an Englishman's home is his castle that is even more true of a Pushtun – is a declaration of war; but to force your way into the women's quarters verges on rapine and slaughter.

Petraeus, who understood the cultural implications, insisted on a complete change, putting 'hearts and minds' above all else. But it is General Jack Keane, a former Vice Chief of Staff, who is credited with persuading Bush himself, if not the top army brass, initially that the only way to avoid a disastrous and demoralising defeat in Iraq was to increase the number of troops on the ground by 30,000, in other words, a 'surge'. This matched Petraeus's ideas on counter-insurgency, which was also to have more boots on the ground, to patrol in strength and thus forge good relations with the local population. With his ratings at rock bottom, Bush was smart enough to recognise a lifebelt when it was thrown to him, so he clung to it with all his might, and no doubt with surprise and gratification found himself being hauled to safety. Petraeus was the man who, by executing the surge, had performed the miracle in Iraq. Could he, despite the loss of McChrystal, pull it off again in Afghanistan?

His doctrine was well thought out and full of catchy aphorisms. For example, he told his soldiers: 'Walk to work; don't ride' – that is, patrol on foot, not in a vehicle – and 'Don't drive by; stop by' – in other words, get to know the local population and try to understand them, their lives, the risks and privations they face, the hopes and aspirations of the ordinary man and woman in the street. In two words, as the British would say, they had to 'muck in'. And only when they proved their humanitarian creden-tials by actually completing the promised house, school or bridge, and by providing medical care for the villagers and their wives and children, would they win them over. And then, as the Americans discovered in Iraq, only when the locals trusted them, would they start providing the intelligence which would make the difference between defeat and victory.

In Iraq, the Americans received a huge bonus when some key Sunni sheikhs decided they wanted to get rid of al Qaeda, and offered to join forces with the Americans to defeat them. It was almost too good to be true, but it was true. At first hundreds and then thousands of Sunni tribesmen switched sides. Although tribal patterns are very different in Afghanistan, General Petraeus hoped to achieve a similar sort of volte-face by winning over the bulk of the ordinary Taliban, starting with the rank and file. Lieutenant General Sir Graeme Lamb, the former commander of the SAS, was recalled by General McChrystal to mastermind the 'reintegration' policy, aimed at persuading middle- to low-ranking Taliban to change sides. General Lamb differentiates between reintegration and reconciliation, defining the latter as 'about high-level talks, invariably cross border. It's the top end of the leadership. It's about the movement as such being brought to a point where it then opens itself to a dialogue to change its course.'[25]

'Lamb' is really a misnomer; one thinks of him more as the lion in the psalm rather than the lamb. He joined the British Army as a Queen's Own Highlander in 1973, later commanding the regiment, but his martial qualities soon led him in the direction of the SAS of which he later became the head, and director of Special Forces. He is a plain speaker, given to robust English and the sort of man whom, one suspects, General Montgomery would have been happy to go into the jungle with, as he once said of Chairman Mao.

Lamb policy, informed by the Petraeus doctrine, divides the Taliban into hardcore 'irreconcilables', starting with Mullah Omar, the seldom-seen, one-eyed Taliban leader and the diehards among his Quetta Shura, or war cabinet, and other hardliners like Jalaluddin Haqqani and his son Sirajuddin; and at the other end of the scale, the rank-and-file potential 'reconcilables' – the '$10-a-day Taliban' – who are fighting because they have no jobs or have been brainwashed in Afghan and Pakistan *madrassas* that it is their duty to go and fight the *jihad* against the 'infidel'.

Of the 'irreconcilables' General Lamb says: 'There are people here who will not accept what we would think [of] as being acceptable. They will not accept what Afghans would wish and they put themselves, in my view, quite clearly to the point which is outlawed. For people like me, I am absolutely comfortable [that] we track them down and we kill or capture them and that's how it is. It's exactly what we did with [al] Zarqawi [the Jordanian head of al Qaeda in Iraq, killed by an American air strike in 2006] and the rest of those worthless individuals in Iraq. His great line [was]: "You obey or we slaughter." It is not a part of negotiation. You have to kill him, his brothers, his uncles, and the friends that are around about him, quite simply and actually quite clinically, because they are in fact an obstacle to any sense of progress.'[26]

Turning to the 'reconcilables' he says: 'There is then a vast range of people – in this case the Afghans use the term "upset brothers", which is a very attractive term, because it gets you away from this term of "the enemy". A great deal of these people are upset because they have genuine grievances. If you drop a 500lb-JDAM [bomb] into a compound, it's somebody's home and they built it, not in this generation but generations ago. They all built it together, it's almost Amish . . . a genuine community enterprise, and you cannot replace that with a pile of dollars. So I will go to my grave only scratching the surface of this complex culture, which is hugely rich in traditions and all the rest. But one needs to try, a little, to understand that and engage with them, understand, in fact, their natural bad behaviour because it is part of these ruthless events of thirty years . . . Make allowances and accommodation for that but at the same time recognise it.'

General Lamb feels strongly that the West imposes 'unrealistic' standards of behaviour on the Afghans, and gives corruption as an example. 'Some people with authority would say: "Zero tolerance, zero corruption". Well, that's ridiculous. It's Afghanistan . . . Will we solve this in a moment? No.' He then cites an example from Iraq. '[One] major oil refinery was losing $1.3 billion of refined product. People would say: "You've got to stop corruption," and I'd say: "No, you've got to reduce it, otherwise they will burn the thing to the ground." So we knocked it down by about a billion dollars, well that's a billion dollars back into the coffers. I said it will get better, it will just take some time and I sense much the same here.'

Being both a pragmatist and an optimist, General Lamb says he does not accept that because Afghanistan's problems were difficult they could not be solved. 'That's really not my style to say it can't be done. I think the question is: is this a long programme? Yes, it is.' But there was corruption in America and Britain too. 'Post-Hurricane Katrina,' resumes Lamb, 'you look at why emergency services [were] in effect bankrupt, so early on? It wasn't because the money had just disappeared. There were levels of corruption.' Then, in a reference to the scandal of British MPs' expenses, which rocked Britain in 2009 and in the run-up to the 2010 election, General Lamb adds: 'You can hardly say that our politicians have covered themselves in glory over this recently. This is how you make your money.'[27]

• Summing up his mission, General Lamb said: 'My view is you have to approach the problems at all levels. Reconciliation is for the government and it's outside my bay because I'm not that fussed about it. But I do need to understand the drive, the dynamics, the concerns, the expectations, the possibilities, opportunities that will sit within the Peshawar Shura, within the Quetta Shura, within the various players who are outside the country. Yes I do. I am interested in their influence on the people. I'm interested in . . . the Afghans who fight well for a bad cause . . . and changing that.'[28]

13

The Protection-Money Racket

We don't trust what they say any more.

Pushtun elder, Kandahar, quoted in the *New York Times*,
26 March 2010

Kandahar is Afghanistan's second city, the historic capital of the Pushtuns and also the birthplace of the Taliban. When they were driven from power after 9/11, the Taliban leadership fled across the border, only sixty-five miles away, to Quetta, the capital of Baluchistan, which became their headquarters in exile – as it had been for many Pushtun *mujahideen* and émigré groups during the Russian invasion and occupation of 1979–89. In 2001, Mullah Omar, the Taliban leader, and the rest of the Quetta Shura, were given sanctuary by the Pakistan authorities and have been there ever since; free to plan, fund and prosecute the war against America, Britain and the rest of NATO with impunity. More recently, however, because of the threat of assassination by drones,* Mullah Omar and his colleagues are reported to have been moved by the ISI to the comparative safety of Karachi.

Just as the North Vietnamese Communists used the sanctuaries of Laos and Cambodia to escape American bombing and to move men and supplies to the front during the Vietnam War, so the Taliban have used the safe havens of Pakistan and its long, porous border for the same purpose. But whereas Laos and Cambodia were more often than not reluctant hosts, the Pakistanis have been enthusiastic allies, using the Taliban insurgency for their own ends. Some observers think that they may be changing their

---

* Drones are unmanned aircraft increasingly used by the American military to target and kill insurgents without warning.

policy, but what is undeniable is that without Pakistan to retreat to for R&R, to rely on for recruiting, training, funding and resupply, medical treatment and accommodation for their families, the Taliban insurgency would not have lasted anything like as long.

If Pakistan were to turn off the tap tomorrow, the Taliban would soon subside to a low-level insurgency as happened for a short period in late 2001 when President Musharraf was given an ultimatum by Richard Armitage, Colin Powell's deputy, on behalf of the White House. One version was that Armitage warned Musharraf the Americans would bomb Pakistan 'back into the Stone Age', ·if they continued to support the Taliban and/or al Qaeda – a threat, needless to say, that Armitage strongly denied making. But Musharraf was a wily operator whose glib protestations of friendship and support certainly took in President Bush and to a lesser extent the British – nervous about the potential terrorist threat from their million-strong Pakistani minority – although probably not Armitage.

In fact, Musharraf was pretending to turn off the tap with one hand and was actually turning it on with the other. Francesc Vendrell, the highly experienced UN and EU representative for Afghanistan in Kabul for many years, classified the Pakistanis as 'the most stupendous liars', although he admitted that others in the area were just as bad;[1] while Amrullah Saleh, the former head of intelligence in Kabul, and an expert observer of Pakistan's reputation for duplicity said, tongue in cheek: 'I admire the Pakistanis. They are masters of deception.' For years, he pointed out, they milked the American cow to the tune of billions of dollars for extremely limited support in the War on Terror, and indeed used part of the subsidy to fund the Taliban. American taxpayers' dollars were being used to kill American and other Allied soldiers – including British.[2]

If Pakistan, or its paranoia-driven policy, is one key to the Afghan puzzle, Kandahar's primacy as the heart and soul of Pushtunism is the other. Kandahar lies at the centre of the Afghan Pushtun mosaic, where the Durrani dynasty came into being in 1747 and where, more than 250 years later, the Taliban movement was born. It was there the flag was raised, and that Mullah Omar donned the cloak of the Prophet and declared himself

Amir ul-Momineen (Leader of the Faithful). The story of the Abdali clan and its rise to power is one of the epics of Pushtun culture, a story of high excitement and romance, of rich and potent symbolism.

Nadir Shah, another of those fearsome conquerors who bestrode Asia in the first part of the second millennium, like Genghis Khan, Tamerlane and the Safavids before him, became ruler of Persia and conqueror of Delhi largely thanks to the military muscle of his Pushtun Abdali mercenaries, above all the cavalry. Their commander was young Ahmed Khan Abdali, who was also the head of his bodyguard and in charge of the treasury, which Nadir Shah had looted from the Moghuls in Delhi, and which contained many priceless pieces including the fabled Koh-i-Noor diamond, now part of the British Crown Jewels.

When Nadir Shah, who had become a murderous tyrant, was eventually assassinated, Ahmed Khan fled, complete with the Koh-i-Noor and his Abdali horsemen, finally reaching Kandahar where they and the other Pushtun tribes held a nine-day tribal jirga to choose a leader. Against all the odds, and despite his youth, they chose Ahmed Khan Abdali, not least, the American scholar Louis Dupree points out, because he controlled the most powerful military force in the area, his 4,000 veteran cavalrymen.[3] After considerable intervention from the floor, led by an excitable holy man, or *darwish*, Ahmed Khan changed his title to Ahmed Shah Durr-i-Durran (Pearl of Pearls), or Durrani, after which dynasty and empire were named. Durranis still rule Afghanistan, since the Popalzais are also Durranis, and President Hamid Karzai is a Popalzai.[4]

Under the Durranis, and surrounded by rich farming land, Kandahar prospered, but is now overshadowed by the Taliban insurgency. It had become a 'city of fear', as one Western journalist who has often visited it since the Taliban were driven out nine years ago, described it in March 2010.[5] When General McChrystal was still in charge, the Americans planned a major campaign to clear out Kandahar and rid it of the Taliban terror. No one was under any illusions that it was a very tough call, but essential if the Taliban hold over the south was to be finally broken. This was not going to be another Fallujah, where US Marines fought a murderous battle in the Iraq War, in which the city would be destroyed first before it was brought under control. This would be done in the classic, Petraeus–COIN manner, winning over the local inhabitants rather than beating them into submission. The bad guys, of course, would be taken care of.

The campaign was planned for early summer 2010, but a similar operation in the smaller town of Marja, another Taliban stronghold, became bogged down and forced a delay. Another reason for the postponement was that the full surge complement of 30,000 fresh American troops was still arriving.

This is how the journalist Carlotta Gall described Kandahar in the *New York Times* in March 2010: 'When American forces all arrive, they will encounter challenges larger than any other in Afghanistan. Taliban suicide bombings and assassinations have left this city virtually paralysed by fear. The insurgents boldly walk the streets, visit shops and even press people into keeping guns and other supplies in their houses for them in preparation for urban warfare, residents say. The government, corrupt and ineffective, lacks almost any popular support. Anyone connected to the government lives in fear of assassination. Its few officials sit barricaded behind high blast walls. Services are scant. Security, people say, is at its worst since the fall of the Taliban government in 2001.'[6]

Her report then quoted a well-known local politician, Haji Agha Lalai, a provincial councillor and former head of the peace and reconciliation commission, who has extensive contacts with the Taliban: 'They are focusing on the city,' he said. 'The Taliban want to show themselves to the world, to show: "We are here."'[7]

The scale of the coming American offensive 'was expected to dwarf the recent operation in Marja, in neighboring Helmand Province, where 15,000 American, NATO and Afghan forces were deployed to secure an area much smaller than this provincial capital of 500,000 people'. The report continued that 'American forces had been preparing for Kandahar since last year, building a presence around the city and along the border with Pakistan to try to secure the province. But as a result, in the most important urban centre in southern Afghanistan, life had rapidly deteriorated, residents said. On 13 March, suicide bombers killed thirty-five people, and the Taliban issued repeated warnings that they were in the city and planning more attacks.'

Residents said they did not 'feel safe in town, and "even for the men it was dangerous to go out", according to a female human rights worker who asked not to be named for fear of reprisals. In the week before the bombings . . . the Taliban conducted a series of attacks on the police and other officials in the city, killing one or two police officers every night for several days and seizing their weapons.'

The same article described how the Taliban's terror regime was exemplified by the following all-too-typical story:

A government official, the well-liked head of the province's Information and Culture Department, Abdul Majeed Babai, was gunned down on his way to work on 24 February. He had received threats from the Taliban, who wanted him to leave his position, relatives said. 'The Taliban can walk around, and government officials cannot,' Hajji Lalai said. The man nominally in charge of Kandahar Province, Governor Tooryalai Wesa, sat alone in his office reading papers on a recent afternoon. The spacious lawns and rooms of his palace, thronged by tribal elders and petitioners a few years ago, stood empty and silent.

Outside the city, it is worse. Government services barely exist. Only five of seventeen districts in the province are accessible to government officials. Four districts are completely under the control of the insurgents, according to Nader Nadery, deputy head of the Afghanistan Independent Human Rights Commission. Administrators and police chiefs are appointed to the districts, but they have so little backup and so few resources, they can do little. With forty to sixty police officers in each district, they can barely guard the district centre. Health services and education are virtually absent outside the towns, and two-thirds of the province's schools are closed, human rights officials say. 'If a single nurse or midwife is working in the districts, you can call me bad names,' a women's activist, Shahida Hussain, said. 'Even in the city, they don't have enough equipment – forget the districts.' On the other hand, Afghan officials in the district of Spinboldak on the Pakistan border said their area was more secure since American soldiers of the Stryker Brigade were deployed there last year to try to close down Taliban infiltration routes, or 'rat lines', as soldiers call them. The road to Spinboldak had grown safer, and a radio tower had been installed that would allow the government to reach Afghans throughout the border region, the governor, Mr Wesa, said on a recent visit. Yet the Taliban have repeatedly hit Kandahar city with roadside bombs.

In Melhajat and Panjwai, agricultural districts to the west and south-west of Kandahar city, farmers say they are under constant threat from mines laid by the militants, as well as from American drones and helicopters combing the skies. Villagers described at least three instances in recent weeks when drone strikes killed farmers digging ditches or bringing goods home from the market, as well as other cases when Taliban fighters were hit. American helicopters swoop in on villagers who are on motorbikes or are working in the fields and hover over them until the men remove clothing and stand with their arms aloft to show they are not militants, said one man who frequently visits his village by motorbike from the city. He asked not to be named for fear of trouble from any side.

In addition to the dangers, residents say they are despairing about the political crisis gripping the province. Real power rests with just two families who have prospered under the presence of American forces in the past eight years. One of them is the family of President Hamid Karzai, who was represented here by his late brother, Ahmed Wali Karzai, who headed the Provincial Council. The other belongs to Gul Agha Sherzai, the former Governor of Kandahar, and his brothers Bacha Shirzai and Razziq Shirzai, who have acquired lucrative security and construction deals with NATO forces.

Residents and elders accuse the families of persecuting rivals and excluding all other tribes from access to power. Their domination has undercut any popular backing for the government or the foreign forces supporting them. 'The first thing Afghans fear is the coming of more foreign troops, and the second thing they fear is the empowering of the current leadership and administration,' said Shahabuddin Akhundzada, a tribal elder from Kandahar city. His Eshaqzai tribe has complained of repeated arrests and political exclusion. The West's acceptance of Mr Karzai's re-election despite widespread fraud was the last straw, he said. 'The Americans, the international community, all the military forces have lost the people's trust,' he added. 'We don't trust what they say anymore.'[8]

In the early part of 2010, in the preparatory stages of the Kandahar operation, President Karzai, it is said, came under considerable pressure from American officials, backed by the British, to remove his brother, Ahmed Wali, from his position as chairman of the Kandahar Provincial Council. This demand – presented as advice no doubt – was rejected by President Karzai. A well-informed resident of Kandahar* pointed out that the demand, or request, was unrealistic.

'Strategically and politically,' he said, it was very important for President Karzai to keep his brother in Kandahar; someone to whom he was 'very close, whom he could trust, whom he could use and refer to when he needed help and support . . . I don't think he would willingly try to remove his brother. I have heard a lot of stories, of tribal elders going to Karzai to complain about his brother. People said that Karzai was so furious and so angry at what the tribal elders told him . . . what his brother was doing in Kandahar. He got really emotional and angry and he said: "As soon as you guys leave here, I am going to remove him [his brother] from power," but nothing happened.' He had always depended on him and always defended him. Despite promising a lot of people he would remove his brother from power, he never did.

The resident said Ahmed Wali was regarded as 'a big boy in Kandahar, known as Kaka Mama [Big Uncle or The Godfather]. There was nobody higher than him. He had his own armed people and used them anywhere. He could basically arrest anybody; he was the most powerful person in southern Afghanistan and had the capability of reaching politicians in Kabul, you know . . . international politicians from international communities. He had the support of [President] Karzai and as well he had the money. He had a lot of money.'**

* He cannot be named because of possible retaliation.
** This description rings truer than General Carter's, on p. 130.

He believes the Americans were not very sure what to do about Wali Karzai, but 'they think . . . [his role] is harming their whole agenda for Afghanistan or for southern Afghanistan, because of what he is doing and what his reputation is, and what people think about Wali Karzai.' On the other hand, he added, 'the international community, Americans particularly, don't have anybody else to refer to. I mean, for example, in Kandahar, if tomorrow they want to start an operation, who are they going to consult? Who are they going to get support from? Ahmed Wali is the only person left for the American and international communities to go and refer to and get information. He had definitely been giving quite good information to the Americans. He had people, he had connections and he had contacts even in the Taliban.'

As to whether the Americans and the British could do the 'Kandahar operation' without him, he said, 'I think they needed someone influential . . . they couldn't do it by themselves, they needed someone influential who could direct them or at least consult with them.'

Had a Loya Jirga (grand assembly), the traditional method for consulting opinion in Afghanistan, been held in Kandahar recently? I asked.

He shook his head: 'Tribal elders [in Kandahar] have mostly been killed – assassinated.'

'By whom?'

'By both parties. Some were killed by the Taliban; some were killed by unknown people. Who knows who these unknown guys are? Some of them [the elders] are sitting quietly at home because they are too scared to speak out . . . Basically . . . the tribal elders are paranoid, because of the insurgency. He [Ahmed Wali Karzai] was the main guy and you know . . . he was the head of the [Provincial] Council. Some tribal elders are part of the Council.' (He mentioned one to me by name but said he does not want it to be published.)

'Would he have been a supporter of Ahmed Wali?'

'He is very careful, from what I have heard about him. These guys, instead of trying to change things for the people, are trying to make money, because there is so much money coming into the country. They have the opportunity to make that money because they are right in there and they can get contracts . . . This guy, they, the people, trusted him in the past. I mean, he was a good guy, but recently I heard, he gets contracts for building roads and that sort of thing, and he makes a lot of money. And once he makes that money, I don't think he will be willing to try to help people, his concentration will be on how to make more money.

'Actually the other day I saw him outside the Canadian Embassy just as it was getting dark. I know him really well, and as soon as I saw him outside the Canadian Embassy, I said what are you doing here? He was not very friendly or open. He said: "I am going to meet some friends." The next day I saw a friend of mine and I said: "I saw this same guy in front of the Canadian Consulate, what would he be doing?" And he said: "He was there to get contracts." I think he felt embarrassed and a little bit guilty . . . you know.'

Like many Afghans, the resident thinks the Americans are funding the corruption and they are funding the Taliban as well, indirectly. 'This is the true story and this is happening right now in southern Afghanistan and almost in all Afghanistan,' he told me. All these transportation companies, he said, 'take logistics [supplies] to American bases around the country, food and everything. They got these contracts from America, then . . . they sell them [subcontract] to someone in Dubai. Yesterday I met one guy who was teaching me how to start this business . . . a guy who does this business, transporting logistics for Americans. He was telling me there is a lot of money in this, you should start it."

The friend then explained there was 'a circle' in Washington where they issued contracts, for example to transport supplies to American bases in Afghanistan. The company which won the contract subcontracts to a regional contractor who hires an Afghan firm, which charges $4,000 per lorry to transport the goods from, say, Kabul to Kandahar. The Afghan firm in turn has to negotiate with the local Taliban who charges them so many dollars to clear, say, fifteen checkpoints (several hundred dollars per checkpoint). 'I think for someone who is illiterate . . . who never went to school and only knows how to use a gun and who [has] gathered some

---

* This sounds remarkably similar to Dr Ashraf Ghani's description of the 'chain of corruption in international contracting' he describes on p. 140.

guys with him and made a group of Taliban . . . and if he is getting dollars
every month, do you think he is going to lay down his gun? Never he is
going to lay down his gun, because he is making money.'

'Was he a Taliban?' I asked.

'He is real Taliban, he is a local gangster and Taliban too . . . that's how
it started. So he is benefiting in both ways, he is doing his *jihad*. He sees
foreigners, he is going to kill them, and that's his *jihad* and he is going to
go to Paradise; and he is making money. In both ways they are benefiting.
So it's very unfortunate.' If the toll was not paid, he said, the Taliban would
burn the vehicle or confiscate it.

The whole system was therefore 'not benefiting and supporting the
Afghan government or people . . . all the money flowing into Afghanistan
on the one hand is corrupting a lot of officials, at a high level, as well as
indirectly funding the Taliban. I know contractors who have been threatened – in Kandahar for example,' the resident explained; 'they get contracts
from Americans or other international companies to build certain things.
They get threats from the Taliban. They say well, we are not going to kill
you if you pay us money, you can continue working. If you pay us we won't
kill you, otherwise we will attack you. So, basically a lot of people, right
now, are paying the Taliban in Kandahar for their own survival and for the
survival of their business. They just pay them a couple of thousand [dollars]
one month and the next month they are all right and no one would attack
them and after some time they will say, we need more money . . . so that's
another way of financing the Taliban.'

The resident then explained how the Taliban's protection racket worked
in Kandahar: 'People say they are getting money from the Gulf, they are
getting money from ISI in Pakistan. I think if they are getting thousands
of dollars from contractors and these kinds of people, I think this insurgency will last for ever. They have the guns, they have the spiritual allowance
[approval] that they are allowed to fight against this government because
it's *jihad* for them and it's freedom. What they need financially, money . . .
they get money right in their streets. It's given [to] them willingly, people
are scared of them . . .'

He knew people who had refused to give money to the Taliban and
describes how, a week later, one of their family members would be

attacked. 'Next time he called and said: "Your money is ready. When do you want to pick it up?" So their world is working and they are making money.'

The other day, the resident said, he was watching President Karzai on television 'complaining about security firms. He has ordered all foreign security companies to close down by the end of the year [2010], saying they are involved in a lot of things happening around the country, the killing and corruption and all that.' As an Afghan, he says, if his President is complaining, who is he going to complain to? 'I mean, you are the President: you can change things. Are you complaining to me? To your people? Your people can't do anything.' The resident thought President Karzai is not very capable. Rather than solving problems, he always complains, he said.

Hamid Karzai was born in Kandahar and had a lot of support there, said the resident. The majority of people voted for him in the first presidential election in 2004 and the election of 2009, but he believed the President had neglected Kandahar. 'He has not been very honest with the people of Kandahar; not only to the people of Kandahar, not very honest to the people over all. He promised a lot of things which he hasn't done.' What people resented most, the resident said, was bad governance and corrupt officials: 'For years and years he supported bad governors and police chiefs including his brother . . . and didn't do anything [about removing them]. So people were quite upset with him. They thought that he didn't really care what was going on; he only really cared about himself and his family and his inner circle.'

The resident is convinced that President Karzai's attempts to negotiate with the Taliban are doomed to failure. 'I don't think you can talk to the Taliban. If they were willing to talk, they would have done it in the last, how many years, that everyone has asked them: "Let's talk. What are the differences? Let's get together and talk [about] what are the differences and how we can solve these problems."'

He believes there are two things that can be done. One is to talk to 'whoever drives these Taliban'; he feels the international community has not 'got it' in the last seven or eight years. 'The Afghans have been shouting: "Look it's Pakistan, they [the Taliban] are there and getting training there and they are getting their safe havens there. It's Pakistan." Now, the international community has begun to "get it", a little bit. "Yes, it's coming from Pakistan!" If you get an agreement with Pakistan . . . there will be peace in Afghanistan. Otherwise, I don't think they will ever come to the table: because they see nothing [to be gained] in making a peace. What are they going to achieve in peace with the Afghan government? If they get a share of the government, what kind of share will they get? They are not educated, are they going to get or accept them in the Ministry of Haj? I don't think Mullah Omar would be happy to get that ministry. What kind of other ministry is there they can run? He can't. His dreams are higher than that, I think. And plus he is saying, I am winning this war and you are going to give me the Ministry of Religious Affairs?'

The second thing is 'the Afghan people. They have always been defending this country, from all the aggressors . . . I think this war can be won by the Afghan people, by the people who live in these villages. If these tribes and villagers are supported wisely and properly, I think they can be very successful in defeating the Taliban.'

There are two possible options in his view. One is: 'If Pakistan stops [their support] the war will eventually stop because the cap is there. If it stops there then it will stop here, too.' The second is internal opposition. The people are 'the one solution that could fight against the Taliban . . . If they talked to people who have been dominated by the Taliban the last couple of years, they'd find they were really tired of the Taliban; because there hadn't been any progress, people were fed up with them checking their mobile phones every day.' He explained that the Taliban were quite paranoid about mobile phones and scared they would give their positions away, like a GPS. 'They check your phone and search houses. But that doesn't mean they [the Afghans] like the Americans . . . I think they are fed up [with them too]. But they would like someone who is on their side. If they see the Americans and the Afghan government are on their side, and have support from them, they can easily fight against the Taliban. Because they are from that area and if a Talib comes and attacks someone or does some bad thing in the area, he [the victim] knows who the guy is. If that Talib escapes from the area, he is going to go and ask for the arrest of [the Talib's] father or brother. This is how things work here.'   •

He gave what he said was a 'good example' from Kandahar. One person was kidnapped so, in retaliation, his family kidnapped five of the kidnapper's relatives and gave their family an ultimatum: 'Return our man within twenty-four hours or there will be trouble.' They got him back. 'This is how things work in Afghanistan. It's not going to work if you say: "Hey, is this person okay? Did you harm him or not?" No, in Pushtu we have an expression: "You can only break metal with metal." So this is how things work in Afghanistan. The tribes need to be engaged in security in Afghanistan.'

The resident's view has to be taken seriously since it comes from an intelligent and well-informed Kandahari, who believes a local police force with local knowledge and proper government support can defeat the Taliban. It also seems to be very close to General Petraeus's plan to set up local village police forces, known as *arbaki*, similar to the local tribal militias the Americans used with such success in Iraq. However, as so often seems to happen in Afghanistan, some units are complaining they have received no money from the government and are consequently losing interest. Once again, Kabul's failure to follow through may prove a fatal weakness.

A Coalition Government, 2010

Life is terrible . . .
> A taxi driver and a farmer from Mehlajat District, Kandahar,
> summer 2010

Gilles Dorronsoro, a French analyst with the Carnegie Endowment think-tank in Washington, who specialises in Kandahar and the south, said in a recent publication entitled 'Worsening Outlook in Afghanistan' that despite the 2010 surge of American troops, 'the coalition's position continues to erode as the Taliban gain strength. Meanwhile, American public support for the war is waning.'[1]

After a trip to Afghanistan in the summer of 2010, he argued, presenting his case in a question and answer format, that Washington's approach was failing and that talking with the Taliban through the Pakistani military establishment was the least bad option available. The best hope for exiting the war was to Afghanise the conflict and establish a coalition government that included Taliban leaders.

His first point was to highlight that the security situation in Afghanistan was clearly deteriorating. When he arrived in Afghanistan in summer 2010, he wrote, he hadn't anticipated a major change in the safety conditions since his earlier trip in April 2010. Even with the surge of US troops, he expected things to have stayed mainly the same within the short window of time between trips. 'I was wrong. There was a palpable regression. The conditions have only gotten worse since the new US counterinsurgency strategy was rolled out. While the coalition is talking about progress in a few districts, the general picture is quite different.'

'In Helmand,' he wrote, 'where the coalition had used its best troops, progress would take at least five years to materialise, according to the

Afghanistan's most brilliant guerrilla commander against the Russians, Ahmed Shah Masud (*centre*) captured Kabul in 1992 and was still fighting the Taliban in 2001 when he was assassinated by two al Qaeda suicide bombers.

A Communist general, Abdul Rashid Dostum joined Masud in 1992 and helped him capture Kabul, but later turned against him. Forced by the Taliban to flee to Turkey, he backed the Americans after 9/11 and became one of President Karzai's vice presidents.

This blurred image is the best of only a handful available of the leader of the Taliban, Mullah Omar. Born in Kandahar to a family of peasants, he lost his right eye fighting the Russians, and is famous for allegedly rescuing two boys (or girls) who had been kidnapped and raped by a local warlord, then hanging him from the barrel of his own tank.

Osama bin Laden, the tall and fanatical Saudi Arabian scion of the hugely wealthy bin Laden family who founded al Qaeda and planned the devastating attack on the World Trade Centre in New York on 11 September 2001. He was killed in his secret hideout in Pakistan on 2 May 2011 in a raid by US Navy SEALs.

Gulbuddin Hekmatyar, head of the extremist Hisb-i-Islami; enemy of Masud and protégé of the ISI with a reputation for eliminating political rivals.

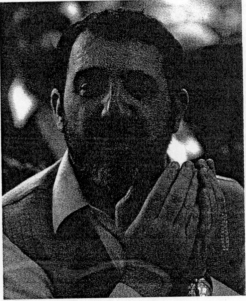

Half-brother of President Karzai and his power-broker in Kandahar and the south, Ahmed Wali Karzai was believed to be deeply involved in drug trafficking – allegations he always denied. Known locally as Kaka Mama (literally Big Uncle), he ran his own private militia, the Kandahar Strike Force, and had close ties to the CIA. He was assassinated by an old family retainer in his own house in Kandahar on 12 July 2011, aged fifty.

A Popalzai Pushtun from Kandahar, Hamid Karzai was chosen by the Americans to lead the first post-Taliban administration in 2001. Seen here with President George W. Bush, Karzai was elected President in 2004, and re-elected amid charges of extensive ballot rigging in 2009. After a promising start his government became increasingly accused of nepotism and corruption, and relations with the Americans steadily deteriorated.

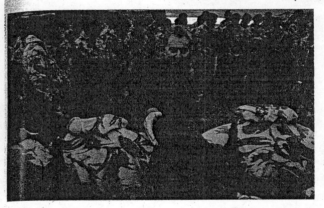

Former Prime Ministers Tony Blair and Gordon Brown visiting British troops in Afghanistan.

The stunning setting of the city of Kabul, which was the Emperor Babur's favourite city, encircled by the snow-capped Hindu Kush mountains.

A normal day in the centre of Kabul.

Northern Alliance Uzbek cavalry commanded by General Dostum, preparing for action in the CIA war against the Taliban after 9/11.

Afghan Pushtun militia, recruited to back up American and British Special Forces Operations against Osama bin Laden and his al Qaeda fighters at Tora Bora. The US Air Force blasted the mountain stonghold for days but bin Laden managed to escape across the border into Pakistan.

As head of US Special Forces Operations in Iraq General Stanley McChrystal caught Saddam Hussein and the head of al Qaeda. President Obama gave him command in Afghanistan but he was forced to resign in June 2010 after he and his aides were quoted criticising Obama's White House team in *Rolling Stone* magazine.

Author of the US Army's counter-insurgency doctrine [COIN], General Petraeus has degrees from the US Military Academy and Princeton. A fitness fanatic, he is best known for the war-winning 'surge' in Iraq. He succeeded General McChrystal in Afghanistan, instituting a robust policy of hunting down and killing Taliban commanders. On retirement, he became Director of the CIA.

General Petraeus, US and NATO Commander in Afghanistan (2010–2011) in the field with his troops.

General Lord Guthrie. After Sandhurst, he was commissioned into the Welsh Guards, served with the SAS, becoming CGS in 1994, CDS in 1997 and a life peer in 2001.

After spending much of his career in Northern Ireland and the Balkans, General Lord Dannatt became CGS in 2006. His outspokenness, especially about soldiers' pay and conditions, is said to have blocked his promotion to CDS.

Britain's top military officer as CDS, General Sir David Richards was the first British general to command American troops since the Second World War when he became NATO commander in Afghanistan in 2006–7. He forged a close relationship with President Karzai, helping him to set up a war cabinet called the Policy Action Group.

Refugees flee the fighting north of Kabul, although at least one young man looks glad to see Northern Alliance fighters advancing against the Taliban.

The root of most of the evil in Afghanistan. Opium is the major source of corruption and of funding for the Taliban insurgency. Farmers in Helmand Province opposed government decrees to stop the cultivation of poppy, stating that they would fight to the death to protect their living

Commandant of the Marine Corps, [General] James T. Conway. With an aggressive counterinsurgency campaign in Marja, coalition troops had been working to suppress the local insurgency. But months after the offensive started, Marja remained unstable and insecure. The lack of progress in Helmand delayed plans to move on to Kandahar, the second largest city in Afghanistan, and forced the United States to rethink its ambitious agenda.'

Dorronsoro states that 'Operations in Kandahar would be even more difficult because the insurgents enjoyed strong popular support west of the city and this was where the most severe fights would take place in the next few months.' The fighting had been strongest 'in a small district north of Kandahar city where there were a series of military bases. While this was a strategically important location for controlling the city, US forces had been unable to extend control beyond their bases – it took hours to go just hundreds of metres outside on patrol. And they had failed to build a local militia or strong ties with influential people.'

'The Taliban are too powerful in the south to defeat,' he states.

Later, in 2011, his comments seem to be rather too pessimistic in general and inaccurate in particular cases.[2] Dorronsoro may be on firmer ground, however, when he claims: 'Things are also going badly in the north. The Taliban are in charge in many places and, even where they are not, the Afghan government has no real support. Of course it's not a situation where areas wholly support the government or the Taliban, it's more complicated than that as there are locations with local commanders who are not dependent on Kabul.' He also gives the Americans some rather guarded credit in Chamkani District of Paktia, previously heavily Talibanised, where US Special Forces had established a tribal shura. However, Dorronsoro adds, while it's too early to tell how these efforts will progress, minor progress in the east won't have any concrete impact on the overall direction of the war itself.

In reply to the question: 'How strong are the Taliban?' Dorronsoro's answer is that they 'are trying to take the fight to every part of Afghanistan and are successfully gaining control as the group becomes more of a national movement. The strategy is working as the conflict spreads across the country. Without many more troops than would ever be feasible for the United States or NATO to supply, the coalition will be unable to face all the threats at once, and it's becoming increasingly difficult to gain a tactical success in a single location that could have wider tangible implications for the war. The progress of the insurgency is now irreversible as the Afghan government is too weak to roll back the insurgents,' he asserts.

'The presence of the Taliban can even be felt in Kabul. They are progressively surrounding the capital and tightening their control in adjacent areas. With the centre of the city remaining safe, even to foreigners, there are fewer and fewer places outside the city that are reachable by car. The Taliban have placed checkpoints on the roads out of Kabul in the north and south. It's dangerous to drive as government employees risk being killed and foreigners are in danger of being captured. The isolation of Kabul is putting further strain on the government and coalition as they cannot easily travel outside the capital,' Dorronsoro says.[3]

My own experience in the first half of August 2010 was rather different. Some friends and I were able to travel as tourists from Kabul on the main road north to Charikar, Jebel-us-Seraj, Gulbahar and then on to the Panjsher Valley and back in a day without difficulty or any security concerns. Another friend, however, who wanted to hire a car to drive from Kabul to Bamiyan, the site of the famous Buddha statues destroyed by the Taliban in 2001, was told part of the road from Charikar through the Ghorband Valley was too dangerous for foreigners. Afghans have no difficulty. The reason is that a few small bombs have exploded near one mainly Pushtun village in Ghorband, causing some casualties. The risk, in my view, is not great; but it does exist.

While some of Gilles Dorronsoro's statements on the low level of Taliban casualties in the south now seem seriously out of date (for example, Anthony Loyd of *The Times* quotes a Western commander in Kandahar as saying in November 2010: 'We're taking them [the Taliban] off the battlefield in industrial numbers'), and his assessment that 'In the south, the Taliban are successfully holding their ground with low levels of casualties in Kandahar and Helmand, despite concerted American campaigns also seem inaccurate (in October, the *New York Times* reported that American and Afghan forces had been 'routing' the Taliban in much of Kandahar). And the Taliban have successfully discouraged local partners from working with the coalition.

This was the result of the 'surge' which only took effect in the autumn. More accurate, however, were his comments on the parliamentary elections of 18 September 2010, Dorronsoro predicted that they would 'in many ways be a rerun of last year's presidential campaign'. The political process would be extremely corrupt and the international community would not be able to monitor the election on the ground. President Karzai would marginalise progressives and use the elections for his own political gain. There was a low turnout, partly because of Taliban threats to cut off voters' fingers if they were caught with ink on them (inking being a device to stop people voting twice).

We then come to the nub of Dorronsoro's argument. This is that the Americans should negotiate as soon as possible with the Taliban through the intermediary of the Pakistani ISI* and Afghanise the war, which is now widely accepted by most parties to the conflict. His suggestion that the Americans should declare a ceasefire before starting negotiations seems, however, very much a step too far, and the 'decapitation' of the Taliban leadership and 'droning' of militants will probably take precedence for some time to come. Dorronsoro has also been overtaken by events, in my view, since America has already begun talks with the Taliban, although few details are available.

Dorronsoro elaborates:

> Negotiations must include the United States, Taliban, Pakistani military, and members of the Afghan government and Northern Alliance. It needs to be relatively small at first, as bringing in too many regional powers would only complicate negotiations. The idea of negotiating only through President Karzai is not a good idea. He is both too weak and surrounded by influential advisers who oppose the United States. He is no longer a partner of Washington and it would be irresponsible to leave the talks in his hands. Plus, neither the Taliban nor Pakistan wants to negotiate with Karzai because he can't deliver results. The United States must play a leading role as it would be dangerous not to.

---

* This seems particularly unlikely since Admiral Mike Mullen and Ambassador Tomsen have heavily criticised the ISI's role in using proxies like the Haqqani Network as a strategic arm.

The talks will need to establish a coalition government in Kabul – that includes Taliban leaders – and security guarantees for the Western alliance that al Qaeda will not return and use Afghanistan as a base to mount terrorist attacks abroad. As negotiations proceed, there will need to be a political agreement detailing the withdrawal of coalition forces. Ideally, 10,000–20,000 troops will stay in the country to defend against external threats, but this would depend on how the talks are going. After a broad-based government is set up, a larger international conference will be needed to garner global support for the new body. This certainly must include India, Russia, Iran, and Saudi Arabia. It could perhaps be under the auspices of the UN, which might provide some of the important outside powers more incentive to cooperate than if the United States were driving it alone. If the United States starts now, it can work. If the international community waits too long, the Taliban will be too strong and will be unwilling to make concessions.

Finally, Dorronsoro comes to the crucial role of Pakistan, which is increasingly perceived in the West as the most important key to the conundrum.

'It's clear,' he argues, 'that the Pakistanis are still supporting the Taliban.' His view of the reasons for the arrest of Mullah Omar's second-in-command are now fairly widely shared, and are confirmed by the interviews with Taliban commanders in Chapter 22. Washington 'continues to funnel money to the Pakistani government to move against the Afghan Taliban, but this is yesterday's policy. It is far too late for the Pakistani army to reverse course. And even if Washington got what it wanted and high-level Taliban leaders were arrested, it would not kill the insurgency. The Taliban are too strong and the remaining players in Afghanistan will refuse to negotiate. In fact, if Islamabad loses influence over the Afghan Taliban, it will be a loss for Washington. Instead of trying to disconnect the Pakistani government from the Taliban, the United States should use the links to start talking. The United States must start using the situation to its own advantage.'

How do Gilles Dorronsoro's views chime with the reaction of local Kandaharis, many of whom, in the past twenty to thirty years, have lived through the Russian War, the *mujahideen* take-over, the ensuing civil war and the emergence in 1994 of Mullah Omar and the Taliban. Some may even have come across Osama bin Laden who lived in Kandahar in the 1990s as the guest of Mullah Omar. Having survived the turmoil of that period, ordinary Kandaharis were caught up in the maelstrom of the autumn 2010 operation. A local journalist recorded his impressions of what it was like to live through this 'make or break' surge by American and Afghan troops in the villages round Kandahar. I cannot name him for his own security. I will simply call him an eyewitness: 'I have been to a taxi station where people from Chelghor, Salawat, Nakhoni and Sanzari [suburbs or villages round Kandahar] are coming to the city for shopping. I talked to a bunch of people about the situation and the ongoing clearing operation in the district of Panjwai and Zhari.' Nazar, forty, a farmer from Chelghor, said:

We have been facing a number of problems in the area, especially since the clearing operation began. There are lots of Taliban in the villages, foreign (mostly American) and Afghan troops are wandering outside the villages, sometimes they are coming down to the gardens where they briefly engage with the Taliban and then retreat. They cannot stay or engage for longer, because of heavy IEDs in the fields and gardens. The foreign troops distributed a letter which you have to fill in with your name, your father's name and village name. They said next time when you carry the letter they won't arrest you, but we did not accept the letter [because] if the Taliban see the letter they would treat you as spying for the foreigners. So people rejected taking the letters.

We are in trouble in the area. The foreign troops make raids and target people. Three days ago an IED exploded beside an ISAF convoy, and as a result they shot a thirteen-year-old boy and he was killed. The Taliban have planted countless IEDs on main roads, in the gardens; we cannot travel in peace, many people have left the area [although] some are still living [there]. I am also looking for a house in Kandahar city, but the rent is too high, I can't afford it. If you bring goods to Kandahar city or home, the helicopters hover over your head and signal you to stop.

They are checking you. If you are on a motorcycle they search you, or if you have a bundle on your shoulder they search you. Life is terrible. Taliban wants everything from us: food, money and help. We cannot reject them, and the government is also not treating us well. They blame us for helping the Taliban, but we are fed up of both. Now Taliban are raising their own white flags to mark their own territories. A policeman told me that he will allow me to go to my garden if I fetch a Taliban flag for him. How could it be possible for me to fetch a Taliban flag for him? This is not my duty; this is the duty of the police to secure the area.

Foreign troops did not bring any benefits for us. I don't think this kind of clearing operation will bring any benefits to people . . . A month and a half ago, the forces launched an operation in Chelghor for three days. When they left, Taliban came again and took their positions in the villages. So this kind of operation is not useful, except to bring destruction, killing and displacement to the people.

Another farmer the eyewitness spoke to was Bismillah, aged fifty-two, from Sanzari in Zhari district. Bismillah explained that where he lives,

ISAF forces are destroying gardens, trees and houses, saying Taliban are staging attacks from them. They have destroyed over a thousand mulberry trees and many more vineyards and houses. We asked them why? They say Taliban are taking shelter [there] and attacking us. We asked them: what is the fault of trees and gardens? But they are not listening. This morning they were going to destroy my trees and garden. I left the area and came to Kandahar city. We are very sad. We will help Taliban if they are unable to defeat Taliban but able to destroy our gardens. We will never help ISAF in the future. I [don't] like Taliban either but the treatment of ISAF makes me [want] to help Taliban. ISAF forces are not useful for us.

The situation is very tough for us: ISAF are targeting people, they are raiding, targeting anyone who drives motorbikes. Taliban are planting mines on main routes which often target civilians. Nevertheless, we are in trouble from both, Taliban and ISAF forces.

Bismillah said the result of the operation was,

> the destruction of people, nothing else, just to bring more violence and
> casualties to the people. We are requesting them to leave Afghanistan
> and let Afghans solve their own problems.
>
> ISAF wants us to defeat Taliban which is a ridiculous idea. You people
> with modern weaponry and power can't drive them away, so how would
> we be able to drive Taliban away from the villages? I am suggesting to
> them [ISAF] if you are really unable to hit Taliban, then [I am] kindly
> requesting you to leave Afghanistan and let Taliban rule in Afghanistan.
> At least we would get rid of night raids and bombing, no matter how
> harsh Taliban would be against us. They have launched similar search
> operations in the area; they have carried out door-to-door searches.
> When they left the area Taliban re-emerged, so they are repeating the
> same things. The Afghan Army and police are unable to hold the areas
> for long alone, and the foreigners cannot stay for longer in the area.
> Taliban cannot be vanquished, they will definitely come again, so the
> operations are useless.

Saifullah, aged forty, from Nakhoni, explained:

> there is fighting in Nakhoni, but there is no significant progress by ISAF
> and Afghan forces. What they are doing now, they are widening a
> narrow . . . [road], which they think will make people happy but actu-
> ally they are destroying our land and burying the gardens. They are just
> widening our street. Now we have a 30-metre street in Nakhoni which
> is a sign of great progress but no security. We don't expect things will
> change. Now they have sent more troops to fight Taliban. If they send
> 50,000 they won't be able to restore peace in the area.
>
> Every person is thirsty for peace; and now everyone [has] lost hope
> that they will have peace in the country, because we don't believe the
> current administration will ever restore peace. We don't have good
> people who really think of Afghanistan and its people's problems. We
> have seen security getting worse day by day; we are not supporting
> Taliban and we don't like them but there is no other option for us. What

can we do? Where can we go? What have the government and foreign forces provided for us in nine years?

We have to be home before 6 o'clock. If not, we will be arrested by the Taliban and the government or picked up by someone else. Taliban [don't allow] us to have a mobile. We are not able to see our lands because of IEDs and fighting. We are just alive. Our children cannot sleep due to the sounds of aircraft and fighting. It's terrible being out there. I have been to Mehlajat in Dand district, south of Kandahar city, where the ISAF and Afghan .forces launched a purification operation yesterday. What I saw there was [local] people with their families leaving the villages. I also saw American forces with heavy armoured vehicles blocking the streets and searching people who were coming out of the villages. This area is full of Taliban and only about five to six kilometres from Kandahar city. They pose a big threat to the city. Almost every day, Taliban attack the police and kidnap people they suspect, or blame, for working for the government and ISAF. Next day, you can see they've either been hanged or their bodies dumped in the area.

The eyewitness also talked to Colonel al Ghulam Farooq Parwani, one of the senior Afghan police chiefs. Parwani said 1,700 Afghan police, security agents and NATO forces had been deployed to clear the Mehlajat area of Taliban. It was the second day of the operation. 'We have blocked all exits and entrances to the area, detained seventy-six suspected Taliban yesterday and forty today who were trying to flee the area. We will investigate them; if it is proved they have a link with the Taliban we will put them in jail. A joint clearing operation will definitely drive Taliban out of the Mehlajat where they are posing a big threat to Kandahar city.' There had been no fighting but they had reports that Taliban were fleeing the area and hiding their weapons. 'But we will pursue them until we drive them away completely from the area,' he said.

Next, the eyewitness said he spent thirty minutes in Rigi Kalacha in Mehlajat where he was told twenty families had left that morning (he counted fifteen). People had been leaving all week. Jalat Khan, forty, formerly from Mehlajat, 'very tired' from loading his belongings on a truck, told him that he and his family were leaving home and going to

Kandahar city. They had heard that an operation was under way against the Taliban: 'There will be severe fighting and we are afraid for our children and women when fighting breaks out, so we're preparing to leave the area,' Jalat explained. 'Every day there is fighting. The Taliban are all around: they are planting mines and government and foreign troops are now taking action against them. We are afraid of losing members of the family and decided to leave. It's very difficult for us in the month of Ramazan, we have left everything behind, and we don't have shelter in the city [Kandahar]. I'm intending to live with my relatives in Kandahar, because I can't afford the cost of the rent.'

Muhammad, who was loading his belongings on a tractor, said: 'We're afraid of the fighting so we decided to leave . . . the place is almost empty, everyone is leaving. The Taliban said that they are planting mines in the villages and going to fight, so we decided to go. I don't have a house in the city. I'm going to stay some days with my family . . . after I will look for a cheaper house to rent. It's very difficult this month [Ramazan]. This month is for recollections of God but for us, the unfortunate people leaving our own homes, [it is] very difficult, God will reward us. The Taliban are planting mines everywhere, the government and NATO are bombing. No one cares for us,' Muhammad said.

A taxi driver from Rigi Kalacha in Mehlajat, also loading his belongings in a vehicle, said the government and NATO were searching the houses and would take you away if you had a link with the Taliban: 'Now the ISAF and Afghan forces are carrying out operations against the Taliban, so there will be fighting and we are afraid of losing our family members, so we decided to go to Kandahar city. We have rented a house for 1,200 *Afghanis* [£20] which is too much for us but what to do? [There's] no other way out of this cataclysm. The government is unable to provide security to the region and the Taliban are killing people and planting mines. Life is terrible,' he said.*

* Names have been abbreviated or omitted for personal security reasons.

PART THREE

WHY WE FAILED IN HELMAND: POLITICIANS OR GENERALS?

Brown and Blair: Double Nemesis, 2006–2009

He [Tony Blair] lacked the moral courage to impose his will on his own Chancellor . . .

General Sir Richard Dannatt, *Leading from the Front,* 2010[1]

In his memoirs, General Sir Richard Dannatt, who was Chief of the General Staff from 2006 to 2009, and never one to pull his punches, is as critical as Lord Guthrie was of Gordon Brown, nor does he spare Tony Blair. Brown's influence on defence spending as Chancellor of the Exchequer he describes as 'malign'; of Tony Blair he says he lacked the 'moral courage' to force his Chancellor to provide the money needed to fight two wars, in Iraq and Afghanistan, to which Blair, as Prime Minister, had committed the country.

The 1997–98 Strategic Defence Review, he starts by saying, was 'hailed as a great success. It was led by policy imperatives, which was good. It set a logical baseline for the future commitment of our armed forces, which was also good. Indeed, it stated that the UK intended to use its armed forces to act on the world stage as a "force for good", which was highly laudable. But did all that really answer every part of the question? The harsh reality was that the review could achieve its aims only if it was fully funded. To do what this review aspired to would cost many billions of pounds but, in the event, something less was provided, a discrepancy exacerbated by a tough year-on-year savings target laid on the MOD by the Treasury very late in the whole process and then further exacerbated by a series of operations embarked on by Tony Blair that broke the planning assumptions made in the review.'[2]

Sir Richard is referring here to Gordon Brown's £1 billion 'complete guillotine' on defence spending imposed in September 2003, at the height of the war in Iraq, but only disclosed by the former Permanent Secretary to the MOD, Sir Kevin Tebbit, in evidence to the Chilcot Inquiry on Iraq in February 2010. He said it was 'arbitrary' and resulted in a 'very major savings exercise'. Gordon Brown, by then Prime Minister, immediately denied in Parliament that he had made these cuts.

Dannatt goes on: 'History will pass judgement on these foreign adventures in due course but, in my view, Gordon Brown's malign intervention, when Chancellor, on the review by refusing to fund what his own government had agreed, fatally flawed the entire process from the outset. The seeds were thereby sown for some of the impossible operational pressures to come. Why didn't Tony Blair resolve this problem, particularly when it put at risk his own aspirations for an "ethical" foreign policy – as Robin Cook described it – that entailed the prospect of significant military operations abroad?' Dannatt asks. 'I was forced to the conclusion that he lacked the moral courage to impose his will on his own Chancellor.' Then in answer to a question put to him by the *Daily Telegraph* when it serialised his memoirs, General Dannatt said: 'Frankly moral courage is what you need. Physical courage is a wonderful thing, but moral courage is actually doing the right thing at the right time.'[3]

Dannatt then describes an extraordinary volte-face by Gordon Brown, whose attitude to soldiers and soldiering, in fact to the services in general, could only be described as aloof, if not antipathetic. In 2008, Gordon Brown wrote a book which extolled the courage of young Britons in wartime. 'I was somewhat bemused a few years later,' Dannatt writes, 'to have a conversation with Gordon Brown when he was Prime Minister about a book he was writing, entitled *Wartime Courage*, which described "the courage, sacrifice and eventual triumph" of the World War generations. Mr Brown wrote that he hoped that he had described a "precious store of moral capital that following generations, inspired by it, can draw on in another age". I am still not sure whether he ever realised that by denying the proper funding of his own government's declared policy, he was condemning more young men and women to the same sacrifices he railed against in a previous generation . . . This sad episode led me to the conclusion that if war is too important to be left to generals, then the funding of war is too important to be left to politicians.'[4]

In his evidence to the Chilcot Inquiry on Iraq in 2009, Sir Richard said that when he took over as Chief of the General Staff in 2006, he was worried about the Army 'seizing up'. Ministers had created a 'perfect storm' by ordering a task force to fight the Taliban in Helmand Province just as the insurgency in Iraq was worsening. As the burden on the Army increased on two fronts, the Military Covenant – the nation's pledge to look after servicemen and women in return for them risking their lives on the battle-field – had become 'progressively out of balance' on pay, conditions, accommodation and equipment.

'You can run hot when you are in balance and there is enough oil sloshing around the engine to keep it going,' he told the inquiry. 'When the oil is thin, or not in sufficient quantity, the engine runs the risk of seizing up. I think we were getting quite close to a seizing-up moment in 2006. My biggest concern was that fragility could be turned into a sharp rise in exits from our trained manpower akin to going over a cliff edge. Once your manning has begun to plummet we would have been in all kinds of trouble trying to man two opera-tions with units that were not fully manned. That would have spiralled into something of a nightmare.' He even hinted he believed Britain was wrong to attack Iraq, a war the Army, he said, had 'no desire' to fight and which under-mined the 'more important' campaign in Afghanistan.[5]

Dannatt said he had been surprised to learn of Tony Blair's decision in 2004 to prepare UK forces for Helmand. And it was an 'error' not to have reconsidered the deployment when the security situation in southern Iraq deteriorated during 2005 and 2006, meaning commanders could not with-draw troops from that front. He also condemned the Ministry of Defence's failure to replace the lightly armoured Snatch Land Rovers, which were highly vulnerable to IEDs (Improvised Explosive Devices), and the govern-ment's failure to fund more helicopters.

He told the inquiry: 'It remains unsatisfactory that it is only now that we have closed with the issue. We worked round the problem; we didn't actually confront the problem. It has been a definitive negative and we are paying to some extent the price for that in Afghanistan.' He continued: 'We were constrained between Afghanistan – misunderstood but in my view extremely important – and Iraq, something that we were doing because it was decided that was the right thing to do.'

Some of General Dannatt's most telling criticism is reserved for the MOD's procurement policy, in particular for one programme called FRES (Future Rapid Effects System). 'There is no better example of how the man on the ground has been short-changed by the MOD's flawed procurement process,' he says. When he took over as Assistant Chief of the General Staff in 2001, the Army was looking for a lightweight mobile transport system which could be deployed to trouble spots by air and fast ships. 'It was to be at the heart of the Army's equipment needs for twenty years. And it is not a happy tale. The intention was to acquire a family of armoured vehicles with a common chassis which would replace a range of ageing ones . . . We were not aiming for a hi-tech solution, merely something that could meet most of our needs in timely fashion.'[6]

To help fund FRES, the Army agreed to cancel two other projects and to save time by buying 'off the shelf'. The Americans had already faced the same problem and to solve it had developed an interim solution called Stryker.

'I spent a day in 2008 in Baghdad with a Stryker battalion,' Dannatt recalled; 'it nearly broke my heart. They had almost exactly what we needed. As I write in 2010, the Army still has no FRES. The acquisition became bogged down in MoD bureaucracy.'[7] External analysts were brought in 'on the mischievous pretext that the Army did not know what it wanted', and the in-service date slipped to 2012. Meanwhile 'the threats to our troops in Iraq and Afghanistan had intensified, necessitating the very rapid acquisition of protected patrol and transport vehicles'.*

Worse was to come. In 2008 the Defence Board decided to proceed with two new aircraft carriers and in 2009 compounded the problem by reluctantly agreeing to procure the full quota of Typhoon fighters. With the fourth major spending requirement – the replacement nuclear deterrent – not really a topic for debate, the only place to go to balance the books was FRES. The project was shunted to 2015 and then to 2018. It was effectively dead.

'We had made a plan in 2001 but intrigue, financial mismanagement

---

* This was the improvident, last-minute, hand-to-mouth apology for a policy criticised by Lord Guthrie, as a result of which the British taxpayer ended up paying hugely over the odds for vital equipment because of lack of foresight by ministers and the MOD.

and other vested interests put paid to it. To me, the whole FRES episode sums up what is worst about MOD decision-making in an environment in which resources are scarce and vested interests loom large, and in the absence of clear political and business leadership. We have to do better in future,' he says.[8]

Because of his forthright, even combative style, General Dannatt was passed over as the next Chief of the Defence Staff (CDS), the head of the country's armed forces, and the uncontroversial Air Chief Marshal Sir Jock (now Lord) Stirrup, who was due to retire, had his period extended by Gordon Brown – in order, it was widely believed, to keep Dannatt out. The *Sunday Times* accused Gordon Brown of personally blocking his expected appointment 'because of his repeated calls for better pay and conditions for servicemen'.[9] In one interview, Dannatt said that British soldiers fighting in Afghanistan were 'paid less than London traffic wardens',[10] a remark which made headlines and caused ministerial apoplexy and finally closed the door on the CDS job, he believes.[11] The *Evening Standard* made the following comparison: 'Soldier: young, single, private, living in barracks, posted to Afghanistan for six months, gets £16,227 a year plus £3,512 overseas allowance and £425 housing subsidy; total: £20,164. Traffic Warden: national average wage including overtime, £20,526.'[12]

Air Chief Marshal Sir Jock Stirrup's reappointment was unpopular above all with the Army, who thought he was unfairly biased in favour of his own service. There was also criticism of spending so much money on fast jets which had no relevance to the conflict in Afghanistan, where the Army was taking the brunt of the fighting. One officer just back from Afghanistan felt Sir Jock had deliberately ignored him when he tried to tell him just how short of helicopters and other vital equipment he and his men had been in Helmand, where the fighting was more savage than anything seen since Korea.[13]

On becoming Chief of the General Staff in August 2006, Sir Richard wrote the equally new Defence Secretary, Des (now Lord) Browne, a long letter voicing his key concerns. How much of the letter Browne understood, Dannatt 'never really knew', he says. 'He had not been in the department many weeks and if he accepted my argument about the centrality of our current operations and the critical need to succeed, he kept this well disguised. I think the wider issues passed him by completely . . .'[14]

.'Frankly,' Sir Richard writes in his memoirs, 'unless you had some background or acquired interest in defence, then, superficially exciting as it was to take on the job as a Cabinet minister, the responsibilities attached when the nation was fighting two demanding wars while only organised, funded and equipped for one, made it a poisoned chalice of some potency.' He then refers to the rapid turnover of Defence Secretaries under the Blair–Brown administrations: 'Perhaps the fact that no fewer than five apparently well-meaning individuals [Defence Secretaries] had sipped from this cup in recent years and succumbed makes the point – especially when Des Browne was given Scotland to look after as well in one of Gordon Brown's hasty ministerial reshuffles! To put the point bluntly, it took me thirty-seven years to be ready to command the Army; I am the first to recognise that it was a terribly tall order to ask very competent lawyers like Geoff Hoon or Des Browne to grasp the essentials in thirty-seven hours.'

Sir Richard Dannatt goes on to ridicule the slowness of the MOD in identifying the very purpose of our presence in Iraq and Afghanistan.

Back in that autumn of 2006, the question of MOD priorities was not clarified until the Defence Board held an 'away day' of discussions in late October, which enabled it to conclude that the primary focus of the department was 'strategic success in Iraq and Afghanistan in the context of countering global terrorism'. Wonderful! But it was little short of a blinding glimpse of the obvious, and begged the second-order question of why this conclusion was not reached and announced until our operations in Iraq were in their fourth year and our major reinforcement of Afghanistan was in its sixth month. To some of us this defied logic. The sad reality of that time was that much of the MOD, in its Byzantine way, was conducting business as usual, in a cocooned environment far distant from the harsh reality experienced by our soldiers on the front line of Helmand or Basra Palace. Sadly, the protection of vested interests within and between the services, others relating to industry or others with a political flavour, seemed to rank higher than the need to succeed in the field.[15]

By 'vested interests' General Dannatt meant the Royal Navy's request for two new aircraft carriers and the Royal Air Force's demand for the full quota of Typhoon fighter jets – both hugely expensive and neither of which would ever be used in Afghanistan. General Dannatt said he felt that 'the top end of the government did not understand or fully appreciate the pressures the Army was under and I tried really hard to get that understanding across. I felt it was pushing a rock up a steep hill pretty much all the way through. It was frustrating because from the land forces' point of view, we always do our job, but we knew we couldn't do it as well because we hadn't got the resources.'[16]

Curiously, he says that his relationship with Gordon Brown improved after he became Prime Minister. 'To his credit, having exhibited very little interest in Defence during his years as Chancellor, Mr Brown invited all of the Chiefs [of Staff] to a working dinner in 2007.' Having agreed beforehand not to talk about money, they had a 'most interesting round-table discussion about foreign and security issues which, of course, included Iraq and Afghanistan'. As an aside, he said he had only a single one-to-one meeting with Tony Blair in his office in Downing Street five weeks before he handed over to Gordon Brown – 'a meeting that was never going to move anything from an army point of view,' Dannatt adds. 'But with Gordon Brown in the chair, things started brightly. Almost against the odds, he felt an apparent desire on his [Brown's] part to want to understand what their concerns were. During the first nine months of the Brown premiership, the Chiefs had three working breakfasts in Number Ten, along with the Secretary of State for Defence, Des Browne, and the Permanent Under Secretary, [Sir] Bill Jeffrey. A rapport seemed to be achieved.'[17]

But, 'ominously', they did not seem to make much progress on the subject of Afghanistan, and then Gordon Brown became distracted by the financial recession. 'The breakfasts at Number Ten stopped.' But in the New Year, 2009, the fundamental difference of opinion within government began to become clearer. The Chiefs of Staff had reached the view that a force level of 'nearly 10,000 British troops [in Afghanistan] was both necessary and sustainable, especially now that the drawdown in Iraq was nearly complete. Dannatt was strongly of this view. Enough boots on the ground meant more soldiers deployed, and that cost money, especially in terms of the mission-specific equipment that was needed. But in the context of a national financial meltdown, with unprecedented amounts of money going to prop up the banking and financial sector, there was never going to be any more money for Defence, despite the fact that the Services were fighting an increasingly bloody war on behalf of, and in the clear interest of the country.'[18]   .

Understandably, General Dannatt writes, Gordon Brown's focus became fixed on the recession, 'to the apparent exclusion of all else. After all, that was his area of expertise. But the cost was paid by Defence, in particular the war in which we were engaged in Afghanistan.'[19]

General Dannatt had not spoken personally to the Prime Minister for more than six months and then one day he saw him walking across Horse Guards Parade with David Miliband to attend the arrival ceremony, with the Queen as host, for the visiting President of Mexico. Seeing his chance, General Dannatt decided that this was 'a good moment for an ambush'. Intercepting the Prime Minister, he excused himself for interrupting their conversation on account of Afghanistan – '"General, I would not have expected anything less" – and briskly made the case for a troop uplift there and then, stressing not only the need from an Afghanistan point of view, but that we had got away with short-changing the Americans in Iraq because of our emphasis on Afghanistan, so we really needed to get this one right. "Ah, well, I am seeing President Obama this week and we will talk about these things," was the evasive answer I got . . .'[20]

Despite having ambushed the Prime Minister so expertly, Dannatt has to admit that Gordon Brown still refused to accept his generals' advice to increase the size of the British contingent in Afghanistan. 'Later that week,' Sir Richard writes, 'Gordon Brown and Barack Obama did indeed talk about Afghanistan. As the Foreign Office telegrams were reporting that the United States was looking for more support in Afghanistan from its European partners, including the British, the President's pitch to the Prime Minister was entirely predictable. I am reliably told that when Mr Brown and Mr Obama did meet, an early part of the conversation was along the lines of: "Hey Gordon, couldn't you do a bit more in Afghanistan?" For whatever reason, Gordon Brown announced a troop uplift of 500 soldiers that week. While the uplift was welcome, it went only part of the way to bringing the force level up to that recommended by the Chiefs of Staff [which was 10,000].'[21]

Although this was only half the increase Dannatt and his colleagues had recommended, it is only fair to Gordon Brown to acknowledge that he was already wrestling with the problems of the recession. 'In my last month in office,' General Dannatt says, 'Gordon Brown and I had a long conversation on the telephone; my wife Pippa and I had lunch at Chequers during which the Prime Minister and I talked in the margins, and I had a one-to-one meeting with him in Number Ten Downing Street.'[22]

But despite the apparent new cordiality between the two men, General Dannatt's farewell visit to British troops in Helmand ended on a sour note. He was forced to fly in an American helicopter to the much fought-over British base at Sangin because, he said, there were no British helicopters available. 'Self-evidently, if I move in an American helicopter, it is because I have not got a British helicopter,' he said when asked by the media why he was flying in a US helicopter. Predictably, some Labour MPs accused General Dannatt of 'playing politics'. One junior minister said: 'This is a very difficult time and he should know better,' and one Labour MP called General Dannatt a four-letter word.[23]

In one of the many clashes over helicopters between David Cameron, then Leader of the Opposition, and Gordon Brown, Cameron asked during Prime Minister's Questions: 'Isn't the reason why we don't have enough helicopters that we didn't plan to have enough helicopters? When he [Mr Brown] looks back to 2004 and his decision to reduce the helicopter budget by £1.4 billion, does he remember that the National Audit Office said that year there was a considerable deficit in the availability of helicopter lift? Does he now recognise that decision was a bad mistake?'

The Prime Minister replied: 'I believe we are making the provision that is necessary both for helicopters and equipment on the ground. We will do everything we can . . . to support our brave and courageous armed forces, who are professional and determined and will have our full support.' He said that the number of helicopters had risen by 60 per cent in the past two years, adding: 'I ask the Conservative Party to look at the statements being made by those who speak for our armed forces on the ground. They have made it absolutely clear that in this particular instance, while the loss of life is tragic and sad, it is not to do with helicopters.' This cut little ice with British troops under fire in Helmand.

General Sir Mike Jackson, General Dannatt's predecessor as CGS from 2003 to 2006, also gave evidence to the Chilcot Inquiry, which released newly declassified documents showing that he had warned five years before that British forces in Iraq were suffering from a lack of helicopters and that both the Americans and the British had underestimated the scale of violence that would flare up after the fall of Saddam Hussein. When security did become a major issue, he said, it became clear British troops were 'too thin on the ground'.

In one declassified document from 2005, General Jackson wrote of a recent visit to Iraq, that 'though there was no sense of defeatism in theatre, the possibility of strategic failure was mentioned (by commanders) in earnest on this visit more than on any before. Our support helicopter fleet is creaking badly,' he added. 'JHF-I [Joint Helicopter Force Iraq] was struggling to meet its tasks even with rigorous prioritisation. The overall picture was one of an SH [support helicopter] force ill-matched to support current operations. If their SH capability was inadequate, their AT [air transport] fleet was worse. The air bridge to theatre was now so fragile that sustaining an efficient R&R schedule was nigh impossible.'[24]

Less vital on a strategic level, but important in terms of personal morale, he delivered a tongue-in-cheek rebuke in another declassified document about shortages of personal kit: 'In the name of accounting orthodoxy,' he wrote in 2005, 'we lack basic items, such as desert clothing. I am unsure whether the cost of storing such items would really have been more than the inflated price we have no doubt paid by procurement under UOR [Urgent Operational Requirement] action but I am certain as to the negative impact on the morale component that failure to provide these items had had.'[25]

A flamboyant figure, General Sir Mike Jackson is best known from the time when, as CGS, he presided over the amalgamation of the British Army's infantry regiments, the result of swingeing cuts imposed on the armed forces by the then Labour Chancellor, Gordon Brown. The disappearance, because of the mergers, of so many historic regiments, including for example The Royal Scots, the oldest regiment in the world, produced a wave of hostile reaction, particularly in Scotland. The other, less contentious, but more dramatic event in General Jackson's career occurred in Kosovo in 1999, when he was deputy to the NATO commander, General Wesley Clark, Supreme Allied Commander Europe (SACEUR). Under the United Nations plan for the peaceful takeover of Kosovo, British troops were ordered to move into Pristina, the capital of Kosovo, but were pre-empted by Russian troops who jumped the gun and occupied the airport. General Clark immediately ordered General Jackson to blockade the runways to stop Russian reinforcements being flown in, but General Jackson refused, in case his soldiers became involved in an 'armed conflict' with the Russians for which he had no authority from London. By refusing, however, to carry out General Clark's order – allegedly saying 'I won't start World War Three for you', a remark which he told me personally he does not remember making[26] – he would be guilty of disobeying an order, which is a court-martial offence. When I quizzed him further about the apparent discrepancy, General Sir Mike Jackson repeated that he could not specifically remember saying the words, but explained these were the words used by General Wes Clark in his book *Waging Modern War*, and since he had no reason to doubt his account, he did not believe he would have made it up.

He recalled that there was no one else present when he and General Clark had 'that very difficult conversation on the morning of 13 June', except for Clark's communications man. He was confident there was no leak from the British side, and surmises Wes Clark must have, as he puts it, passed it on through Washington. 'In summary, I do not specifically remember saying the words, but I have no reason to doubt the account given by Wes Clark, and so used it in my own narrative.'[27] Eventually the impasse was resolved when the Americans persuaded the Hungarians, Romanians and Bulgarians to bar the Russians from using their airspace to fly in reinforcements. As a result, the tabloids dubbed Jackson 'Macho Jacko'.

Labour's record of six Defence Secretaries in thirteen years – three of them for a year or less – contrasts unfavourably with the Americans who in the same period, under two different administrations, had only three, the last of whom, Robert Gates, appointed by President Bush in 2006 after twenty-six years with the CIA and the National Security Council, and kept on by President Obama, retired in July 2011 after nearly four and a half years at the Pentagon. The Americans might be forgiven for thinking the British were no longer a serious ally who, although small in terms of numbers, could always be relied on to punch above their weight. Little wonder that a military insider, speaking before the British general election in June 2010, with Labour still in power, said: 'I feel that we have stumbled, lurched from one fighting season to the next [in Afghanistan] and we haven't got an army big enough to take this on; and even less we don't have a government that says: "Let's get in there and do it." You can't not resource an issue, and at the same time want them to fight above their weight.'[28]

He went on: 'It's telling, I thought, that in the last two party conferences it took Gordon Brown forty minutes before Afghanistan was mentioned. We sat there in the office waiting for him to talk about Afghanistan. David Cameron mentioned it immediately; it was his opening sentence practically. Okay, it's easy being the opposition, but that implied to me that someone realises what a state we are in and is going to grip it. He may actually go in reverse and say we are not up to this, this is all we can do. He may not dance, perhaps, to the American tune and feel it is so important, as part of the special relationship. Because that smacks at the moment of what this is, of doing a "keeping in with the Americans" and just 500 [soldiers] at a time will help and we are going to do our bit.'[29]

While the Conservative–Lib Dem Coalition government, which came into power on 11 May 2010, is probably more sympathetic to the armed forces than Gordon Brown's Labour, and in Dr Liam Fox, the ex-Secretary for Defence, had someone prepared to fight their corner, the drastic cuts in the MOD budget, in line with Tory policy across the board, is bound to make life for the services increasingly difficult. What may have seemed at first sight to be a relatively minor exercise, helping to set up and maintain a 'no-fly zone' in Libya, approved by the Security Council on 17 May 2011, revealed weaknesses in the RAF's and Navy's ability to carry out what transpired to be a bigger and lengthier operation than was first anticipated. But Afghanistan remained Britain's main military priority and it soon became apparent that Prime Minister David Cameron was taking his cue from President Obama in wanting to scale back the size of their respective NATO contingents in Afghanistan. Both leaders had their eye on the dates of their next election – Obama in November 2012, and Cameron in the spring, presumably, of 2014; and both have said they want their combat troops out by the end of 2014. The emphasis had changed from war-war to jaw-jaw, in the Churchillian phrase, and talks with close aides of Mullah Omar, who in the past had always rejected them, were said to be under way.

General Richards Takes Over, 2006–2011

Cometh the hour, cometh the man.

Anon.

General Sir David Richards, who became Chief of the Defence Staff in September 2010, is a 'soldier's soldier'. Matey, funny and articulate, he has seen action in East Timor, Kosovo and Sierra Leone, where a particularly nasty civil war was in progress when he arrived on the scene and saved President Kabbah's neck. But it was in Afghanistan, in 2006, where 3 PARA were fighting almost non-stop, that he really showed his mettle. The roll call of battle honours in the opium towns of Helmand – Sangin, Musa Qala, Kajaki and Naw Zad – all names to conjure with, is long and impressive. As everyone now knows, 3 PARA's 'Toms' gained many decorations for valour. Their courage, alas, came at a heavy price. Both their Victoria Cross and their George Cross were posthumous. In all, fifteen were killed in action and forty-six wounded.

In *Danger Close*, 3 PARA's commander, Lieutenant Colonel Stuart Tootal, criticises NATO's command structure as being cumbersome and incompetent, but he adds that, to his credit, David Richards soon gave it a rapid and drastic overhaul. He also took in hand President Karzai's virtually non-existent administration and set up a 'war cabinet'. Above all, he brought an awareness of how close to 'institutional failure' the British armed forces had come, under-financed by years of Gordon Brown parsimony, overstretched by Tony Blair interventionism, and maladministered by MOD incompetence, culminating in the British Army's sorry exit from Basra.

In the following interview with Sir David Richards, conducted in 2010, he gives his own frank and outspoken account of the campaign in Helmand, in 2006–07. He criticises the British military establishment for being ill-prepared and with a 'rather amateurish approach to high-level military operations verging on the complacent'. He also characterises NATO as being often disorganised and unhelpful. Then a lieutenant general, Richards was ISAF (NATO) Commander in southern Afghanistan. His record of the misconceptions and errors that preceded the Helmand venture, when he was the first British general to command American troops since the Second World War, makes disturbing reading. His comments, however, depressing though they may be, are countered by his belief that the struggle in Afghanistan can and must be won and his 'clear faith' that 'the British armed forces are now handsomely proving that they have the ability to reform and adapt'.[1]

A few months before, General Richards, then Chief of the General Staff, was equally critical in a previous interview about the lack of resources which have dogged our presence in Afghanistan. 'Firstly,' he told me, 'we have never had sufficient troops to dominate the physical and human terrain in the manner successful COIN [counter-insurgency] operations demand; and secondly, there was a conspicuous failure to follow up tactical military success with high tempo "civilian effect", i.e. reconstruction, development and governance. On top of that, the reconciliation, or reinte-gration [of the Taliban] effort had been woeful . . . I made many attempts to reinvigorate it [when NATO Commander], but it languished through a lack of interest in Washington and London. For a while, because of alleged corruption, funding was stopped altogether in 2007/8.'[2]

Richards is the only recent CDS to have fought in Afghanistan, which gives him unique authority, especially since President Obama, soon after taking office, said that whereas Iraq was a disastrous mistake, Afghanistan was the 'necessary war' that America, and by implication its allies, must fight and win.

We spoke for about an hour in September 2010, in the sunny sitting room of an elegant apartment in London, after the Richardses had given lunch to an enterprising British agriculturist who was just leaving to grow pomegranates commercially in Kandahar. General Richards retains a lively interest in all things Afghan, as does his wife Caroline, who started and runs a charity, the Afghan Appeal Fund, with a branch in America, which raises money to build and staff schools for Afghan children. He has a distinguished record in putting out military 'bush fires' in disparate parts of the world, but Afghanistan will be his greatest challenge.

That day he was between jobs. He had just ceased being Chief of the General Staff, head of the British Army, and was about to become Chief of the Defence Staff, head of all three services: the most important military figure in the country.

He began by saying he thought the initial ISAF military operation in Afghanistan in 2001 and 2002 was excellent and had 'very successfully pushed the Taliban out . . . before all eyes turned to Iraq'. He had reservations, however, about the UN Secretary General's Special Representative in Afghanistan, Lakhdar Brahimi. 'I don't mean to sound too critical of him, but Lakhdar Brahimi's "light touch", I think is at the heart of a lot of these problems.' Brahimi, a former Algerian Foreign Minister, who was charged with establishing a democratic Afghan government in Kabul, advocated the United Nations and the international community adopt a 'light footprint' approach, meaning less top-down control and encouraging the Afghans to run their own affairs as far as possible.

'If in 2002 the West had realised the state Afghanistan was in after twenty years plus of fighting,' General Richards said, 'many of whose most talented people, the ones with the most initiative, had departed, leaving behind two generations who hadn't been educated, and we had really done then what we are belatedly trying to do now, I suspect we wouldn't have the problem today and the military would not have had to play a major part.'

He recalled Donald Rumsfeld – President Bush's Secretary of Defense, from January 2001 until December 2006 – asking him in the summer of 2006: 'Well, why are things deteriorating, General Richards?'

What followed must have been one of the longest answers the normally impatient Rumsfeld ever had to listen to. Rumsfeld is famous for not suffering fools gladly. A man with a sharp mind, he likes to categorise problems into 'Known Unknowns' and even 'Unknown Unknowns'. It says a lot for David Richards's persuasiveness and fluency that apparently he did listen.

'I said, well I think in 2002/3/4 a vacuum was created through a shortage of resources and understanding, both military, civilian and political and the Taliban began to think "actually, they have forgotten about us" as they sat in Pakistan watching. The [Afghan] people, at the same time, began to get a little bored, disappointed about our inability to meet the promises that we had made to them which were well-intentioned but hopelessly ill-resourced. So a combination of a poor performance – clearly there were not enough troops there to do whatever was required in Lashkar Gah – there were only about fifty Americans at one stage, which actually was fine, while things went well – but as the promises were or appeared to be being broken, the security situation started to deteriorate. The warlords were still there, all the things we promised wouldn't happen, did. I think it fed an environment in which, actually, the Taliban could naturally come back; and as we realised that was happening we should have quickly, militarily stepped in to restore that vital sense of security without which all our efforts actually are pointless.'

But this failure to act, which General Richards emphasises – was it due to a lack of intelligence or, as Lieutenant Colonel Tootal suggests, was it because of the wishful thinking he claims then dominated opinion in Whitehall? 'What was the most important thing to all of us?' Richards asked rhetorically with that familiar quizzical look over the top of his spectacles. 'It was the ability to get up in the morning and if you want to go shopping you go shopping, or for a drive to see your family, or whatever it is. If you can't do that, to begin with you will think: "What are the police doing? Oh, they'll sort it out the next day." But if after three years that isn't happening, you begin to lose complete faith in your government, and in this case in the international community. I think all those things came together, and Iraq certainly didn't help because of the huge amount of focus on it.'

General Richards makes plain his frustration at being caught between the rock of a shortage of resources and the hard place of the almost exclusive focus on Iraq. 'And so by the time I started getting interested [in planning his NATO mission in Afghanistan] in 2005 – because we, [I and] my headquarters in particular, had been nominated as the man and organisation that was going to not just look after relatively quiet and successful Kabul, the north and the west – Mazar and then Herat – [but] the dodgier bit in the south and the east as well. So we put real effort into our analysis, and I have to say we might as well have not bothered, judging by the degree to which the international community and NATO collectively listened to us.'

In fact, what emerged from the analysis should have made the establishment sit up straight. 'It made it quite clear that we didn't have enough troops, and the international effort in the south in terms of reconstruction and development was also going to be inadequate – so I made these points very clear up my chain of command, but perhaps quite understandably Iraq was absorbing virtually everyone's interest.'

'As a soldier,' General Richards said, a hint of resignation in his voice, 'you make the best of whatever you are given and anyway, you don't have much option.' He became overall NATO commander in Afghanistan on 4 May 2006, but such was the complexity of the NATO command structure that area command handovers followed at different times: the south, for example, on 31 July, from General Karl Eikenberry (later US Ambassador in Kabul), the east (where the American hunt for al Qaeda remnants was concentrated) also from Eikenberry on 4 October. 'So progressively we went anti-clockwise around the country . . . I often say if in the late autumn of 2004, when Tony Blair agreed that Britain would lead the expansion of NATO across the whole country, if when he and other NATO leaders took that decision in late 2004 in Istanbul, they had known then what it was going to be like in 2006, they almost certainly would not have done it.'

General Richards was probably too polite to answer Donald Rumsfeld's question as to why things were deteriorating in Afghanistan by saying that it was because of the demands of the war in Iraq, but spoke instead of a massive institutional failure: 'So as a long answer to your question: Were they naive? Did they really understand what they were getting into, when the die was cast for that move of NATO into the south-east?' Undoubtedly they did not, was General Richards's unequivocal answer and he wasn't even involved then, he adds. 'But as soon as we did the analysis, we . . . realised that it was inadequately resourced and the command and control arrangements were very weak.'

General Richards went on to paint a picture of an MOD and defence staff that seemed, in 2005, to be held in thrall, like Ulysses's sailors, by a bewitching siren song – that there was going to be no trouble. 'To give you a feel for it, when I took over my new headquarters in January 2005, many people in it, including some very senior officers, said there is absolutely no need to worry about this till next November: then you will have to do some work and go. I remember taking what I suppose was a morally courageous decision, because it was contrary to the advice that I was getting from my staff. I said: "No, no, we are going to turn our attention to Afghanistan now." And I have to say a very good American who had been part of the other school of thought, said to me, not many months later: "That was the best decision you ever took, because otherwise we would be hopelessly unready for it." So this is why I would say it was an institutional failing both in government, NATO and across the senior elements of the armed forces.'

General Richards remembers in 2005 going across to the Foreign Office or the Cabinet Office 'to speak to the woman who was in charge of our policy for that part of the world, when she wanted to tell me what I would be doing in terms of the British government approach, and I said: "What about NATO's plan and NATO strategy?" and she said: "Well that doesn't matter, and anyway I don't even know what it is." They didn't know that what we had actually signed up to wasn't a bad strategy. But we weren't, like every other nation, helpful in delivering it. So it was an institutional misunderstanding as usual; arrogance about what was involved; and just genuine ignorance of the whole issue of the country. And at that stage things did not look too bad. There weren't that many casualties. We had lost very few in Mazar and because there were virtually no Americans in the south, they were not really losing any people either. And there is a message in there, perhaps.'

Surprisingly, General Richards found himself receiving assistance from an unexpected quarter and pays a handsome compliment to the man responsible, Dr John Reid, the main architect of the Blair-inspired tripartite development plan for Helmand, based on British Army-supplied security, Foreign Office-supplied governance and DFID-supplied development. General Richards said he was a defender of Dr John Reid, Secretary for Defence, for the remark he made and for which he was later ridiculed – 'We would be perfectly happy to leave in three years' time without firing one shot' – pointing out that the famous quote reflected the perceived wisdom at the time that the Army was going not to fight but to protect the governance programme.*

What particularly impressed General Richards, however, was that Dr Reid 'had responded to my appeal to give us more fighting equipment in case our hopes proved pious'. They arranged to meet, with some difficulty, in Berlin – Richards was then at his new headquarters, the Allied Rapid Reaction Corps (ARRC), at Rheindahlen, British HQ in Germany – to have a 'completely off-the-record breakfast where Reid sat patiently with his special adviser, Josh Arnold Foster, and I explained what, after the best part of a year's analysis, we [Richards and his team] thought was going to happen.' Reid was very helpful and 'agreed to make sure we did have the equipment we needed, or at least as much as was available'. For example, 'it was his decision to agree to my request to take Apache helicopters to deploy for the first time with the British armed forces, artillery and so on'. Richards explained they did not want to use them, but they might just have to. 'It would be folly to go to Afghanistan, given the history of the place, without something to stop us being massacred. So I am a defender of John Reid.'

NATO as a whole, however, General Richards said, was 'with a few notable exceptions' probably even worse at that time than the British defence and security establishment.

When I was thinking, perhaps subconsciously, about this book, I remember asking General Richards in late 2005 or early 2006, how his preparations were getting on. His reply was that he had no strategic reserve, perhaps the first time that had ever happened, and that the MOD were being exceedingly difficult about arranging for him to have his own helicopter or aircraft, without which he said he could not do his job properly. His headquarters would be in the capital, Kabul, and his troops often many hundreds of miles away, including the British task force in Helmand.

---

* What John Reid said at a press conference in Kabul in April 2006, according to the BBC, was: 'We're in the south [of Afghanistan] to help and protect the Afghan people, to reconstruct their economy and democracy. We would be perfectly happy to leave in three years' time without firing one shot.'

'It is a cardinal principle in a military operation,' he said, 'that the commander must have a reserve. I had no proper reserve. I had a company of light Portuguese troops, one company, who couldn't possibly go into the most demanding environments – if they materialised, as we thought they inevitably would – because they didn't have the protection and the fire-power. They were very gallant, by the way. I did use them wherever I could . . . I am the biggest fan of the Portuguese armed forces to this day because they did as much as they possibly could. But NATO was abso-lutely resistant to the idea that we should have anything more capable.'

I wondered aloud why NATO had been so unresponsive. Who was giving the orders? General Richards's answer was that while the overall commander, the Supreme Allied Commander Europe (SACEUR), was always American, NATO was 'only as good as the nations that it comprises want it to be'. The military chain of command was slow in understanding what was at stake, and 'I had some trouble persuading my immediate superiors in this pretty archaic chain of command' – a German air force officer in Brunssum and General Jim Jones, then SACEUR and later President Obama's National Security Adviser. 'They understood the risks we were running and both became progressively much more active in argu-ing my case, although I have to say it took them time.' The only people who did understand it were his own headquarters because they had been 'charged with this task which was clearly very important for NATO and our nations'. Only they had really done their homework, which he described as a year-long 'very swept-up process of analysis and deduction' on which you base your planning.

We did that: we gave our proposals, our plan in and got no response, except there is no money and anyway we don't agree with you etc. They just had to go in [to Afghanistan] with what they had . . . but at least then they knew they had quality fighting troops [3 PARA] and because of John Reid, much maligned, we had the heavier and more capable equipment if it should go bad. Goodness me, what we would have suffered if John Reid had not agreed to that, so you can see why I actu-ally defended him. Three PARA did have artillery, [but] quite a lot of people in the MOD at the time said why do you want artillery? It's a peacekeeping operation. So it very much affected 3 PARA. There were undoubted equipment failures at the time . . . most of the equipment was going to Iraq anyway. Three PARA were a light infantry organisation; when they needed protected mobility they had the infamous Snatch [Land Rover] . . . that was virtually all we had.

It was obviously fortunate that, as General Richards himself pointed out, 'the Taliban were . . . quiescent, passive in Helmand to begin with'. It was only when 3 PARA 'started to push out to those platoon houses' – government district centres garrisoned by small detachments of British soldiers which came under heavy and repeated Taliban attack – a strategy to which Richards says he was 'bitterly opposed', that 'suddenly the Taliban realised that they could take them [the British] on and they found themselves often hard pressed. I remember very well the first KIA [killed in action] was a very fine artillery officer called Jim Philippson and I thought, "Christ, it has started". That is why we had persuaded Reid it was not going to be as easy as he and others had hoped. I hoped it would be easier, but all my military life I have hoped for the best but planned for the worst; and for the first time in my life I was being asked to do it the other way around.'

General Richards arrived in Camp ISAF in Kabul on 4 May 2006, knowing his headquarters was as well worked up as it could possibly be. He had spent over a year preparing for this despite people, including some of the most senior serving officers, advising him he only needed a few months. Thank goodness, he says, he rejected that. He gave up arguing for more resources at some point, probably around April, until they got there. He didn't personally get the equipment he needed as commander of a major theatre of operations. Historically, he should have had a plane to fly himself around in, or helicopters, and he should certainly have had a reserve, and he had none of them.

Explaining why he never had his own helicopter, he says 'because Britain and the British establishment doesn't understand what command is; a lot of people in the defence establishment are naturally but unjustifiably envious of the man getting the glory, if you like, who's in the spotlight. The attitude was: "Oh, you will manage and anyway you don't need it. It is all about your ego." They don't say it, but that is what you pick up, whereas actually having an aircraft to fly around a country as large as Afghanistan is a *sine qua non* of successful command.' Without it he could not visit his troops.

'You have to use a fixed-wing aircraft for the long distances and helicopters for the shorter ones. Of course the Americans were very good and lent me both most of the time I needed them. Sometimes the French had a few helicopters in Kabul and they knew our approach to these things, so helped out. I just put up with it. But it was a sad reflection on how little some in London understood the practicalities of high command.'[3]

NATO's British-dominated HQ Allied Rapid Reaction Corps, under Richards's command, deployed at the beginning of May and 'to begin with it was all quite peaceful. I only had responsibility for Kabul and the north and west which was pretty minimal in terms of conflict or fighting . . . Then I remember in late May there was a riot in Kabul as a result of an American convoy going out of control and ploughing into a market, killing some locals,' an accident which led to serious trouble. The brakes on the lead vehicle failed as the convoy was driving down the steep hill into Kabul's northern suburb of Khairkhana, causing extensive damage. The Americans opened fire as crowds blocked the road, and in the resultant carnage about twenty Afghans were killed and more than 150 injured.

To General Richards the incident acted as an SOS. 'The ensuing rioting made the international community, foreign ambassadors and Karzai's government realise people were getting fed up . . . I had been saying we are in the middle of a fool's paradise at the moment . . . We are about to go into the south and the east and this [accident] has brought home to us – the international community and the government – that things were fragile.' Richards then had the idea, with the help of some English-speaking Afghan politicians like Hanif Atmar, the Education Minister, and General Abdul Rahim Wardak, Defence Minister, and a few other people, of persuading Karzai to establish a war cabinet, to which they gave the name of Policy Action Group. It was known colloquially as the PAG, or as the *Economist* said jokingly in an article in November 2006, simply 'Please Ask the General'. The other General, Wardak, who trained in America, had, during the Russian occupation of 1979–89, been military commander of one of the smaller *mujahideen* parties, Pir Sayed Ahmed Gailani's Mahaz (the National Islamic Front of Afghanistan). I met him for the first time in 1984, at night, in enemy territory, near Jalalabad, when both of us were taking part in separate *mujahideen* operations: Wardak as the leader of a Mahaz group that was blowing up electricity pylons; I as a film-maker with the Yunus Khalis group. He asked me to join them but I explained we were already fully committed. General Wardak is larger than life, speaks good English and gets on well with both the American and British military.

His purpose, General Richards explained, 'was to use the rioting as a catalyst to get the international community, the government and the military to start working together more closely. And still to this day, he says, he believes that one of the glaring omissions of the Western approach to Afghanistan has been – because the PAG really fell into disrepute or disrepair after the British left – the failure of the leaders out there to get together in a methodical manner. Because, unless you force yourselves together and debate the issues in an open manner, everyone is hiding things from each other. Knowledge is power. One country goes in to see Karzai, then another. He owns the knowledge; he is not ill-intentioned, but he will say one thing to them, a different thing to someone else. He hasn't got his government around him to say whether he has got any money.'[4]

The PAG allowed them to take a much more comprehensive approach and actually to start work on an international level. 'It was a sort of big war cabinet,' General Richards said. 'We needed it, because we couldn't get any sense out of anybody. I remember saying to myself: "I have got to work this through" . . . I put a wet towel round my head for a couple of days and I came out with the concept of the Policy Action Group. Having read a bit, I knew that you had to get together, you had to have committees . . . We did that and I think it began to flourish and I have to say nothing that I have heard since was not broadly one way or another discussed then . . .'

The great power of the PAG, General Richards maintains, was that you sat down once a week. 'About one in four [meetings] was chaired by President Karzai. He flourished in the chair actually – we helped him, advised him – but he chaired it. He would get proposals for action, we would then debate it; the Afghan side would say why our proposals couldn't work, or how long it would take, where the money would come from.'

David Richards believes something like a PAG is essential to successful counter-insurgency operations, 'and to this day there is no real equivalent in Kabul', he asserts. 'The most influential foreigners, the Americans and the Brits and others, individually and sometimes together, talk to President Karzai and occasionally one or two of them will go along to their equivalent National Security Council.' But it was no longer a regular systematic event with a joint Afghaninternational secretariat. He appears still very conscious of the benefits it conferred. 'I know today Afghan government ministers better than people who have been there longer, because of the PAG,' he says. One is tempted to speculate that if the PAG had continued, in one form or another, the breakdown in relations between Karzai and the Americans, and to a lesser extent the British, might have been prevented. The PAG, after all, was really about networking. 'You mingle beforehand,' David Richards recalls, 'you talk afterwards, you become friends, all that sort of thing has gone, largely. We had representatives of the World Bank say, all the military, the major ambassadors were there, twenty internationals depending on the subject, all the key ministers, about twelve, the National Security Adviser, finance, economics, defence, interior, agriculture, communications, it really was the comprehensive approach, it was what you needed.'

I wondered what had happened before. Even General Richards was not entirely sure. It was all done, he thought, by the Americans who, not surprisingly, 'liked being in charge'. To Richards, the 'whole point of the PAG was that you had to share authority and influence with others', but it dwindled in importance after the HQ Allied Rapid Reaction Corps left because a few key nations didn't play by the rules. If you did not involve everybody in the analysis and decision-making process, he argues, others who were not part of it would, either unwittingly or deliberately, undermine a lot of what you were proposing, for no better reason than that 'they simply don't know about it or don't agree with you'. The PAG system, with everyone having a say, did take a bit longer, but on the other hand you then had an agreed plan. 'We agreed things that were quite difficult but people saw were necessary.'

It took General Richards about a month to set up the Policy Action Group. 'Hanif Atmar said we need this very badly but you will never persuade President Karzai to do it, because knowledge is power and he likes to work with the mobile phone, which I think Khalilzad* really taught

---

* Zalmay Khalilzad, an Afghan-American academic and State Department official, who

him to do.' The riot and its aftermath, however, persuaded Karzai he did need a body like the PAG, David Richards says, 'and I was on a bit of a crest of a wave in terms of influence, so I remember going back to Hanif Atmar. He had a big grin on his face and said: "I didn't think you would ever do it but fantastic."' He became 'a big ally' and adviser and still visits the Richardses in London.

One of the conundrums which puzzles Afghan watchers is the reason why Britain took over Helmand instead of Kandahar. When General Sir Mike Jackson, another former Chief of the General Staff, was asked, he is said to have thrown up his hands and replied: 'Search me, guv.' At the NATO leaders' conference in Istanbul in 2004, Britain decided that they, the Canadians, the Americans and the Dutch would all go into the south, according to General Richards. The Americans would probably look after the east as well (as part of the continuing and largely fruitless hunt for al Qaeda remnants). The Canadians, after a conference in Ottawa, were 'very keen' to go to Kandahar, Richards says. 'I said to the MOD, having done the analysis: "We should go to Kandahar. It's a crucial province and the Canadians, as capable as they are, are very unlikely to have the numbers and resources needed to handle it. Helmand is very complex and best simply contained for now." Much to my annoyance, back comes the message that as a result of the Ottawa Conference, we [the British] will go to Helmand.'

David Richards thinks the reason was 'partly over some misguided association with the fact that Britain had said they would lead on the drugs side', but mainly because the Canadians understandably perhaps given the commitment they were making wanted a prestigious role, ideally in the key province. 'But Canada, as we knew, would never have the resources and the manpower to do that as well as we thought it should be done. Yet, it had to be us or Canada because America was going to lead in the east and the two of us were going to share the lead in the south. So basically we are in the wrong province.' In Richards's view, Britain should have said: "'Are you certain you are big enough to do Kandahar? Should we swap?" We were the

---

worked with the 'Neo-Con' Republican Paul Wolfowitz, Rumsfeld's deputy, advised President Bush after 9/11 and was Bush's ambassador to Kabul, in 2003–05.

only ones, of the three nations involved – the Dutch, Canadians and British – that potentially were. Anyway we ended up with Helmand.'[5]

That was one muddle. Another was NATO's complicated and clumsy command and control system in Helmand which, until General Richards put it right, drew the ire, among others, of Lieutenant Colonel Stuart Tootal, Commander of 3 PARA, who perhaps suffered most.

This is how David Richards described the snakes-and-ladders type of NATO command structure he inherited when he took over in Helmand at one of the turning points of the war:

[Brigadier] Ed Butler was not actually in command formally of 16 Air Assault Brigade in Helmand, he was under a chap called Colonel Charlie Knaggs, and Tootal, formally, was under him and Knaggs was meant to answer to the American chain of command until I took over at the end of July. (We didn't know it was going to be the end of July but that's when we did it.) I was very critical of this because we had a British brigadier, very fine brigadier, Ed Butler. I am not blaming him. He was not formally responsible for what was happening, but in practice was dictating it. So he wasn't actually in our chain of command . . .

Ben Freakley, an outstanding American major general who was formally responsible still at that stage for what was going on in the south, didn't go through Ed Butler in his chain of command, he went to Charlie Knaggs, and then dealt with Tootal. In practice, Ed Butler was running the British operation but he wasn't in that American-led chain of command, so he was an irritant to Ben Freakley. I think Ed spent more time up in Kabul as a national contingent commander, which he wasn't really, but pretended to be, than he did down in Helmand which he rather left to Knaggs and Tootal. But as far as Ben Freakley was concerned he wanted him down there. Anyway, he [Butler] actually had his little headquarters in Kandahar, not even in Helmand.

Butler, who wasn't formally in command 'but in practice was', General Richards says, agreed under pressure from Governor Daud to push into the north and establish the 'infamous' platoon houses. 'He didn't ask me; I wasn't responsible at the time but I heard about it and I said this is actually contrary to what our own doctrine is.' Richards and Tootal had agreed at Christmas in a bar, 'funnily enough', up in Wiltshire, that Tootal would focus on Lashkar Gah and Gereshk in the south of Helmand, 'do good works and show what was possible' by way of development. 'If he started by distributing his small force [3 PARA] in these penny packets, he wouldn't have the critical mass to do what was required even in Lashkar Gah.'

Far from achieving in those first few months what they wanted to, 'which was to use Lashkar Gah as a beacon of what could be achieved [in development terms] and around which you would create an information operation to demonstrate to the Taliban and mainly to the Afghan people what was possible if they went down a peaceful route,' General Richards explains, 'we ended up going into these little villages, places like Musa Qala, Sangin and Naw Zad, and threatening their livelihoods with no alternative, because it was all wrapped around the poppy. Then they said: "Well, we are not having this," and they started fighting back, for the next two or three months. They [the Taliban] fought themselves to a standstill.' So did the British. But when the British first went in, they did not meet any serious opposition. There was a lull before the storm. 'It was only after about three weeks,' General Richards says, 'that the platoon houses started coming under increasingly heavy attack.'[6]

The arrival of the Paras must have been a fearsome sight to the Pushtun farmers and traders of the little opium towns; the terrifying clatter of the twin-rotor Chinooks, the choking clouds of dust, steel-helmeted and flak-jacketed British 'squaddies' leaping off the ramps, rifles at the ready, like a scene from *Apocalypse Now*. And yet the Taliban did not turn and run. They shot back and gave as good as they got. The Paras, the *crème de la crème* of the British Army, had to hold on for dear life. Even the pessimists were taken aback. The optimists who had misread it so badly, kept silent. The PBI – Poor Bloody Infantry – took the brunt. In General Richards's words: 'For the soldiers concerned they conducted themselves magnificently. You know the tales of derring-do under the command of Stuart Tootal. But on a strategic level we were absolutely dismally failing. We had gone in there to do what I have just described, that was our plan.'

But then the fog of war seems to have descended.

'Our orders were not clear,' General Richards says, and although 'it wasn't difficult working it out', he admits that 'in practice, we ended up killing a lot of people, destroying lots of bazaars and mosques. We absolutely knew it was not what we were there to do, and would not be helpful.'

He summarised the dilemma of the platoon houses: 'Now that would have been fine, going to these platoon houses, if we had enough troops. But we didn't, so I have to say, everyone agrees, that was a big error. Ed Butler will tell you – I think he has agreed it probably wasn't the right thing – that at least we established some sort of military equivalence if not superiority, because they never beat us, in a tactical sense. I don't agree with that view but I can understand why some people might say it.'[7]

As to the calls for help to Butler and Tootal by Governor Daud, reinforced by frequent long-distance lobbying by President Karzai in Kabul, Richards said the answer should have been: 'Mr President, I will address this as soon as I can. I do not have the resources at the moment.'[8] But it was a dilemma.

The Battles of Panjwai and Musa Qala, 2006–2007

The Taliban were so confident they thought . . . they would defeat us.
General Sir David Richards, London 2010

On 31 July 2006, General Richards inherited responsibility for southern Afghanistan from General Karl Eikenberry, who was the three-star American general above Major General Ben Freakley, the tough American commander in the south. He also inherited a blazing row, or rows, between Freakley and the British brigadier, Ed Butler, who had formerly commanded the SAS in Afghanistan in 2001 and 2002. Butler referred to Freakley as 'heavy metal'. David Richards tells the following story: 'Ben came back from a meeting where there were British officers – I know this is true – and said: "I nearly punched that damn Limey's [Butler's] lights out, he was so arrogant and he wouldn't listen."'[1]

Butler played it all down, saying American commanders like Freakley did not understand the British concern with the political process at home, and pooh-poohed the suggestion of a punch-up.[2] Basically, the British were not acting in line with the US and then subsequently the NATO chain of command, General Richards said.[3] This was not a criticism just of the British; it was a criticism of many nations contributing to the NATO operation. 'You have individual fiefdoms known as national contingents that too often do whatever their individual capitals are telling them, rather than following the operational designs of the NATO commander, because it doesn't suit that nation's agenda.'[4]

Richards admits: 'I'm afraid at that stage the UK were, on and off, rather guilty of it and this was an occasion. Anyway I took over on 31 July and I remember saying to Air Chief Marshal Sir Jock Stirrup, who by then was Chief of Defence Staff, "I am not prepared to accept these command and control arrangements. Butler must get into the chain of command." I made it clear that it must be done, "or I am not having anything to do with it".'

This was strong stuff; Jock Stirrup was CDS. However, Richards says, 'Jock Stirrup saw the point, changed the command and control arrangements immediately – my argument was it should have happened some time before – but he changed it and put Butler formally inside my NATO chain of command. The problem was, however, it was too late in the day in terms of the platoon house concept, because by then there was a lot of fierce fighting going on and they basically did – as you know – fight themselves to a standstill.'

General Richards recalls a 'fatal or full week' in September 2006, during which three main things happened:

'The North Atlantic Council [NATO's ruling body] chose to visit and I had to handle that as well. It was the only three-day period when I didn't keep a record of what I was doing. I was so busy I got little sleep, but in essence we, NATO, were being very badly challenged in the Arghandab Valley and Panjwai, south-west of Kandahar. This was an area of very fertile ground, small villages set by rivers, and one big road, the Kandahar to Lashkar Gah road. Mullah Omar came from this area, so there was a sort of "instinctive sympathy" with the Taliban. About two years earlier, well-intentioned NGOs had told the locals if they gave up poppy and marijuana growing they would give them seed and everything would be perfect. Two years later none of those promises had been met and in the meanwhile the bitterness had fed back into the return of the Taliban, who said: "You can't trust this lot, leave us to look after you. Furthermore, we will now inflict a decisive military defeat on NATO in their first month of the campaign."'

It did not help that the Helmand operation was delayed by political disagreement in Holland. The Green Party, which was opposed to military intervention in Afghanistan, refused to support the move, which set the mission back by several months.

'Don't forget,' General Richards said, NATO had been 'very equivocal' about the deployment to Helmand. 'There had been a lot of unease about it in the Netherlands and in Canada and Britain about taking this on . . . and they had actually sent the wrong signals about their determination to succeed. The Taliban had put about a thousand fighters into a very defensible piece of ground in the Panjwai – the river down one side and the road the other – and they dug themselves into Second World War defensive positions. There were well-sited, deep trenches, communication trenches, a little hospital, and ammunition dumps within it. They basically said, "Come and attack us, we will prevent any movement down this road." They were just there,' General Richards explains, 'demonstrating you can't touch us, but we'll prevent you travelling on the road, with all the psychological impact that would have on everyone in the area, given it is only ten miles from Kandahar.' The Taliban threat was casting a 'spectre' over the whole of Kandahar, so he knew he had to do something about it.

A senior commander, he reflected, often takes only two or three decisions in a year that are really critical, 'otherwise he is managing a campaign, explaining it and all the rest of it, and the real work is being done at a lower level. Anyway, I gave orders that they had to take out this position [Panjwai], because otherwise NATO would have been defeated in its first month.' He recalled 16 Air Assault Brigade had taken over at the end of July. The crisis came to a head in early September. NATO's whole reputation was at stake and although the mission was about reconstruction and development, the current crisis was 'really all about security'.

The local people 'above all else wanted security . . . so they could drive around without being robbed and beaten'. The Taliban had to be removed, otherwise the insurgency would have grown and grown and taken over Kandahar. 'So militarily and politically it was a no-brainer.'

General Richards is refreshingly frank about his modus operandi. 'I didn't ask NATO, by the way, if I could do it. I have learned a few things in my life; one is: don't ask, don't tell; get on with it.' He only told them later that that was his plan when it was too late for them to stop him. He admitted they would probably have let him do it after much discussion, 'only it would be two months too late'. He put the Canadian Brigadier General, David Fraser, in charge of the tactical operation, made the American Major General, Ben Freakley, his own deputy commander of operations, and in early September the Canadians launched the attack. It faltered to begin with but in the end, with help from the Americans, a small number of Dutch, a small number of Danes and a few British and 'some great fighting' by the 'fledgling Afghan Army' they 'completely trounced' the Taliban with hardly any civilian casualties. They had warned the locals they were coming, and advised them to leave their homes.

'The Taliban were so confident they thought . . . they would defeat us,' Richards says, 'and it was a close-run thing.' He did not want to go into the details, but 'it was a faltering attack and it took ten days, a lot of air power and a lot of artillery was used and we killed – and I did not take any pride in one sense in this – around 800 Taliban . . . There had never been a pitched battle like it since. They [the Taliban] stood their ground and instead of leaving, they reinforced it and people were coming in to join the battle . . . It was a proper World War Two battle and it is the only one ever in Afghanistan: we called it Operation Medusa.* That's what I call psychological ascendancy over the Taliban. They have never fought a pitched battle since – they basically do shoot-and-scoot type stuff. Occasionally, they do stand and fight for a bit, but never for very long because they know they cannot beat us in that sort of battle.'

At this stage, Richards explains, General Sir Richard Dannatt, CGS, arrived on a visit and was alerted to the fact that the situation was not good in the places where the British were 'hunkered down' in their platoon houses. Even more worrying, there was a possibility of a Chinook helicopter being shot down while flying in or out of Musa Qala to reinforce a platoon house or 'medevac' a wounded soldier. That would have had a catastrophic strategic impact back in Britain, given that things were 'looking fragile'. Dannatt's advice was 'that we should get out of Musa Qala – "just get out". Dannatt went back to Britain and said: "We can't take that risk, we must get out of Musa Qala."'

At this point General Richards recalls how he had to intervene strongly. 'Orders started to be given to Butler from the UK,' Richards continues, 'yet I was the operational commander, and I said "Don't you forget I have got a say in this and I will not agree to you leaving Musa Qala at this stage because if you do be quite clear it will be portrayed by the Taliban and

---

* In Greek mythology, Medusa was one of the three Gorgons, so hideous that anyone who looked at her was turned to stone.

sceptics – and it will be – as a defeat of British arms."' Reluctantly, Richards says, Air Chief Marshal Sir Jock Stirrup 'accepted my advice because it was really him or, you know . . . back me or sack me time. I did not want to be in Musa Qala, I never liked the platoon houses, but having gone in there and, if you like, taken them on, to leave in the way they were proposing would have been a defeat of British arms. It would have had a catastrophic effect on our reputation as a fighting power. Actually, they just hadn't thought of it in that way and of course, if that had happened our whole future would have been undermined within the first few months.'

So General Richards said to Stuart Tootal, through Ed Butler, he was not leaving, they would find another way. And that led to the so-called Musa Qala deal, the ceasefire. 'At the time people were critical of it, some people, particularly the Americans, saw us as being "surrender monkeys" – a very pejorative term in their lexicon, Richards notes. 'They didn't know what it was like down there. There was a lot of counter-briefing . . . but luckily, six months later in Iraq, of course, David Petraeus and others were doing exactly this. They were seeking and reaching accommodation with essentially disenfranchised tribal elders. In the case of Musa Qala, some were Taliban, but weren't necessarily hard-line Taliban, so I authorised, well, I told Ed Butler, there has got to be another route. By then, to their great credit, the chaps in 16 Air Assault Brigade had fought the Taliban in Musa Qala to a standstill; both sides were exhausted and both the Taliban and the elders were equally keen to find a route out.'

The Musa Qala ceasefire was a godsend for the embattled British and may have been a psychological turning point in the war, in the sense that it showed, possibly for the first time, that negotiation and compromise were the only way forward. David Richards tells the story with a suitable sense of drama: 'The elders went to both parties and then to Governor Daud and said: "This is hopeless. Our town is being destroyed in front of our eyes. You are getting nowhere, Oh Taliban, and you [British] are not getting anywhere [either] . . . The Taliban must have said: "No, you are right. This is hopeless, we are all knackered anyway."'⁵ The elders then sent a delegation to Daud. Daud asked Butler and Richards what they thought. Richards said it sounded like the sort of thing they ought to be exploiting 'because this has got to be the future'. Richards asked President Karzai and

Karzai said: "'Yes, I have been saying we need a local solution." So they all agreed to give it a go.'

Richards was on good terms with Karzai, not least because of his creation of the PAG, which no one else, no government, politician or diplomat, had had the wit or energy to set up before. Karzai, General Richards says, was 'absolutely in the know' about the Musa Qala ceasefire. He denied he liked it later, 'but that is the way, because the Americans got at him. Most Afghans were absolutely with us. It was a hopeless impasse [at Musa Qala] we had to break and this, I would argue, was an imaginative and pioneering attempt to do it, which was used repeatedly in Iraq in a different format, but essentially the same principle. And it is, of course, what everyone is looking to do today. But back in 2006, 2007, I think at that stage a lot of people thought they could still defeat . . . [the Taliban] militarily.'

Two or three weeks later, Ed Butler did some very good work talking to the elders, General Richards says, so he, General Richards, and Ed Butler went down and had 'a clandestine meeting in the desert – a very barren wilderness, quite Boy's Own, and agreed it and a few days later we got out [of Musa Qala] with the elders' help, actually'.

General Richards says he would argue that the Musa Qala ceasefire was something of a pioneering example of what they should be doing on a grander scale, as Petraeus was doing in Iraq. Shortly afterwards, in fact, the American military in Iraq asked him for details of how this had been done, to feed into their own understanding. Other Americans were very critical of it. General Dan McNeill, who took over as NATO commander from General Richards in February 2007, 'was not happy'. Most Americans weren't, says Richards; 'I wouldn't want to particularly pick on McNeill, but the Americans were very keen that I finished this thing before they took over because they didn't want on Day One, as was their intention, to stop it, to break the ceasefire with the Taliban; that was a key part of the deal. We debated it through the Policy Action Group and we agreed to a series of measures that would test the ceasefire and its bona fides.'

One of these was that 'the police had to go in and a second was that the type of governance regime acceptable to the Governor had to be agreed. Another was that we wouldn't occupy the town, but that we could patrol through it. And we did all these things to test their intent. I am not saying it was perfect, it was a very Afghan solution and some of those involved were ex-Taliban and no doubt the Taliban were to a degree exploiting it for their own ends. But so were we and of course, militarily, one of the most important things to me wasn't to do with this being an experiment, but the fact that I had so few resources, so few troops that we were absolutely pinned solid in static positions, with no what we call "manoeuvre capability" – we couldn't do anything. So I could free up at least one company, pathetic really, which [Lt Col] Stuart [Tootal, commander of 3 PARA] was very keen to do and that gave me a bit more military flexibility as well as a chance to see how we could do things differently. Anyway, in January – I was handing over on 4 February – I came under increasing pressure to break the ceasefire.'

Ironically, other similar things were actually happening in the east. The difference was the Americans led that, the CIA probably; he didn't know. 'So that was okay, but when the Brits did it in Helmand, that was different. Surprise, surprise: as we got through to late January, and it was within the rules, a bomb was dropped on the leader of the local Taliban who was living just outside the five-kilometre radius. So he was a legitimate target, but it was absolutely against the spirit of the deal. It didn't kill him but it killed his brother and I think twenty other members of his group.'

The local Taliban leader hit the roof, not surprisingly, General Richards recalls. 'He went into Musa Qala and arrested the tribal elders and said: "You have broken the deal. Your allies, the Brits and Americans, have broken the deal." Then, very courageously, the elders arrested him because he went in with very few people. Most had been killed. Then he escaped, went to Naw Zad and came back and reasserted control over Musa Qala.'

'On 4 February, my last act virtually – I take no great pride in this – was to endorse a recommendation that the car he was travelling in from Musa Qala to Naw Zad could be attacked and it was attacked and he was killed . . . We were then back to square one. The rest you know about: Operation Snakebite a bit later under [Major General] Andrew Mackay, who commanded a force of British, American and Afghan troops which recaptured Musa Qala in December 2007. The big difference was of course that by then we had enough troops to do these things. Back in 2006, early 2007, there were no troops.'

Looking back, General Richards says, he thinks the ceasefire was the right thing to do; throughout the history of counter-insurgencies there always comes a point when you negotiate with someone. The issue was when. 'Someone like Ahmed Rashid and I share this view, and believe that now is a good time because even if you are achieving what some seek, which is clear military ascendancy over the Taliban, whether or not that is the case, they can destroy the perception of such military ascendancy. And anyway they [the Taliban] know we have to get out at some stage, so they'll just lie low again. We learnt that in 2001.' Hoping that it was going to get better, and more on your terms in a year or two years was not necessarily wrong, but you couldn't be certain you would achieve it.

General Richards's prescription was to get your 'mailed fist in one hand and your negotiating doctrine in the other, and go forward on both lines and I think it doesn't mean you are defeated: who knows what those nego-tiations will lead to. But the knowledge that it could get worse . . .' He would say today for example, General Petraeus, whom he admired hugely, was only now, midsummer 2010, getting the resources and troops he needed to do what they all agreed even then was necessary – 'there is noth-ing new in this stuff [counter-insurgency doctrine]'. Whether it was called Afghan development zones, the British term, or population-centric strate-gies, the American phrase, Richards says, 'it was all the same stuff in which you looked after the bulk of the population as best you could, let them feel good about themselves and you isolated, marginalised, the Taliban both psychologically and physically. In Malaya they did it by physically moving people into protected encampments – you can't do that in Afghanistan. So you have a different route to achieve the same thing.'

The ingredients for successful counter-insurgency, he says, are broadly the same the world over: 'The formula building on those ingredients was going to be different in any particular counter-insurgency and that was what we were doing here. Musa Qala was accidentally a pioneering attempt because we made a virtue of a necessity. But it was the sort of thing we ought to be doing. If, perhaps, we had started with that ceasefire and held it a bit longer and seen how you could build on it – I am not saying that you shouldn't do it with your eyes open because you should and if the Taliban started using it as a sort of training centre or base for a bomb factory then you were going to have to do something about it – but at that stage and right up to the time of the end of January there was no proof that that was the case . . . The tribal elders were obviously very keen to keep the experiment going. But I am afraid that bomb caused the Taliban leader to go in and that was the end of it.'[6]

He reverted to the vexed question of platoon houses. He thought there was right and wrong on both sides, but 'the original crime, or mistake, was going into the platoon house concept when we didn't have the mass of troops and resources generally .to make such a concept work'. He says he was 'very much on the record at the time as saying I was opposed to the platoon house concept. When I took over I said to Stuart Tootal, "What the hell . . . this is exactly what we said you wouldn't do." Governor Daud was undoubtedly under huge pressure from President Karzai to take down the [Taliban] black flags. My argument was: "We will deal with it, Mr President, when we are able to deal with it" and that was actually Ben Freakley's advice to the British. That advice was ignored and I think it was ignored because of a conceit that they knew better than people like Ben Freakley. Our ambitions were too big for our ability to deliver . . .'[7]

General Richards flew back to the UK in July 2006 to see the Prime Minister, Tony Blair. He gave a talk at the Royal United Services' Institute, which he thought was off the record, in which he said: 'the international community's efforts in Afghanistan are close to anarchy'. This was headlined in the *Guardian* the next day, 21 July, as 'Afghanistan close to anarchy, warns General. NATO Commander's view in stark contrast to Ministers'; Forces short of equipment and "running out of time",'[8] which got him into trouble.

'The point of saying it,' General Richards explains, 'was a direct attempt to address that problem.' But he also said that we were not doing enough ourselves in terms of resources. We hadn't got enough troops. 'I felt my duty was to be quite vocal and strong with my chain of command,' and he did not disguise it from the media, because he was trying to get messages through them back to the top people that this wasn't going very well, and we hadn't been resourced because they hadn't listened. 'But they began to realise it when the body bags started coming back.'[9]

So, General Richards reflects, 'I had an uneasy 2006. I loved it actually, but the media pressure; it wasn't the media itself, it was the pressure from political and very senior military people wanting me to shut up. I had the responsibility to continue to ask for the things I knew I needed even though I knew I was unlikely to get them. And of course I felt a huge responsibility to my soldiers who were in that position.'

Finally, I asked this most approachable, friendly, easy-going, bright, but when it matters, iron-fist-in-a-velvet-glove general, CDS and now Britain's most important military figure, how he sees the further unfolding of the war against the Taliban. I prefaced the question by alluding to the pessimistic assessment by the Carnegie Endowment analyst Gilles Dorronsoro, written after a late summer 2010 trip to Kandahar. I asked David Richards specifically if he thought it was possible to conceive of winning through to a satisfactory conclusion in Afghanistan with a corrupt and weak government on the one hand, the Taliban apparently increasing in strength on the other, and Pakistan's support for the insurgency not really changing?

'Well first of all, it is so easy as an analyst with the benefit of 20/20 hindsight to say what you should have done. I don't want to fall into that trap. People like me have to live in the world as it is today and our job is to find a solution today.' The root of the problem, he says, was to try and impose a Western style of government on a country that never had it, and then singularly failing to teach them how to work it. The fact that there was still not a school of governance or administration worth its name in Afghanistan was a signal failure of the West. Also, what he calls the 'formula in the civilian sphere' – reconstruction and development – was far too complicated and 'did not recognise the nature of the average Afghan and their culture: Islamic, agrarian . . .'

David Richards undoubtedly believes that a common-sense approach is the answer to many of Afghanistan's problems, a view that few who know the country well would disagree with. 'There were only four things they really wanted,' Richards continues. 'Most of all, funnily enough, they want security. Who wouldn't? It's a very basic need for us all and is too often lost in an over-focus on governance. Secondly, irrigation, then roads and electricity all of which leads to the next most important thing overall after physical security which is jobs. A failure to deliver this is why we soldiers feel very let down by our civilian partners who are far too quick to blame 'the generals' for their failings. Of course the security strategy early on was flawed but this was largely determined by politicians not generals. If we had deepened the early security effect things would have been much better but, with the focus turning to Iraq, nations took their feet right off the pedal and the Taliban came back. If the generals had been allowed to sustain the early impact on security and the civilians in charge had just focused on roads, irrigation and electricity with governance being devolved to the local level rather than too much held centrally, things would be much brighter. And where there is a need for central government at least, over five intensive years, train them how to run it and pay them for it, then we would never be in this position today . . . And you would have grown the Afghan Army and police aggressively at the same time. We now know that that was our crime, if you like, our error. We didn't do what I have just described, we are now trying to do it. So effectively, we have only really been grappling with it the way we should and resourcing it properly for the last year and a half.'

Was it too late, first of all, to establish a proper relationship with President Karzai, I asked?

'I think we had better wake up to the fact that President Karzai is part of a political culture; that is what it is. I am not suggesting he personally is corrupt. I know the rumours. But the fact is probably whoever was in that position is going to be accused of corruption as are all the officials and everybody else and the government themselves even. So better grow up boys: that is the world as it is . . . Would a change in government, in President, make any great difference? I am not convinced and anyway, he is a formally elected President. Now I do know that there are those who would rather he wasn't President. What I am saying is I am not certain the alternatives are going to be any better. So let us go with the flow and work with the grain of reality rather than necessarily stand back and have nothing to do with it. By the way, we have undermined him and then we played him up again because we suddenly realised what I just said is true. So we have got to be consistent over President Karzai and help him progress.'

At least, General Richards says, with 25,000 troops in Helmand, mainly American, plus the Afghan National Army, 'at last we have got the critical mass we needed'.

We had not gained 'strategic traction', however, he says. 'People here and in Afghanistan, through a complete and abject failure of communication, believe – and I understand that there is some justification for it – that we are losing or we can't win anyway and therefore it is some sort of stalemate. I don't think we are losing, by the way; we are just not succeeding in the timeframe that suits and is acceptable to Afghanistan or Afghans and is acceptable to our population and our politicians. So what can we do? Well, since we have only now got the resources to do this correctly, I think we have got to give ourselves more time. People talk about a bit more strategic patience. I think next year [2011] in July, President Obama has said we will have a proper look at it. By then, I think we will know whether or not we have turned a corner, in perception terms.'

He then showed what I read as a qualified optimism about the future. 'I believe where we have got the balance right we are already turning the corner in practical terms, but we hadn't got that across to people.' In Kabul, for example, Richards says, 'there had not been a major incident for months, as far as I know – and don't forget there are bombs going off in all sorts of places around the world whether it is Kampala or elsewhere, so it's not quite the singular failure that some have portrayed . . . The Haqqani Network [allied to al Qaeda and the Taliban and based in Pakistan's North Waziristan tribal area] is constantly trying to do a dramatic incident in Kabul and usually failing; Lashkar Gah very few [incidents]. Tomorrow there could be a bomb but the real test is how do the Afghans, for a while yet with our help of course, respond to such shocks? But the essence is: there is very little problem, certainly strategically, where we have got it right.' General Richards was, of course, speaking well before the assaults on the Kabul Intercontinental Hotel on 28 June 2011, in which at least twenty-one people were killed, including three Afghan policemen and nine Taliban or Haqqani terrorists; and on the British Council building two months later, on 19 August 2011, in which none of the four British staff were hurt but at least eight Afghan police, three guards and one New Zealand Special Forces soldier were killed as well as all the terrorists.

'Can we now, five years on from when I tried to develop the Afghan Development Zone concept, can we employ the same precepts to demonstrate that where you get the formula right, a combination of resources

– troop numbers, police, governors, a sense of growing prosperity even though it is not huge but it is getting better? Where you get that right you give people hope and it is certainly a more hopeful future than that offered by the Taliban. Now it is that equation that we have got to get right and I can't tell you whether we will succeed. I just feel that we need a bit longer and I know everyone says: "Well, you have had long enough." But I just reiterate we have only been doing it properly really for about a year and a half. I would also say, the very people who are saying "It is time to get out" will be often the very people who will subsequently say: "You have got to do something about the fact that these women are being brutalised and raped and the children are not being educated . . ." I would also like to say of the [British] Army that there is no doubt in the minds of most, I would say the vast majority, of British soldiers, that this is a just war.'

Turning to Pakistan, seen by most foreign observers as being the Taliban's godfather, General Richards admitted it was difficult to read. Were their assurances that they no longer wanted to interfere in Afghanistan to be taken at face value? He poses the question, 'Is there a policy from the very top in Pakistan to see the defeat of the West and the rise of the Taliban in Afghanistan? I do not think that is the case but anyway, as I have said publicly, we all know there will at some stage have to be a political process of reconciliation, which will include the Pakistanis as well as the Taliban.'

He also underlined why he thinks we must turn the corner:

I want to give you a reason it is important we do succeed [in Afghanistan] . . . If we leave precipitately there is a good chance there will be a civil war because the Northern Alliance . . . are not going to suffer a Taliban government again or certainly they are going to fight very hard to avoid it. The Pushtun south will broadly have no option but to be ruled by the Taliban. You could divide the country but Afghanistan has got no record of being divided. Despite being of different ethnic backgrounds they all seem to count themselves as Afghan. So there would be a huge risk and a risk which some might say we should take of a civil war happening in Afghanistan, a very brutal one as it has been in the past.

Today that civil war, because you have to add Baluchistan [provincial

capital: Quetta, near the Afghan border and long a Taliban safe haven]
into this mix, could turn into a proxy war between India and Pakistan.
That proxy war could start to be fought perhaps in other ways, not
directly but . . . there was a risk it would appear in the east on the Indo-
Pakistan border. That is between two nuclear armed states. It is not out
of the realms of possibility. Add Kashmir into that pot. Is the Pakistan
government, after the floods [in July 2010] in particular, not already
being seriously challenged in some parts anyway by some of these *jihad-
ist* groups, who on the surface are doing rather good work as well as
adopting when it suits them the terrorist tactics for which they are better
known. Suddenly all this, this melee of plausible risks, goes hot. You
think that is bad enough, [to] inflame Muslim versus Hindu. Well, take
it one step further: India is backed by America, Pakistan backed by
China . . . Things could get very fraught on a much bigger scale. And
then as things deteriorate in the region you have got, closer to home,
diasporas from both the Hindu and Pakistan Islamic communities in
this country. Are they just going to sit there in Bradford as their cousins
fight it out brutally on our television screens? Chances are they are going
to remind us what's what and suddenly you have got a bit of a proxy war
on the streets of this country. So this is a very important thing to try
hard to get right; for geo-strategic reasons.

In conclusion, he sounded another note of warning. 'I also say, if we get it
wrong – and I am not after perfect solutions here – if we get it wrong, it
has all sorts of implications for us downstream: our broken promises; what
price our pledges to other countries. And as future threats develop, do we
hunker down into some sort of defensive crouch and hope it doesn't come
our way? David Miliband [Labour Foreign Secretary from June 2007 to
May 2010] said that would be hopeless. So all these things have to be
factored into it. Which is why, I think, give us a bit longer; 2015 is probably doable, for example. We have just started to get it right and we might
yet succeed.'

His optimism was echoed by the views expressed by General David
Petraeus, the outgoing American Supreme Commander in Afghanistan
just before his departure in July 2011. Speaking to the *New York Times* in

the last interview he gave in Kabul, he was guardedly optimistic about the outcome of the war: he said he was leaving in the belief that his plan to turn around the war and hand over security to the Afghans could be achieved, and added: 'It is very hard, but it is doable.'[10]

PART FOUR

END GAME AND THE PAKISTAN CONNECTION

McChrystal Brought Down by *Rolling Stone*

Most damaging was the impression Team McChrystal gave of despising
the 'wimps' on Capitol Hill.

•

As if the war against the Taliban was not producing enough shockwaves,
a totally unexpected bombshell exploded on 8 July 2010 when *Rolling
Stone* magazine published a story about the commander of US and
NATO Coalition forces in Afghanistan, General Stanley McChrystal, in
which he and his staff were quoted making disparaging remarks about
some of President Obama's most senior colleagues, above all his Vice-
President, Joe Biden. Another target was the legendary Richard
Holbrooke, the negotiator of the Dayton Accords which brought peace
to the Balkans in 1995 and who died of a heart attack on 13 December
2010. General McChrystal had already been in hot water for another dig
at the Vice-President when, after a speech in London in autumn 2009,
he told a questioner that Joe Biden's criticisms of the proposed 'surge' of
30,000 American troops in Aghanistan were 'short-sighted' and would
lead to 'Chaos-istan'. McChrystal was recalled by Obama and repri-
manded. But the *Rolling Stone* gaffe was of a different order and the result
was inevitable. Summoned to Washington by the President, McChrystal
ate humble pie and offered his resignation of his commands in
Afghanistan, which was accepted. Days later McChrystal announced his
retirement.

The story betrayed a surprising lack of awareness on the part of
McChrystal's team of just what sort of image they were portraying, and
what the effect of a warts-and-all portrait – *Rolling Stone*'s stock-in-trade
– would have on a White House whose Democratic supporters were

already disenchanted with what had become America's longest war; longer even than Vietnam, with which it invited unfortunate comparisons. Most damaging, one imagines, was the impression Team McChrystal gave, in its hard-swearing elitism, of despising the 'wimps' on Capitol Hill: the contempt of the warrior for the politico.

In many ways, McChrystal's departure was a minor tragedy. He was an exceptionally able Special Forces officer, with an outstanding record in Iraq where he planned and oversaw the tracking down and capture of Saddam Hussein, and later hunted and killed the leader of al Qaeda in Iraq, Abu Musab al Zarqawi, a Jordanian extremist who carried out a violent campaign of bombings and beheadings before being traced to a safe house – which turned out to be vulnerable to two 500lb bombs dropped by US Air Force F-16Cs. But despite this background, General McChrystal was determined to pursue General Petraeus's COIN policy of protecting and winning over the local population.

One of the first decisions General McChrystal made after receiving his appointment was to recruit Lieutenant General Sir Graeme Lamb, the former head of the SAS, with whom he had worked closely on Special Forces operations in Iraq. 'I knew General Stanley from way back,' General Lamb told me when I interviewed him in Kabul in 2010. 'We fought together for twenty years, one might say . . . People see General Stanley as a warrior; you don't see any body fat, it doesn't appear, he's a lean machine type. I first came across Stan in 1990/1991 before we went into Iraq the first time around, and at that point in time I had served for twenty years and Stanley McChrystal was the fastest and sharpest staff officer I had ever come across.'

Lamb describes McChrystal as 'hugely well read' and recalls the American General kindly giving him a copy of Anton Myrer's 1968 novel, *Once an Eagle*. The book's main protagonist is Samuel Damon, 'who in many ways', Lamb says, 'is Stanley McChrystal: stoic, sense of duty, service, sacrifice in a way that is a hugely attractive . . . humility, humbled by the exertions and the commitment of others; but he himself absolutely at point, leading by personal example and commitment to what he believes in. What you see is absolutely what you get. I know Stanley of old . . . there's not a British general that could have got me out of retirement and out here [Afghanistan]. McChrystal was the only fellow that could do that.' General McChrystal appointed Lamb to run the 'reintegration' programme, persuading former Taliban fighters to lay down their arms and join the government side. He left Afghanistan soon after McChrystal stepped down, having, he said, completed his mission.

If General McChrystal's dismissal was not a complete surprise, the choice of his successor was. General David Petraeus had been the US Commanding General in Iraq (January 2007–September 2008) and is the author of the US Army's official counter-insurgency manual. He had overseen and executed the successful surge in Iraq in 2007, which turned a disaster into a winning strategy and gave him an aura of near-infallibility. From Iraq, Petraeus had been promoted Commander of CENTCOM (Central Command) in Florida, with responsibility for Afghanistan as well as Iraq, and was thus General McChrystal's boss. His appointment as McChrystal's successor was therefore, in one sense, a step down; but the Obama administration hoped it would turn out to be a stroke of genius.

———

One of the most urgent problems Petraeus had to deal with, although not an essentially military concern, was the corruption that had been growing rapidly since early in Karzai's first presidency (2004–09). By June 2006 it was serious enough to prompt Mahmoud Saikal's resignation as Deputy Foreign Minister.

Afghanistan's presidential system, devised by the French constitutional lawyer Professor Guy Carcassonne, on the instructions of Lakhdar Brahimi, the UN Secretary General's Special Representative, resulted in too much power being concentrated in the hands of one man. With few checks and balances, Karzai could do more or less what he liked. Under American pressure, he repeatedly promised to take action against corruption but in effect did virtually nothing about it. In desperation, the Americans, with the help of the British, took the initiative and set up two anti-corruption bodies, the Major Crimes Task Force, trained by the

FBI [Federal Bureau of Investigation] and the Sensitive Investigative Unit trained by the DEA [US Drug Enforcement Administration].

In January 2010, Afghan agents from both organisations raided the Kabul headquarters of New Ansari Exchange, Afghanistan's largest *hawala*, or money-transfer business, seizing 42,000 documents. *Hawalas* like New Ansari move money globally using a network of dealers. A customer in Kabul, for example, might hand cash to a local *hawala* with instructions to send it to someone in Dubai. Five minutes later, the designated recipient can walk into a *hawala* in Dubai and pick up the money. When New Ansari was founded in the southern city of Kandahar in the early 1990s, it was one of dozens of *hawalas* scrambling for a piece of the money-transfer business, a lucrative industry in an economy that at the time had no formal banks, and even today remains largely cash-based.

New Ansari's fortunes rose at least in part through the relationship it developed with the Taliban, whose leaders governed most of Afghanistan from their headquarters in Kandahar. Some were among the *hawala's* biggest customers. Haji Muhammad Jan, one of New Ansari's founding partners and the chairman of Afghan United Bank, acknowledges working with the Taliban when they were in power. 'Everybody did business with the Taliban,' he says. 'They were the rulers.'[2]

Anti-corruption agents also arrested Mohammad Zia Salehi, a veteran Karzai 'fixer' and negotiator with the Taliban, who was taped allegedly soliciting a bribe to block the corruption investigation. Karzai gave orders to have him released next day and, according to the *Wall Street Journal*, he was soon back in the Presidential Palace, free, pending trial. In fact, at the time of writing, he has not been brought to trial. The raid caught many people by surprise, the *Journal* said, including New Ansari's well-connected executives and even President Karzai himself, who was reported to be 'furious'.[3]

What the investigators found as they combed through the 42,000 documents in the next four days, confirmed rumours of a vast money-laundering operation which had couriered $3.18 billion of cash out of Kabul airport between the start of 2007 and January 2010 – $2.78 billion of it carried by New Ansari couriers. One New Ansari courier, identified in the documents only as 'Rahmatullah', personally carried at least $2.3 billion out of Kabul airport between the start of 2008 and the middle of 2009, much of it to Dubai, according to a senior American official. American and Afghan officials say they found evidence that New Ansari was helping to launder profits from the Afghan drug trade generally, as well as specifically for the Taliban, which also benefited from extortion. Investigators said they had found links between the money transfers and some of the most powerful political and business figures in the country, including relatives of President Karzai.

If true, this would explain why President Karzai reacted with angry surprise. According to the *Washington Post*, after the raid 'wiretaps picked up conversations indicating that there had been a frantic meeting involving Karzai aides at the Presidential Palace'. American officials said members of Karzai's administration; as well as members of parliament, held subsequent meetings with Mr Mohammed Ishaq Aloko, the Attorney-General pressuring him to ensure that certain New Ansari executives not be charged.

The *Post* claimed that 'among those protected was Haji Muhammad Rafi Azimi, deputy chairman of Afghan United Bank, the New Ansari subsidiary . . . "It's clear to everyone involved he should be indicted and charged," an American official said of Azimi. But Azimi is "a businessman who knows a great deal about the finances of government officials",' the official said.[4] Aloko claimed the American ambassador, Karl Eikenberry, had told him if he did not arrest Azimi, he should resign. But Aloko said he did not have enough evidence to arrest Azimi.

In yet another attempt to persuade Karzai to carry out his promises to fight corruption, Senator John Kerry, who had been successful in making Karzai see reason in the past, having heart-to-heart talks with him in the gardens of the Presidential Palace, was asked by the White House to return to Kabul in August 2010 to exercise his persuasive powers again. After two separate meetings with Karzai, Senator Kerry said the President had again promised to 'take action' and 'make changes' to his anti-corruption campaign.[5] But Afghan politicians like Daud Sultanzoy, a vocal critic of Karzai in parliament, was reported in the local press as saying: '"These statements are a bit too late for the situation we are in. In Afghanistan, we are suffering from larger problems" . . . Sultanzoy, who represents the Pushtun province of Ghazni, where the Taliban control more territory than the government, added: "These statements are good when a problem is beginning, but when we are nose deep in problems, we need action. The government of Afghanistan needs to fix problems yesterday; we cannot afford seminars.'"[6]

Fawzia Koofi, one of the sixty-eight women in the Afghan parliament, said: 'When it comes to President Karzai's commitment to [fighting] corruption and the rule of law, .I'm not very hopeful. There's very little sense of accountability; there's no checks and balances . . . Their efforts against corruption don't prevent corruption. It is just words to make it look like they are doing something.'[7]

Because of lapses of security in the run-up to the execution of previous raids, there was tight security before the New Ansari swoop. Even the now-sacked Interior Minister, Hanif Atmar, did not know about it until he was telephoned by the head investigator from the doorstep of New Ansari's offices to tell him the raid was about to start. The New Ansari probe did nothing to improve relations between the Afghan President and his American allies. At one point Karzai intervened to try to take more direct control of the anti-corruption units, ordering a handpicked commission to review scores of past and current cases. Senior American military and civilian officials regarded his move as an effort to protect those close to him and, in the process, to quash the investigation into New Ansari. They described it as a blow to American anti-corruption policy.

One of the American officials called the situation 'a real reality check' for both the United States and its European allies. President Karzai had promised for years to clean up high-level corruption, but little was done. Things started to move only after the *Wall Street Journal* reported in June 2009 that huge sums of cash were being flown out of the country. 'We need to investigate whose money it is and whether it is legal,' the Finance Minister, Omar Zakhilwal, said in July 2009. Afghan officials had known since the January 2010 raid, if not earlier, that New Ansari played a central role in moving the cash. Before the raid, so much money was passing through New Ansari in so many different currencies that, according to the Bank of Afghanistan, it effectively set Afghanistan's exchange rates. New Ansari's manager, Haji Muhammad Khan, said in a recent interview that the company had done nothing wrong. The money being flown out of the country was declared, so moving it was legal.[8] Preliminary evidence collected by Afghan and American investigators, however, indicated that while some of the money came from legitimate businesses, some was diverted Western aid and logistics money, opium profits and Taliban funds. Investigators were trying to uncover the exact sources of the money and determine who was benefiting. Although customs records were incomplete, the sum carried out of the country over that period was probably much larger than $3.18 billion, they believed. Following the *Wall Street Journal* article in June 2009, a US Congress panel froze some $4 billion in non-urgent aid to Afghanistan.

Corruption in the Afghan government and business establishment has become a major source of tension between President Karzai and Washington, threatening to derail the coalition's counter-insurgency strategy. American officials say it is crucial to restore the trust of ordinary Afghans in their own government, which has been shaken by pervasive commercial and government graft. Because law enforcement is so lax, according to Amrullah Saleh, the former head of Afghan intelligence, 'anybody can choose his or her own law. New Ansari is not unique.'

By the late 1990s, New Ansari had become one of the major *hawalas*. After the American intervention that ousted the Taliban in 2001, New Ansari developed relationships with the new rulers and it continued to grow. By 2007, New Ansari's owners opened Afghan United Bank, now the country's third-largest financial institution, by soliciting deposits. Haji Muhammad Jan, the New Ansari founding partner and chairman of the bank, is an investor in a huge suburban housing development that the President's brother, Mahmood Karzai, is building outside Kandahar. Another key player in New Ansari, Haji Muhammad Rafi Azimi, the deputy chairman, is suspected of playing a role in a corruption case involving Mohammad Siddiq Chakari, the former Minister for Haj and Islamic Affairs. Chakari was allowed to leave the country while under investigation for allegedly taking hundreds of thousands of dollars in bribes to steer the business of flying pilgrims to Mecca to certain airlines. Afghan and American investigators allege that Azimi, who hasn't been charged, was the middleman who passed some of the alleged bribes from the airlines to the minister.

President Karzai wanted to disband the Sensitive Investigative Unit, but he was talked out of it by his then intelligence chief, Amrullah Saleh. After the raid, American and Afghan investigators went through the tens of thousands of seized documents as fast as possible. 'We were afraid that if they couldn't get back into business, the financial sector could collapse,' says a senior American official whose staff helped oversee the document analysis. Among other things, the documents revealed that between July 2009 and the day of the raid, New Ansari moved almost $1 billion out of Afghanistan, most of it to Dubai. New Ansari's books were returned four days later. The company's Kabul offices soon reopened, only to close for good a few weeks later. 'Whatever I was doing was legal and in accordance with Afghan laws,' says the New Ansari manager, Haji Muhammad Khan. 'The Americans,' he adds, 'continued their pressure on me and forced me to leave my business once and for all.'[9]

Khan claims the business remains closed, but there has been evidence to the contrary. Although its headquarters in Kabul is shuttered, its office in Kandahar was up and running after the raid in January 2010, with long lines of people waiting to send money, according to American and Afghan officials. New Ansari offices in other parts of Afghanistan and in the Pakistani city of Peshawar are also still open, as are the *hawala*'s affiliates in the United Arab Emirates and other Middle Eastern and European countries. The co-founder of New Ansari, Haji Muhammad Jan, says he cut ties to New Ansari in 2007.

His claim is disputed by US and Afghan investigators, business associates and even political allies in Kandahar, where New Ansari got its start. They say he still owns a major portion of the business and oversees its operations, although day-to-day management falls to Mr Khan. Mr Jan, the co-founder of New Ansari, insists neither the *hawala* nor Afghan United Bank has any existing relationship with the Taliban. Again American investigators disagree, saying they have evidence the *hawala* has been moving money for the Taliban. US officials also say they have recorded phone conversations between Haji Muhammad Rafi Azimi and members of the Taliban. In one recent conversation, a Taliban commander in Kandahar was heard apologising for accidentally kidnapping Azimi's brother; the Taliban commander promises to release the man immediately, and pleads with Mr Azimi to forgive him, the officials say.

Whatever the figures, no one disputes that huge amounts of cash, which could benefit the Afghan economy enormously if put to work locally, are being exported to buy property and invest generally in Dubai and other Gulf States. This is happening legally, since Afghanistan has virtually no currency exchange restrictions, provided the exporter has paid his or her taxes and can prove the money is not from a corrupt source. Judging by the volume of money leaving the country every day, it would seem that these qualifications are not hard to meet.

Some Afghans shrug off Western complaints about corruption. The owner of the most successful television station in Afghanistan, Tolo TV, Saad Mohseni, a still-youthful entrepreneur who spent the war years in Australia where he learned excellent English, says corruption is simply another way of doing business. Having to pay a bribe to import, say, a television set, is just 'another tax'. This free-wheeling attitude is not shared by the Western coalition. The international community sees corruption as the main reason the Afghan people, especially in the south, prefer the Taliban's rough-and-ready, but straightforward, justice to the dilatory and above all hugely corrupt government variety, where it is commonly said the biggest bribe wins the case.

Although the people of Kabul are nothing if not resilient, the lack of security, complemented by the seemingly unstoppable growth of corruption, continue to undermine public support for the Karzai government, as well as NATO's presence and morale generally. Bribery flourishes at every level. Afghans say they have to pay bribes for every service they use, even to pay their electricity bill, for example. A driving licence costs $50; obtaining one used to involve twenty different steps, each requiring a bribe. 'But there has been a big improvement,' one American official joked sarcastically. 'It now needs only three.'[10]

Departing from Kabul airport in August 2010, I was invited to pay baksheesh by one of the men behind the ticket desk. He nodded his head in the direction of a baggage handler, probably a relative or friend, so I said: 'Why? He's only doing his job.' Then a policeman made not much of a show of ushering me through, shaking my hand beseechingly at the gate, an invitation I also declined. This was the first time in nearly thirty years I had been asked to pay baksheesh at the airport, although friends say it is now common. In mitigation, one has to say that wages for those in lowly jobs, including the police, are still often abysmal, despite the billions of dollars pumped into the country by the United States.

The row between President Karzai and the Americans took a turn for the worse at the end of August 2010. The former Deputy Attorney-General, Fazel Ahmed Faqiryar, told the *New York Times* that he had been fired by Hamid Karzai the week before 'after he repeatedly refused to block corruption investigations at the highest levels of Mr Karzai's government'.

Faqiryar said 'investigations of more than two dozen senior Afghan officials – including Cabinet ministers, ambassadors and provincial governors – were being held up or blocked outright by President Karzai, the Attorney-General, Mohammed Ishaq Aloko, and others'. President Karzai's office denied Mr Faqiryar's version of events, but it had been 'largely corroborated' in interviews with five Western officials familiar with the cases, the *New York Times* said.[11]

The five officials, none of whom was named at their own request, 'said President Karzai and others in his government had repeatedly thwarted prosecutions against senior Afghan government figures. An American official, also speaking anonymously, said that Afghan prosecutors had prepared several cases against officials suspected of corruption, but that President Karzai was "stalling and stalling and stalling". "We propose investigations, detentions and prosecutions of high government officials, but we cannot resist him," Mr Faqiryar said of Mr Karzai. "He won't sign anything. We have great, honest and professional prosecutors here, but we need support."'[12]

He also confirmed President Karzai had intervened to stop the prosecution of one of his closest aides, Mohammed Zia Salehi. Mr Karzai's chief of staff, Mr Umar Daudzai, however, disputed Mr Faqiryar's account of the President's involvement, saying that the President had instructed the prosecutors to move cases forward "appropriately". "I strongly deny that the President has been in any way obstructing the investigations of these cases," Mr Daudzai said. "On the contrary, he has done his bit in all these cases, and it is his job to make sure that the justice is not politicised. And, unfortunately we see in some of these cases that it is politicised."[13]

The *New York Times* said that the former Deputy Attorney-General had made his accusations amid a growing sense of alarm in the Obama administration and in Congress over President Karzai's failure to take action against officials suspected of corruption, but also as the administration debated whether pushing too hard on corruption would alienate a government whose cooperation it needed to wage war. The Karzai government, the paper continued, 'awash in American and NATO money, is widely regarded as one of the most corrupt in the world. American officials believe the corruption drives Afghans into the arms of the Taliban.'[14]

In a two-hour interview at his home, Fazel Ahmed Faqiryar said he and the other prosecutors in his office 'were demoralised by the repeated refusal of Mr Karzai and Mr Aloko to allow them to move against corrupt Afghan leaders'. His prosecutors, he said, 'had opened cases on at least twenty-five current or former Afghan officials, including seventeen members of Mr Karzai's Cabinet, five Provincial Governors and at least three Ambassadors. None of the cases, he said, had gone forward, and some had been blocked on orders from Mr Karzai . . .'[15]

For his part, the *New York Times* added, President Karzai 'said he had intervened in the case of Mr Salehi, who worked for the National Security Council, because the American-backed anti-corruption agencies were violating the civil rights of those they detained. He blamed foreign contractors for the corruption, and threatened to take control of the anti-corruption agencies, summoning the head of the one that arrested Mr Salehi to the Presidential Palace for questioning.'

Subsequently, under 'intense Western pressure', President Karzai appeared to back off, saying he would allow the anti-corruption units to do their jobs. Fazel Ahmed Faqiryar, a seventy-two-year-old career prosecutor, said he was fired by President Karzai after sending a mid-level prosecutor to speak about public corruption on Afghan television. After Mr Karzai watched the broadcast, he called for the papers to authorise his dismissal, Mr Faqiryar said, adding that his abrupt departure was the culmination of a long-running tug-of-war between him and his prosecutors on one side, and Mr Karzai and Mr Aloko on the other. The dispute began last year, Mr Faqiryar said, when he went before the Afghan parliament and read aloud the names of at least twenty-five Afghan officials who were under investigation for corruption. The list included some of the most senior officials in President Karzai's government, including Siddiq Chakari, the former Minister for Haj and Islamic Affairs, and Rangin Spanta, a former Foreign Minister who was the National Security Adviser.

After Mr Faqiryar returned from parliament, he claimed 'he was summoned by Mr Aloko, who told him that Mr Karzai was furious. "He told me the President was not happy about this," Mr Faqiryar said. "He said, 'I told you not to divulge this.'" Mr Daudzai, the President's chief of staff, insisted that Mr Faqiryar was not dismissed. He said Mr Faqiryar had been due to retire and that his papers 'were signed weeks ago but just now came to the surface.'

'Some of the corruption cases involved relatively minor transgressions. But Mr Faqiryar said his prosecutors had unearthed serious allegations of corruption against several senior Afghan officials. In many of those cases, he said, the prosecutors had substantiated the claims with ample evidence. Only three of the twenty-five Afghan officials have been charged, he said, and in no case had a verdict been delivered. The cases of the other twenty-two have either been blocked or were lying dormant for inexplicable reasons, he said.

'One of the most serious cases involved Khoja Ghulam Ghaws, the Governor of Kapisa Province, who was appointed by Mr Karzai in 2007. According to Western officials, Afghan prosecutors compiled a dossier against Mr Ghaws that included telephone intercepts and sworn statements from Americans and Afghans working in the province. According to these officials, prosecutors had enough evidence to charge Mr Ghaws with colluding with insurgents and demanding kickbacks from contractors working on American and Afghan-financed development projects. Mr Ghaws is also a suspect in the killing of five members of a Provincial Reconstruction Team last year.

'Prosecutors turned over the Ghaws case to Mr Aloko, four months ago, according to a Western official who insisted on remaining anonymous. Mr Aloko had refused to sign either the warrant to arrest Mr Ghaws or the warrant to search his house, the official said. "He's the President's ally," the official said. "Obviously, Karzai doesn't want the case to go forward."

'Mr Daudzai, according to the *New York Times* report, insisted that Mr Karzai had made the first move against Mr Ghaws weeks ago by signing a letter suspending him from his job and asking him to appear before the Attorney-General. He could not explain why Mr Ghaws was still running the province and residing in the Governor's compound, where he was interviewed last week by the *New York Times* . . . The case against Mr Ghaws was raised two weeks ago by Senator Kerry, the Massachusetts Democrat, who travelled to Kabul in part to urge Mr Karzai to take action against corrupt officials.

'In the interview, Mr Faqiryar confirmed the Western official's account, saying that Mr Ghaws has been allowed to remain free at Mr Karzai's insistence. "Mr Karzai has not agreed [to the arrest]," Mr Faqiryar said of the Ghaws case. "Aloko said to me, 'You have to follow the President.'" Mr Aloko signed the arrest warrant of Mr Salehi, the Karzai aide who was later released, but only after Western officials insisted that he do so, Mr Faqiryar said . . . Mr Aloko was also blocking the arrest of Mr Azimi, a key figure in the . . . New Ansari case, Mr Faqiryar said . . .

'American officials in Kabul confirmed that Afghan prosecutors had tried to arrest Mr Azimi but had been prevented from doing so by key figures in the Karzai government. In his interview, Mr Faqiryar said Mr Salehi had emerged from his office in the Presidential Palace and asked the Attorney-General, Mr Aloko, to block Mr Azimi's arrest. "The reason Mr Aloko does not sign the arrest warrant for Mr Azimi is because Salehi told him not to," he said.

'Mr Faqiryar listed three cases of corruption among senior Afghan diplomats posted in Canada, Germany and Britain, and said there were other cases as well. In each of the three cases he said, they were suspected of stealing public money. None of them, including two former ambassadors and a consul general, had been prosecuted . . . An official at the Afghan Foreign Ministry confirmed that the three diplomats had in fact taken public money. But at least two of them, the official said, the former ambassadors to Britain and Germany, had "paid the money back". After a career spanning forty-eight years, Mr Faqiryar said he was looking forward to retirement. "It's good to be away from them and not held accountable for their wrongdoings," he said.'[16]

During the past year or so, from the end of 2010 until the autumn of 2011, the atmosphere in Kabul has become, if anything, more febrile and more uncertain, as if the capital and the country at large are living on borrowed time.

Everyone is tired of war, longing for peace and a sense of security. There seems to be an exhaustion of the spirit, a sense of desperation caused by what most ordinary people see as a failure of government, a failure of the West and its forces, as well as a deep distrust and dislike of the barbarians waiting at the gate. Perhaps because of the general exhaustion, there is no anti-war movement, few, if any, demonstrations or protest marches, just the murderous insurgency with its IEDs and suicide bombs, its assassinations and threatening Taliban night-letters.

One senses that corruption and the headlong pursuit of the dollar have grown like Frankenstein's monster out of the collapse of a moral code on the one hand, and the availability of the vast sums of money the Americans have been pouring into Afghanistan on the other, in a belated attempt to buy their way to victory, or at least to an agreement that will stop al Qaeda regaining a foothold in Afghanistan. An apparently endless supply of dollars is the panacea, a solution for all the country's woes. Being rich, full of dollars, is a suit of armour, the best insurance policy there is, although available only to the few. If the Americans suddenly get up and leave, the rich can jump in their jets and head for the safety of Dubai and the good life of the Gulf. Corruption, Amrullah Saleh used to say, is bad and must be brought under control; but it is the lesser of two evils, the greater being al Qaeda and the Taliban. Their defeat comes first. That is where he parted company with his President.

19

The Afghan Mafia, 2009

To me our government is like a Mafia syndicate . . . do anything you want, it's okay – loot, steal, kill, grab . . . and we'll protect you as far as we are getting what we want.

Sultana, Kabul, 2009

At the end of October 2009, there was the crispness of early autumn in the Kabul air, but it was still warm in the middle of the day. The political temperature, however, had plummeted. It was positively wintry. Most Afghans I talked to, old friends and new, were scathing about the blatant rigging of the presidential election of August 2009, in which President Karzai's supporters were accused of falsifying the results to the tune of more than a million votes. So gross was the fraud that even the weak-kneed United Nations Office in Kabul insisted on a recount and Karzai was forced into a run-off. He refused, however, to alter the biased composition of the grotesquely misnamed Independent Election Commission (IEC) – staffed entirely by his own cronies and yes-men.

Not surprisingly, his sole challenger, Dr Abdullah – formerly the right-hand man of the assassinated Ahmed Shah Masud, the leader of the Northern Alliance, demanded the reform of the IEC. When Karzai ignored him, Abdullah refused to stand. The failure of the United Nations and the international community at large to intervene led to fierce recriminations in the UN's Kabul office. Its number two, Peter Galbraith, the outspoken son of the renowned American economist and ambassador, J. K. Galbraith, was first of all asked to leave Afghanistan by his boss, the Norwegian diplomat, Kai Eide, and later sacked by the UN Secretary General, Ban Ki-Moon. Galbraith was a close friend of Richard Holbrooke, Obama's special envoy to Afghanistan and Pakistan, who was widely reported to have had a blazing row about the fraudulent elections with President

Karzai, over dinner in the palace. Karzai weathered the storm and won by default; but what little credibility he still had vanished overnight, like François Villon's *neiges d'antan*,* a fact exploited to the full by the increasingly effective Taliban propaganda machine.

The prospect of five more years of President Karzai's corrupt and incompetent rule filled almost every politically conscious Afghan – and foreign national – I met with equal amounts of derision and dismay. His morally bankrupt administration seemed to offer no escape from what was widely seen as a sinking ship. Everyone spoke of the rampant corruption and the deteriorating security situation, which seemed to go hand in hand. The political and moneyed 'elite', for want of a better word, I was told, all had their escape plans ready. Many had already bought their flats or houses in Dubai, Qatar or Abu Dhabi, and no doubt the really well-off had their pads in London, New York or San Francisco – where for many years there has been a large Afghan colony, the product of the diaspora which began with the Communist Revolution of 1978 and has reflected every crisis since.

The sense of impending collapse, accompanied by the fear of a Taliban victory, was everywhere. When I asked Sultana, a Kabul architect who grew up in America but came back to Kabul in 2002 after the fall of the Taliban, what she thought about their possible return, she poured out her fears in an almost Joycean stream of consciousness:

'It's scary. It's too scary to think about it. It's mind-boggling. And at the same time, after almost ten years of tremendous effort by the international community, by the private sector of the international community, by the people of the Western world, the attention, the love, the affection, the care that people showed to Afghanistan was remarkable, unbelievable. Not to mention that the soldiers came here and money came here and Afghans themselves, like me, came here who left for fear of their lives. They came back here hoping with so much hope that there was a new era, after all the killing, all the fighting, all the bombing and getting rid of this horrible dark force . . . And all of a sudden we have them back . . . They had made some really big mistakes since 2001,' Sultana told me, and now, in her

---

* From the haunting poem by François Villon (*b.* 1431): '*Mais où sont les neiges d'antan?*' (But where are the snows of yesteryear?)

opinion, in 2009, they were making the same mistakes again. 'What I see right now . . . is exactly what happened in 2001: bringing an incompetent government in place, with the warlords, and impose it on the Afghan people. We saw that happen and it didn't produce any good results for eight years and now we did it again so anything is possible. I am surprised the Taliban are not already here.'[1]

I interrupted to suggest there were quite a lot of American troops in Afghanistan.

Sultana agreed. 'We have quite a lot of American troops but the American population are having less and less support for this war.' American support had declined because, in her view, 'the American government are realising that they didn't have a partner [Karzai] to work with . . . and a lot of their efforts were just being nullified and diverted'.

So the question was, Sultana added: Were we going to fix this along with the rest of the Western forces, with more troops? 'The answer in my opinion: No, based on what I have seen in the past eight years. It may help militarily by blocking them or pushing them or doing some new strategy, it may help in some way, but in the long run, in terms of the overall security and development of Afghanistan, you have got to have a completely new way of thinking and new way of operating within the Afghan government. We need a rethinking of how we have done things and who is in a position of power, what kind of authority do they have, how are they using this authority, what is the result of their actions and activities. So far it has been empire-building, to be honest with you.'

To Sultana the government was like a Mafia syndicate, sitting at the top, and giving protection to people below: 'but do anything you want, it's okay – loot, steal, kill, grab, do anything you want, don't challenge us, just do what you want and we'll protect you as far as we are getting what we want – it is completely like that. I know that's how criminal organisations work and we have an exact replica.'[2]

Sultana's judgement, that the Afghan government was an exact replica of a Mafia syndicate, was damning; but the more I heard, and the more Afghans I talked to, the more accurate it seemed to be. I got the same sense of foreboding from another well-educated middle-aged woman who had also been brought up in the United States and spoke good English. Mina's family had been close to the royal family, no doubt the reason they were among the first victims of the bloody Communist Revolution of April 1978. Her father, who was the first Afghan to learn to fly, rose to be head of the air force and became the King's personal pilot. According to Mina, after his arrest 'he simply disappeared'. 'We still don't know what happened to him. Nor where he is buried. Nothing,' she told me.[3]

This was a period when literally thousands of Afghans perceived as political enemies by the Communists were arrested, taken to the huge, Russian-built Pul-i-Charki prison, on the eastern outskirts of Kabul, interrogated, tortured and executed, or just executed.

Her family managed to flee the capital and escaped to America where Mina, now in her early fifties, grew up. She had come back to Afghanistan recently to start a charity project on a piece of land she inherited from her father. As with many educated Afghan women, the thought of the Taliban returning to power fills her with dread. She feels especially vulnerable because she has no husband – she is divorced – and the Taliban, when in power, displayed a narrow-minded attitude to women leaving the house without their husband, or another 'male relative' to chaperone them, even if they were only going shopping or visiting friends. Going out to work was absolutely taboo, with the exception of the few women employed in the medical profession. This Taliban edict, combined with the compulsory closure of all girls' schools, practically paralysed teaching in schools and universities, where the majority of staff were women. Kabul University, for example, virtually closed because of lack of women staff in many faculties and departments. Being an American citizen, Mina can always go back to the United States, but she has put her roots down in Afghanistan now and wants to stay in her own country.

She is, however, appalled by the corruption, which she says is everywhere. 'People are just out for themselves. They want to make as much money as possible, as quickly as possible and they don't care what happens to anyone else, or to the country. You find this attitude everywhere. Right up to the top. Even among the people in the palace, Karzai's people . . . They're just as bad as everyone else. Worse even.'

Did she think President Karzai himself was personally corrupt?

'Yes, of course. The whole clan is corrupt.'[4]

Not everyone thinks so, of course. I spoke to one Member of Parliament, Shukria Barakzai, a striking-looking woman in her forties. A member of the one of the grandest Pushtun tribes, the Barakzai, she is a personal friend of the President. Unlike Mina, Shukria Barakzai defends Karzai as not being 'personally corrupt'. She admits the system is corrupt, however, and criticises it frankly. Speaking in her office in a well-protected compound near parliament, she told me: 'Corruption is a disease, a cancer, it affects a whole part of the governmental and non-governmental organisations, both.' Thirty per cent of international aid money, she claims, went to the Afghan government, which was responsible for accounting for it; but 70 per cent went to 'international organisations and local NGOs', who were similarly responsible. 'I am glad that the USA recently wants to know with whom they contract, who is their contractor and where are the old projects.'[5]

In her opinion, the problem of corruption could be solved by enforcing the rule of law, dealing with 'the culture of impunity', and by 'removing corrupt people from high official positions'.

'It is solvable,' she maintains, 'with a new system . . . because bureaucracy itself, directly and indirectly is supporting corruption. If you want to simply buy milk for a government office you need eight signatures, so it is ridiculous.' She repeats the now well-known mantra for what needs to be done: 'to build capacity, punish people for the bad work, give honour for the good work, [provide] good jobs, an equal rule of law for everybody and available access to justice for everybody and having professional people. These are really important for corruption.'

But first of all, she insists: 'There is a strong need for an [anti-corruption] body, independent of the government,' an investigative body with teeth, with powers to track down and presumably bring charges against 'illegals', because, she adds, 'today those who are corrupt, there is no investigation on them'.[6]

Critics point out that it is easy to see what is wrong, but doing something about it is another matter. The corruption of the justice (or injustice) system has been notorious for, literally, years. You have no chance, I was told, even if you are completely in the right and have a watertight case, unless you bribe the judges in advance. As the Karzai government has slid downhill, becoming increasingly corrupt and incompetent, the Taliban's alternative government, with its own 'shadow' administration in place from provincial governors down, has become steadily more effective. Many of the Afghans I talked to think, and fear, the shift in power is now irreversible.

• _____

Zaid Siddig was born in Berlin, where his father, a former Foreign Minister, was twice Ambassador. As a result of a political feud, his uncle, General Ghulam Nadir Charkhi, was murdered on the orders of King Nadir Khan, who imprisoned the rest of the family, including a number of the children. Nadir Khan was later assassinated by a student on the palace lawn.

The full story, related to me by Zaid Siddig himself, makes grim reading even by Afghan standards: .

After the fall of King Amanullah [1919–29] and the ascension to the throne of Mohammed Nadir Khan my father was reappointed as ambassador to Germany and Ghulam Nabi Khan [his brother and Siddig's uncle] was invited to Kabul by the king. The king's brother Shah Wali Khan personally travelled to Istanbul to guarantee a safe conduct written into a Koran. Once in Kabul Ghulam Nabi Khan was suspected of working for the return of Amanullah by King Nadir, although no proof existed. An insurrection of the Jadran tribe in Paktia province served as an excuse to have General Ghulam Nabi appear before the king. In a prearranged incident, he was confronted on the steps of the Dilkusha Palace by the king . . . and accused of treason which my uncle denied forcefully. Tempers flared and the king gave orders to the guards to beat my uncle with their rifles shouting 'beat him until he is dead'. His body was then thrown into our family compound for immediate burial. No evidence was ever produced by the government of any culpability on the part of our family. Our entire family was thrown in jail where they remained for 17 years and a further 5 years under house arrest. All family property was taken away. My other uncle, my cousins and other relatives were successively taken out of jail and executed, specifically after the son of General Nabi's personal servant, a student at the German High

School shot and killed King Nadir Shah almost exactly on the anniversary of [Siddig's uncle] Ghulam Nabi's violent death. My father naturally remained in exile in Germany where he died in 1968. We were able to get permission to bury him in Kabul. By invitation of King Zahir Shah I returned to Kabul in 1967, and worked as senior geologist at the Geological Survey of Afghanistan.

Despite this violent past, Zaid is charming and mild-mannered, with a Masters degree in geology and mining engineering. Brought up in Germany, he speaks fluent German and almost as fluent English, and is a successful farmer and horticulturist. A few years ago he planted 150,000 fast-growing almonds, apples, pears and non-fruit trees near Darulaman Palace, built for King Amanullah on the outskirts of Kabul by a French architect in 1923, but today a ruin.

He recalls the period after 9/11 and the American intervention as being 'a shambles.' Thousands of NGOs poured into the country. 'No one talked to each other. There was a dormitory for girl students at Kandahar built by one NGO; then down the street another NGO built another . . . But the first dormitory had only one girl in it. There was no coordination, no cooperation, everybody did their own thing, money poured in . . .'[7]

Money was spent by 'the foreigners', not by the Afghan government, which lacked capacity. 'It wasn't just the fault of the foreigners. They didn't have any capacity in the ministries because the people who were empowered by the US invasion, after the Taliban were run out, took over and flooded the ministries. [Jobs] were parcelled out by the old *mujahideen* leaders [warlords]. Everybody brought their own ethnic group into the ministry. So the Ministry of Agriculture officials were all Hazaras, the Ministry of Commerce were all Uzbeks and so on . . .'

The old civil servants had vanished, were refugees, had died or were abroad, Zaid explains, so there was no one in Afghanistan to do the work. 'The foreign aid community didn't trust the Afghan government [enough] to give them a lot of money,' but the Afghans were 'screaming: "Let's channel all the funds for reconstruction through the government."'

'The next thing was priorities. For the Americans the most important thing was [to act] very fast to show something as a success story. So the first

thing that happened was that the roads were built . . . The Kandahar–
Kabul road was built so quickly it had to be rebuilt . . . $260 [£170] million
was spent rebuilding the Kandahar–Kabul road [but] it didn't last long.
The first road, built in the early sixties by Morrison-Knudsen, an American
company [which built the Helmand Valley Project, based on the Tennessee
River Valley Authority], lasted for sixty years – craftsmanship was involved.
But this time they used the wrong asphalt. There was no priority given to
the agricultural sector which is one of the most important. The mining
sector and the agricultural sectors are the most important to bring up the
level of prosperity.'[8]

Another serious problem, he says, was that 'thousands of students graduated from Kabul University . . . but they were all unemployed. The
country needed vocational schools [to train] motor mechanics, plumbers,
carpenters, electricians, masons and the rest to bring up the level. If you go
around the construction sites in Kabul city, where these mansions are
being built, 80 or 90 per cent of the workforce are from Peshawar [in
Pakistan], from the border, from the tribal area because they have skills.
We have only non-skilled workers. This is where money comes in, where
employment comes in.'

Having been a successful farmer before the Communist coup and the
Russian invasion in the late 1970s, Zaid says it is very important to replant
orchards that have been destroyed by thirty years of warfare. 'For example,
five acres of almond orchard will yield the family farmer about 130,000–
140,000 Afghanis [£1,850–£2,000] a year, which works out at about 12,000
Afghanis [£170] a month.' A government employee makes a maximum of
3,000–4,000 Afghanis (£42–£57) a month. 'The man in the countryside,
the family farmer, has no rent to pay, he probably doesn't have any electricity, so no power bill, so he can live quite handily with the money he can
make from five acres of orchard.'

From 1970 to 1980, Zaid Siddig farmed wheat and sheep in Farah
Province, in the remote south-west corner of Afghanistan, between
Helmand Province and the borders of Iran and Pakistan. Then one day, he
says, 'the Communist Afghan government confiscated everything and
threw us off our land. There were 247 farms there [before] the Russian
invasion of 1979. In 1979 and 1980, I dug my own wells and was a very

successful farmer. There is a big desert, the Bakva, [but] unfortunately it is all opium there now . . . and there are 5,000 wells.'

Zaid Siddig therefore understands the need for water resources and 'modern irrigation systems like drip irrigation and so on', and is critical of the Karzai government for having done little to exploit it. Afghanistan had plenty of water but a lack of water where it was needed for agriculture. 'Take, for instance, the Oxus River, the Amu Darya [Afghanistan's northern border]. It could be pumped and brought up through pipelines to hundreds of thousands of acres of fertile land in the north that could be irrigated.' Only in the last year or so have plans been worked on 'to give hundreds of thousands of acres of fertile land to farmers without land, not only in the north but everywhere. The government is now cataloguing all the government land which can be used for agriculture. Once it is catalogued, then we have a one-stop office where the applicants can come and get their land allocated in the area they live in, if there is any land . . . and they will be assisted with water systems and fertiliser and seed so they can start.'

Things that should have been done immediately after the departure of the Taliban and the arrival of Western forces were only being done now. Zaid blames the American preoccupation with Iraq, and the handover of power to the warlords. That, however, he says is all 'water under the bridge'.

He is a believer in 'small is beautiful', and advocates projects which benefit the ordinary Afghan. 'A lot of things can be done in Afghanistan which do not cost billions of dollars.' For example, a cousin from France with limited resources came back to Afghanistan to finance a pilot project. 'He engaged five farmers or labourers with no land, gave them each a cow and five *jerib* [two acres] and provided them with seed and fertiliser . . . The whole thing cost about 1 million Afghanis [£11,000] including the cows, and they sustained themselves for nine months until the harvest, by selling milk and yogurt . . . The second year they made a surplus, one saved 20,000 Afghanis [£250] in the bank.'

Sooner or later, every conversation in Afghanistan seems to come round to corruption. Zaid Siddig believes that to achieve good government there has to be 'a crackdown', but that this is 'very difficult [because] of all the corruption in the judiciary and the administration. Every government office which has customer relations, like the tax office, the electric power company, wherever you pay a bill, everyone is taking bribes and it is upsetting people. In the countryside there is no justice, it is all [about] money . . . It's who gives the most money, wins the lawsuit. People get very frustrated, people have no work, are unemployed in the countryside. The Taliban offer $200 a month and the Afghan Army soldier gets $100 a month. So you can imagine a lot of people are being diverted to the Taliban. They [the government officials] say there are no Taliban, but they [the young men] are being brainwashed and indoctrinated by obscurantist mullahs.'

As someone who benefited from a German education, he is critical of the poor educational standards in Afghanistan. 'We have about 70,000 teachers with only eleventh-grade education who are teaching tenth- and eleventh-grade children, so there is no educational level, there is no standard.' Government propaganda claims 6 million children go to school. 'Well, it's just a kindergarten. They go to school for only three hours a day so the level is still low. We need to train up teachers, and have more teacher training colleges. It all takes time. Everything takes time. I am looking at a [period] of fifteen to twenty years to bring it [education] up to a level where it can sustain itself and [we can] have a much better educational system than now.'

Eighteen months later, in late 2011, I asked Zaid Siddig for his views on the current situation. They were frank, to say the least:

'Afghanistan is sliding from one crisis into another,' he began. 'First the Kabul Bank fiasco which has not been resolved to date.'* (Kabul Bank, the country's biggest, with many influential shareholders, including Mahmood Karzai, a younger brother of the President, went bankrupt in September, 2010, with debts of about $850 million. This caused a national crisis since it handled the salaries of most public servants, including the police. The Central Bank had to step in to make good the payments.) The drawback, Zaid Siddig said, was that the International Monetary Fund refused to operate in Kabul 'until the mess is cleaned up, the culprits brought to justice and the outstanding loans repaid' to the bank 'as far as possible'.

But that was not all, he added: 'Now we have the Parliament debacle

---

* It was subsequently.

brought on partially by Mr [President] Karzai himself.' After the last elections, 62 losing candidates claimed they had lost because of massive fraud
and demanded to be reinstated. Accepting their claims, Karzai 'went ahead
and inaugurated the new Parliament, giving it legitimacy. This year [2011]
he appointed a special court to resolve the matter. The court's decision
invalidated the tenure of 62 sitting MPs claiming fraud and giving the
mandate to the 62 protesters.' Parliament 'balked' and vowed not to let a
single MP lose his or her seat.

Then Karzai abolished the special court and handed the matter over to
the Independent Election Commission to decide. 'They came back with a
decision that nine MPs should be kicked out and nine protesters given
their seats. This decision was not accepted by either side and so the
saga goes on. What a mess indeed.'

Security around Kabul had recently 'deteriorated considerably', especially in Logar and Wardak, Zaid Siddig said. Taliban, Arab and Chechen
insurgents who had been 'pushed out' of the south had found their way up
to Kabul and the surrounding provinces, where they were operating with
local insurgents.

'In all it is not a pretty picture,' Siddig summed up. 'Eid al Fitr [the
holiday that marks the end of Ramazan] will be tomorrow or the day after
depending [on] whether the Saudis will see the new moon. Why we can't
look for the new moon ourselves just beats me . . .'

At least Zaid Siddig seems to think – or perhaps merely hope – that time
can solve Afghanistan's problems. I found a more pessimistic view when I
talked to a man who, paradoxically, might be considered the greatest optimist in the country. An architect turned diplomat and minister, Mahmoud
Saikal, a former Afghan Ambassador to Australia, was appointed Deputy
Minister for Foreign Affairs by President Karzai in 2005. He resigned the
following year, donned his architect's hat again and started planning a
satellite city of 3 million inhabitants, in the foothills north of Kabul airport.
The Japanese offered to provide the finance and the project took off,
despite initial security worries. On the political front, Saikal says things
began to go wrong after Karzai's first election as President. This led, he
says, to a cult of personality.

'In January 2006 we put the Afghanistan Compact together and I was the focal point, because I was the Deputy Foreign Minister at the time.' As such, he was responsible for negotiating with about eighty foreign countries which had pledged assistance to Afghanistan. He describes it as a 'joint document between Afghanistan and the international community: what should we Afghans do, and what would you do to support it in the form of cash and technical cooperation'.[9]

The Afghans pledged to meet certain 'benchmarks', in a given time, and the international community pledged to provide the finance and technical cooperation in the field of security, anti-corruption, counter-narcotics, governance and all those things; clear benchmarks, all with timelines. Also included in the agreement was a 'blueprint for the development of this country for the next five years'. What happened, however, according to Mahmoud Saikal, was that 'personalities' started taking advantage of and abusing the system, 'a bit like the Shah of Iran, who between the 1950s and his fall in the late 1970s, had taken advantage of American aid to strengthen his own position instead of building [up] Iranian institutions. Karzai and his brothers and the cronies around him started taking advantage of the aid available to strengthen their own power,' Saikal claimed. In the Afghan constitution 'we have a highly centralised presidential system'. It was not working for Afghanistan, Saikal said, but it was working for Karzai, because it gave him a lot of power. He could 'fire, hire, appoint ministers, deputy ministers, governors, district officers, police chiefs, everything was at his disposal and what he did he actually started picking up people who saluted him, *his* men, *his* women who could strengthen his base, so that he could have a good grip of power.'[10]

Saikal said the signs were so obvious that he asked for a meeting with the President in June 2006. 'I went to his office – he had a new office at the back of his office which was really private. I said "Mr President, I can see signs of trouble, if we don't have quality governance everything will fall apart."' He gave the President some 'good examples' from within the Foreign Ministry, including two people he had had dismissed 'and he rose up and he shook hands with me and said: "We will take care of it."' Two months passed, nothing happened. One day, Saikal said, he went to his office and found himself the 'most unproductive guy on planet Earth. It took me half an hour to draw up my resignation and I resigned . . . In my letter I wrote I cannot be part of a corrupt government. I really do not want to bring myself down to this level.'[11]

Saikal recalls that in early 2007 the Lower House of Parliament passed a vote of no confidence in the Foreign Minister, Rangin Spanta, by a majority of 144. Any 'decent' President 'would have said: "I respect the constitutional right of parliament and I will introduce another Foreign Minister to you." . . . But no, because Spanta was his buddy . . . he wrote a letter to the Supreme Court and the Supreme Court came back to him and said it is okay . . . That hurt our MPs' dignity, to the point that they wrote a letter to all the embassies in Kabul to say that Mr Spanta was not their Foreign Affairs Minister.' But despite that, Rangin Spanta remained as Foreign Minister until he was replaced in January 2010.

Mahmoud Saikal is also critical of the delay in holding the 2009 presidential election. Karzai's term having expired in May, the international community should have insisted on a transitional authority, he says. 'But no, Mrs Clinton gave the green light and said it is okay. Then one after the other we could see the collapse of the rule of law in this country. When people saw that they said: "If the President is doing it, then why can't we? Let's do anything . . ."'

Mahmoud Saikal described the current situation (November 2009) as 'chaos'. 'My feeling is . . . it is primarily the fault of the Afghans,' but it was the duty of the international community to put Karzai on the spot and hold him to the terms of the 2006 Compact, 'and since he had failed to comply, they should have said: "There is no budget for you or your government until and unless you come to your senses." . . . Now Mr Gordon Brown and [President] Obama have given him six months to hurry up and get rid of corruption. But let's come to now . . . there is no way we can get rid of corruption, there is no way he can re-establish the institutions of Afghanistan . . . It is way too late.'

Saikal argues the international community could have acted before the August 2009 election, but the fraud and unconstitutional decision of the so-called independent election commission to give Karzai the presidency had made things worse. 'I feel that the government is no longer there to serve the people; the government is a burden on the shoulders of the people. It is a corrupt government and therefore . . . serving this government is a disservice to Afghanistan . . . But the way he is going he will have an eventual fall and that fall, I hope it's not very tragic for him' – an apparent reference to the fate of the Communist ex-President Najibullah, who in 1996 was tortured and killed by the Taliban, and his body hung up outside the Presidential Palace. 'I hope it will be a peaceful fall, but the Afghan people cannot afford to see the continuation of this kind of stubbornness that we have experienced in the last couple of years.'[12]

The Beginning of the End? Summer 2010

The only phenomenon in which people still trust is God
Amrullah Saleh, Kabul, August 2010

In the unusually steamy heat of Kabul in August 2010 – caused they say by the tail end of the abnormally late Indian monsoon – the Afghan government of President Karzai seemed to be spiralling out of control. If there were reliable opinion polls in Afghanistan, the government's popularity would almost certainly be in the low single figures. Overwhelming personal greed and corrupt political practice at the top of government had sent public confidence to a new, rock-bottom low, according to sources and officials who had worked with and for the mercurial President and his entourage in the past decade.[1]

The immediate cause was a big shake-up in the key security sector when the British-educated Minister of the Interior, Hanif Atmar, and the pro-Western, long-serving Head of Intelligence, Amrullah Saleh, resigned from President Karzai's government after a rocket attack on the opening of the Peace Jirga in Kabul on 2 June 2010. The President had made it clear he had lost confidence in them, after the Taliban – or was it the Taliban? – penetrated the police cordon and fired three rockets at the opening ceremony. The rockets fell about a hundred yards from Karzai. No one was hurt and the jirga continued without the delegates as much as getting out of their seats, according to the United Nations envoy, Staffan de Mistura, who was present.

While the incident was fairly predictable for Kabul, what came as a surprise was the reaction of the President, although his behaviour had become increasingly erratic over the course of the year. Diplomatic and media gossip portrayed him as a manic-depressive, who was now 'on his meds', then 'off his meds', a figure almost of derision, although his outbursts against the West and the United States in particular were seen by some as understandable given the criticism he has had to face.

Although the Taliban claimed responsibility for the attack and three heavily armed militants dressed as women in burkas were identified as the attackers – two of whom were killed and one captured – President Karzai was in denial. He told the Interior Minister and the Intelligence Chief he did not believe the Taliban were guilty, according to a very senior security source. He implicitly suggested that the Americans were responsible, saying 'nobody was a factor' except the Taliban and the Americans, adding: 'I know it is not the work of the Taliban. Even if it is good for them that they can come so close to us . . .'[2] (A curious remark, since he denied they were involved.)

That seems to have been the breaking point and the two officials resigned immediately after the meeting with Karzai. The whole incident, the bizarre blame game that followed and the shakiness of the Karzai regime, conjured up visions to the more historically minded of the last days of Rome before the onslaught of the barbarians.

The resignations were seen by the West as the serious loss of two exceptionally able senior Cabinet members with years of experience. Hanif Atmar lost a leg fighting in the *jihad*, not as a *mujahid* but for the Afghan Communists who repulsed the *mujahideen* attack on Jalalabad in 1989, soon after the Russian withdrawal. After the war, he studied at York University in Britain, gaining two degrees, then worked for several foreign NGOs in Afghanistan before entering the post-Taliban government after 2001. Amrullah Saleh, a protégé of Ahmed Shah Masud, the famous Afghan guerrilla leader, was sent by Masud to America to set up a liaison office and was trained by the CIA – although he learned his almost flawless English, he says, in Kabul in the late 1980s. He became head of the NDS (National Directorate of Security) in 2004. The Americans in particular thought highly of him. Both he and Hanif Atmar had high reputations for professionalism, which was more than could be said for some members of the Karzai government.

It was after the 2009 presidential election, when Karzai and his supporters were accused of rigging the election to the extent of more than one million votes, that Karzai's views seem to have undergone a dramatic shift. 'All of a sudden after the presidential election,' Amrullah Saleh told me, President Karzai 'made it very clear that he was not happy with NATO, had lost confidence in NATO, that he thought democracy had hurt him and shattered his prestige in Afghanistan and he was very unhappy with the Americans putting things in their media against him. So he said: "This is it, and I want to make it with Pakistan and with the Taliban."'[3]

Saleh agreed that approaches to both parties were needed, but argued that they should be well planned, not abrupt.

'The Taliban had become very, very strong and he [Karzai] had not consolidated his post-election government yet. [Karzai had appointed a number of ministers, most of whom had been rejected by Parliament.] Now that you go and reach out from such a weak position it will further weaken the state.' Even government in Kabul was declining; there were clashes in the capital. 'But the President was not prepared to listen to any of this. He had made his decision. Then came the jirga and the attack on the jirga which the President insisted was not the work of the Taliban.' So, Amrullah Saleh says, 'he ridiculed all the evidence and that was it'.[4]

The weakness of the government in Kabul in the summer of 2010 led one source to comment that it was unable to guarantee the safety of its own subjects. 'The current government says: "I cannot protect you." That is the message of this government . . . [it] is all about complaining about foreigners, about Taliban, about everything but itself. Even [of] itself it says: "We are so weak we cannot protect you."' The unnamed source went on: 'I have lost hope in the top . . . By the top I don't mean Karzai, [but] whoever is the top, the elite, the Kabul theatre let's say, political Kabul. It is hopeless. They have become so greedy and they are so detached and they live in a balloon. They think the Americans are here for some reasons not known to the Afghans, and that they will continue to fight for them for ever. So you go and preach to them and it doesn't work.'[5]

After his resignation, Amrullah Saleh formed what he calls a 'grass roots' movement. The response, Saleh told me, was 'overwhelming'. These were people who had 'lost belief in politics and politicians and reconstruction and the government and the contracts and the NGOs and the Americans. The only phenomenon in which people still trust is

God. That is why you see everywhere, in the villages, there is nothing but prayers and mosque-going, and reading the Koran. There is no other meaningful activity. So once you go and jump into that disbelief and allow yourself to be burned, grilled by the people and you create new confidence, they trust you . . . But it doesn't make news, because it is with the very margins of society who are not tainted, who are not manipulated yet. Not necessarily all young; [but] those who have not benefited from anything; and those who . . . share our view.'[6]

Amrullah Saleh's view is very clear. 'Democracy is dying in Afghanistan and the country needs settlement,' he says. 'People who said that, came under fire from the government press, but it was true. Democracy is dying and is already dead in twenty provinces. [There are thirty-four provinces in Afghanistan.] Okay: holding elections in Wardak, what does it mean? Holding elections in Ghazni, what does it mean? It means nothing. Even now you have the Taliban gun, you have the government gun. In between, there is no civil society. So democracy in 50 per cent of Afghanistan is already dead . . . Not necessarily under Taliban control, but dead. Psychologically, there is no government. People do not recognise an authority. There are people who are paid by the government, who protect themselves and there are Taliban groups who go around and spread intimidation and fear. In between, the population is caught between two fighting forces and they do not go to [either] for a solution. So where is democracy there? There is no democracy.'[7]

Could General Petraeus have organised another 'Sunni Awakening', as he did so successfully in Iraq, with militias, village forces, I asked?

'It is extremely difficult to see things change in Petraeus's time,' Saleh replied. 'And he would need partners in Kabul, not spoilers.'

'And the Karzai government, they wouldn't cooperate?'

'I wouldn't say, wouldn't cooperate. The present government both at national and sub-national level is detached. They are detached from reality. What do I mean by that? You have the district commissioners or governors completely living in a box. So Petraeus creates a militia for them or amongst the people who will partner with him. If he creates it amongst the people it means he will divide the government at district level. If he creates it for the district commissioner he is already hated.'

Speaking several months before Ahmed Wali Karzai was assassinated in Kandahar on 12 July 2011, he cited him as an example. 'Let's be very frank. In Kandahar, who were the militia working for? Wali Karzai. Kandahar is key, so in Kandahar if General Petraeus creates a militia outside of the domain of Wali Karzai it means he creates the third problem: Taliban, militia, Wali Karzai. But if he creates it for Wali Karzai . . . Why are they against Wali Karzai in the media? So if he is a bad man, now they want to further empower a bad man? You see that is why I say the policy is not very clear.'

I asked about President Karzai's rejection of the West, and above all of America. How had he got into this situation?

There were too many reasons, Saleh said, but to summarise it: President Karzai believed that America had no policy on Pakistan and thought the Americans were being hypocritical. They had 100,000 troops in Afghanistan 'yet knowingly they do not do anything vis-à-vis the Taliban leadership in Pakistan . . . "Why should I burn my country because the expendable Taliban are here? Why are the Americans not burning Pakistan although they know the valuable targets are there?" That is reason number one.'

'Reason number two,' he says: '"I am their partner as a leader but they have not been protective of me. They have discredited me, bringing my vote below 50 per cent and calling my brother a drug this and that." And reason number three: He [President Karzai] thinks a lot of times his administration is bypassed and PRTs [Provincial Reconstruction Teams] are better resourced, more powerful, etc. etc. But if you talk to the Americans they [reject] all of these [complaints]. They say he . . . should have emerged as a leader capable of managing resources and managing expectations and uniting his country.'

Saleh said that among all President Karzai's criticisms and complaints he agreed with him fully and without question on Pakistan. 'On the Pakistan issue: Yes, I agree.' He added: the 'Americans to this date, as you and I are talking, don't have a policy. What is their policy?'

Counter-insurgency? Get the people on your side?

'Are they sticking to it? They don't have a policy. I have not seen an American policy. Yes, they fight with dignity and honour. They help us with dignity and honour. They are very dedicated but they are like this [waving his hands] all over the place.'[8]

Another well-informed, reliable intelligence source was critical of appointments made to top security posts in Kabul after the resignations of Atmar and Saleh. Some of the new appointees, he said, were 'thieves'. 'How can it work like that?' the source asked. 'It is all about their greed. Look at the appointments they are making. Look at the Deputy Chief [of Intelligence] in Kabul . . . illiterate. In 2004, he was fired from Kabul airport because he had allowed gold to be smuggled through the airport, using the VIP [lounge].' The deal was for more than $2 million. Because he had powerful backers the official involved in the gold smuggling was fired but not arrested, the source said. 'Now, five years later, he becomes Deputy Chief of Kabul NDS.' The source raised the appointment of the Police Chief for Ningrahar. Both the British and the Americans had 'thick files' on him, alleging widespread corruption.[9]

One question that foreign nationals in Kabul often ask of their Afghan colleagues: 'Is President Karzai losing his influence? Is he weaker?'

'Absolutely,' the source said. 'I do not believe in power politics, I believe in honesty and transparency. It is not that I don't know how power politics work. I did not believe in them because at the end of the day what is at stake is the future of Afghanistan . . . All I am saying is you do not see a single positive trend in governance and security and economic development or any national cohesion. In the last three to six months is there a positive trend to be seen?' It was now 'a matter of greed for all of them', the source added. 'There is no vision. The vision has crumbled. Whoever is there, they are trying to enlarge their own nepotistic influence and [to promote] their very narrow interests. Some powerful officials were finding jobs for their relatives in embassies abroad, including London, despite them having no diplomatic experience.'

As a former long-serving senior official, Amrullah Saleh commands considerable authority. And he gave the following 'very small example' of the dysfunction of government: 'The biggest achievement of the US is the Afghan government and it is imploding. Their biggest achievement is not the defeat of the Taliban; they are not defeated, they are back in Wardak [just south of Kabul]. Their biggest achievement is not the defeat of al Qaeda; it is not defeated. What they could say to their public, to the Afghans here: we have a government and that government is being spoiled by the very masters who own it.'

What he called the 'policy of appeasement', of reaching out to the Taliban, was 'a fatal mistake and a recipe for civil war', endangering democracy and women's rights. The decision of Karzai to give remission to Taliban prisoners was also controversial, but on one thing he did see eye to eye with the President, Saleh said. 'The ISI is part of the landscape of destruction in this country, no doubt. So it will be a waste of time to provide evidence of ISI involvement. They are a part of it.'[10]

A few months later, in December 2010, Amrullah Saleh, speaking at the National Press Club in Washington, went further than he had ever done before in public and laid down the conditions for meaningful peace talks with the Taliban. The talks would lead to a disaster, he said, unless the Taliban were first disarmed, their support from Pakistan cut off, and they began to operate as a normal political party. 'Demobilise them, disarm them, take their headquarters out of the ISI's basements,' he was quoted as saying. 'Force the Taliban to play according to the script of democracy,' he added, predicting the party would ultimately fail 'in a country where law rules, not the gun . . . not the law of intimidation'.[11]

Saleh's strongest demand was that the United States should give Pakistan a deadline of July 2011 to pursue top insurgents inside their borders, or threaten to send in US troops to do the job. He warned that failure to cut off Pakistani support for the Taliban would allow them to pretend to make peace, and then sweep back to power after NATO troops had left. He claimed that the 2010 surge of US troops had accomplished a 'temporary effect' of securing some territory in Kandahar and Marja, but had failed to change the 'fundamentals'.

'The Taliban leadership has not been captured or killed,' he stressed again. 'Al Qaeda has not been defeated . . . The current strategy still believes Pakistan is honest, or at least 50 per cent honest [in their attitude to fighting the Taliban].'[12] But he predicted Pakistan would continue to support the Taliban and other proxies to try to maintain its influence in Afghanistan. He criticised the Karzai administration, without naming Karzai, claiming that 'political Kabul' was out of touch with the rest of the country, and too often publicly at odds with NATO.

Kabul today – chaotic, dirty and dilapidated – is the symbol of the failed state of which it is the capital. The roads and traffic are horrendous. Almost without exception every road is full of potholes, some six inches deep. Drivers who know their potholes swerve from right to left and back again to avoid the worst of them, often at speed, avoiding head-on collisions at the last moment. Afghans seem impervious to this dicing with death but it reduces less-hardened passengers to nervous wrecks.

The rush hour, which starts at 6 a.m. and hardly abates until the evening, often brings near gridlock. One sits, powerless, hardly moving, sweating in the heat, dust and diesel fumes, deafened by the continuous and pointless blaring of horns for, it seems, hours on end. In the ten years since 9/11, I have noticed very little development of any quality – mainly cheap-looking blocks of offices and flats, garish wedding halls (an Afghan speciality, the jerry-built equivalent of our conference centres) and hideously ugly millionaires' mansions. The latter are mainly in the suburb of Sherpur, once the old British cantonment dating back to the Second Anglo-Afghan War. Sherpur was once Afghan Ministry of Defence property but when Marshal (now Vice-President) Fahim became Minister (2002–04) he had it converted into a township and pressured the municipality to sell it off. He and his friends are said to have done well out of the scheme. The plots now sell at a premium. Although no one has bothered to put in a decent road, and the mansions are built almost on top of one another, Sherpur has become a byword for conspicuous consumption and corruption in high places. Fahim and his brother Hasin are the biggest players in the importing of gas and oil – Hasin's gas distribution company, Gas Group, is a national concern – and have invested heavily in real estate in Dubai. Both men are reputedly multi-millionaires.

Because of governmental chaos in general and the failure to provide an urban plan for Kabul in particular – and there are plenty of talented Afghan architects who could do it – the city's amenities have been allowed to degenerate into a disgraceful shambles. One of the reasons traffic is so appalling in Kabul is that there are still virtually no traffic lights in the capital. Of the three I can think of offhand, one is on the main road between the Turkish and Iranian Embassies, and a second is a stop light at the end of Jade Maiwand, beside the bridge across the river leading to Babur's Gardens. This is not just any old traffic light but a sophisticated piece of equipment which, starting at thirty, counts down the seconds remaining on red, before the light changes to green. I don't know who installed this masterpiece of regulatory technology but its uniqueness only serves to underline the otherwise almost total lack of a traffic control system. The third I know of is at the intersection of Darulaman and University roads, although Kabulis know plenty of others. The point is that they are often not working, like the rest of the city.

In the middle of the city, in busy Pushtunistan Square, leading to the handsome old mausoleum of the founder of modern Afghanistan, Amir Abdul Rahman, where half a dozen roads pour their rivers of vehicles into a central pool, there are no traffic lights and usually only one or two traffic police on duty. Cars, whether big Land Cruisers and SUVs, ramshackle buses and lorries, or small saloons like the one I usually travel in, come at you from every direction, weaving and thrusting their way through the melee with what appears to be reckless abandon. There are no rules of the road, nothing like *priorité à droite*; all that is required is eyes in the back of your head and nerves of steel. Driving in Kabul is in many ways a motorised version of the national game, *buzkashi*, literally, 'pulling the goat', when twenty or thirty horsemen dispute the possession of a headless kid or calf, tugging and wrenching the heavy corpse as their horses plunge, barge, kick and bite in the race to drop the 'ball' into the winning circle, painted in white chalk at one end of the field. Said to have been invented by Genghis Khan's horsemen, it is one of the wildest and roughest games ever devised.

The *chapandaz*, the best players, the riders who are most successful at dropping the headless kid into the winning white circle, are rewarded with hundreds of dollars, handed to them in wads of notes when they canter up at the end of the game. The best horses fetch thousands. Vice-President Fahim has his own team, one of the best in the country, and his own ground just outside Kabul, on the edge of the Shomali plain.

To watch a *buzkashi* game, played with verve and skill for high stakes, is to begin to understand the Afghan character and culture. Afghanistan today, despite the sophistication of Kabul's small intellectual elite, once so prominent in the days of the monarchy in the 1960s and early 1970s, is the equivalent of Dickens's or Hogarth's England. It is a macho, male-dominated society in which most women, whatever the constitution may say, are at best second-class citizens, and in the poorer, rural areas, are more often treated as slaves and beasts of burden. As in England in the sixteenth and seventeenth centuries, dog fights are hugely popular. The sight of powerful mastiffs bred and trained for the purpose, tearing at one another so that the spectators can satisfy their passion for gambling, excites and pleases rather than disgusts the audience. Seen as a sport rather than unacceptable cruelty to animals, dog-fighting is officially banned – but everyone, including the police, turns a blind eye. On 17 February 2008, more than eighty men and boys, including Abdul Hakim, a tribal leader and former Police Chief of Kandahar, were killed and ninety injured when a suicide bomber blew himself up at a tribal festival near Kandahar just as a dog fight was about to start. The Taliban were accused of being responsible for what was the bloodiest bombing since 2001.

The Taliban in Quetta, 2007

All Taliban are ISI Taliban.

On 21 January 2007, the front page of the *New York Times* carried an article datelined 'Quetta, Pakistan', and rather cautiously headlined 'At Border, Signs of Pakistani Role in Taliban Surge'. But the thrust of the article was much stronger, saying that after more than two weeks of reporting along the Afghan frontier, and dozens of interviews with residents on each side of it, there was little doubt that Quetta was an important base for the Taliban, and that there were many signs that Pakistani authorities were encouraging the insurgents, if not sponsoring them. The evidence was anecdotal, provided in 'fearful whispers'.

At the Jamiya Islamiya, a *madrassa*, or religious school, in Quetta, Taliban sympathies were on 'flagrant display', the article reported. Residents said students had gone with their teachers' blessings to die in Afghanistan. Three families whose sons had died as suicide bombers in Afghanistan said they were afraid to talk about the deaths because of pressure from Pakistani intelligence agents, the ISI. Local people said dozens of families had lost sons in Afghanistan as suicide bombers and fighters, the article continued. 'One former Taliban commander said in an interview that he had been jailed by the ISI because he would not go to Afghanistan to fight. He said that, for Western and local consumption, his arrest had been billed as part of Pakistan's "crackdown" on the Taliban in Pakistan. Former Taliban members who had refused to fight in Afghanistan had been arrested – or even mysteriously killed – after resisting pressure to re-enlist in the Taliban, according to Pakistani and Afghan tribal elders.'[2] A Western diplomat, speaking in Kabul, confirmed the Pakistanis were 'actively supporting' the Taliban, the article continued. The diplomat said he had seen an intelligence report of a recent meeting on the Afghan border between a senior Taliban commander and a retired colonel of the Pakistani ISI. Pakistanis and Afghans interviewed on the frontier, the *New York Times* report added, scared of the 'long reach' of Pakistan's intelligence agencies, spoke only with assurances that they would not be named. Even then, they were still cautious. The ISI and its fellow intelligence services have for decades used religious parties as a convenient instrument to keep domestic political opponents at bay and for foreign policy adventures, the *New York Times* said, quoting Husain Haqqani, a former adviser to several of Pakistan's prime ministers and the author of a book on the relationship between the Islamists and the Pakistani security forces.

'"The religious parties were recruited for the *jihad* in Kashmir and Afghanistan during the 1980s, when the ISI funded and armed the *mujahideen* resistance and channelled money to them from the United States and Saudi Arabia to fight the Russians in Afghanistan," Mr Haqqani said. In return for help in Kashmir and Afghanistan, the ISI would rig votes for the religious parties and allow them freedom to operate. "The religious parties provide them with recruits, personnel, cover and deniability," Mr Haqqani said. The Inter-Services Intelligence once had an entire wing dedicated to training *jihadis*, he said. Today the religious parties probably had enough of their own people to do the training, but, he added, the ISI so thoroughly monitored phone calls and people's movements that it would be almost impossible for any religious party to operate a training camp without its knowledge.'[3]*

The article went on to describe the suburb of Pashtunabad, 'a warren of high mud-brick walls and narrow lanes', where the ties between the

---

* This last assertion, made more than four and a half years ago, is particularly relevant to today's debate on whether the ISI knew that Osama bin Laden was hiding in the compound in Abbottabad. The latest information (August 2011) suggests he or his 'trusted courier' were in touch with Harakat-ul-Mujahideen, one of the more extreme religious 'proxies' that Husain Haqqani describes.

government, religious parties and Taliban commanders to a local
madrassa are thinly hidden, according to a local opposition party
member who lives in the neighbourhood. 'Three students from the
madrassa went to Afghanistan recently on suicide missions, he said. The
family of one of the men admitted that he had blown himself up but
denied that he had attended the school. The man's brother suggested
that he had been forced into the mission and that someone had recruited
him for payment. "Nowadays people are getting money from somewhere and they are killing other people's children," he said. "We are
afraid of this government," he said. His father said he feared the same
people would try to take his other son and asked that no family names
be used in the article.'⁴

The irony of the situation is that both President Musharraf and General
Zia before him banned the big political parties, the PPP (People's Party of
Pakistan), founded by Zulfikar Ali Bhutto, and the Muslim League,
supported by Mohammed Ali Jinnah, the father of the nation, and whose
last prime minister, Nawaz Sharif, was ousted by Musharraf. To fill the
void they both promoted the religious parties, some of them very extreme,
although they had never polled more than 10 per cent of the popular vote.
They and the ISI formed an unholy alliance, which included the Taliban
and prompted shrewd political commentators like author and journalist,
Ahmed Rashid, himself a Pakistani, to warn that the Taliban embrace
would eventually radicalise Pakistan, a forecast which has proved all too
tragically accurate.

The *New York Times* points out that President Musharraf relied on
the religious party, Jamiat Ulema-i-Islam, or JUI, which dominates the
province of Baluchistan, as an important partner in the provincial and
national parliaments. It also points out that the Jamiya Islamiya
madrassa, on the 'winding Hajji Ghabi Road, displays a board in the
courtyard which proudly declares "Long Live Mullah Omar", in praise
of the Taliban leader, and "Long Live Fazlur Rehman", the leader of
JUI. Members of the provincial government and JUI were frequent
visitors to the school, said the local opposition party member, who also
asked that his name not be used . . . People on motorbikes with green
government licence plates visit at night, he said, as do luxurious sport

utility vehicles with blackened windows, favoured by Taliban commanders.'

The *New York Times* report by Carlotta Gall continues: 'Maulvi Noor Muhammad, a JUI representative from Baluchistan in the National Assembly, recently received a guest barefoot while sitting on the floor of a grubby district office in Quetta, a map of the world above him painted on the wall to represent his belief in worldwide Islamic revolution. He denied providing the militants with any logistical support. "The JUI is not supporting the Taliban any more," he said. "We are only providing moral support. We pray for their success in ousting the foreign troops from the land of Afghanistan." On a recent morning, the deputy director of the Jamiya Islamiya *madrassa*, Qari Muhammad Ibrahim, declined to meet a female reporter of the *New York Times* but answered a question from a local male reporter. He did not deny that some of the *madrassa's* 280 students had gone to fight in Afghanistan. "In the Koran it is written that it is every Muslim's right to fight *jihad*," he said. "All we are telling them is what is in the Koran, and then it's up to them to go to *jihad*."'

The deputy director is being disingenuous when he says that the *madrassa's* mullahs are merely telling their students their rights, as it were. All the evidence shows that the *madrassas* exert huge pressures on young students to go to Afghanistan to fight or to enrol in suicide bomber camps.

In September [2007], Gen. James L. Jones, then NATO's supreme commander, told the Senate Foreign Relations Committee that Quetta remained the headquarters of the Taliban movement. 'NATO officials and Western diplomats in Afghanistan had grown increasingly critical of Pakistan for allowing Taliban leaders, commanders and fighters to operate from their territory, which had given an advantage to the insurgency in southern Afghanistan. Yet, Pakistan insists that the Taliban leadership is not based in Quetta. "If there are Taliban in Quetta, they are few," said Pakistan's minister for information and broadcasting, Tariq Azim Khan. "You can count them on your fingers,"' he told Carlotta Gall.[5]

Even if this was only barely believable in 2007, it certainly is not today. Ever since the 2 May 2011 Abbottabad raid by US Special Forces' SEALs which killed Osama bin Laden, the scales have dropped from American eyes. Although the top leadership – at least since President Obama took over – must have been fully aware of the hugely devious 'double-game' which the Pakistani establishment, in the shape of the ISI, had been playing since 9/11, it apparently felt powerless to stop it. Abbottabad has changed all that.

In 2007, the *New York Times* pointed out, President Musharraf had 'acknowledged that some retired Pakistani intelligence officials may still be involved in supporting their former protégés in the Taliban. Hamid Gul, the former director general of Pakistani intelligence, remains a public and unapologetic supporter of the Taliban, visiting *madrassas* and speaking in support of *jihad* at graduation ceremonies. Afghan intelligence officials, it said, recently produced a captured insurgent who said Mr Gul facilitated his training and logistics through an office in the Pakistani town of Nowshera, in the former North-West Frontier Province, west of the capital, Islamabad. NATO and American officials in Afghanistan say there is also evidence of support from current midlevel Pakistani intelligence officials. Just how far up that support reaches remains in dispute.'[6]

But since that was written in 2007, it has become absolutely clear that it does go right up to the top, and that the old excuse of a handful of 'rogue officials' simply does not wash. The *New York Times* Quetta report continued: 'At least five villages in Pishin, a district northwest of Quetta that stretches toward the Afghan border, lost sons in the recent fighting in Kandahar between the Taliban and NATO forces, opposition politicians said. One village, Karbala, is a main center of support for the *jihad*, local people say. Unlike the other villages, which blend into the stark desert-like landscape with their mud-brick houses and compound walls, Karbala has lavish houses, mosques and *madrassas*, suggesting an unusual wealth. Further on, in the village of Bagarzai, lies the grave of Azizullah, a religious scholar who used only one name and acquired fame as a Taliban commander. Only twenty-five, he was killed with a group of fifteen to twenty men in an air strike in the Afghan province of Helmand on May 22 [2007], said his father, Hajji Abdul Hai. Thousands of people attended his funeral, including senior members of the provincial government, the father said.'

Poor families in particular are vulnerable to the pressure and brainwashing of having their sons become *jihadis*. The family receives a lump sum and the kudos of having had a son who has gone to paradise as a suicide bomber or fighter 'martyred' in Afghanistan. The *New York Times* continues:

Mr Hai, fifty, who is a JUI member, denied that his son had been persuaded to fight by anyone. 'From the start it was his spirit to take part in *jihad*,' his father said. 'It's all to do with personal will. If someone agrees, then he goes. Even if someone wishes to, no one can stop him.' It is an argument that supporters of the *jihad* use frequently. But for some of the families mourning their sons, there is no doubt that the *madrassas* and the religious parties are the first point of contact.

That was the conclusion reached by the family of Muhammad Daoud, a twenty-two-year-old man from Pishin who disappeared more than a year ago. 'In our search we went to many places and everyone said different things,' said his father, Hajji Noora Gul. 'We went to the *madrassa* in Pashtunabad, but no one was ready to tell us his whereabouts. Even the *madrassa* people did not know,' he added. 'Behind the curtain of the *madrassa*, maybe there are other people who do this. Maybe there are some businessmen who take them.' Then, he said, a Taliban propaganda CD came out showing his son with a group of others taking an oath before the Taliban commander, Mullah Dadullah [since killed by British Special Forces]. 'He had a shawl over his head and was preparing for a suicide bombing,' Mr Gul added. 'He said, "I am fighting for God, and I am ready for this."'

His eldest son, Allah Dad, thirty-three, blamed the *jihadi* groups and the ISI. 'We don't know how he made contact with those *jihadi* groups,' he said. 'There are some groups active in taking people to Afghanistan and they are active in Quetta. All Taliban are ISI Taliban,' he added. 'It is not possible to go to Afghanistan without the help of the ISI. Everyone says this.'[7]

A number of families are clearly unhappy about their sons being brainwashed to become suicide bombers and in certain areas it is undoubtedly fairly common. There are many cases of worried parents appealing to local authorities to reclaim their sons, but it's an uphill battle against the influence and power of the religious parties and the *madrassa*s they largely control.

Being a foreign correspondent often means reporting in difficult circumstances. In the days of the Cold War, for example, reporting in the Soviet Union or in one of its 'Satellites' (East Germany, Poland, Czechoslovakia, Hungary, etc.) presented some serious challenges. One was that as a journalist you were automatically considered a spy. I spent two and a half years as Reuters Correspondent in Hungary, after the 1956 Revolution. Luckily, I never got into serious trouble, but there were many pitfalls. Hungary then was a police state and the AVO, the secret police, were all-powerful. They tapped your phone, monitored your movements and generally watched and listened to everything you did. They would set little traps for you, usually involving women or money, hoping to compromise you. Once you were compromised, they would try to blackmail you. That was how the system worked.

They trapped an Austrian colleague – I will call him Heinz – who bought a radio for a Hungarian journalist 'friend' as a favour, and then, when he was handing it over in his flat, the AVO burst in. An AVO colonel appeared on the scene, accused Heinz of illegal currency transactions and made threats of a possible jail sentence. In return for dropping the charges he wanted details of the layout of the American Legation and in particular the area occupied by Cardinal Mindszenty, the head of the Roman Catholic Church in Hungary who had sought asylum there during the 1956 Revolution. Heinz* managed to wriggle out of that; but they did not give up. He had a very attractive Hungarian fiancée, and as a keen photographer had, rather unwisely, taken lots of pictures of her in the nude. The AVO found out about it, raided his flat and stole the photographs. The colonel reappeared and threatened, if Heinz did not cooperate, to have someone outside the church when the couple were married and offer the photographs for sale to members of the

---

* Heinz worked for an American news agency and had professional access to the Legation.

congregation, including her family as they left the church after the wedding. (In fact they did not carry out the threat and Heinz and his bride departed on their honeymoon to Vienna, where, alas, after a short interval, his beautiful wife, now an Austrian citizen, left him.)

I myself was caught up, against my will, in another typical police state scenario, in which the former head of the Hungarian air force, through the intermediary of a British acquaintance, asked me to help him defect. Reluctantly, I agreed, knowing that if it went wrong I would probably be fired by Reuters, since as they used to say, I was there to report the news, not to make it. I passed on my new friend's plans to the British Legation at his request and he duly defected. I went on holiday and forgot all about it. When I returned to Budapest a few weeks later, I discovered to my surprise and, I must confess, horror that the defector had re-defected and was back in Budapest. I took it for granted he would have been interrogated and would have divulged the whole story including my name and role in his escape, which had been simply to say he might seek asylum, and tell him what to do if he did. I expected at any minute to be summoned to the Interior Ministry or simply handed the expulsion order. Luckily I was near the end of my assignment, and perhaps they decided not to make a fuss, although that was hardly in character – but to my surprise there were no repercussions.

Describing it later, I wrote: 'I did not really feel safe until my plane touched down in Vienna. I took a taxi to the Hotel Bristol, where [my wife] Eleanor and I always stayed, went straight to the American Bar and ordered a champagne cocktail. To arrive in Vienna from the grim, prison-like atmosphere of Hungary always made me feel deliriously happy. It was like having your birthday, the first day of spring and falling in love, all rolled into one. On this occasion, I felt that was probably an understatement.'[8]

Pakistan is in many ways, especially for journalists and opposition politicians, also a police state where military intelligence, the ISI, is all-powerful. Local journalists are particularly at risk; some have disappeared for long periods, some have never reappeared. Colleagues who know of their cases believe they are either in prison or dead. The families are not informed.

This behaviour is typical of the way the secret police system works in many totalitarian countries. It does in Pakistan too, as my daughter Carlotta discovered. By investigating the ISI–Taliban connection in Quetta, something that would be considered a perfectly legitimate journalistic activity in a democratic society, and although working for a highly respected American newspaper, she also fell foul of 'police state' behaviour. In her report on Quetta and the Taliban presence there for the *New York Times* of 21 January 2007, she wrote of her experience:

> My photographer, Akhtar Soomro, and I were followed over several days of reporting in Quetta by plainclothes intelligence officials who were posted at our respective hotels. That is not unusual in Pakistan, where accredited journalists are free to travel and report, but their movements, phone calls and interviews are often monitored.
>
> On our fifth and last day in Quetta, Dec. 19, four plainclothes agents detained Mr Soomro at his hotel downtown and seized his computer and photo equipment. They raided my hotel room that evening, using a key card to open the door and then breaking through the chain that I had locked from the inside. They seized a computer, notebooks and a cell phone.
>
> One agent punched me twice in the face and head and knocked me to the floor. I was left with bruises on my arms, temple and cheekbone, swelling on my eye and a sprained knee. One of the men told me that I was not permitted to visit Pashtunabad, a neighborhood in Quetta, and that it was forbidden to interview members of the Taliban. The men did not reveal their identity but said we could apply to the Special Branch of the Interior Ministry for our belongings the next day.
>
> After the intervention of the Minister of State for Information and Broadcasting, Tariq Azim Khan [the same minister who told Carlotta there were so few Taliban in Quetta 'you can count them on your fingers'], my belongings were returned several hours later. Mr Soomro was released after more than five hours in detention. Since then it has become clear that intelligence agents copied data from our computers,

notebooks and cell phones and have tracked down contacts and acquaintances in Quetta. All the people I interviewed were subsequently visited by intelligence agents, and local journalists who helped me were later questioned by Pakistan's intelligence service, the Inter-Services Intelligence.

Mr Soomro has been warned not to work for the *New York Times* or any other foreign news organization.[9]

The Sun in the Sky

I hate the big suicide attacks that kill Afghan civilians; I hate the killing of NGO workers.

Senior Haqqani commander, 2009/2010[1]

In June 2010, Matt Waldman, a British researcher and currently a UN official-cum-analyst in Kabul, formerly attached to the Kennedy School of Government at Harvard University, published a paper entitled 'The Sun in the Sky: The relationship between Pakistan's ISI and Afghan insurgents'. Although many of its findings were foreshadowed in previous American press reports, its strength lay in its timing, comprehensiveness and detail. This made it ring true. Its thesis is brutally simple: no solution of the insurgency is possible without the cooperation and support of Pakistan and the ISI. Their influence has been, and still is, so great that not even the United States can win without their approval. That approval always has been, and still is, glaringly absent, despite developments in the later part of 2011, many of which back up the Waldman thesis.

On the question of whether the ISI literally 'controls' the Taliban, as many interviewees told him, Waldman says it 'may not actually control the Afghan insurgency, which implies power over all major dimensions of the movement and its campaign, and the ability to bring it to an end. However, as the provider of sanctuary, and very substantial financial, military and logistical support to the insurgency, the ISI appears to have strong strategic and operational influence – reinforced by coercion. There is thus a strong case that the ISI and elements of the military are deeply involved in the insurgent campaign, and have powerful influence over the Haqqani network.'[2] Waldman states that the 'ISI gives sanctuary to both Taliban

and Haqqani groups and provides huge support in terms of training, funding, munitions, and supplies'. In the interviewees' words, this is 'as clear as
the sun in the sky', he says, a Pushtun proverb equivalent to the English 'as
clear as daylight'.³ Matt Waldman's case could be summarised as suggesting
that Pakistan, via the ISI, may not have total control over the Taliban, but
its influence is so great that the difference is virtually one of semantics.

He argues that the relationship, in fact, goes far beyond contact and
coexistence, and 'although the Taliban has a strong endogenous [self-
generating] impetus ... the ISI orchestrates, sustains and strongly
influences the movement, according to Taliban commanders. Directly or
indirectly the ISI appears to exert significant influence on the strategic
decision-making and field operations of the Taliban; and has even greater
sway over Haqqani insurgents. According to both Taliban and Haqqani
commanders, it controls the most violent insurgent units, some of which
appear to be based in Pakistan.'

Even more significantly commanders had claimed that the ISI are even
represented, as participants or observers, on the Taliban supreme leadership council, known as the Quetta Shura, and the Haqqani Command
Council. Indeed, the agency appeared to have circumscribed the Taliban's
strategic autonomy, he argues, precluding steps towards talks with the
Afghan government through recent arrests (a reference to the arrest in
Karachi in February 2010 of Mullah Baradar, then Mullah Omar's military
commander and deputy, who was said to be engaged in peace talks with
the Kabul authorities).

'One individual who was a deputy minister under the former Taliban
regime and who frequently liaises with the Taliban, said that three to seven
ISI officials attend the Quetta Shura as observers' according to Waldman.
'He believed that the ISI had responsibility for organising the meetings
and that it exerted pressure on individual participants beforehand, especially if major decisions were to be taken ... An Afghan conflict analyst,
with years of experience in southern Afghanistan and contacts with the
Taliban, concurred, pointing out that the ISI, "use people who have the
same appearance, language, behaviour and habits as Afghans, They
wouldn't be strange to the Talibs, [and] seem to them to be Muslims, also
fighting infidels. In fact, both he and other interviewees suggested that the

ISI observers could be Afghans, possibly even Taliban leaders who are working closely with, or for, the ISI" . . . An ISI presence on the Shura is consistent with the agency's heavy involvement in the movement's inception and augmentation . . . indeed, a detailed assessment of the history and composition of the Quetta Shura indicates that the ISI "maintains a hand in controlling its operations".'

Another proof of Pakistan's closeness to the insurgents, Waldman asserts, is that its President, Asif Ali Zardari, had 'apparently assured captive, senior Taliban leaders that they are "our people" and have his backing. He has also, it seems, authorised their release from prison. The ISI even arrested and then released two Taliban leaders, Qayyum Zakir, the movement's new military commander, and Mullah Abdul Raouf Khadem, reportedly now head of the Quetta Shura, who are among the three or four highest ranking in the movement below Mullah Omar.'⁴ Waldman goes on to conclude that 'Pakistan's apparent involvement in a double-game of this scale could have major geopolitical implications and could even provoke US counter-measures'. This now appears to be happening, judging by recent remarks by Admiral Mike Mullen and Ambassador Peter Tomsen. It also suggests that progress against the insurgency, or towards political engagement, requires Pakistan's support. The only sure way to secure such cooperation, he says, is to address the fundamental causes of Pakistan's insecurity, 'especially its latent and enduring conflict with India'.⁵

'The Sun in the Sky', published in London by the London School of Economics, is based on a series of interviews Matt Waldman conducted with nine Taliban field commanders, one high-level Taliban 'intermediary', and two Haqqani commanders, in or near Kabul and Kandahar, between February and May 2010. The commanders were drawn from different parts of Afghanistan, interviewed separately and anonymously and without the knowledge of any other Taliban. In addition, an Afghan research assistant interviewed six other insurgent commanders, three in Kandahar and three in Quetta. Waldman says he also interviewed ten former senior Taliban officials – six ministers, two ambassadors, a high-ranking civil servant and an ex-military commander; twenty-two Afghan elders, tribal leaders, politicians and analysts; and thirteen foreign diplomats, experts and security officials. Although the Taliban is a broad church consisting of seven separate armed groups, Waldman concentrated on two of the most significant: 'First, the core Taliban movement led by Mullah Mohammad Omar, which is relatively hierarchical and has national reach but is strongest in southern Afghanistan; and, to a lesser extent, the Haqqani network, led by Jalaluddin Haqqani, which is based in Waziristan, in some of the wildest of Pakistan's Federally Administered Tribal Areas [FATA], but operates largely in its home tribal area of south-east Afghanistan.'[6]

At this juncture the reader may be asking: how accurate, even how genuine, are Waldman's interviews, and even if they are, how truthful is the information and the opinions expressed by the various commanders interviewed. The short answer is that 'The Sun in the Sky' carries the imprimatur of two of the world's leading academic institutions, the LSE and the Carr Centre for Human Rights, at the Harvard Kennedy School of Government. It would also seem to be backed up by a wide range of general intelligence and, not least by the fact that Osama bin Laden lived under cover for at least five years in Abbottabad, at the heart of Pakistan's military establishment, supported by an ISI terrorist proxy group, until he was killed in the US Navy SEALs raid, undertaken without Pakistani knowledge, before dawn on 2 May 2011.

Waldman argues that after the loss of East Pakistan (now Bangladesh) in 1971, and its recognition by India, 'Pakistan took steps to counter a perceived threat from India and growing Pushtun nationalism. Part of the response was an increasing Islamicisation of society, reflected in the proliferation of *madrassas*, and greater support for militant Islamist groups that could be used as proxies in Kashmir and Afghanistan.'[7] This radicalisation, encouraged first by General Zia and later by General Pervez Musharraf, both of whom banned traditional political parties and gave free rein to religious parties, led eventually to the creation of the Pakistani Taliban.

The ISI, as we have seen, and as Waldman emphasises, 'played a pivotal role' in the emergence of the Afghan Taliban, later providing it with 'significant political, financial, military and logistical support' from 1996, when it took Kabul, until 2001 and its collapse after 9/11. This support comprised not only arms, ammunition, equipment, fuel and other supplies, but also military advisers and trainers, as well as economic support. 'Even in 2001, in breach of UN sanctions,' Waldman points out, quoting Ahmed Rashid, '"up to thirty ISI trucks a day were still crossing into Afghanistan",' with all sorts of equipment and supplies.[8]

So much for Pakistan's oft-repeated claim that the Taliban is a home-grown Afghan insurgency and owes nothing to Pakistan. By providing sanctuary and support to the Afghan Taliban, and arresting those who step out of line, the ISI appears to have been able to exert significant influence on Taliban strategy, Waldman quotes Taliban commanders as saying. 'The Taliban–ISI relationship is founded on mutual benefit. The Taliban need external sanctuary, as well as military and logistical support to sustain their insurgency; the ISI believes that it needs a significant allied force in Afghanistan to maintain regional strength and "strategic depth" in its rivalry with India.'[10] A former Taliban minister is quoted as saying: 'The ISI are helping the Taliban a lot, but they only give for their own gain. There is a reciprocal issue: Kashmir. The root of the problem in Afghanistan is the Pakistan–India competition.'[11] 'Pakistan's fundamental strategic calculus did not appear to have altered significantly since the 1970s,' Waldman writes. Quoting articles by Steve Coll in the *New Yorker* in spring 2010, he says that Pakistan submitted a briefing to the US on its national interests in the Afghan conflict which reportedly 'reflects one overriding concern: India.'[12] According to Coll: 'Pakistan's generals have retained a bedrock belief that, however unruly and distasteful Islamist militias such as the Taliban may be, they could yet be useful proxies to ward off a perceived existential threat from India. In the Army's view, at least, that threat has not receded.'[13]

Western observers, including diplomats, put it more bluntly when they describe Pakistan as being 'paranoid' about India. Many in the Pakistan establishment believe that India has significant and 'increasing economic and political influence in Afghanistan', Waldman states. 'India enjoys close relations with the Karzai administration, has four regional consulates, and is providing substantial reconstruction assistance, including plans to rebuild the Afghan parliament, and construction projects on the Pakistan border. Senior Pakistani officials also believe the withdrawal of US forces from Afghanistan, due to begin at the end of 2011, could open up a power struggle from which India could benefit – a major incentive for Pakistan to maintain, or even strengthen, its Afghan allies.'[14]

In addition, Matt Waldman says, the ISI may be able 'to exert influence by exploiting tribal fractures within the Shura . . . other fissures, and significant levels of mistrust in the Taliban leadership'. His interviews suggest that there is a rivalry or latent power struggle between, on the one hand, Qayyum Zakir, who replaced Mullah Baradar as Mullah Omar's deputy and military commander of the movement, his deputy, Mullah Akhtar Mohammed Mansour, and his close associate, believed to be head of the Quetta Shura, Mullah Abdul Raouf Khadem; and, on the other, the 'old guard figures' of Amir Khan Muttaqi, Mullah Mohammad Hassan, former Governor of Kandahar, and Mullah Gul Agha. 'Although the extent of this dissension is not clear, it may well have generated opportunities for manipulation.'[15]

It certainly seems to have done so in the case of Mullah Mansour, or the man MI6 seems to have mistaken for Mullah Mansour. Far from being the deputy to the military commander, Qayyum Zakir, it turned out that MI6's 'Mullah Mansour' was an imposter, not a high-ranking Taliban official but in real life a Quetta shopkeeper. He was reported to have been flown by MI6 from the border to Kabul, supplied with large sums of money, and, according to one account, taken to the Presidential Palace in Kabul to see President Karzai, who later insisted he never met him. He was finally exposed when an Afghan who had met the real Mullah Mansour said he did not think it was the same man. MI6 had been made to look foolish. Their failure, however, was not as disastrous as the CIA blunder with an al Qaeda suicide bomber, a Jordanian doctor-cum-double agent, Humam al Balawi, who promised to provide access to a top al Qaeda figure – Osama bin Laden's deputy, the Egyptian Dr Ayman al Zawahiri. So convinced were the Americans that he was the real thing, they dropped their guard and without a body search, allowed him into a secret CIA base on the Afghan–Pakistan border, where he blew up and killed himself and seven CIA agents including the head of the base. (It was thought the ISI may have planned both stings.)

The case of Mullah Baradar reveals just how great the ISI's influence over the Taliban is. Baradar's alleged contact with the Kabul government, without the ISI's approval, was seen as breaking the rules. ISI influence went as far as establishing 'parameters of Taliban conduct and strategy, reinforced by the threat of arrest. Independent contacts between the Taliban's former military commander, Mullah Baradar, and the Afghan government, possibly with a view to negotiations, were clearly considered to have breached these boundaries, and so he and at least seven other Taliban leaders were arrested by the ISI in early February 2010. It would appear that the arrests were intended to send a message to both the Taliban and the United States that negotiations could only take place if the ISI had a major role in, if not control over, the negotiating process.'

Waldman found this view 'was echoed by Taliban commanders, most of whom doubted Pakistan's support for negotiations. As a commander from a central province said: "The ISI arrests [of Taliban leaders] were done for their own interests; they don't want peace in Afghanistan, and they don't want them to talk to the Afghan government. If there is peace, it is not to Pakistan's benefit."'[16]

Since the ISI had a powerful hold over the *mujahideen* movement during the Russian occupation, it is hardly surprising that it has an even stronger one on the Taliban and its fellow insurgents, the Haqqani network. Some of the old *mujahideen* leaders, like Jalaluddin Haqqani and his son, Siraj, are still major players, above all with the ISI who have provided them with a base in North Waziristan. According to the Afghan conflict analyst, quoted by Waldman: 'There is not an equal relationship between the ISI and Taliban – the ISI are far more powerful. The Taliban don't have any choice except to live in Pakistan; where else can they go?' One former Taliban deputy minister said he thought Taliban leaders in Pakistan were 'living under pressure . . . they fear the Pakistan government, that their families will be taken to prison'.[17] This is confirmed by a joint US, NATO and Afghan intelligence assessment from June 2006, which concludes: 'A large number of those fighting are doing so under duress as a result of pressure from the ISI.'[18]

NATO's International Security Assistance Force has a 'deliberate decapitation strategy', Waldman says, that uses 'Special Forces to target Taliban commanders'. According to a majority of commanders interviewed by Matt Waldman – and, one might add, Western press reports, especially from the Kandahar area – this strategy has been 'remarkably effective. Thus, to some extent, Taliban leaders are caught between pressure and the threat of imprisonment from the ISI, and Afghan and international forces north of the border.'

Waldman's interviews suggest 'that Talibs deeply resented the ISI pressure. Indeed, one interviewee who had frequent contact with Taliban leaders and commanders said the only people they hated more than the Americans were the ISI. Analysts were divided on the extent to which ISI policy towards Afghan insurgents was determined independently of civilian officials, especially after Pakistan's newly elected government attempted, and failed, to bring the ISI under the control of the Interior Ministry in July 2008.'[19]

Probably the most controversial of all Waldman's claims mentioned above is his report that President Zardari paid a friendly visit in 2010 to a group of imprisoned Taliban. 'According to a Talib who has regular contact with members of the Quetta Shura,' he says, 'in late March or early April this year [2010] President Zardari and a senior ISI official visited some fifty high-ranking Talibs who were held in a prison in a secret location in Pakistan. Some thirty to thirty-five had been arrested in recent months, and ten to fifteen were longer-term prisoners. Reportedly, he told them they were arrested because he was under a lot of pressure from the Americans and that they were "our people, we are friends, and after your release we will of course support you to do your operations".'

'Disturbingly,' Waldman comments, 'Zardari's words echo what the ISI's head, General Mahmud Ahmed, said to the Taliban's ambassador to Pakistan, Abdul Salam Zaeef, in late 2001: "We want to assure you that you will not be alone in this *jihad* against America. We will be with you."'[20] This is the same General Ahmed who was dispatched by President Musharraf after 9/11 to ask Mullah Omar on behalf of the Americans to hand over Osama bin Laden and who, after delivering his official message, advised Mullah Omar that he should ignore the request and refuse to hand him over.

At least one senior diplomat cast doubt on the Zardari story. When I raised the question of its authenticity in Washington with the late Richard Holbrooke, President Obama's Special Envoy for Afghanistan and Pakistan, he expressed reservations, saying: 'I know Zardari. I don't believe he would have done and said that.' On the other hand, one well-informed Afghan journalist commented: 'Zardari does and says what the ISI tell him.' Whatever Richard Holbrooke's reservations, there is little doubt that despite being President, Zardari is virtually a prisoner of the Pakistan Army and the ISI. Their power was demonstrated by the refusal of General Kayani, the head of the Army, to allow Zardari's new civilian government, elected in 2008, to appoint the head of the ISI and to bring it under the control of the Interior Ministry.

According to Waldman's informant, 'President Zardari told the prisoners he would release them in two categories: first, those who are not well known to the media, who would be released shortly, and, second, those who are better known, who would be released later in prisoner exchanges. He strongly urged them not to report the meeting to the media. Consistent with Zardari's promise, just three days after the visit, around a dozen Taliban figures were released (including an individual who is the indirect source for this account).'

Waldman claims the Zardari report is 'consistent with Pakistan's political history, in which civilian leaders have actively backed *jihadi* groups that operate in Afghanistan and Kashmir', and quotes the researcher Christine Fair as saying: 'The army does not operate alone . . . Previous civilian governments tolerated and even supported some militant enterprises.'[21] It also 'gives credence', Waldman argues, 'to the claim of two American analysts, Thomas H. Johnson and M. Chris Mason, that "Pakistan is in fact following its own perceived strategic interests, which do not coincide with those of the United States". They even argue that the arrests constitute, "not cooperation against the Taliban by an allied state; it is collusion with the Taliban by an enemy state [Pakistan]".'[22]

The release in February 2010 of seven or more Taliban leaders – including Qayyum Zakir and Mullah Abdul Raouf Khadem, two of the most powerful individuals in the movement – just days after their arrest by the ISI, was, says Waldman, 'a strong indication of significant ISI influence over the movement and it is highly likely that the release was on ISI terms or at least on the basis of a mutual understanding'. Referring to his research with commanders and informed individuals, he says that 'all eight Talibs interviewed (seven field commanders and one senior intermediary) believe that the ISI has heavy influence on their leadership, four of whom believe that this amounts to control. One of the southern commanders commented: "If anyone rejects that the ISI backs or controls the Taliban, he has a mental problem . . . all our plans and strategy are made in Pakistan and step by step it is brought to us, for military operations or other activities. Pakistan [the ISI] does not have only one representative on the Quetta Shura, they have representatives everywhere. As for Mullah Baradar's arrest, do you think they didn't know where he and others were before that?"'

The outspoken southern commander was in no doubt as to who was really in charge. 'The reality is that the ISI controls the leadership. Omar has the strong support of Pakistan; he has to listen to them and do what they say. This view was echoed by leading community, tribal, civil society and political figures in Kandahar,' Waldman says. 'Fourteen interviewees lived in Kandahar, all of whom had first-hand knowledge of, or connections to, the insurgency; ten of them believed that the ISI was represented on the Quetta Shura and had either control of the movement, or something that approximated to control. (The other four believed that the ISI has control or significant influence over the movement, but were not sure if it had representation on the Shura.)'[23]

To someone like myself, who while travelling with the *mujahideen* during their war against the Russians in the 1980s saw their relationship with the ISI at first hand, and knew President Zia and his views well, it was clear that the ISI, which he had put in charge of the Russian War, became steadily more powerful and ruthless. The most recent example is the killing in May 2011 of a Pakistani journalist, Saleem Shahzad, allegedly by the ISI, according to Admiral Mike Mullen who said Pakistan had 'sanctioned' his murder.

One unnamed political figure interviewed by Waldman, possibly a Taliban ex-minister or ambassador, said: 'Everything is controlled by the ISI. Without the agreement of the ISI, the insurgency would be impossible . . . The big problem is that Pakistan created the fundamentalists;

the government, military and ISI supported them; yet while the first two have stopped supporting them, the ISI continues to . . . of course the ISI are on the Quetta Shura . . .' Waldman concludes that 'although many informed Afghans interviewed argued that the ISI was *controlling* the Taliban leadership, this was probably an exaggeration, given the powerful internal force and dynamics of the movement. The Taliban leadership also has a record of resisting Pakistani pressure, he says (citing the refusal of the Taliban regime to recognise the Durand Line or to hand over Osama bin Laden to the US).'

It is at least questionable, Waldman says, that President Musharraf wanted to see Osama bin Laden handed over to the Americans. He was the one, after all, who, knowing well General Ahmed's extreme Islamicist views, chose him to pass on the American request to Mullah Omar. And we know from Kathy Gannon's account in *I is for Infidel* that he did so coupled with his own advice which was to reject the request.[24] Also, the suggestion that the Pakistan military had turned against the fundamentalists, distancing itself from the ISI, is equally unlikely. Before becoming Chief of Army Staff – head of the Pakistan Army – General Ashfaq Kayani had been head of the ISI and presumably would not have tolerated the ISI following a policy he did not approve of. The ISI may have been the tail that wagged the dog, but it was still part of the dog.

Despite resisting the conclusion that the ISI controls the Taliban insurgency, Waldman says that nonetheless 'indications of significant ISI involvement at a strategic level are compelling, and are consistent with reports of their influence in the field. Insurgents believe the ISI shapes their operations in a powerful, surreptitious and coercive way. They even believe that the ISI is represented on their operational command councils, although one, from a central province, told him: "We heard the ISI are on the Quetta, Miranshah and Peshawar Shuras, [the operational command councils for the south, south-eastern and eastern Afghanistan] and we're not happy about this," which argues a certain independence of spirit. Insurgent skills and capabilities at the operational and tactical level suggesting the involvement of trained military personnel, would also presuppose ISI involvement. As a former senior security official said: "They give them the plans, the strategy and new techniques. The chain goes back to the

ISI." This was also consistent with reports that the ISI had provided tactical, operational and strategic intelligence to the Taliban.'[25] One should
bear in mind, Waldman points out, that 'insurgents might seek to shift the
blame for some of their most egregious activities, such as the execution of
elders or attacks on schools; they might misapprehend and overstate ISI
power; or they might in fact be in a state of denial. However, it was hard
to discount the consistency, cogency and force of commanders' views.'[26]

To anyone reading Waldman's interviews with their descriptions of
how closely intermeshed the Taliban and the ISI are, and as a result how
serious a threat to Afghan independence this presents, it is hard to see
how the Americans can disentangle themselves from their alliance with
Pakistan. But, increasingly, in the eyes of many Americans, disentangle
themselves they must.

Waldman quotes the comments of one southern commander which he
says echo those of many others: '"There are a lot of ISI Taliban and they are
very strong. It is very hard to recognise them . . . Both foreign [meaning
non-Pushtun] and Afghan Talibs are working for the ISI." The ISI make
plots to kill commanders who do not obey their orders . . . They have their
groups and commanders, to whom they pay a lot, very secretly. They reach
their interests through these commanders."' If true, this would suggest the
Taliban are another, very powerful, ISI proxy army.

The Afghan conflict analyst interviewed by Matt Waldman described
how he had spoken to foot soldiers and low-level commanders, who all
said they had no independence: 'if we do not obey [the ISI] we are fired,
replaced or transferred', they told him. ISI control didn't extend to all
levels, but there was a hierarchy that was disciplined. 'Arguably,' Waldman
writes, 'such influence is facilitated by the movement's fragmentation. As
one commander put it: "I can't say the Taliban are all united, there are
different groups, and different ideas . . . different leaders, which makes it
very complex." Southern Taliban commanders all complained of heavy ISI
involvement, which they say is often responsible for attacks on civilians . . .
A south-eastern Taliban commander said: "They [the ISI] have specific
groups under their control, for burning schools and such like. The ISI
[also] has people working for it within the Taliban movement – it is clearer
than the sun in the sky."'[27]

ISI." This was also consistent with reports that the ISI had provided tactical, operational and strategic intelligence to the Taliban.'²⁵ One should
bear in mind, Waldman points out, that 'insurgents might seek to shift the
blame for some of their most egregious activities, such as the execution of
elders or attacks on schools; they might misapprehend and overstate ISI
power; or they might in fact be in a state of denial. However, it was hard
to discount the consistency, cogency and force of commanders' views.'²⁶

To anyone reading Waldman's interviews with their descriptions of
how closely intermeshed the Taliban and the ISI are, and as a result how
serious a threat to Afghan independence this presents, it is hard to see
how the Americans can disentangle themselves from their alliance with
Pakistan. But, increasingly, in the eyes of many Americans, disentangle
themselves they must.

Waldman quotes the comments of one southern commander which he
says echo those of many others: '"There are a lot of ISI Taliban and they are
very strong. It is very hard to recognise them . . . Both foreign [meaning
non-Pushtun] and Afghan Talibs are working for the ISI." The ISI make
plots to kill commanders who do not obey their orders . . . They have their
groups and commanders, to whom they pay a lot, very secretly. They reach
their interests through these commanders."' If true, this would suggest the
Taliban are another, very powerful, ISI proxy army.

The Afghan conflict analyst interviewed by Matt Waldman described
how he had spoken to foot soldiers and low-level commanders, who all
said they had no independence: 'if we do not obey [the ISI] we are fired,
replaced or transferred', they told him. ISI control didn't extend to all
levels, but there was a hierarchy that was disciplined. 'Arguably,' Waldman
writes, 'such influence is facilitated by the movement's fragmentation. As
one commander put it: "I can't say the Taliban are all united, there are
different groups, and different ideas . . . different leaders, which makes it
very complex." Southern Taliban commanders all complained of heavy ISI
involvement, which they say is often responsible for attacks on civilians . . .
A south-eastern Taliban commander said: "They [the ISI] have specific
groups under their control, for burning schools and such like. The ISI
[also] has people working for it within the Taliban movement – it is clearer
than the sun in the sky."'²⁷

ISI." This was also consistent with reports that the ISI had provided tactical, operational and strategic intelligence to the Taliban.'[25] One should bear in mind, Waldman points out, that 'insurgents might seek to shift the blame for some of their most egregious activities, such as the execution of elders or attacks on schools; they might misapprehend and overstate ISI power; or they might in fact be in a state of denial. However, it was hard to discount the consistency, cogency and force of commanders' views.'[26]

To anyone reading Waldman's interviews with their descriptions of how closely intermeshed the Taliban and the ISI are, and as a result how serious a threat to Afghan independence this presents, it is hard to see how the Americans can disentangle themselves from their alliance with Pakistan. But, increasingly, in the eyes of many Americans, disentangle themselves they must.

Waldman quotes the comments of one southern commander which he says echo those of many others: '"There are a lot of ISI Taliban and they are very strong. It is very hard to recognise them . . . Both foreign [meaning non-Pushtun] and Afghan Talibs are working for the ISI." The ISI make plots to kill commanders who do not obey their orders . . . They have their groups and commanders, to whom they pay a lot, very secretly. They reach their interests through these commanders.'" If true, this would suggest the Taliban are another, very powerful, ISI proxy army.

The Afghan conflict analyst interviewed by Matt Waldman described how he had spoken to foot soldiers and low-level commanders, who all said they had no independence: 'if we do not obey [the ISI] we are fired, replaced or transferred', they told him. ISI control didn't extend to all levels, but there was a hierarchy that was disciplined. 'Arguably,' Waldman writes, 'such influence is facilitated by the movement's fragmentation. As one commander put it: "I can't say the Taliban are all united, there are different groups, and different ideas . . . different leaders, which makes it very complex." Southern Taliban commanders all complained of heavy ISI involvement, which they say is often responsible for attacks on civilians . . . A south-eastern Taliban commander said: "They [the ISI] have specific groups under their control, for burning schools and such like. The ISI [also] has people working for it within the Taliban movement – it is clearer than the sun in the sky."'[27]

One southern commander described their predicament to Matt Waldman, saying another group of Taliban was directly supported by the ISI and would never stop fighting in the country; they wanted to destroy the government and bring chaos. Behind all the attacks – on NGOs, schools, teachers, doctors – was Pakistan. 'We cannot deny that it is Taliban,' he told him, 'but there are Pakistan-controlled groups among us. They want destabilisation. They are the enemies of our nation and our country. The people in charge of these factions are members of Pakistani intelligence [the ISI]. The fighters are Afghans, but they are not true Afghans. We have spoken to them, and they feel that only the Taliban are Muslims, but those who are just normal, working Afghans – who die in the suicide attacks – they think they are all infidels. The ISI Taliban are stronger than us, they have more money, and are supporting us. We have few resources, so we have to follow them. We have no backers in order to resist them. I was never given an order to blow up a bridge or burn a school, because they know who is suitable. Even if they tell me I would not tell my fighters to do it. The Pakistan Taliban is perhaps about 30 per cent of the Taliban in our district [in Kandahar], but they are much stronger than the others, who have to follow them.'[28] Matt Waldman spoke to two other southern commanders who echoed these claims. One told him: 'The assassination of tribal leaders, of *maulawis* [religious leaders] has ruined the foundation of our country. The ISI stand behind all this – the burning of schools, keeping children out of education, the beheadings – all are related to the ISI Taliban. The Emirate [the Taliban movement] and Islam never order these innocent people to be killed. When we are ordered to do these things, we cannot say no, but try to persuade our commanders that we shouldn't do it. If I don't do it, they will make me powerless or a foot soldier.' He ended on a sinister note: 'Many [Taliban commanders] have been assassinated by the ISI.'[29]

Another southern commander told the British researcher that the ISI 'gives the orders to the Taliban to attack road contractors, schools or aid workers. They tell our commander and he orders us. They say it is the Taliban's plan, we know it is their [the ISI's] plan. We know the projects are for the welfare of communities, we know that burning schools is not against the [Afghan] government; they benefit the community, so we know they are ISI activities. If he [their commander] doesn't accept he will be dismissed or killed . . . On the Kabul–Kandahar highway all the bridges are destroyed: this is on the orders of the ISI. Our country is like their house; nobody from the family wants to destroy their own home. If you see such destruction, you should know your neighbour [Pakistan] has done this.'[30]

Although Waldman does not speculate on the split which seems to divide the Taliban movement into ISI killer squads and nationalist Taliban who do not want to see their tribal leaders and elders killed (the beheadings and suicide bombs) and the infrastructure wantonly destroyed (burning of schools and blowing up of bridges), this dichotomy does seem to suggest deep differences of opinion exploitable by General Sir Graeme Lamb's policy of reintegration – reconciling the reconcilable and eliminating the irreconcilable which, the latter part of the equation, coalition spokesmen claim has been highly successful in 2010. Waldman does however argue that reports of Pakistani commanders operating in Afghanistan, such as a Taliban commander killed by British Special Forces in late 2008 who was identified as a Pakistani military official, 'reinforces claims of ISI participation in Taliban operations and raises the possibility that the ISI may be supporting the most violent commanders or units within the movement. Arguably too, it is consistent with the arrest of Taliban leaders that showed an interest in talks with the Afghan government, and with the ISI sanctioning, perhaps even orchestrating, the replacement of Mullah Baradar with the more hard-line Qayyum Zakir.[31]

'ISI involvement in the early stages of the insurgency has been widely acknowledged. From 2003–04, the ISI operated training camps for Taliban recruits, and facilitated the supply of funds, equipment and arms from Gulf countries. The Pakistani Army established medical facilities for Taliban fighters, and even provided covering fire at border crossings. Communications intercepts showed that Taliban commanders were liaising with Pakistani military officers to ensure safe passage across the border. The scale of ISI support was evident from the major Taliban offensives launched in southern Afghanistan [against the British] in 2006. In June that year, a joint US, NATO and Afghan intelligence assessment (noted above) concluded that the ISI not only provided a vital sanctuary for the Taliban, but also paid and pressured them to fight. As Ahmed Rashid puts it, "over time evidence slowly collected by US and NATO intelligence officers on the ground showed a systematic and pervasive system of ISI collusion".

'A number of analysts suggest that due to American and international pressure in 2006, 2007 or later, Pakistan has curtailed its support for the insurgents,' Waldman continues, but he considers 'there is little evidence to support this. Indeed, in February this year [2010],' he points out, 'the US Director of National Intelligence admitted that the "Pakistan safe-haven is an important Taliban strength", and made no mention of any change in their behaviour vis-à-vis the Afghan insurgents.' Waldman quotes a former Taliban minister as saying that there continues to be close cooperation on cross-border movement between the Taliban and ISI or military, of which he had seen written evidence: he says he had 'seen a letter from the Taliban [shadow] governor in Helmand to Pakistani officials one year ago [2009], which asks for them to let some vehicles go through the border, giving their type and number plate. ISAF officials readily accept that insurgents continue to cross the border in significant numbers. And as one southern commander confirmed: "When we need ammunition we go to Miranshah [in North Waziristan]; our base is there and we get ammunition and expenses. If I go across the border, even if the Pakistani authorities know I am a commander, they open the way for me, all the way to the base."'[32]

A Policy Action Group analysis from as long ago as 2006 says: 'The insurgency cannot survive without its sanctuary in Pakistan, which provided freedom of movement, safe havens, logistics and training facilities, a base for recruitment, communications for command and control, and a secure environment for collaboration with foreign extremist groups. The sanctuary of Pakistan provides a seemingly endless supply of potential recruits for the insurgency.'[33]

Similarly, Waldman says, his interviews 'suggest that Pakistan continues to give extensive support to the insurgency in terms of funding, munitions and supplies. As a south-eastern commander put it: "We receive a lot of training, weapons, ammunition and expenses from the Pakistan government . . . Everyone knows Pakistan gives money, it goes centrally, then flows down." Another commander from a central province said: "Of course, it's a huge project [the insurgency], it needs huge funding, IEDs [improvised explosive devices], ammunition, training . . . all of this has been given by Pakistan. We do not have facilities to produce any of this . . . We get 10,000 Pakistani rupees [$120] per month for each Talib.'"

While it is clear that Pakistani funding keeps the Taliban insurgency going, what does not seem to have been so widely understood, at least by the general public in America, is that huge amounts of the billions of dollars the United States – particularly during the two terms of the Bush Presidency – has given Pakistan to fight the War on Terror has in fact been passed, under the counter, by the ISI to their protégés, the Taliban, to fund their War of Terror on the Americans themselves, the rest of NATO including the British, and their Afghan allies – a point not lost on some Taliban commanders. If that were to be stopped or substantially reduced, and the Americans put pressure on the Gulf States and Saudi Arabia not to continue to fund the Taliban, things could change radically.

Waldman quotes one commander on this very subject. 'This money comes from Pakistan, first to the [shadow] provincial governor, then to the district commander, then to the group commander. It is from the Pakistan government – but maybe other countries too, are paying from behind the curtain.' One southern commander reported that groups were paid bonuses for successful attacks against coalition forces, usually of $2,000–$3,000 [£1,500–£2,500], which he believed were derived from ISI sources. Likewise, a commander from a central province said: 'The ISI help our commanders, they come occasionally, and meet secretly. They give money and advice. I don't like them – they are not honest people, they are fighting for their own purposes. Most Taliban think this. But we have to work with them – we don't have any other choice. If we get injured or sick we have to go to Pakistan for treatment, or for training.' Waldman's account states,

These accounts were corroborated by former Taliban ministers, a Western security analyst, and a senior UN official based in Kabul, who said the Taliban largely depended on funding from the ISI and groups in Gulf countries. The ISI also appears to be funding groups of Taliban fighters who are based in and operate from Pakistan. One southern commander said that when he and comrades were living in Pakistan they used to solicit donations for fighting in Afghanistan, but: 'The ISI and Pakistan government [also] paid. Charity was small money; it didn't even pay the rent. Groups going to Afghanistan [from Pakistan] had a lot of expenses. For sure the ISI were paying a lot of money: groups of 20–30 people got 2–3 million Pakistani rupees ($24,000–$36,000) [£16,000 to £24,000] each a year.' Some Afghan and Western security officials believe that the ISI is also covering the living costs of the families of Taliban fighters who live in Pakistan.

'The sheer scale of the insurgency,' in Matt Waldman's judgement, 'appears to have convinced Afghan officials that it is supported by Pakistan.' An Afghan minister also argued: 'The ISI control the Taliban – otherwise there couldn't be this level of insurgency, with huge logistical and military needs. How can we . . . take this out of Pakistani hands?' Likewise, a former senior Afghan security official observed: 'For fighters, when they move to fight it's essential that they have logistical support. They need vehicles, fuel and food. They need ammunition. They need money and guns . . . They need a hospital to take their casualties to for treatment.'

So who is providing these things to the Taliban if it's not Pakistan? This argument is reinforced by the fact that the Afghan insurgency might be over 35,000 strong, as reported by Jerome Starkey (*The Times*, 3 March 2010) and last year [2009] launched an average of 620 attacks a month. Assuming costs associated with each Talib averaged $150 (£100) per month, manning costs alone would exceed $60 (£37.5) million a year.

The impact of the details of funding, its extent and the scale of the insurgency only reinforces the argument for a drastic reappraisal of NATO [i.e. American] policy which can bring under control and one day, one hopes, dismantle the ISI war machine – encompassing training camps, both for fighters and potential suicide bombers, and *madrassas* – targeting Afghanistan.

The interviews suggest that the ISI continues to sanction and support military training centres for insurgents and a large number of *madrassas* that actively encourage their students to fight in Afghanistan. All commanders reported that significant numbers of their fighters attend training camps in Pakistan that are run or backed by the ISI. One southern commander described how in his district, where there are some 600 fighters, around 70–80 fighters had gone to Pakistan for training in the winter of 2009 to 2010. Emphasising the continuing importance of such training, a south-eastern commander said that 'of the 280 fighters in our district, some 80 per cent were trained in Pakistan'.

Commanders described their own experiences in Pakistani *madrassas* and training camps . . . which suggests a large-scale, well-organised system. One southern commander attended a *madrassa* in Quetta for four years (from 2004 to 2008). There were 500–600 students, most of whom were Afghan, and some 60–70 graduated every year. He said: 'Everyone was saying *jihad* (in Afghanistan) is good. All our teachers were saying this as well. Every day *jihad* was discussed.' Apparently, *jihad* in Afghanistan was raised and endorsed not only in political classes but also in both religious and religious law classes. At certain times, groups of students from the *madrassa* would attend military training camps in Pakistan (to learn how to make and lay IEDs, for example), or spend a period fighting in Afghanistan, which could range from 10–20 days to several months.

The commander described one round of training that took place at a house in Wana, in South Waziristan Agency, FATA, in 2005. There were between twenty to fifty people (at different times), who were being instructed in how to make suicide vests and car bombs. 'The trainers were ISI. One of the trainers had two jobs: he worked with us and in the Pakistan military. There are very good relations between the Pakistan military and Taliban, a good friendship; we'd often sit together and exchange ideas on how best to attack . . . The man was definitely ISI, he told some of us. When some of our friends were arrested by the Pakistani authorities, he went and got them freed.'[34]

One of the commanders from a central province described how he spent a year in a Pakistani *madrassa* in 2008, describing it as 'a big camp, really big, like a university with 2,000–4,000 people' (although he believes it is now much smaller). It included a military training camp, where they were taught combat techniques, such as how to lay IEDs, attack or ambush. He said two-thirds of the students were Afghans, and that their Afghan and Pakistani teachers were continually telling them, 'it was our duty to fight in Afghanistan'. The other commander from the centre of Afghanistan described how he spent four years in a Pakistani *madrassa* in Karachi with 600–800 others, one third of whom were Afghans. He said that every day, either in formal classes or informal discussions, '*jihad* against the infidel American invaders' would be condoned and encouraged. Often students would go for two or three months' military training, and then some months' fighting in Afghanistan, after which they would return to the *madrassa*.

He said that the camps were 'huge'. Indeed, in 2007 he attended a camp in the mountains near Mansehra,* in Khyber Pukhtunwha [the new name for North-West Frontier Province, or NWFP]. The training was comprehensive: covering attacks, ambushes, escapes, firing rocket-propelled grenades (RPGs), and PKMs [heavy machine guns], although IED training was conducted elsewhere. He said that all those attending the camp were being trained for fighting in Afghanistan. He also believed that most of the Pakistani military trainers were ISI: 'The ISI is hard to recognise,' he wrote; 'we could tell, but we kept it secret.'

'Given that the Taliban commanders' experiences are from some years ago,' Waldman states, 'it is impossible to verify the continuance of this form of insurgent recruitment and training in Pakistan. However, most of the commanders believed that the only significant change is that the military training camps are now smaller, more dispersed and better concealed – a point which also emerged from research on the Haqqani network, an Afghan terrorist organisation controlled by the Haqqani family.'[35]

Waldman says his study 'is not intended as a detailed analysis of the group . . . but focuses on its links to Pakistani officials, as described by Haqqani commanders'. Two such commanders were interviewed: one was jointly responsible for operations in three districts, the other was one of the

---

* Mansehra is just north of Abbottabad and at one time Afghan intelligence apparently thought Osama bin Laden was hiding there.

two or three most senior Haqqani commanders, in charge of eight other commanders, with about a total of a thousand fighters.

Estimates of the strength of the Haqqani network vary widely from 4,000 to a possible 15,000 fighters, some of them Arabs, Pakistani, Chechen and other al Qaeda recruits. One attack not attributed by Admiral Mike Mullen to the Network in his address to the Senate Armed Services Committee inclued a 2008 raid on the Aga Khan-owned Serena Hotel in Kabul in which six people died, including a Norwegian journalist who was covering the visit of the Norwegian Foreign Minister, Jonas Stoere, who was also staying in the hotel with a delegation but was not hurt.

'Western analysts and intelligence agencies have long been aware of ISI support for the Haqqani Network,' Waldman says, 'which is founded on historic ties' and 'symbiotic relations'. These go back to the Russian War.[36] Indeed, the ISI has long considered the Haqqanis as 'strategic assets' of the first order, and has stubbornly resisted American pressure to attack them. 'Both Haqqani commanders confirmed this relationship.'[37]

The senior commander described how the Network was led and resourced by a command shura comprising Maulawi Jalaluddin Haqqani, his son Sirajuddin Haqqani and a small group of former senior ISI officials (at least one of whom is Afghan), who were, in his words, contracted by and working for the ISI. 'If the Pakistani ISI were not with him [Jalaluddin Haqqani] then he can't do anything,' the other district commander remarked. These views are consistent with the clandestine network, described by Ahmed Rashid and quoted by Waldman, comprising former ISI operatives or army officers who were hired by the ISI 'on contract' after 2001, to train Afghan insurgents, one of the best known of whom was a certain 'Colonel Imam', real name Sultan Amir Tarar. Colonel Imam trained Afghan *mujahideen* fighting the Russians in the 1980s, including Mullah Omar, and maintained contact after they formed the Taliban.

The *New York Times* reported that he and another ISI officer, a journalist and his driver, were kidnapped by renegade Pakistani Taliban and that while the journalist and his driver were released, both ISI men were murdered. Colonel Imam was killed in January 2011 in North Waziristan, in the Pakistan Tribal Areas. It was a brutal and hardly believable death for the 'Godfather of the Taliban', a grim example of the spectre of the revolution devouring its own. 'Colonel Imam had helped the Taliban stage a remarkable comeback', Carlotta Gall reported in the *New York Times*. Waldman goes on to say that the ISI had a central role in the re-emergence of the Haqqani group after the American intervention in 2001. The district commander described how he and many former Talibs and *jihadi* fighters were living in Pakistan, doing ordinary jobs. But in 2003–04 the 'Pakistani military and ISI' were actively 'trying to reconnect us, encouraging us to join back together, and urging us to fight. They said if you go back we will give you money, weapons, support.

'With regard to relations with the Taliban, the senior commander said that neither Sirajuddin or Jalaluddin Haqqani were any longer a member of the Quetta Shura: "Before, we got all [strategic] decisions from the Quetta Shura, but recently because they started talking to the [Afghan] government, we stopped being involved with them."' The district commander said that in his area Haqqani fighters sometimes had 'problems' with Taliban and Hizb-i-Islami fighters, which led to fighting. He was critical of both groups, which he accused of co-opting criminals. He also said that there were a number of Arabs working for the Haqqanis, sometimes as commanders. Although he did not believe these were al Qaeda operatives, there are reported to be close links between the Haqqanis and al Qaeda. The senior commander described how the ISI had significant influence within the ranks of the Network, claiming: 'Yes, there are ISI people inside the Taliban, even in the Afghan government. Three of my (eight) commanders have close relations with the ISI.'[38]

The commander described his reluctance to carry out attacks which targeted Afghan civilians. 'Our fighters got orders from the command group [of former ISI officials and Sirajuddin Haqqani] it goes step by step down the hierarchy. The top command gives the orders. We get orders to attack American, ANA (Afghan National Army), ANP (Afghan National Police) bases, whoever works with the Afghan government and the Americans – even aid workers – all of them. This is an order I've been given.' The commander, according to Waldman, went on to say that construction and logistics workers didn't get attacked if they gave money to Sirajuddin. If they didn't, then they were attacked. 'Taliban are not all the same. Some groups never attack Afghans; some others, run by the ISI, even attack schools, everybody. I support the ANA and ANP; so many times I sheltered them in the fighting. My view is that we should fight Americans; the ISI are telling us to kill Afghans. In Afghanistan, a lot of commanders were trained by the ISI so when they get orders from the ISI, they always listen to them. I hate the big suicide attacks that kill Afghan civilians; I hate the killing of NGO workers.'[39]

Whether these assertions are true is debatable (the caveats mentioned with respect to the Taliban also apply here). However, there is certainly a consistent view among analysts that the Haqqani Network is one of the most ruthless, aggressive and powerful insurgent groups. Echoing comments of the senior commander, the district commander described how certain groups, comprised of mainly Pakistani fighters, are based in and operated from north-west Pakistan. 'There are secret places in Miranshah and Quetta . . . Before, the bases were open but now they are secret. Apart from the Pakistani authorities no one knows they are there . . . Police or military vehicles transport fighters to the border at night . . . Other trucks loaded with guns and ammunition arrive separately, which are distributed at the border. The Pakistani army, police, intelligence all cooperated . . . Only the group commander knows where they will fight.

He described how he was involved in such operations about once a month: in 2010 he had undertaken four such missions by May, and one just a fortnight before. He said that around 40 per cent of all the attacks in his area were undertaken by these groups, and that they were increasing . . . Many were led by 'Pakistani ISI or military officers', apparently often Punjabis, who comprised the majority of the officer corps of the Pakistani army. He said that although they didn't wear uniforms, they (the Haqqani fighters) knew who they were because of their particular appearance and manner. They were well educated, well trained, gave strong orders . . . used advanced techniques . . . and develop good plans.' He said they participate in almost all important operations, but if it was a major operation, then there might be up to three such commanders involved. He confirmed that from his district he would regularly communicate by radio with people in Pakistan whom he believed to be military.

Directly or indirectly, the ISI appeared to have a major role in sustaining the Haqqani group. The senior commander said that in every three weeks he would usually spend two in Pakistan and one in Afghanistan. Every month he would receive sixty to eighty boxes of AK-47 rounds and two or three large boxes of grenades and IEDs. If he required further supplies or munitions, he would go to the command group (the Haqqanis and former ISI officials) who would issue him with a letter of credit, which he could present to arms dealers in Khost (in south-east Afghanistan) or Miranshah. For operating expenses, he received a monthly cheque of between 500,000–1 million Pakistani rupees [$6–12,000 or £3,800–£7,640]. He believes the money comes from two sources: Gulf countries, especially Saudi Arabia – that is accessed through the Saudi Bank; and from the ISI, accessed from the Islamic Bank of Pakistan, in which the Haqqani network apparently has a representative. Indeed, the former claim is corroborated by a recent report that over $920 million has flowed from Saudi Arabian donors to Afghan insurgents, mainly via Waziristan, over the past four years.[40]

The Haqqani district commander, according to 'The Sun in the Sky' report, 'described how arms and ammunition would sometimes arrive in his area by trucks, and sometimes on horses, donkeys or camels, which was "from the Pakistani military". He said that they were paid salaries: fighters receive around 9–10,000 Pakistani rupees ($110–120) a month and he, as a commander, receives 15–20,000 Pakistani rupees ($170–220) a month, through the *hawala* system. When asked from whom the money came, he replied: "The Americans. From them, to the Pakistani military, and then to us." He was baffled as to why, in his eyes, the Americans were supporting their activities. (In fact, many Afghans believe that the United States is deliberately funding the insurgency. Although this seems barely credible, it is hardly surprising given America's massive and sustained support of the Pakistani military.) Separately, the commander confirmed that groups receive a reward for killing foreign soldiers, usually $4–5,000 [£2,550–£3,180] for each soldier killed.'[41]

All the details of the arms shipments and budgetary costs of the insurgency mentioned above, support and reinforce, to this reader at least, the

credibility of 'The Sun in the Sky'. The explanation of how America's funding of the Pakistan Army finds its way into the coffers of the Haqqani and
Taliban insurgents must have raised a few eyebrows in the Pentagon and
Congress, one imagines. But only now through the outspoken remarks
made in September 2011 by Admiral Mike Mullen and Ambassador
Tomsen, have the Americans apparently woken up to what is really
happening.

Waldman says, 'There are apparently a number of small, covert
Haqqani bases in North Waziristan and Kurram Agencies, and in Quetta,
staffed by serving or former Pakistani military officials. They are often
combined with a *madrassa*, provide a broad-based military training, and
include suicide bomber cells'. 'The senior commander described how
until recently there were insurgent training camps in Pakistan for 2,000–
3,000 fighters, but due to drone strikes they are now far smaller, capable
of training only 120 Taliban each, usually for twenty days at a time. He
said there are now three major camps, two in Kurram Agency and one
near Miranshah. 'The trainers are all Pakistan ISI – they are well trained,
well educated. The Taliban have strong support from the ISI. Training is
in all military tactics: attacks, ambushes, IEDs – but not suicide bombers. This training is separate, very specialist . . . they have 200 standby
suicide bombers; it's run by Pakistanis, Arabs, Chechens, Saudi Arabians,
people who use foolish, uneducated boys of 13–15 years, and most of
these come from *madrassas*.[42]

'This account is consistent with events on the ground in Afghanistan.
For example, a suicide attack in Kabul on 18 May 2010, which killed eighteen people including twelve civilians, has been widely attributed to the
Haqqani network. A spokesman for the Afghan intelligence directorate
said: "The intelligence service of our neighbouring country has definitely
had its role in equipping and training this group."

'The district commander also described Haqqani bases in Quetta and
Miranshah: "The base I use [in Miranshah] is in a house, with a huge basement, for around fifty people. Outside is a big board saying it is an office.
The basement is divided into sections, for example some groups are being
trained in IEDs; they sleep and eat in these rooms. People being trained for
suicide attacks are kept separate. There's also a big *madrassa* hall. Groups

are taken off to other places to practice shooting or whatever. People stay for around a month." He described the people there as "young boys, who cannot discern good from bad, who don't know history but are very good fighters. They want to die for Islam."

'Both Haqqani commanders echoed the comments of Taliban commanders about the presence of ISI representatives on the Quetta Shura. According to the senior commander: "Yes, the ISI control the Quetta Shura. When Mullah Baradar and Mullah Omar talked directly to the Afghan government – peace talks – the ISI arrested Baradar . . . because they want peace talks to fail. I don't know how many ISI are on the Quetta Shura . . . Honest Afghans who want *jihad* and are honest to their country, were disarmed, detained and became powerless . . . I know many good high-ranking [former] Taliban who are not supporting the fight in Afghanistan . . . the rest are listening to the ISI, [and] still have the control. I don't like this. Without the support of the ISI, Afghans cannot do anything, can't even have meetings. Both former and current ISI are on the Quetta Shura. New ISI members are not so reliable and do not have such a strong role in it; the former ISI have more credibility and influence. All the Taliban interested in the peace process are detained."

'Perhaps surprisingly, he argued, "Peace talks with the Afghan government are a good idea. The most important condition for the Afghan Taliban is the withdrawal of foreign forces. They should say how long they will be here, and when they will withdraw, and keep to the date exactly. The ISI Taliban will never come to peace – they always want instability and weak government here."

'Similarly, the district commander said: "The Taliban get all their plans and strategy from the ISI, if they don't cooperate, they can't live for a day there." He doubted that negotiations with the Afghan government would succeed because in his view: "The Taliban is in the hands of Pakistan. They have to do what Pakistan tells them to do; they do not have autonomy. Pakistan wants a weak, puppet government in Afghanistan".'[43]

In his conclusion, Matt Waldman says: 'Taliban and Haqqani fighters are motivated by a range of factors, many of which relate to government predation, corruption or injustice, and the perceived aggression of foreign military forces . . . Thus, despite the claims of many interviewees, the ISI (and elements of the Pakistani military) may not actually *control* the Afghan insurgency, which implies power over all major dimensions of the movement and its campaign, and the ability to bring it to an end. However, as the provider of sanctuary, and very substantial financial, military and logistical support to the insurgency, the ISI appears to have strong strategic and operational influence – reinforced by coercion. There is thus a strong case that the ISI and elements of the military are deeply involved in the insurgent campaign, and have powerful influence over the Haqqani network. This relationship appears to be of a different nature, or at least order of magnitude, than suggested by most studies.'[44]

As the American talks with the Taliban progress, and include, one imagines, some Pakistan Army involvement, not least that of their top soldier, Chief of Army Staff, General Kayani, whom the American military talk to regularly and the British from time to time – General Sir David Richards, Chief of the Defence Staff, knows him well – the extent of ISI control over the Taliban will become clearer, as will the possibilities of a wider settlement including not only the Taliban and Pakistan but eventually India and other neighbouring states such as Iran as well. It will be a matter of skilful negotiation and no doubt hard bargaining with all parties. But it would seem to be the only way forward.

Matt Waldman states he asked 'three experienced Afghan analysts and two senior Western security officials' to examine his assessment and they agreed with the principal findings. 'It means that without a change in Pakistani behaviour it will be difficult if not impossible for international forces and the Afghan government to make progress against the insurgency. It also means that, as one southern commander put it, "if the ISI doesn't support negotiations [with the Afghan government], then they won't succeed". Perhaps more significantly, it is hard to see how the international coalition can continue to treat Pakistan as an ally and "effective partner" . . .   Only last December [2009],' Waldman continues, 'President Obama affirmed that "we are committed to a partnership that is built on a foundation of mutual interest, mutual respect and mutual trust".'

The discovery in May 2011 that Osama bin Laden had been hiding in Abbottabad, two hours' drive from the capital, Islamabad, under the noses of the Pakistan military, for at least five years, has blown the partnership, or alliance, sky high. The immediate reaction of many American politicians – 'not a dime more' – reflects the growing disillusionment at Pakistan's duplicity, and its exorbitant price. As Waldman points out, since 2001 America has provided Pakistan with $11.6 billion in security-related assistance and $6 billion in economic aid. It is due to provide at least $7.5 billion more over the next five years. American and other Western intelligence agencies must be aware of Pakistan's conduct, Waldman says, yet Pakistani officers are even represented on the Tripartite Joint Intelligence Operation Centre situated in ISAF headquarters in Kabul.

The apparent contradiction – backing the enemy's backer – is perhaps a reflection of the United States' preoccupation with the threat it faces from al Qaeda and associated groups, Waldman suggests, rather than the Afghan Taliban. It may reflect a reluctance to confront an unstable, nuclear-armed country that faces a serious internal threat from Pakistani Taliban groups. It may also reflect a concern not to jeopardise Pakistani cooperation in preventing terrorist attacks against Western targets; or a fear of galvanising extremism among Pakistani immigrant communities. 'Nevertheless, Pakistan appears to be playing a double-game of astonishing magnitude,' Waldman concludes.

The conflict, at August 2012, had led to the deaths of over 1,939 American servicemen and women, 422 British and 628 other NATO personnel; thousands of Afghan soldiers, police, officials and civilians; and an unknown number of Afghan, Pakistani and other foreign insurgents. It has already cost America nearly $300 billion, and now costs over $70 billion a year. As a Haqqani commander put it: 'Of course Pakistan is the main cause of the problems [in Afghanistan] but America is behind Pakistan.'[45]

The Pakistan government's apparent duplicity – and awareness of it among the American public and political establishment – could have enormous geo-political implications. It could jeopardise American financial support: security-related assistance is conditional on Pakistan's cooperation on Afghanistan. Moreover, it could trigger punitive counter-measures by the US and its allies, or direct military action against the Afghan Taliban in Pakistani territory.

However, an aggressive American response to Pakistan's conduct is only likely to generate further instability, especially given the Army's ongoing battle against Pakistani militant groups and widespread anti-American sentiment among the population. The priority must be to address the fundamental causes of Pakistan's insecurity, in particular its latent and enduring conflict with India. This requires a regional peace process and, as the former CIA analyst Bruce Riedel has argued, American backing for moves towards a resolution of the Kashmir dispute. It should be accompanied by support for military and political reform, and a combination of incentives and disincentives to persuade Pakistan's elite that support for Islamic militants is no longer in Pakistan's national interests.

'Even this is no panacea for the Afghan conflict; it merely makes treatment possible. So long as the root causes remain – especially a corrupt, exclusionary, unjust [Afghan] government, and the perception among some Afghans of an aggressive, self-serving foreign military presence – then the violence will continue,' Waldman concludes.[46]

In July 2010, only a month or so after the publication of 'The Sun in the Sky', Matt Waldman's findings seemed very largely vindicated by the revelations of the WikiLeaks website, which published 75,000 classified documents obtained from internet hackers. Some prompted the New York Times to comment that 'Pakistan's military spy service [the ISI] has guided the Afghan insurgency with a hidden hand, even as Pakistan receives more than $1 billion a year from Washington for its help combating the militants.'[47] The documents, it adds, 'suggest that Pakistan, an ostensible ally of the United States, allows representatives of its spy service to meet directly with the Taliban in secret strategy sessions to organise networks of militant groups that fight against American soldiers in Afghanistan, and even hatch plots to assassinate Afghan leaders', including, among others, President Karzai.

'Taken together,' the New York Times says, 'the reports indicate that

American soldiers on the ground are inundated with accounts of a network of Pakistani assets and collaborators that runs from the Pakistani tribal belt along the Afghan border, through southern Afghanistan, and all the way to the capital, Kabul.'[48]

Turning the Tide

We're taking them off the battlefield in industrial numbers.
Senior Western commander in Kandahar, November 2010[1]

The last five years or so in Afghanistan, since British troops deployed in Helmand in 2006, and despite a major surge by American forces in 2010, taking their total strength to 100,000, have seen a seemingly unstoppable escalation of the Taliban insurgency. Battle casualties have risen sharply – for NATO, Taliban and civilians: the UN says 2010 was the 'deadliest' year with 2,777 civilian deaths recorded, 75 per cent of which were caused by the Taliban. Each year there have been more IEDs, more suicide bombs. The overall impression has been one of continuing deterioration and expansion of the war which has spread into areas that were previously peaceful, such as Kunduz and other parts of the north, including Badakhshan in the north-east where a team of medics, most of them expatriates – one British, Dr Karen Woo – were murdered in August 2010, in a brutal and senseless attack. In October, another aid worker, Linda Norgrove from the Scottish Highlands, who was kidnapped in the restive province of Kunar and taken to the notorious Korengal Valley, was killed accidentally when a US Special Forces raid to rescue her went wrong.

Politically, things are just as grim: parliament hamstrung; corruption sweeping the country like a tsunami, with vast sums of money that have been laundered and couriered to Dubai over the past three years by the *hawala*, New Ansari, money-launderers to the elite; and a President less and less in touch with reality, sacking his intelligence chief and telling him it was not the Taliban who shot rockets at the Kabul Peace Jirga. When the chief asked him who did, he got the Delphic reply: 'Why should I tell you

who did it?' It appeared the oracle meant the Americans. That same intelligence chief, Amrullah Saleh – one of the few incorruptibles – says Karzai
has turned his back on the West, blaming NATO and the Americans for
all his troubles, and turning to Iran and the Taliban for his salvation. In
November 2010, only a few days before the NATO meeting in Lisbon,
Karzai called on the coalition to reduce all military operations and to ban
all Special Forces missions in the south. General Petraeus was reported to
have greeted the announcement with 'astonishment and disappointment'.
One report, unconfirmed, suggested that Petraeus threatened to resign if
the President insisted.

And then suddenly, at the other end of the country, with winter approaching, a few green shoots began to appear. Everyone was rubbing their eyes.
Were they really green shoots? Was it a mirage? The first person to report
their presence publicly was Anthony Loyd of *The Times*, who wrote in early
November 2010 about the big operation, involving mainly American and
Afghan troops, then under way in Kandahar. It was startling stuff. After years
of heading for the rocks, the tide of battle seemed to be turning.

'The Taliban's best war captains are either dead or held captive,' Loyd's
report began. 'Their soldiery are harried and on-the-run, subject to
constant attack and betrayal; under-equipped, overwhelmed, demoralised:
losing. If in Britain and America doubt and confusion prevail over the
future of the Afghan war, in southern Afghanistan the description of the
Taliban insurgency by senior figures at the forefront of fighting against it is
bold and unequivocal. Surge works, they say. The Taliban are at breaking
point. An Iraq-style watershed may be nigh – a skein of hope for NATO
aims in the war's darkest and tenth year.'[2]

Pie in the sky? Anthony Loyd is a highly experienced journalist who has
spent a lot of time in Afghanistan over the years. His report continued:
The Taliban are getting an absolute arse-kicking," said one top-level
Westerner, deeply involved with Operation Ham Kari in Kandahar, "their
worst since 2001–02. We're taking them off the battlefield in industrial
numbers. We're convinced that the initiative has really shifted."'[3]

Loyd quoted the President's controversial but powerful late half-brother
Ahmed Wali Karzai as saying the Taliban were in a 'miserable state', their
best commanders dead and their fighters running 'here and there'

in disarray. Loyd describes NATO and Afghan commanders as being exceptionally upbeat, but they also urge caution – saying that much in the end depends on the ability of the Karzai government to ensure good local government is brought in fast to consolidate the territorial gains, something that Kabul has been notoriously bad at in the past. In fact, it has been NATO's Achilles' heel.

The usually more sober and careful *New York Times* also detected a number of green shoots, reporting that: 'American and Afghan forces have been routing the Taliban in much of Kandahar Province in recent weeks, forcing many hardened fighters, faced with the buildup of American forces, to flee strongholds they have held for years.'[3] The completion of President Obama's full surge of 30,000 fresh troops in late summer 2010 allowed a force of 12,000 American and NATO troops and 7,000 Afghan Army to saturate Kandahar. The successes that October and November persuaded Afghan and Western officials that the Taliban would have a hard time returning to areas they had controlled in what had been their main base. Some of the gains came from a new mobile rocket that has pinpoint accuracy – like a small cruise missile – and has been used against the hideouts of insurgent commanders around Kandahar. That forced many of them to retreat across the border into Pakistan. Disruption of their supply lines made it harder for them to stage retaliatory strikes or suicide bombings. The *New York Times* quoted Major General Nick Carter, the then British commander of NATO coalition forces in southern Afghanistan who oversaw the Kandahar operation in 2010, as saying: 'We now have the initiative. We have created momentum. It is everything put together in terms of the effort that has gone in over the last eighteen months and it is undoubtedly having an impact.'[4]

'Shock and awe', in Donald Rumsfeld's famous phrase, seems to have been the effect of this new secret weapon on the Taliban. Residents 'talk with awe of a powerful new rocket that has been fired from Kandahar air base into Panjwai and other areas for the last two or three weeks, hitting Taliban compounds with remarkable accuracy. The rocket curls and turns in the air as it zooms in on its target and sets off secondary explosions, often burning the trees and foliage around buildings,' the *New York Times* quoted one landowner from the Panjwai District as saying. General Carter identified it as probably the High Mobility Artillery Rocket System, or HIMARS, a relatively new device. They are extraordinarily precise, he says, accurate to a metre.[5]

Again, however, there was a note of caution. Mindful of past setbacks NATO forces have experienced, some military officials say the advances in Kandahar may not represent a turning point in the overall war effort. One American commander, however, did emphasise Taliban losses. '"A lot are getting killed," he said. "They are not receiving support from the local population." They are complaining that the local people are not burying their dead, and they are saying: 'We are losing so many we want to go back home.' Military and civilian officials say there are also signs of a crisis in command: the Taliban are said to be struggling to maintain logistics and supply routes; suicide bombers have failed to turn up for attacks; and even senior commanders were showing reluctance to follow orders from their leader, Mullah Muhammad Omar, to go in to fight the NATO onslaught in Panjwai.' The *New York Times* reported that one local police chief was in no doubt. 'We broke their neck,'[6] said Haji Niaz Muhammad, the Police Chief in the Arghandab District, home of the powerful Alikozai tribe, one of the most important districts of Kandahar and traditionally anti-Taliban.

Another, parallel, development in Kandahar raises hopes of a different nature. The Petraeus plan to recruit 30,000 former police and other villagers via the old, anti-Soviet *mujahideen* networks to which they all belonged is also seen as an encouraging new sign. Although many Afghans are suspicious of the *mujahideen* past, it is increasingly being perceived that they are probably the only force at village level that can keep out the Taliban and stop them intimidating the villagers. Petraeus has persuaded President Karzai to sanction a pilot project in which 10,000 police will be recruited at village level – an Afghan home guard under the control of the local elders.

'On a recent day,' the *New York Times* reported, 'Major General Carter sat with Afghan and American commanders on the roof terrace at the district headquarters of Arghandab, discussing how to consolidate their hold over areas cleared three weeks before. "How quickly can you recruit

300 local police?" he asked a former *mujahideen* commander, Haji Hafizullah. "Can you bring them for training by tomorrow?" By the end of the meeting, the district governor was signing the papers of several dozen local men who will form the local police force.'[7]

In one of his last acts as NATO Commander in the south, General Carter called the new forces the 'Sons of the Shura' because, as the *New York Times* points out, 'they require approval by everyone on the traditional council of elders to prevent them from becoming what he called "one bloke's militia". The plan has clear echoes of the Sons of Iraq' – the tribal levies which General Petraeus so successfully recruited and armed in the battle against al Qaeda. Five months later, in early April, I was told by a reliable source from Kandahar that at least one new police force, which had been originally full of enthusiasm, had become disenchanted because of lack of money and support from Kabul.

There are other echoes of Iraq here, in Kandahar, too. One is David Kilcullen, a former Australian infantry lieutenant colonel, who now works for the American State Department and is a specialist in counterinsurgency. He advised General Petraeus in Iraq and is now doing the same in Afghanistan. While sitting waiting for his plane at Kabul airport, he jotted down some thoughts, which duly appeared in *The Times* on 30 October 2010. Reflecting on his recent visit, he said that for the first time in five years, he thought: 'We just might be starting to turn the tide . . .' Recent reports suggested that roughly 300 Taliban leaders had been killed or captured between June and late September in the so-called decapitation programme, he said, with another 2,000 insurgents arrested and almost 900 killed.[8]

Cracks had also started to appear in Taliban networks – specialists like bomb makers were under pressure; discord was growing between harried lower-level leaders and senior commanders safe in Pakistan; and, perhaps most significantly, groups of Taliban were defecting to the government, and laying down their arms. But encouraging as this was, David Kilcullen said, none of it would make a real difference unless it was matched by similar progress against corruption and the reform of local government. And could it be done in the 'short self-imposed time frame' the coalition faces, and with the Karzai government as a partner? Big ifs. We would not be in a position to know, he suggested, until early summer 2011.[9]

At the end of November 2010, I had a chance to put a question to General Stanley McChrystal, the former NATO Commander in Afghanistan, when he was on a flying visit to Britain. Given the optimistic reports from various commentators about the progress of the Kandahar operation (which McChrystal planned), I asked him if he shared the view that the Taliban were being 'routed' and that, in David Kilcullen's phrase, 'the tide might be beginning to turn'.

He began by saying he had been out of the Army for several months, so he was not fully in touch but he did get emails from people who were. 'Security wise, I think that is absolutely correct,' he told me. 'Everything I get from people that communicate with me confirms what the news says. We knew that would happen, we knew the security would get better, absolutely, and I know people were doubting that, but we absolutely knew that would happen.' The question was: Did the Afghan people view that as a change, as a significant change? Did it build their confidence that we were going to move forward in governance and part of that was: could the national government and some of the other actors at the provincial and district levels step up enough? McChrystal's sense was that they could; that the turn in the security in the south was an opportunity for them to step up. But he did not think it was a done deal, until they actually did that. He thought it could backslide if 'malign actors' got a disproportionate amount of power in certain areas like Marja.[10]

'Cleaning out Marja,' he continued, 'you had to clean out the Taliban and then you had to clean out the people who were running the show . . . that was going to be true around Kandahar – although not quite as bad as in the Marja area.' So he was 'pretty optimistic' about that; and the one thing he would tell people was that Afghanistan, in his view, was a situation of confidence. 'Once the Afghan people felt it was tipping the right way, it would go very quickly. Because that was the way they wanted it to go . . . But they were rational about it – they were staying on the fence until they were sure which way it was going to go. Because you were the big loser if you went the wrong way and then it didn't work.'[11]

Even if the coalition, under the spell of General Petraeus's wizardry, informed by people like David Kilcullen, succeeds in turning the tide in a decisive way, there will still need to be some sort of solution and settlement of the problem. Two men who were eminently qualified to negotiate such a settlement are, alas, no longer available. One was Richard Holbrooke, President Obama's Special Envoy to Afghanistan and Pakistan, the architect of the Dayton Peace Accords which brought peace to Bosnia, who died suddenly of a heart attack on 13 December 2010. The other was Sir Sherard Cowper-Coles, who was, first, British Ambassador to Kabul from May 2007 to February 2009, and then the Foreign Secretary's Special Representative to Afghanistan and Pakistan from February 2009 to September 2010. He resigned from the Foreign Office in October 2010.

Ambassadors are no longer expected to write a valedictory when they leave the service, but Sir Sherard's evidence to the House of Commons Foreign Affairs Committee on 9 November 2010 seemed to be just that – a deft analysis of the problem and a classic recommendation of what needs to be done now. Sir Sherard started off by saying that 'the peace that was negotiated at the Petersberg outside Bonn in December 2001 was a victor's peace – the vanquished [the Taliban] were not present. The constitution which we are fighting and dying for and spending getting on for £6 billion of British taxpayers' money a year to support, is an unstable constitution because it is highly centralised. I am glad to say it was designed by a Frenchman [Professor Guy Carcassonne] and imposed by an American [James Dobbins].'* But it was not sustainable, he said, because it didn't go with the grain of Afghan tradition.[12]

'We needed something much more decentralised,' Sir Sherard added. In the end, what would bring security to the Pushtun areas, indeed the whole of the region, he said, would be the solution Lord Curzon adopted as Viceroy on the North-West Frontier, when he pulled our troops back east of the Indus and decided, rightly, that the policy for pacifying or stabilising (he hesitated to say pacifying) the Pathan tribal areas was one of empowering the tribal leaders, under the supervision of the government, to secure and govern those areas for themselves with a representative shura of local tribes and punishing them if they misbehaved and rewarding them with bags of gold if they succeeded. And the modern-day equivalent of the

---

* Guy Carcassonne is Professor of Constitutional Law at Nanterre University, Paris; Ambassador James Dobbins was an experienced 'troubleshooter' for the State Department.

Curzon formula had to be the right approach. Garrisoning these areas with alien troops might produce temporary suppression of the symptoms but it wouldn't cure the underlying disease, he said. And he knew that General Richards and General Petraeus understood that. 'What had been missing was that political strategy which ... might sound a little like Liberal Democrat community politics – it had to be top down and bottom up.

'Easy to say, difficult to do,' but no other solution would work, he believed. 'We needed to remember that the Afghan Army, which was only 3 per cent southern Pushtun, was almost as alien to the farmers of the Helmand Valley as the 3rd Battalion The Rifles or the 82nd Airborne Division of the United States Army. Only the United States could succeed in this venture,' he said. 'America was necessary, but not enough for a solution. And one of our chief roles and one of the chief benefits of our massive contribution was the influence it gave us with the American military and in Washington ...'

A month or so after he took office, President Obama stated publicly that America sought no long-term permanent presence in Afghanistan. 'Of course,' Sir Sherard continued, 'most Afghans believed that we were there, or America was there to seek some long-term military presence; to seek some sort of neo-colonial long-term hegemony over the area.' That was as irrational, he said, as people in Helmand believing we were there to avenge the battle of Maiwand (1880). But they did believe it. So announcing 'that we were going, that we were getting out of combat' was, in his view, a good thing. It was a courageous thing for the Prime Minister to do, but in his view the right thing. 'The tragedy of our policy,' Sir Sherard stated, not just British policy but NATO policy in Afghanistan, was that 'we'd had far too much of the right hand' and 'not enough of the left hand'. You needed them both. 'You needed the political process to harvest the success politically which our military were delivering.'

Sir Sherard said he was always against an over-hasty withdrawal. 'If we were to leave precipitately, there would be chaos. There would be civil war

---

* Some of Sir Sherard's previous colleagues disagree with him on this point, arguing that in fact we have little influence in Washington. One cited Bob Woodward's latest account of Washington politics, *Obama's Wars*. If you examine the index, he says, you will find the names of no British politicians or generals.

and there would be a battle across the south between the Taliban and the narco-mafia . . .' What many southern Afghans wanted to know, in his view, was who was going to be in charge of their village or their valley five months or five years from now and they would back the winner. And for many of them the Taliban were harsher but fairer than a predatory narco-mafia Afghan government. So he was strongly opposed to precipitate withdrawal of troops. He thought that would do a great dishonour to the sacrifice of our troops and undo or threaten everything that had been achieved for the people of Afghanistan.[13] The key question, he said, was how you accompany a military drawdown with a serious political process . . . not whether there was a negotiated withdrawal – there would be a negotiated end to this conflict as to all conflicts – but did we get ahead of the tide of history? Did we have the confidence and the courage to say, 'Look, this needs a comprehensive negotiated solution, regionally and internally'? Or did we say: 'We didn't want to get involved. We'll subcontract it to the Afghans and the Pakistanis.' In the end, we wanted what the Taliban wanted, which was the withdrawal of foreign forces.

The conversation, he said, was about the conditions accompanying those foreign forces. 'If we wanted to protect what had been achieved, we did it best . . . (and David Miliband [Labour Foreign Secretary, June 2007–May 2010] and he believed the present [Coalition] ministers shared the view) by having the confidence to take the initiative ourselves, rather than saying "After you, Claude", as it were, and letting it drift on . . . It was terribly easy to say [this] in a committee room of the House of Commons, difficult to deliver on the ground. But the truth was the Afghans knew how to do it. The system was called *jirga* – in Arabic it was *shura* – sitting together and thrashing out your differences.'[14]

Finally, he was asked if NATO and the British had a policy that could deal with the Taliban policy of intimidation and assassination they were using to gain control in Kandahar. 'No, clearly . . . we don't,' he replied. 'But, as in Northern Ireland, Malaya, Palestine, Vietnam or Algeria, the solution was not going to be to try to suppress it by force alone. You needed to protect the population. But you needed to make the young men who were mounting that violence . . . feel they had a political stake in modern Afghanistan. The truth was in 2001, when our Special Forces, and our intelligence services, helped the northern warlords push the Taliban out of power, first in Kabul, then in Kandahar, the Taliban weren't defeated, they were pushed south and east and down. But they were never defeated. They were pushed out of power . . . And they were not part of the subsequent political settlement.'[15]

Sir Sherard, across whose desk reports of dozens of examples of Taliban brutality must have passed while he was Ambassador and then Britain's Special Representative to Aghanistan and Pakistan, admits the Taliban are violent and unpleasant. But for many southern Pushtuns, in his view, they represent a less bad alternative. And that was why the West needed to use military force but it had to be accompanied by a political outreach and a sense that these people could be brought into 'a fair political settlement', he concludes.

Epilogue

Attacking Iraq after 9/11 was like attacking Mexico after Pearl Harbor.
Max Cleland, ex-Senator for Georgia

After well over a hundred interviews with a wide cast of actors in the Afghan drama, many visits to Afghanistan, mainly to Kabul, but also to Bamiyan in the centre-north and Kandahar in the south, as well as to Washington and New York, I am convinced there is only one answer to the question: Why did it all go wrong in Afghanistan?

It can be summed up in one word: Iraq.

President George Bush's reaction to the al Qaeda attack on the United States on 9/11 – bombing Afghanistan and then using the Northern Alliance to overthrow the Taliban – was quick, cheap and eminently successful, certainly to begin with. Invading Iraq was a very different proposition: ill advised, poorly planned and in the end a near disaster which did enormous damage to the Western cause. And to cap it all, there was no connection with al Qaeda.

As Max Cleland, the ex-Senator for Georgia and Vietnam veteran, shrewdly remarked: attacking Iraq after 9/11 was like attacking Mexico after Pearl Harbor. It made no sense. It was totally irrational: a Neo-Conservative (Neo-Con) agenda in which a novice President, George W. Bush, with little if any knowledge of world affairs – and his ultra right-wing Praetorian Guard, Vice-President Dick Cheney, Secretary for Defense, Donald Rumsfeld, his deputy Paul Wolfowitz and an assortment of like-minded acolytes – decided regime change and the removal of President Saddam Hussein from power would 'democratise' the Middle East, and remove Saddam's threat to America's two allies, Saudi Arabia and Israel.

There was even a suggestion, advanced by Maureen Dowd of the *New York Times*, that Bush was motivated by a personal vendetta, saying of Saddam in a speech in 2002: 'After all, this is the guy who tried to kill my Dad.'[1] The attempt was said to have been planned to coincide with President Bush Senior's official visit to Kuwait in 1993, after the First Gulf War. Most commentators, however, do not believe there was ever a serious plot.

The Neo-Con agenda certainly cut no ice with the assembled wisdom and knowledge of fifty-two former British diplomats, from ambassadors down, who wrote to *The Times* in April 2004, rejecting British Prime Minister Tony Blair's support of George Bush. They pointed out the British were now portrayed throughout 'the Arab and Muslim world as partners in an illegal and brutal occupation in Iraq' and said the conduct of the war had made it clear that there was 'no effective plan for the post-Saddam settlement'.[2] Later, as the casualties mounted – the diplomats remarked it was disgraceful that the coalition had no idea of their number – the highly respected medical journal, the *Lancet*, estimated that almost 655,000 Iraqis, mainly civilians, had been killed and presumably two or three times as many wounded between the start of the war in 2003 and June 2006, while the 2007 Opinion Research Business Survey (ORB) estimated that 1.2 million Iraqis had been killed.

Quite apart from the fifty-two retired diplomats, practically the whole serving Foreign Office must have shared their views but could not say so publicly. I know that my friends in the Foreign Office, some very senior, all thought it was a disaster. But Blair did not take advice, it would seem, except from George Bush, and perhaps God.

The invasion of Afghanistan, as justified as Iraq was unjustified, reflects the same reckless lack of planning in terms of the aftermath – something that Bush seems to have left to Rumsfeld and never bothered to follow up. Kabul, however, suffered much less from looting than Baghdad, partly because there was nothing to loot, and also because the Northern Alliance controlled Kabul better than the Americans did Baghdad.

Tony Blair committed more than 40,000 British troops to the invasion of Iraq, against the better judgement of at least some of his senior generals. British Special Forces acquitted themselves with outstanding skill and courage, but suffered heavy casualties. And although the British

Army as such performed well, their lack of resources and poor political leadership led to serious failures, above all in Basra where they allowed the Shia militias to impose a Taliban-like regime. This made life intolerable for ordinary citizens, especially women, and led Prime Minister Maliki, angry at British inaction, to send in Iraqi troops who, when they got into trouble, had to be baled out by the Americans. It was a shameful situation for the British, relegated to impotence at their airport headquarters in one of Saddam's old palaces.

As the military situation deteriorated in Iraq, President Bush's ratings fell week by week, lower than those of any predecessor apart from the impeached and disgraced Richard Nixon. At the last minute, a retired general, Jack Keene, urged Bush to stake all in the form of a 'surge' of additional troops, and in desperation, one imagines, the President agreed. David Petraeus, then the commander in Iraq, who had rewritten the Army's counter-insurgency manual, took over the plan, and in a brilliant demonstration of how to snatch victory from the jaws of defeat, made it work.

Every British commander in Afghanistan I have spoken to, beginning with General Sir John McColl, who was the first ISAF Commander in 2001–02, to General Sir David Richards in 2006–07, has agreed that the demands of Iraq were all-consuming. McColl, who, as deputy commander in Iraq in 2004 had a ringside seat, recalled that 'the resources flowing in from the US to try and resolve the crisis – and it was a crisis in Iraq at that time – were immense'. Afghanistan did not just take second place. 'It wasn't just a second order, it was of a different order totally . . . The allocation of resources in the widest sense – hardware, men, money and brainpower – between Iraq and Afghanistan, were worlds apart.'[3]

But for the Afghans it was much worse. Their hopes were pinned on Western aid. The news of the American invasion of Iraq was a crippling blow. Dr Ashraf Ghani, the Finance Minister, told me it was the single most important reason for the failure to get Afghanistan back on its feet after 2001. It was 'the worst day for me and the Afghan government', he said in an interview. He knew what it would entail: 'All the oxygen was taken out . . .'

Then there was the refusal of George Bush and Donald Rumsfeld to

have anything to do with 'nation-building'. General McColl soon discovered this was official policy. Choosing his words carefully, he said it was a
'doctrinal thing' and that it 'flowed, I suspect, from higher, probably from
Rumsfeld'.⁴ McColl's deputy, Brigadier White-Spunner, confirmed this,
saying: 'from Rumsfeld's point of view, he didn't want to do nation-building'.⁵ Having overthrown the Taliban, Rumsfeld saw no need to put
anything in its place. They would continue to rely on the warlords who
had helped them to unseat the Taliban while the United States got on with
the more pressing business of getting ready for war with Iraq. Someone,
however, had to do something, so McColl started to train the new Afghan
Army. He recalls the first battalion duly passed out on time in 2002.

But because of the growing demands of Iraq, resources for the new army
dried up and it was only much later the Americans realised that a functioning Afghan Army and police force were crucial to their exit strategy. The
same was true of other forms of institution building. General Richards, for
example, when he arrived in Kabul in 2006, was shocked to find that nothing was being done to train a future civil service, nor did President Karzai
have any sort of war cabinet to help him run the country. As a result
General Richards set up the Policy Action Group (PAG), which did much
to improve the existing lack of government. But, again, when he left and
handed over command to the Americans in 2007, they let it lapse.

Many Afghans, and diplomats like the former British Ambassador in
Kabul, Sir Sherard Cowper-Coles, consider the presidential system
imposed under the Bonn Agreement to have been a mistake, since it
went against the 'grain' of Afghan tribal practice and tradition.
Concentrating all power in the hands of one man – without sufficient
checks and balances – inevitably led to a dictatorial system in which
Karzai had almost absolute powers.

The cult of personality was born.

Mahmoud Saikal, the former Deputy Foreign Minister, resigned in
2006 when he realised Karzai had no intention of curbing corruption.
Since then things have got much worse. The American practice of award-
ing large contracts initially to American companies, and then by extension
to the Afghan mafia families that surround and feed off the Karzai administration, has set a bad example. 'If that is how the Americans themselves

operate, who are they to criticise us if we do the same?' Afghans may well ask. This has given ammunition to the Taliban with its shadow government in half the country's provinces and its system of Sharia law, which is seen as being harsh, but fair. The Western belief that despite the weaknesses and corruption of the Karzai government, most Afghans still prefer it to the Taliban may no longer be true, as Sir Sherard Cowper-Coles told the House of Commons Foreign Affairs Committee in November 2010: in his view, for many southern Pushtuns, Taliban rule may be preferable to a 'predatory narco-Mafia Kabul government'. In my opinion, the attitude is more 'a plague on both your houses'.

Even as the Americans and the British make every effort to achieve the daunting task of putting Humpty Dumpty back together again, one obstacle may make it impossible: the continuing support of Pakistan's spy agency, the ISI, for the Taliban. As President Obama reviews his war strategy after nearly three years of his presidency, he would seem to face two realities: only a negotiated settlement will put an end to the conflict; and such a settlement will only be possible if there is a reversal of, or at least a major change in, Pakistani policy.

So as the Americans, the British and the rest of NATO get ready to start moving out their combat troops in 2014, will Pakistan – meaning the ISI – change its policy and stop playing a double-game? Stop taking billions of American dollars with one hand and supporting, funding and arming the Taliban with the other? Stop helping the Taliban to kill NATO troops, to be brutally frank? Some British experts believe that the ISI will not change. Never, they say. So where does that leave the West – the Americans and the British? No one really knows. Perhaps to another Mumbai and what former Chief of the Defence Staff, Lord Guthrie, that wise old soldier who has seen it all, calls his Doomsday scenario? It goes like this:

There is an incident like the Taj Hotel [in Mumbai] or the Delhi parliament. The armies mobilise like they did in 2001/2 and then there is another incident and the Indians will probably say: 'Well, we will sort it out once and for all, we will have a limited war.' But limited wars often slip into something else. India wouldn't actually do very well in Kashmir to start with, because they would have very little air support. The cloud base is low. Very difficult to advance in that mountainous area against some good troops of Pakistan and soon the people in India will say: 'Well, we aren't winning are we?' So they'll be pressured to do something else and stream across the desert with a million men or go into the Punjab. That would be unstoppable except for nuclear weapons and most Pakistanis believe the Islamic bomb is what's kept them safe. So it is a bad situation. We have got a very sensible Prime Minister [Manmohan Singh, the Indian PM], who calmed things down last time. But he had to talk a lot of his Cabinet out of going to war . . . and he will find it harder next time if there is another time. Quite soon I think there will be pressure to do something.[7]

To avoid the Doomsday scenario, which must be the aim of any rational politician, India and Pakistan must somehow be brought together, persuaded to solve their differences and encouraged to make peace. This will have to start with the Kashmir issue, the principal source of conflict, which, as we have seen, has its origin in Partition. The history of past attempts to defuse it, mainly by means of United Nations resolutions, is, however, one of repeated failure.

The problem seems as intractable today as it has ever been. Just how intractable was defined to me by a very senior Pakistani general, ex-Sandhurst, now retired, under whom the current head of the Pakistan Army, General Ashfaq Kayani, served. 'We cannot rely on Indian intentions,' he says, 'because Indian intentions can change overnight.' India is seven times the size of Pakistan and 90 per cent of their army is mobilised against them. 'Why do they have 90 per cent of their armed forces bearing down on us?' he asks. He insists India remains a threat and is gloomy about a possible settlement. 'It is all related to the Kashmir issue, but the Indians won't budge. They don't have to and they won't budge . . . I think of course Pakistan would appreciate that at least this should remain on the agenda . . . But to be honest I don't think anyone can really do anything about it – the Indians won't budge and nobody in the world can make them budge, least of all Pakistan.'[8]

India's military and economic superiority of three or four or even seven to one over Pakistan, has led to an arrogance of power which, in turn, has bred a reluctance to compromise. In Pakistan, the smaller, weaker neighbour, it has created the paranoid fear of domination and even invasion by India. Being a military dictatorship, despite periods of civilian rule, Pakistan has reacted in two ways. One, by establishing or supporting a viper's nest of terrorist organisations – like Lashkar-e-Taiba (LeT, The Army of the Pure) and Jaish-e-Mohammed (JeM, The Army of Mohammed) – originally to fight the Indians in Kashmir. The other was to develop the policy of strategic depth. If India were to invade, the theory goes, the Pakistan Army would have only one place it could retreat to – Afghanistan. Hence the long-standing and ruthless determination to have a pliant vassal state on its western border, with a client government in Kabul. This was the reason they favoured the unsavoury Gulbuddin Hekmatyar, the founder of the Hisb-i-Islami Party. When he failed to prove a winner, they put their money – or rather the Americans' and Saudis' money – on the even more extreme but bigger and more successful Taliban.

'Strategic depth' became the Pakistan Army's mantra, and the Taliban fitted the bill in every way. When President Musharraf said, before 9/11, that recognition of the Taliban government in Kabul was in Pakistan's national interest, he was expressing the considered view of the Pakistan Army and the ISI. When he publicly reversed his stance after 9/11, under intense American pressure, it was a front; there was no change of heart. And when the opportunity for the resurrection of the Taliban offered itself in 2002, and later, the ISI seized it with both hands.

The policy of 'strategic depth' is the key to understanding Pakistan's *Weltanschauung*. It informs the whole war effort on behalf of the Taliban insurgency – the *jihad* mentality which starts in the *madrassas* and brainwashes young Pakistanis to join the Taliban and fight NATO in Afghanistan, and others to enter the suicide bomber camps. Unless this phobia can be overcome by better education and a more liberal outlook at home, and a concerted diplomatic offensive by the rest of the world, the immediate future will continue to look grim.

In the last resort, only an American President, with the support of Britain, France, Germany and the rest of NATO, plus the regional powers of China, Russia, Iran and Saudi Arabia, has the power and influence to bring India and Pakistan to the negotiating table, and to persuade them to make a peace in South Asia which will embrace Afghanistan. That means persuading India to compromise over Kashmir and Pakistan to abandon its out-and-out support for the Taliban. The brutality with which the ISI is conducting the Taliban insurgency – a brutality only matched by that of the Indian Army in suppressing the resistance in Kashmir – must be stopped. ISI encouragement, in fact deliberate ordering, of the methodical destruction of Afghanistan's infrastructure – schools, hospitals, bridges, roads – revealed by Taliban commanders interviewed by Matt Waldman in 'The Sun in the Sky' is wholly unacceptable. Especially if it is being financed by American dollars, as it appears to be.

It is time America got tough. Pakistan is broke. American dollars keep it solvent – just. America therefore has enormous leverage over Pakistan. It is time the most powerful country in the world started to use its muscle to persuade Pakistan, above all its army and the ISI, that it is in their best interests to abandon jihadism, and to cooperate with the United States and the Afghan government in finding a solution to the Afghan War.

But India is also blameworthy. It has consistently refused to discuss the Kashmir problem and commits a large part of its army to crushing opposition in Kashmir – much as Israel tries to crush Palestinian opposition in the West Bank and Gaza. Both are pointless exercises in that they will never achieve a peaceful solution. Only negotiation and compromise can do that, as Britain discovered after the expenditure of much blood and money in Northern Ireland; and whatever his other failings that is one success no one can deny Tony Blair, although not without the able assistance of his fellow-negotiator, Senator George Mitchell. To the outside observer Northern Ireland often seemed insoluble and yet peace, apart from the actions of a few hotheads, was finally achieved – which must give us all hope. Kashmir and Palestine remain sources of world tension, incendiary situations which have repeatedly burst into flames, leading to war between India and Pakistan on the one hand, and Israel and the Arab world on the other; wars which have led to the death, destruction and displacement of hundreds of thousands of innocent civilians and further poisoned relations between Islam and the West.

As in Northern Ireland, the killing in Afghanistan needs to be brought to an end. Many Afghans, as well as Westerners, feel that it is time to put away the mailed fist of military action and replace it with the velvet glove of diplomacy. As Winston Churchill said at the White House in 1954, and he usually got it right: 'To jaw-jaw is always better than to war-war.' It is time to restore the balance.

. One final thought. In the five months, from May until the end of October 2011, there has been a dramatic sea change in high-level American thinking, both military and political, caused first by the clinical extermination of Osama bin Laden, killed like a rat in a trap on 2 May in Abbottabad, Pakistan; an event which changed the world. And largely as a consequence, what might be called the Mullen-Tomsen school of thought has emerged, which basically says that the Pakistan Army, in the shape of its all-powerful spy agency, the ISI, is playing and has been playing for a very long time a dirty game of double cross with its hugely generous American allies, and this has to stop. Right now. 'Or else,' as Ambassador Tomsen put it.

So far the White House and Hillary Clinton have taken a softer line, holding out at least a sort of olive branch. But to back down now would merely encourage Pakistan to deny everything, as they have always done, on the principle that the bigger the lie the more people will believe it.

Will the Americans finally get tough? Impose sanctions? Cut off the funding? We shall see. The future not only of Afghanistan but of much of the world may depend on it.

Notes

Foreword

1 Much of the historical detail in this Foreword is taken from Isobel Shaw's *Pakistan Handbook*, Local Colour Ltd, Hong Kong, 1998.

Chapter 1: Zia and the ISI

1 Personal communication from General Zia, Rawalpindi, 1984.
2 Personal communication from Zaid Rifai, London, 1970–71.
3 Interview with King Hussein of Jordan, Amman, 1971.
4 Interview with British Army sources, Amman, 1971.
5 Interview with General Zia, Rawalpindi, 1977.
6 Minutes were taken of conversations and typed up as the official record.
7 'It might be Afghanistan today, but it could be Pakistan tomorrow, even if it's in fifty years,' he told me. Personal communication 1984–5.
8 Like the Americans in Vietnam, the Red Army in Afghanistan was a conscript army, most of whom did not want to be there.

Chapter 2: The Coming of the Taliban

1 Nancy Hatch Dupree, *An Historical Guide to Afghanistan*, Afghan Tourist Organization, Kabul, 1977, pp. 269–70.
2 Louis Dupree, *Afghanistan*, Princeton University Press, New Jersey, 1980, pp. 77, 314.
3 Nancy Hatch Dupree, *An Historical Guide* p. 467.
4 Kathy Gannon, *I is for Infidel*, Public Affairs, New York, 2005, pp. 92–3.
5 Ibid.
6 Louis Dupree, *Afghanistan*, Princeton University Press, New Jersey, 1980; Dupree describes him as 'a brutal, brilliant, military tactician on a scraggly Mongol pony', p. 316.

Chapter 3: Tora Bora 1

1 Interviews with Panjsheri *mujahideen*, Panjsher Valley, 1982.
2 Personal communication from one of Haji Zamar's former *mujahideen*, Kabul, 2010.
3 Interviews with local eyewitnesses, Astana, Panjsher Valley, 2001–3.
4 Quoted by Bruce Riedel, *The Search for Al Qaeda*, Brookings Institution Press, Washington DC, 2008, p. 1.
5 Personal communication.
6 Interview with Haji Zahir, Jalalabad, 2005. He was certainly on the spot but whether his information is as accurate as that of the senior intelligence source in Kabul is doubtful.
7 Ibid.
8 Ibid.
9 Quoted in Peter Bergen, *The Osama bin Laden I Know*, Free Press, New York, 2006, pp. 330–31.
10 Ibid., p. 330, quoting Commander Musa.
11 Dalton Fury, *Kill Bin Laden, A Delta Force Commander's Account of the Hunt for the World's Most Wanted Man*, New York, 2008.
12 Bergen, *Osama bin Laden*, p. 330.
13 Ibid.
14 Fury, *Kill Bin Laden*, p. xxiii.
15 Personal communication.
16 'Tora Bora Revisted: How We Failed to Get bin Laden and Why it Matters Today'. A Report to Members of the Committee on Foreign Relations, United States Senate, 30 November 2009.
17 Interview with the author, London, 2010.
18 Ibid. p. 142.
19 Ibid., p. 142.
20 Ibid., pp. 142–3.
21 Senate Foreign Relations Committee Report, p. 42.
22 Ibid.
23 The United States Special Operations Command History, 6th edition, quoted in the US Senate Foreign Relations Committee Report on Tora Bora, March 2008, p. 33.
24 Senate Committee Report, p. 11.
25 Ibid.
26 Personal communication.
27 Ibid.
28 Dalton Fury, Senate Foreign Relations Committee Report, p. 12.
29 Fury, *Kill Bin Laden*, p. 287.
30 Ibid.
31 Ibid.
32 General Tommy Franks, *American Soldier*, Regan Books, New York, 2004.
33 'Tora Bora Revisited: How We Failed to Get Bin Laden and Why it Matters Today', US Senate Committee on Foreign Relations, Washington, 30 November 2009, p. 12; hereafter 'US Senate Report on Tora Bora'.

Chapter 4: Tora Bora 2

1   Gary Berntsen and Ralph Pezzullo, *Jawbreaker: The Attack on Bin Laden and Al Qaeda*, Crown Publishers, New York, 2005, p. 86.
2   US Senate Report on Tora Bora.
3   Ibid.
4   Ibid., p. 2.
5   *Al Majalla*, October 2002.
6   Ibid.
7   Bergen, *Osama bin Laden*, 2006, pp. 383–4.
8   General Michael DeLong, *Inside CentCom*, Regnery, Washington DC, 2004, and US Senate Report on Tora Bora, p. 5.
9   *Inside CentCom* cited in the US Senate Report on Tora Bora, p. 8.
10 Bergen, *Osama bin Laden*, pp. 333, 334, 335.
11 Berntsen, *Jawbreaker*, pp. 86, 307.
12 Ibid., pp. 290–1.
13 Ibid., p. 277 and see p. 291.
14 Quoted in US Senate Committee Report on Tora Bora, p. 7.
15 Berntsen, *Jawbreaker*, pp. 290–1.
16 Ibid., p. 307.
17 Interview on PBS Television's *Frontline* programme.
18 US Senate Committee Report on Tora Bora, p. 8.
19 Personal communication.
20 Fury, *Kill Bin Laden*, p. 254.
21 Ibid.
22 Ibid.
23 Ibid., pp. 256–7.
24 Ibid., p. 257.
25 Ibid., pp. 292–3.
26 Personal communication from Dalton Fury to author.
27 Ibid.
28 Ibid.
29 Fury, *Kill Bin Laden*, p. 294.
30 US Senate Committee Report on Tora Bora, p. 2.
31 Ibid.
32 Ibid., pp. 2–3.
33 George Tenet, *At the Center of the Storm*, HarperCollins, New York, 2006, cited in US Senate Report, p. 13.
34 US Senate Committee Report on Tora Bora, p. 13.
35 Ibid.
36 Ron Suskind, *One Percent Doctrine*, cited in US Senate Report, p. 13.
37 Personal communication.
38 Ibid.
39 US Senate Committee Report on Tora Bora, p. 15.
40 Ibid.
41 Ahmed Rashid, *Descent into Chaos*, Penguin Books, London, 2008, p. 99.

42 OBL audio tape broadcast by Al Jazeera TV 11 February 2003, cited in US Senate Committee Report on Tora Bora, p. 14.
43 Ibid., p. 2.
44 Frank Leeson, *Frontier Legion: With the Khassadars of North Waziristan*, The Leeson Archive, West Sussex, 2003.
45 Personal communication.

Chapter 5: The British in Kabul, 2001–2002

1 Rashid, *Descent into Chaos*, pp. 104–5.
2 Ahmed Rashid, *Taliban*, Yale University Press, New Haven and London, p. 72.
3 Interview with General John McColl, London, 2009.
4 Interview with Brigadier Barney White-Spunner, London, 2010.
5 Ibid.
6 Peter Levi, *The Light Garden of the Angel King*, Palla Athene Arts, 1999.
7 Interview with White-Spunner.
8 Ibid.
9 Ibid.
10 Interview with McColl.
11 Ibid.
12 Ibid.
13 Interview with Lakhdar Brahimi, Paris, 2010.
14 Interview with Lord Boyce, London, 2010.
15 Interview with McColl.
16 Ibid.
17 Interview with White-Spunner.
18 Ibid.
19 Ibid.
20. Christina Lamb, 'US friendly fire almost killed Karzai', *Sunday Times*, 2 October 2011.
21 Interview with White-Spunner.
22 Interview with General John McColl, ISAF HQ, Kabul, 2002.
23 Ibid.
24 Interview with White-Spunner.
25 Interview with McColl, London, 2009.
26 Ibid.
27 Ibid.
28 See Chapter 12.
29 Matt Waldman interview (March 2010) for 'The Sun in the Sky', see Chapter 22.
30 Ibid.
31 Interview with McColl, London, 2009.
32 Ibid.
33 Ibid.

Chapter 6: The Great Game in the South

1   Interview with Lieutenant Colonel Henry Worsley, London, 2010.
2   Ibid.
3   'British Troops "will be targets in Afghanistan"', *Sunday Telegraph*, 29 January 2006.
4   Interview with Worsley.
5   Ibid.
6   Press conference, Kabul, June 2006.
7   *The Times*, 9 June 2010.
8   Ibid.
9   Interview with Lieutenant Colonel Stuart Tootal, London, 2010.
10 Ibid.
11 Ibid.
12 Ibid.
13 Ibid.
14 Ibid.
15 Ibid.
16 Private communication with Brigadier Ed Butler.
17 Colonel Stuart Tootal, *Danger Close*, John Murray, London, 2009, p. 10.
18 Ibid., pp. 44, et seq.; interview with Tootal.
19 Interview with Tootal.
20 Ibid.
21 Ibid.
22 Christina Lamb, *Sunday Times*, 10 September 2006.
23 Ibid.
24 Interview with Tootal.
25 Ibid. Middle-ranking officers in the field were told not to complain about shortages, particularly helicopters, when talking to visiting VIPs (private conversation with senior British Army source, UK, 2010).
26 Interview with General Lord Guthrie, London, 2010.
27 General Lord Guthrie in *The Times*, 25 July 2009.
28 Ibid.
29 Interview with Lord Guthrie.

Chapter 7: Ed Butler and Musa Qala

1   Interview with Lieutenant Colonel Worsley, London, 2010.
2   Tim Ripley, *16 Air Assault Brigade*, Pen and Sword, London, 2008, p. 238.
3   Ibid.
4   Personal communication with senior British Army source.
5   Interview with Brigadier Ed Butler, London, 2010.
6   Ibid.
7   Ibid.
8   Ibid.

9   Ibid.
10   Ibid.
11   Ibid.
12   Ibid.
13   Ibid.
14   Tootal, *Danger Close*, pp. xiii–xiv.
15   Interview with Butler.
16   Ibid.
17   Ibid.
18   Ibid.
19   Ibid.
20   Ibid.
21   Ibid.
22   Quoted by Butler in ibid.
23   Ibid.
24   Ibid.
25   Ibid.
26   Ibid.
27   Ibid.
28   Ibid.
29   Ibid.
30   Ibid.
31   Ibid.

Chapter 8: Patronage or Corruption

1   Entitled 'Afghanistan Then and Now: What We Can Learn from History', the lecture was based on the essay of the same name published in 2008.
2   Michael Semple, *Afghanistan Here and Now*, Sarsen Press, Winchester, p. 48.
3   Ibid., p. 41.
4   Ibid.
5   Ibid.
6   Semple quoting Elphinstone in ibid., p. 41.
7   Ibid., p. 42.
8   Ibid., p. 42.
9   Semple quoting Elphinstone in ibid., p. 41.
10   Ibid., p. 42.
11   Ibid., p. 43.
12   Ibid.
13   Ibid., pp. 43, 44.
14   Ibid., p. 44.
15   Ibid.
16   Ibid.
17   Ibid., pp. 44–5.
18   Ibid., p. 45.

19 Ibid., pp. 46–7.
20 Ibid., p. 47.
21 Ibid., pp. 47–8.
22 Ibid., pp. 48–9.
23 Ibid., p. 49.
24 Victoria Schofield, *Afghan Frontier: Feuding and Fighting in Central Asia*, Tauris Parke Paperbacks, London, 2003, p. 116.

Chapter 9: The Narco State

1 'Brother of Afghan Leader said to be paid by CIA', *New York Times*, 27 October 2009.
2 Carlotta Gall, 'Afghan Poppy Growing Reaches Record Level, UN Says', *New York Times*, 19 November 2004.
3 Former CIA officer, Kabul, quoted in the *New York Times*, 27 October 2009.
4 Quoted from Drew Pearson's column in the *Washington Post*, 30 April 1952, mentioning Somoza's impending visit.
5 Gretchen Peters, *Seeds of Terror*, St Martin's Press, New York, 2009, p. 136.
6 Ibid.
7 Ibid., pp. 136–7.
8 Interview with General Nick Carter, Kandahar, August 2010.
9 Ibid.
10 Peters, *Seeds of Terror*, p. 20, quoting Thomas Schweich, 'Is Afghanistan a Narco-State?', *New York Times* magazine, 27 July 2008.
11 Schweich, 'Is Afghanistan a Narco-State?', *New York Times* magazine, 27 July 2008.
12 Ibid.
13 Ibid.
14 Ibid.
15 Ibid.
16 Ibid.
17 Ibid.
18 Ibid.
19 Interview with Dr Ashraf Ghani, Kabul, 2010.
20 Ibid.
21 Interview with Dr Ghani.
22 Ibid.
23 Ibid.
24 Ibid.
25 Ibid.
26 Ibid.
27 Ibid.
28 Ibid.
29 Peters, *Seeds of Terror*, p. 29.
30 Interview with Dr Ghani.
31 Ibid.

32 Ibid.
33 Antonio Mario Costa, 'Corruption in Afghanistan', UNODC Drug Report, January 2010.
34 Peters, *Seeds of Terror*, p. 186.
35 Ibid., p. 209.
36 Ibid.
37 Ibid.
38 Ibid.
39 Interview with Amrullah Saleh, Kabul, 2010.
40 Peters, *Seeds of Terror*, p. 21.
41 Personal communication, Helmand, 2010.

Chapter 10: Sherard and the French

1 Sir Sherard Cowper-Coles as quoted in *Le Canard Enchaîné*, Paris, September 2008.
2 Ibid.
3 Ibid., but denied by Sir Sherard Cowper-Coles (see later in chapter).
4 Ibid.
5 Quai d'Orsay spokesperson, reported in Elaine Sciolino, 'Afghan "Dictator" Proposed in Leaked Cable', *New York Times*, 3 October 2008.
6 Interview with Sir Sherard Cowper-Coles, *Today* programme, BBC Radio 4, 16 November 2010.
7 Afghan official, anonymous.
8 Italian government spokesperson, reported in Tom Coghlan and Nico Hines, 'Silvio Berlusconi issues denials over Afghanistan bribe scandal', *The Times*, 15 October 2009.
9 Leaked to Agence France-Presse (AFP) by Afghan official on condition of anonymity.
10 Interview with Brigadier Mark Carleton-Smith, London, 2010.

Chapter 11: The Girl Who Ran Away from Her Husband

1 *Time* magazine, July 2010.
2 Ibid.
3 Ibid.
4 Quoted in local media at the time.
5 Ibid.
6 Zareen Taj, *Hazaristan Times*, 1 May 2009.
7 Private information.
8 Ibid.
9 Karl Eikenberry telegram to Hillary Clinton, 6 November 2009.
10 Eikenberry telegram to Clinton, 9 November 2009.
11 *New York Times*, 'US Envoy's Cables Show Worries on Afghan Plans', 28 January 2010.

12 *The Times*, 'Karzai Feels Chill After Rants at the West: Pressure Grows on Afghan Leader over "Erratic" Outbursts', by Jerome Starkey, 7 April 2010.
13 Ibid.
14 Ibid.
15 Ibid.
16 Private communication, May 2011.
17 Philip Crowley, press conference, Kabul, August 2010.

Chapter 12: The State of the Insurgency

1   Private conversation with senior Western diplomat.
2   Ibid.
3   Ibid.
4   Ibid.
5   Ibid.
6   Ibid.
7   Ibid.
8   Rashid, *Descent into Chaos*, pp. 134 et seq.
9   Private conversation with senior Western diplomat.
10 Ibid.
11 Interview with Vendrell, London, 2010.
12 Ibid.
13 Ibid.
14 Private conversation with senior Western diplomat.
15 Ibid.
16 Ibid.
17 Ibid.
18 Private information.
19 Private conversation with senior Western diplomat.
20 Ibid.
21 McChrystal's review of the war and request for more troops to President Obama.
22 Carlotta Gall, 'Afghan Raid Leaves Trail of Shock, Grief and Anger', *New York Times*, 5 July 2002.
23 BBC news website (www.bbc.co.uk/news/world-south-asia) 9 March 2011.
24 Interview with Amrullah Saleh, Kabul, November 2009.
25 Interview with General Sir Graeme Lamb, Kabul, 2010.
26 Ibid.
27 Ibid.
28 Ibid.

Chapter 13: The Protection-Money Racket

1   Interview with Francesc Vendrell, London, spring 2010.
2   Interview with Amrullah Saleh, Kabul, 2010.
3   Dupree, *Afghanistan*, pp. 334 et seq.

4 Ibid.
5 Carlotta Gall, 'Kandahar, a Battlefield Even Before US Offensive', in the *New York Times*, 26 March 2010.
6 Ibid.
7 Ibid.
8 Ibid.

Chapter 14: A Coalition Government

1 Gilles Dorronsoro, 'Worsening Outlook in Afghanistan', Q&A, Carnegie Endowment for International Peace, 9 September 2010 (www.carnegieendowment.org/2010/09/09/worsening-outlook-in-afghanistan).
2 Cf. reports in *The Times*, including article by David Kilcullen, and the *New York Times*, 'Coalition Forces Routing Taliban in Key Afghan Region', Carlotta Gall, 20 October 2010.
3 Dorronsoro, 'Worsening Outlook'.

Chapter 15: Brown and Blair: Double Nemesis

1 General Sir Richard Dannatt, *Leading from the Front*, Bantam Press, London, 2010, p. 184.
2 Ibid.
3 Ibid.
4 Ibid.
5 Ibid.
6 Ibid., p. 209.
7 Ibid., p. 210.
8 Ibid., p. 212.
9 Ibid.
10 Personal communication.
11 Ibid.
12 *Evening Standard*.
13 Personal communication.
14 Dannatt, *Leading from the Front*, p. 247.
15 Ibid., p. 248.
16 Ibid.
17 Ibid., p. 316.
18 Ibid., p. 345.
19 Ibid.
20 Ibid., p. 346.
21 Ibid., pp. 346–7.
22 Ibid., p. 350.
23 General Sir Richard Dannatt, reported in *Daily Mail*, 16 July 2009.
24 Documents declassified in 2005 for the Chilcot Inquiry.
25 Interview with author, London, 2010.

26 Interview with General Sir Mike Jackson, London, 2010.
27 Personal communication, 2011.
28 Ibid.
29 Ibid.

Chapter 16: General Richards Takes Over

1 Interview with General Sir David Richards, London, September 2010.
2 Interview with General Sir David Richards, Dorset, spring 2010.
3 Interview with General Sir David Richards, London, 2010.
4 Ibid.
5 Interview with Richards, London, September 2010.
6 Interview with Richards, London, 2010.
7 Ibid.
8 Ibid.

Chapter 17: The Battles of Panjwai and Musa Qala

1 Interview with Richards, London, 2010.
2 Interview with Butler, London, 2010.
3 Interview with Richards, London, 2010.
4 Ibid.
5 Ibid.
6 Ibid.
7 Ibid.
8 Richard Norton-Taylor, 'Afghanistan Close to Anarchy', *Guardian*, 22 July 2006.
9 Interview with Richards, London, 2010.
10 Carlotta Gall, 'Petraeus Confident as He Leaves Afghanistan', *New York Times*, 10 July 2011.

Chapter 18: McChrystal Brought Down by *Rolling Stone*

1 Interview with Lamb.
2 Matthew Rosenberg, 'Afghanistan Money Probe Hits Close to President', *Wall Street Journal*, 12 August 2010.
3 Ibid.
4 'Karzai officials seen hindering bribery probes', *Washington Post*, 28 June 2010.
5 American media reports, August 2010.
6 Ibid.
7 Ibid.
8 Rosenberg, 'Afghanistan Money Probe Hits Close to President', *Wall Street Journal*, 12 August 2010.
9 Ibid.

10 Private conversation with US anti-corruption official, Kabul, 2010.

11 'Graft-Fighting Prosecutor Fired in Afghanistan', Dexter Filkins and Alissa Rubin, *New York Times*, 28 August 2010.

12 Ibid.

13 Ibid.

14 Ibid.

15 Ibid.

16 Ibid.

Chapter 19: The Afghan Mafia

1 Interview with Sultana, Kabul, summer 2010.

2 Ibid.

3 Interview with Mina, Jalalabad, May 2010.

4 Ibid.

5 Interview with Shukria Barakzai, Kabul, May 2010.

6 Ibid.

7 Interview with Zaid Siddig, Kabul, 2010.

8 Ibid.

9 Interview with Mahmoud Saikal, Kabul, 2009.

10 Ibid.

11 Ibid.

12 Ibid.

Chapter 20: The Beginning of the End?

1 These sources, all of whom are reliable, cannot be named for personal security reasons.

2 Senior security source who does not wish to be named.

3 Quoted by Amrullah Saleh in interview with author, Kabul, August 2010.

4 Interview with Saleh, Kabul, August 2010.

5 Private information, Kabul, 2010.

6 Interview with Saleh.

7 Ibid.

8 Ibid.

9 Private information, Kabul, July/August 2010.

10 Interview with Saleh, Kabul, August 2010.

11 Report in US media, Washington DC, December 2010.

12 Interview with Saleh, Kabul, August 2010.

Chapter 21: The Taliban in Quetta

1 Quoted in Carlotta Gall, 'At Border, Signs of Pakistan Role in Taliban Surge: Link to Religious Parties', *New York Times*, 21 January 2007.

2 Ibid.
3 Ibid.
4 Ibid.
5 Ibid.
6 Ibid.
7 Ibid.
8 The incident is described in detail in Sandy Gall, *Don't Worry About the Money Now*, Hamish Hamilton, London, 1983, pp. 68–74.
9 *New York Times*, 21 January 2007.

Chapter 22: The Sun in the Sky

1 Quoted in Matt Waldman, 'The Sun in the Sky: the relationship between Pakistan's ISI and Afghan insurgents', Carr Center for Human Rights Policy, Kennedy School of Government, Harvard University, June 2010, p. 18.
2 Ibid., p. 21.
3 Ibid., p. 11.
4 Ibid.
5 Ibid., p. 1.
6 Ibid., p. 2.
7 Ibid., p. 6.
8 Ibid., p. 2.
9 Ibid., p. 3, and quoting Rashid, *Descent into Chaos*, p. 60.
10 Ibid., p. 4.
11 Waldman interview March 2010, in ibid.
12 Steve Coll in *New Yorker*, 24 May 2010, quoted in ibid.
13 Coll in *New Yorker*, 1 March 2010, quoted in ibid.
14 Ibid., p. 5.
15 Waldman interviews March 2010, in ibid., pp. 6–7.
16 Ibid., pp. 7–8.
17 Ibid.
18 Waldman interviews in ibid., p. 8, and quoting Special Security Initiative of the Policy Action Group's 'Insurgency and Terrorism in Afghanistan: Who is Fighting and Why?', June 2006, and Rashid, *Descent into Chaos*, p. 368.
19 Waldman, 'The Sun in the Sky', p. 9.
20 Ibid., p. 8, quoting Coll in *New Yorker*, 1 March 2010.
21 Ibid., p. 9, quoting Christine Fair, 'The Time for Sober Realism: renegotiating US relations with Pakistan', *Washington Post Quarterly*, Vol 32: 2, pp. 161–3.
22 Ibid., p. 9, quoting Thomas H. Johnson and Chris M. Mason, 'No Sign until the Burst of Fire; Understanding the Pakistan-Afghanistan Frontier', *International Security*, Vol. 32: 4, 2008.
23 Ibid., p. 10.
24 Kathy Gannon, *I is for Infidel*, p. 93.
25 Waldman, 'The Sun in the Sky', pp. 10–11.
26 Ibid., p. 12.

27 Waldman interviews, March 2010, ibid., p. 12.
28 Ibid.
29 Ibid., pp. 12–13.
30 Ibid.
31 Ibid., p. 13.
32 Ibid.
33 Ibid., fn. 55, quoting Special Security Initiative of PAG, 'Insurgency and Terrorism in Afghanistan'.
34 Ibid., pp. 14–16.
35 Ibid., p. 16.
36 Jalaluddin Haqqani was a famous *mujahideen* commander against the Russians. The network is now run by his son Siraj.
37 Waldman, 'The Sun in the Sky', p. 19.
38 Ibid., p. 20.
39 Ibid., p. 21.
40 Cf. report by FinTRACA (Financial Transactions and Reports Analysis Center of Afghanistan), the anti-money-laundering agency in Kabul, on the transfer of about $1 billion (£636 million) in Saudi riyals from private donors in Saudi Arabia to Pakistan where it was changed into dollars and rupees and then smuggled into North Waziristan. The FinTRACA representative in Kabul said since there was no real industry or business in North Waziristan, they presumed the money was destined for terrorist purposes; interview with author, August 2010, Kabul.
41 Waldman, 'The Sun in the Sky', p. 19.
42 Ibid., pp. 19–20.
43 Ibid., pp. 16–20.
44 Ibid.
45 Ibid., p. 21.
46 Ibid., pp. 21–2.
47 Mark Mazzetti in the *New York Times*, 26 July 2010.
48 Ibid.

Chapter 23: Turning the Tide

1 Quoted by Anthony Loyd in 'Taliban on Verge of Collapse', *The Times*, 8 October 2010.
2 Ibid.
3 Carlotta Gall, 'Coalition Forces Routing Taliban in Key Afghan Region', *New York Times*, 20 October 2010.
4 Maj. Gen. Nick Carter quoted in ibid.
5 Ibid.
6 Ibid.
7 Carlotta Gall, 'Coalition Forces Routing Taliban in Key Afghan Region', *New York Times*, 20 October 2010.
8 David Kilcullen, 'Unless We Beat Corruption This is All For Nothing', *The Times*, 30 October 2010.

9 Ibid.
10 Q & A with General McChrystal at a public dinner in the UK, November 2010.
11 Ibid.
12 Transcript of Sir Sherard's Cowper-Coles' speech to the House of Commons' Foreign Affairs Committee, 9 November 2010.
13 In a dig at Rory Stewart, Conservative MP for Penrith and the Borders, Sir Sherard added: 'I'm glad to see some of the members of the Troops Out movement with whom I have debated in the past, have adopted a more nuanced approach recently and that's a very good thing,' (Cowper-Coles to Foreign Affairs Committee, 9 November 2010).
14 Ibid.
15 Whether the Taliban were defeated or not is arguable. Intensive American bombing and heavy casualties inflicted by Northern Alliance ground troops forced the Taliban to surrender en masse in Kunduz in November 2001. General Dostum's Uzbek troops imprisoned thousands, although many senior Taliban, including one particularly brutal commander, the one-legged Mullah Dadullah, bribed their way out and hundreds of Pakistani and Arab fighters were evacuated in a Pakistani airlift cleared by the Americans. Mullah Dadullah was later tracked down and killed by British Special Forces. See Ahmed Rashid's *Descent into Chaos*.

Epilogue

1 *New York Times*, 'Who's Your Daddy Party?', Maureen Dowd, 28 March 2004.
2 Letter to *The Times*, 'There Was No Plan for the Post-Saddam Settlement', 27 April 2004.
3 Interview with General John McColl, February 2010.
4 Ibid.
5 Interview with White-Spunner.
6 Cowper-Coles to Foreign Affairs Committee, 9 November 2010.
7 Interview with General Lord Guthrie, London, 2010.
8 Interview with retired senior Pakistani general, Islamabad, 2010.

Select Bibliography

Articles and Reports

Various articles from *The Times*, the *Telegraph*, the *Evening Standard*, the *New York Times*, the *Washington Post*, the *Wall Street Journal*, *Time* magazine.

Dorronsoro, Gilles, 'Worsening Outlook in Afghanistan', Q&A, Carnegie Endowment for International Peace, 9 September 2010 (www.carnegieendowment.org/2010/09/09/worsening-outlook-in-afghanistan)

Semple, Michael, 'Afghanistan Here and Now', Sarsen Press, 2008.

Waldman, Matt, 'The Sun in the Sky: the relationship between Pakistan's ISI and Afghan insurgents', Carr Center for Human Rights Policy, Kennedy School of Government, Harvard University, June 2010

Books

Allen, Charles, *God's Terrorists: The Wahhabi Cult and the Hidden Roots of Modern Jihad*, Da Capo Press, London, 2006

————(ed.), *Plain Tales from the Raj: Images of British India in the Twentieth Century*, Andre Deutsch, London, 1975

Bergen, Peter L., *The Longest War: The Enduring Conflict between America and al Qaeda*, Free Press, New York, 2011

————*The Osama bin Laden I Know: An Oral History of al Qaeda's Leader*, Free Press, New York, 2006

————*Holy War Inc.*, Free Press, New York, 2002

Berntsen, Gary, and Pezzullo, Ralph, *Jawbreaker: The Attack on bin Laden and al Qaeda: a Personal Account by the CIA's Key Field Commander*, Crown Publishers, New York, 2005

Bin Laden, Najwa, bin Laden, Omar, and Sasson, Jean, *Growing Up bin Laden: Osama's Wife and Son Take Us Inside Their Secret World*, St Martin's Press, New York, 2009

Bradsher, Henry S., *Afghanistan and the Soviet Union*, Duke Press Policy Studies, Durham, N.C., 1983

Byron, Robert, *The Road to Oxiana*, Macmillan, London, 1937

Caroe, Olaf, *The Pathans 550 BC–AD 1957*, OUP, Karachi, 1958

Chandrasekaran, Rajiv, *Imperial Life in the Emerald City: Inside Baghdad's Green Zone*, Bloomsbury, London, 2007

Coll, Steve, *Ghost Wars: The Secret History of the CIA, Afghanistan and Bin Laden, from the Soviet Invasion to September 10, 2001*, Penguin Books, London, 2004

Dannatt, General Sir Richard, *Leading from the Front*, Bantam Press, London, 2010

DeLong, General Michael, *Inside CentCom: The Unvarnished Truth About the Wars in Afghanistan and Iraq*, Regnery, Washington DC, 2004

Dobbins, James F., *After the Taliban: Nation-Building in Afghanistan*, Potomac Books, Inc., Washington DC, 2008

Dorronsoro, Gilles, *Révolution afghane*, Karthala, Paris, 2000·

Dupree, Louis, *Afghanistan*, Princeton University Press, Princeton, New Jersey, 1980

Dupree, Nancy Hatch, *An Historical Guide to Afghanistan*, Afghan Tourist Organization, Kabul, 1977

Franks, General Tommy, *American Soldier*, Regan Books, New York, 2004

Friedman, George, *America's Secret War: Inside the Hidden Worldwide Struggle between the United States and its Enemies*, Little, Brown, London, 2004

Fury, Dalton, *Kill Bin Laden: A Delta Force Commander's Account of the Hunt for the World's Most Wanted Man*, St Martin's Press, New York, 2008

Gannon, Kathy, *I is for Infidel, From Holy War to Holy Terror, 18 Years Inside Afghanistan*, Public Affairs, New York, 2005

Grey, Stephen, *Operation Snake Bite: The Explosive True Story of an Afghan Desert Siege*, Viking, London, 2009

Hennessey, Patrick, *The Junior Officer's Reading Club: Killing Time and Fighting Wars*, Allen Lane, London, 2009

Hosseini, Khaled, *A Thousand Splendid Suns*, Bloomsbury, London, 2007

——— *The Kite Runner*, Bloomsbury, London, 2003

Kilcullen, David, *The Accidental Guerrilla: Fighting Small Wars in the Midst of a Big One*, Oxford University Press, Oxford, 2009

Lamb, Christina, *Waiting for Allah: Pakistan's Struggle for Democracy*, Hamish Hamilton, London, 1991

Leeson, Frank, *Frontier Legion: With the Khassadars of North Waziristan*, The Leeson Archive, Ferring, West Sussex, 2003

Macrory, Patrick, *Signal Catastrophe: The Retreat from Kabul, 1842*, Hodder & Stoughton, London, 1966

Neumann, Ronald E., *The Other War: Winning and Losing in Afghanistan*, Potomac Books, Inc., Washington DC, 2009

Newby, Eric, *A Short Walk in the Hindu Kush*, Secker & Warburg, London, 1958

Peters, Gretchen, *Seeds of Terror: How Heroin is Bankrolling the Taliban and al Qaeda*, Thomas Dunne Books, St Martin's Press, New York, 2009

Rashid, Ahmed, *Descent into Chaos: The world's most unstable region and the threat to global security*, Penguin Books, London, 2008

——— *Taliban: Militant Islam, Oil and Fundamentalism in Central Asia*, Yale University Press, New Haven and London, 2001

Ricks, Thomas E., *The Gamble: General David Petraeus and the American Military Adventure in Iraq, 2006–2008*, The Penguin Press, New York, 2009

————*Fiasco: The American Military Adventure in Iraq*, The Penguin Press, New York, 2006

Riedel, Bruce, *The Search for al Qaeda: Its Leadership, Ideology, and Future*, Brookings Institution Press, Washington DC, 2008

Roy, Olivier, *Islam and Resistance in Afghanistan*, Cambridge University Press, Cambridge, 1986

Scheuer, Michael, *Marching Towards Hell: America and Islam after Iraq*, Simon & Schuster, New York, 2008

————*Imperial Hubris: Why the West is Losing the War on Terror*, Brassey's Inc., 2004

Schofield, Victoria, *Afghan Frontier: Feuding and Fighting in Central Asia*, Tauris Parke Paperbacks, London, 2003

Schroen, Gary C., *First In: An Insider's Account of how the CIA Spearheaded the War on Terror in Afghanistan*, Ballantine Books, New York, 2005

Stark, Freya, *The Minaret of Djam: an Excursion in Afghanistan*, John Murray, London 1970.

Thesiger, Wilfred, *Among the Mountains: Travels Through Asia*, HarperCollins, London, 1998

Tootal, Colonel Stuart, DSO OBE, *Danger Close: Commanding 3 PARA in Afghanistan*, John Murray, London, 2009

Woodward, Bob, *Obama's Wars*, Simon & Schuster, New York, 2010

Acknowledgements

It was the almost daily sight on television, in the summer of 2009, of the black hearses carrying the coffins of British servicemen and occasionally women, covered with the Union flag, driving through Wootton Bassett past grieving crowds, which first made me consider writing this book. It was a shocking ritual which prompted the question in my mind: *why?* Why was it that, despite the most liberal and honourable of intentions, we were paying such a bitter price to rebuild Afghanistan, and replace its fanatical government with something more humane?

To try to find the answer I have interviewed well over a hundred participants, covering a wide range of soldiers, sailors, politicians, diplomats and ordinary citizens, British, American, Spanish and Afghan, asking them all the same question: what went wrong? What were the mistakes made by the West, and by the Afghans themselves, after 9/11? Who and what is to blame for the mess we find ourselves in today?

To all these interviewees, British, American, French and above all Afghan, great and small, men and women, I owe a huge debt of gratitude because it is their knowledge, their wisdom, their experiences and their memories which underpin this book and lend it whatever merit it has. I am also deeply grateful to Gretchen Peters for giving me free access to *Seeds of Terror*, her brilliant exposé of the drug business in Afghanistan and the alleged involvement of Ahmed Wali Karzai; to Richard Will, the British Customs veteran who introduced us and guided me through the Afghan drug maze; to Bill Keller, Executive Editor of the *New York Times*, for his generosity in allowing me to quote freely from its detailed record of the Afghan War, not least the reports written by my daughter Carlotta, particularly her treatment at the hands of the ISI in Quetta; to James Harding, editor of *The Times*, and Geordie Grieg, editor of the *Evening Standard*; also to the *Daily Telegraph* which, day by day, have delivered superb coverage of the war; thanks too to the *Sunday Telegraph* for permitting me to quote from their serialisation of Richard Dannatt's memoirs, and to Michael Semple who allowed me to quote extensively from his monograph, 'Afghanistan Then and Now', and how he was declared persona non grata by President Karzai in 2007. Other sources from which I have greatly benefited are the US Senate Foreign Relations Committee Report on Tora Bora, and Matt Waldman's remarkable paper 'The Sun in the Sky' about ISI influence on the Taliban, published by the London School of Economics in 2010. There are many lesser but not less important sources too numerous to mention.

Selecting and tracking down the interviewees, in Afghanistan, Britain and America, was a task in itself and I was hugely lucky to have the invaluable assistance in Kabul of Nasir Saberi, a distinguished engineer who knows everyone in Kabul and served as a deputy minister in the Ministry of Urban Development under the late Vice-President of Afghanistan, Haji Qadir, who was assassinated leaving his office one day in 2002, and my young secretary, Zari, who talked our way through apparently endless checkpoints; while here, at the other end of the spectrum, in Kent, I owe an equally enormous debt to Diane Steer, who transcribed all the interviews, despite some opaque accents, with stunning speed and precision; and to Virginia (Ginda) Utley, researcher par excellence who produced in a short time a series of rabbits out of unlikely hats.

Some interviewees who gave me the benefit of their time and expertise may not, alas, find themselves included, not because they did not have something valuable or interesting to say, but for lack of space or incompetence in marshalling the material on my part. Regrettably, they ended up, as we used to say in the television business, on the cutting-room floor: a fate I know only too well myself. The paucity of politicians on these pages may puzzle some readers. This is not entirely my fault. I received at first no reply from Tony Blair, then a refusal; a fairly abrupt turndown from

Gordon Brown, although admittedly some letters went out in the run-up to the May 2010 election; Dr John Reid, after a third letter, finally said no, although General Sir David Richards, CDS, pays him a handsome compliment in the book for the help he gave him before he went out as NATO commander to Afghanistan in 2006. There was no reply from Geoff Hoon, and Des Browne cancelled, also because of the election. The only former Defence Secretary who came through was John Hutton. Servicemen, on the other hand, many of whom have served in Afghanistan, and many of them very senior, have given me unstinting assistance.

Another perhaps more serious omission is the lack of an interview with President Karzai. His press officers ignored several requests and in the end I felt there was more than enough about him already in the public domain. I did interview him briefly several years ago for Channel 5 on the possible restoration of the Bamiyan Buddhas. He said all the right things about the Buddhas, in excellent English. But more important at this critical juncture, it would seem to me, is his state of denial about the rampant corruption that is eating the heart out of Afghanistan; and on that he does not care to be interviewed. Similarly his brother, the late Ahmed Wali, accused of being in the drug business, also declined.

Finally, underpinning all, and without whose unstinting help I could never have got this far, is my family; above all my wife, Eleanor, chef, chauffeur and senior adviser; daughters Fiona and Carlotta both of whom lived in Kabul for years, and my invaluable third daughter, Michaela, who unsnarled my frequent computer glitches and read much of the manuscript, aided part-time by granddaughter Charlotte, who at sixteen is already a computer whizz. Even Freddy, her younger brother, had to come to the rescue once or twice when no one else was around.

Last but not least I am indebted to my friend and agent Dinah Wiener, who was always encouraging, and of course to my wonderful publisher Bloomsbury and its editorial wizards Michael Fishwick, Anna Simpson and Kate Johnson. They have all in their different ways been invaluable.

Sandy Gall,
Penshurst, October 2011.

Index

Rumsfeld, Donald, 35, 37, 40, 44–5, 48–54,
    56–7, 68–9, 74, 222, 224, 333, 341–4
Russia, 172, 198, 347

Sadozai, Shah Mahmud, 25
Safavid dynasty, 183
Saikal, Mahmoud, 255, 278–80, 344
Salang, 32, 67, 168
Salawat, 199
Saleh, Amrullah, 122, 145, 160, 176, 182,
    259–60, 266, 282–8, 332
Salehi, Mohammad Zia, 256, 263, 265
SAM7 missiles, 10, 15, 17
Samangan, 33
Sangin, 20–3, 87, 91–2, 103, 107–8, 110–11,
    116, 216, 234
Sanzari, 199–200
Sarkozy, Nicolas, 149
Sarobi, 149–50
SAS, 11, 96, 178, 236, 254
satellite surveillance, 98, 169
Saudi Arabia, 20, 37, 147, 172, 198, 278, 324,
    341
    and bin Laden, 29–31
    support for Taliban and ISI, 28–9, 63, 317,
    347
SBS, 39, 51–3
Scheuer, Michael, 50, 54
Schofield, Victoria, 126
Schroen, Gary, 35, 49–51
Schweich, Thomas, 131–2
Scotland, 217
security companies, private, 161–2, 191
Semple, Michael, 119–26
Sensitive Investigative Unit, 256, 260
Shad, Gowhar, 26
Shahzad, Saleem, 311
Sharia law, 155, 345
Sharif, Nawaz, Prime Minister, 294
Sherzai, Governor Gul Agha, 73, 186
Shia Family Law, 155–6
Shiburghan, 33
Shuja, Shah, 120
Shura-i-Nazar, 33
Siddig, Zaid, 273–8
Sierra Leone, 61, 94, 220
Sind, 161
Singh, Manmohan, 346
Six Day War, 4
Skrzypkowiak, Andy, 9

Snatch Land Rovers, 209, 228
Somalia, 42, 133, 143
Somoza, Anastasio, 129
Soomro, Akhtar, 300–1
Spain, 137
Spanta, Dr Rangin, 138, 264, 280
Spin Boldak, 161, 185–6
Stark, Freya, 24
Starkey, Jerome, 318
Stewart, Rory, 365, n13
STINGER missiles, 10
Stirrup, Air Chief Marshal Sir Jock, 110,
    112–13, 211, 236–7, 240
Stoere, Jonas, 321
Sultana, 268–9, 270
Sultanzoy, Daud, 257–8
Sunday Telegraph, 83
Sunday Times, 9, 90–1, 211
supply convoys, 161–2
Suskind, Ron, 55
Swat, 79
Syria, 6

Taj, Zareen, 156
Tajikistan, 28, 35
Takhar, 33
Taliban
    author's introduction to, 18–19
    bribery of, 149–50
    casualties, 108–9
    defeat of, 35–6, 64, 99
    disbandment, 75
    and drugs trade, 109, 129, 132–3
    escape to Pakistan, 39, 49
    and foreign fighters, 104
    and money-laundering, 260–1
    negotiations with, 197–8, 288, 326–7
    possible return of, 269–70
    prisoners, 288, 304, 309–10
    propaganda, 269, 297
    protection rackets, 190–1
    'reconcilables' and 'irreconcilables', 152,
        168, 178–9, 315
    reintegration policy, 119–25, 154–5, 158, 178,
        221, 315
    resurgence, 76–81, 170–1, 223, 237, 246
    and safe havens, 151–2
    strength of, 195–6, 318
    and supply routes, 161–2
    surrender, 61